# DRESS CODES

PALEIS HET LOO, APELDOORN

WAANDERS PUBLISHERS, ZWOLLE

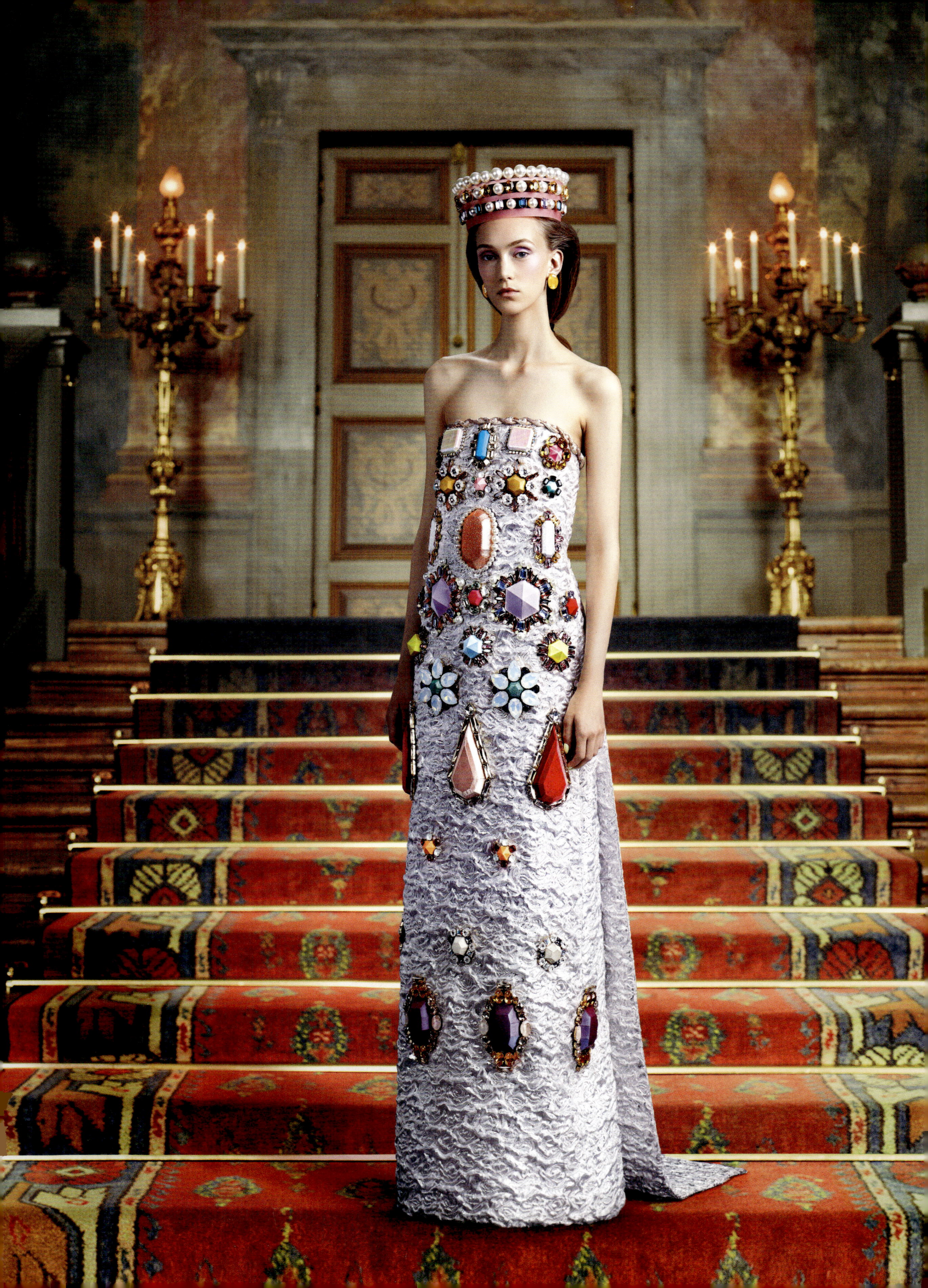

FROM STATEMENT TO STYLE ICON

# DRESS CODES

PAUL REM
MADELIEF HOHÉ
TIRZA WESTLAND
CÉCILE NARINX

# FOREWORD

Nothing is more personal than clothing. It is literally right next to our skin. It is tangible, and makes its presence felt. The fabric, texture, line, colour, sheen: they all contribute to the overall effect. It stimulates all our senses. The rustling of gowns at a ball – what more immediate evocation of history could one imagine? Clothes make us who we are, or who we want to be. It is no coincidence that costume dramas are so popular, and fashion exhibitions attract such a wide range of visitors.

Dress codes: rules about what to wear. Sometimes specified on an invitation, but often in the form of unwritten rules about 'the done thing'. Dress codes have always been important at court. A gala dinner, wedding or a tennis match – there was a dress code for every occasion. Those who ignored the rules would exclude themselves from the group. There have always been dress codes, and they play a role not only at court, but also in daily life. We dress in a style we feel comfortable with, whether consciously or not. We dress to belong, or to set ourselves apart.

This exhibition explores dress codes from the past and from the present day. And what do we find? Rules change. Dress codes that in the past applied only at court are now part of popular culture, having shifted from the palace to the red carpets of Hollywood, Cannes and New York. Celebrities, today's style icons, appear on the red carpet like kings and queens. A star wishing to make a statement will generally look to royal dress codes.

*'Dress Codes – From Statement to Style Icon'* is the first major fashion exhibition to be staged at Paleis Het Loo since it reopened in 2023. It has been developed in collaboration with Kunstmuseum Den Haag. We would like to express our gratitude to the Kunstmuseum and, in particular, to fashion and costume curator Madelief Hohé, fashion and costume historian Tirza Westland, and head of photography and design Alice de Groot for their pleasant and professional collaboration with our project team. The core team at Paleis Het Loo consisted of senior curator Paul Rem, programme designer Adjo Tjon-A-Tsien, marketing manager Laura Meerveld and project lead Marijntje Knapen. The project team was supported by many other staff at Paleis Het Loo, including conservator Hans Schuite.

This book, published to accompany the exhibition, will make the unique costume collection at Paleis Het Loo – whose core consists of items generously provided on long-term loan from the Royal Collections in The Hague – permanently accessible to the public, as well as linking it to contemporary fashion. Many of the works on show can also be accessed via our online collection and Modemuze. The publication is divided into three sections: historical court dress from 1880 to 1940 (by Paul Rem), dress codes today (by fashion journalist Cécile Narinx) and the impact of court dress codes on popular culture (by Madelief Hohé). These sections are interspersed with highlights from the Royal Collections, and the collections of Paleis Het Loo and Kunstmuseum Den Haag, the latter showcasing court outfits and clothes worn in circles close to the court. Many of the clothes and accessories were recently photographed for this publication, most of them in the historic setting of Paleis Het Loo, Paleis Lange Voorhout (Queen Emma's palace) or at the Royal House Archives in The Hague. The publication also includes some historical photographs of the Dutch royal family that have never previously been published.

The exhibition has been made possible thanks to items loaned by many museums and private collections. We are particularly grateful to H.M. the King, H.M. the Queen and Their Royal Highnesses Princess Amalia, Princess Irene and Princess Mabel, who have all generously loaned us items of personal property. Thanks also to the Royal Collections in The Hague for the many examples of royal clothing and accessories on long-term and short-term loan. Our partner Kunstmuseum Den Haag has also loaned a significant number of costumes worn in circles close to the royal family. The other lenders are: ABN AMRO History Department / long-term loans from the Dutch Silver Museum, MoMu | ModeMuseum Antwerpen, Dries van Noten Antwerp, Princess Diana Museum | The Princess & The Platypus Foundation Los Angeles, Givenchy Patrimoine Paris, Viktor&Rolf Amsterdam, Dutch Cavalry Museum Amersfoort, Gucci Archive Florence, Elie Saab France (SARL), Guo Pei Peking/Paris, Frans Hoogendoorn The Hague, Patrimoine Schiaparelli, Paris, Christian Siriano New York, Geschiedkundige Vereniging Oranje-Nassau, Stichting tot Instandhouding van het Museum van de Kanselarij der Nederlandse Orden, Edwin Oudshoorn Leiden, Toppers in Concert, Studio Exactitudes Rotterdam and various private lenders.

The beautiful exhibition design is the work of Tatyana van Walsum (spatial design) and Marline Bakker (graphic design). Marline also designed the catalogue. Our collaboration with Marloes Waanders and Stefanie Klerks of Waanders Uitgevers was as enjoyable and professional as always. Thanks also to the authors listed above and to picture editor Angelique van den Eerenbeemd.

The museum of Paleis Het Loo would like to take this opportunity to express its gratitude to its main benefactors, the Ministry of Education, Culture and Science and the VriendenLoterij lottery. We would also like to thank the following funds and sponsors for supporting the *Dress Codes* exhibition and publication: Cultuurfonds, Fonds 21, the Mondrian Fund, Apeldoorn municipal authority, Zabawas, Gravin van Bylandt Stichting, Stichting Hendrik Mullerfonds and the Dutch Costume Association.

We hope you enjoy your visit to *Dress Codes* and the publication that accompanies it.

Frans van de Avert, Director
Annette de Vries, Head of Research, Collection & Programmes

← ← **'Size Queen' ensemble by Viktor&Rolf ◆**
Autumn/winter 2021, courtesy of Viktor&Rolf, Amsterdam;
background, interior of Paleis Het Loo, Apeldoorn

→ **Gown ◆**
Worn by Princess Maria of Prussia (1855–1888) in 1878,
on her engagement to Prince Hendrik (1820–1879,
brother of Willem III.
Maker unknown, 1878
Silk, cotton, metal
Kunstmuseum Den Haag

TABLE OF CONTENTS

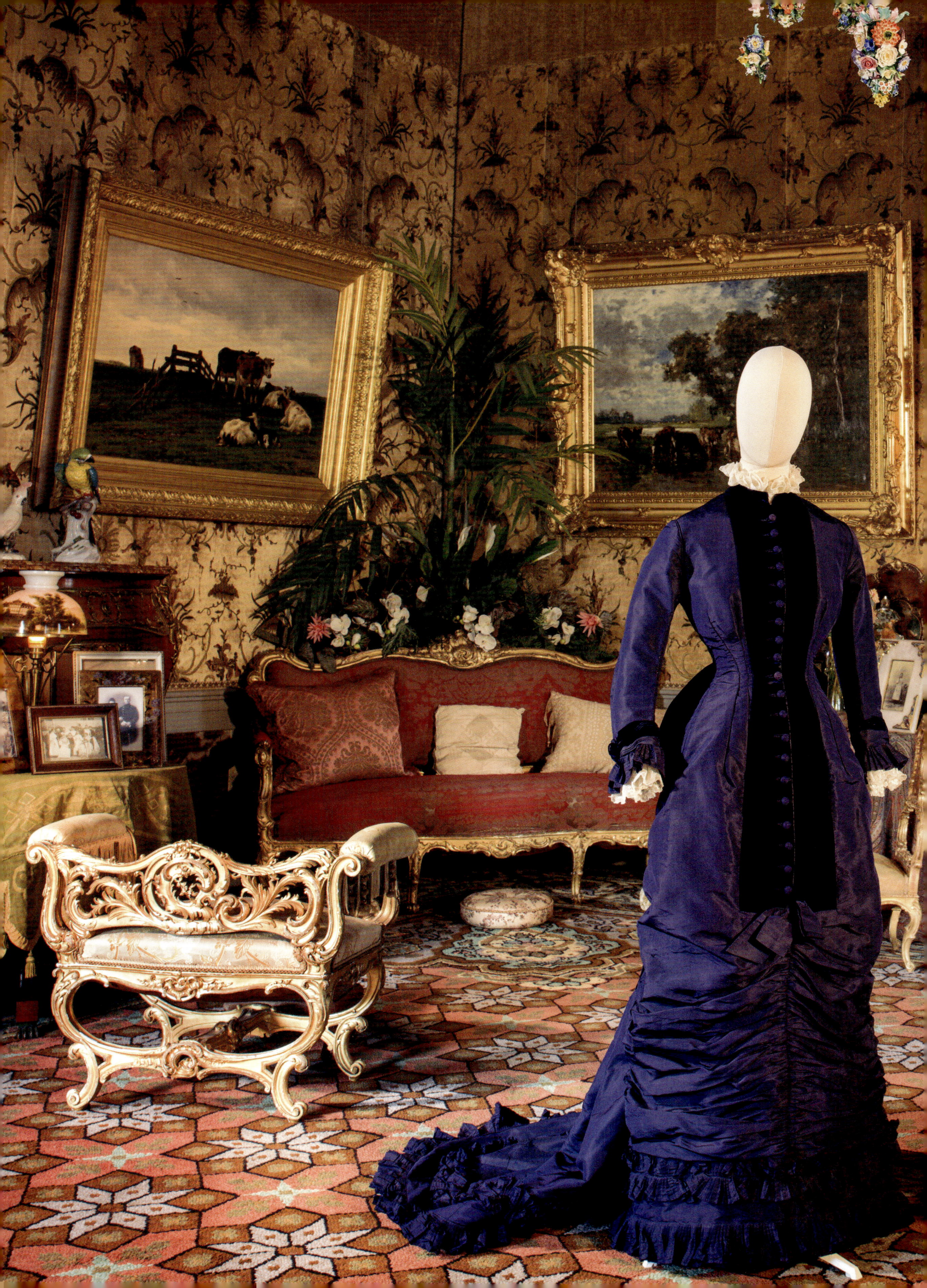

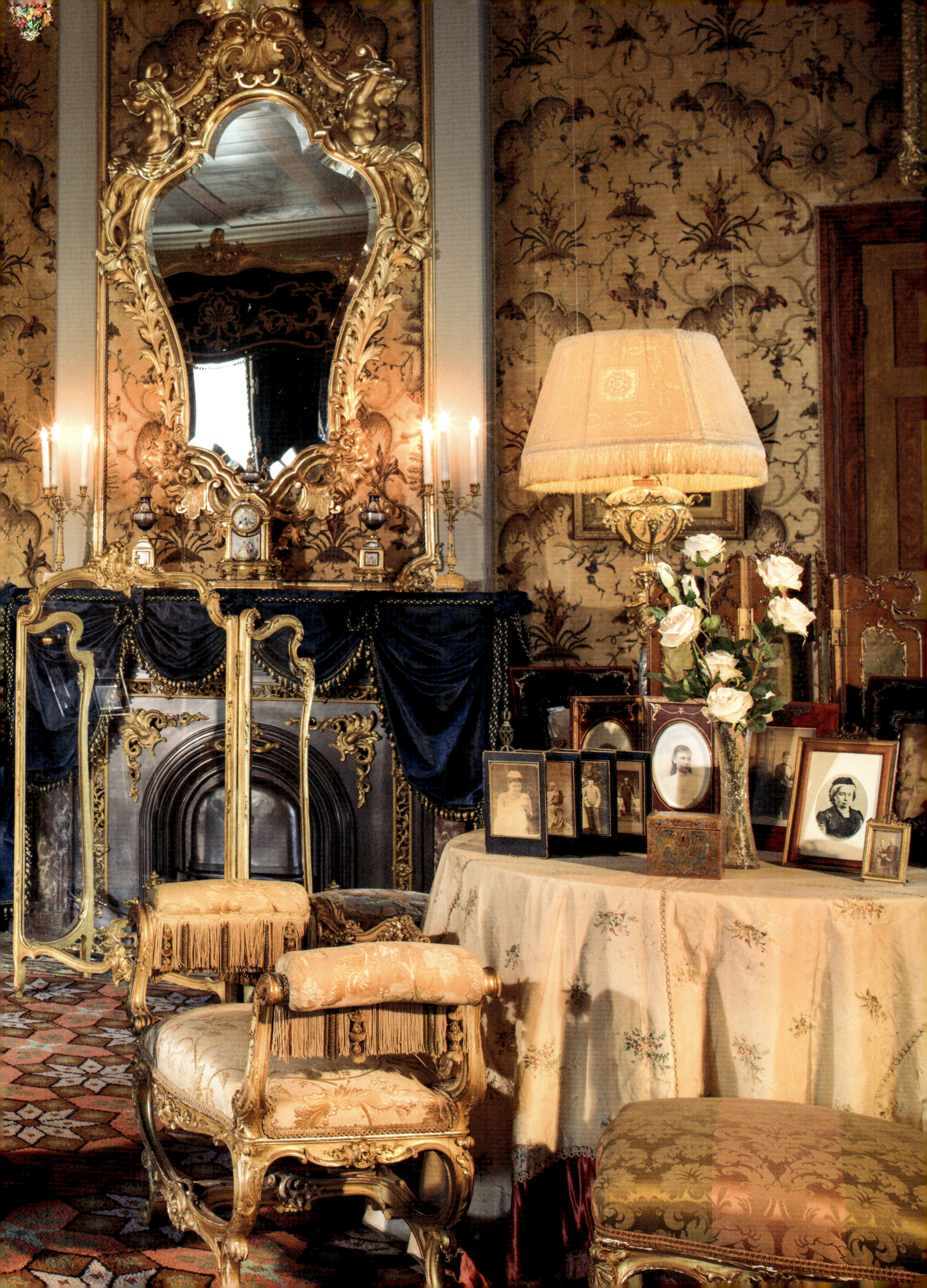

# DRESS CODES FROM STATEMENT TO STYLE ICON

Dress codes are not exclusive to any particular period. This is the story of the Dutch court in the period 1880-1940. This was the age of three female monarchs: Queen Regent Emma (1858-1934), Queen Wilhelmina (1880-1962) and Princess Juliana (1909-2004). Their wardrobes have largely been preserved as part of the Royal Collections. The clothes and accessories were worn at important occasions like weddings and investitures, and also at court festivities or out horseriding – always in line with protocol and the appropriate dress code for the event. Fashion was important in court culture. The right clothes allowed a monarch to stand out from the rest of the court, its staff and visitors. There were dress codes for all kinds of events, from grand ceremonies to outdoor sports, either defined on paper or existing as an unwritten rule. There could be no court life without a dress code in those days, and to be a player, a person had to know the codes and have the money to comply, otherwise they would be excluded. This raises many questions. What exactly were those dress codes? Who wore what at court? How did people ensure they didn't commit a fashion blunder? And who made the fashionable attire worn by monarchs, ladies-in-waiting and footmen?

The exhibition *Dress Codes* answers all these questions. The project, initiated by Paleis Het Loo, is a collaboration with Kunstmuseum Den Haag, which has the largest fashion collection in the Netherlands. A logical partnership for this venture, given that the royals' clothes are kept by Royal Collections and Paleis Het Loo, while those of their 'entourage' (ladies-in-waiting and others in court circles) are at Kunstmuseum Den Haag. The two institutions have collaborated on fashion projects in the past. In 1998 Paleis Het Loo in Apeldoorn organised an exhibition and published an accompanying catalogue entitled *In Royal Array: Queen Wilhelmina 1880-1962*, combining the knowledge and skills of the museums' costume curators, Elizabeth Braam and Ietse Meij. In 2006 curators Trudie Rosa de Carvalho of Paleis Het Loo and Madelief Hohé of Kunstmuseum Den Haag worked together on *Hague Court Fashions*, staged at Kunstmuseum Den Haag (then Gemeentemuseum Den Haag). These two institutions, in Apeldoorn and The Hague, have joined forces again for *Dress Codes*. And the costumes are travelling back and forth again between the two places, just as they did in the days when they were in use, and were transported by carriage or train to ensure that the wearer looked absolutely perfect, whether outdoors in the summer at Apeldoorn, or at one of the many parties and other events that took place at the court in The Hague in the winter months.

→ King Willem-Alexander and Queen Máxima on Prinsjesdag (official opening of parliament) in 2016. The king is wearing a morning suit, Queen Máxima is wearing an evening dress by Claes Iversen. ◆

Dress codes might seem like something from the distant past, but nothing could be further from the truth. Dress codes are all around us, whether we are aware of them or not. People often like to express who they are, or the group they belong to, or would like to belong to, through what they wear. Cécile Narinx, fashion journalist and former editor-in-chief of *Harper's Bazaar* draws on her many years of experience to discuss today's dress codes. Her essay ties in seamlessly with the *Exactitudes* series, in which Dutch photographers Ari Versluis and Ellie Uyttenbroek have been documenting unwritten dress codes for years. But that is not all. Over the years, court dress codes have increasingly become part of pop culture. While the strict protocol at the Dutch court declined after the Second World War, international dress codes also changed. Fashion became more democratic, as popular culture grew in importance. And who did the film stars, pop stars and, later, even reality TV stars, influencers and YouTubers imitate in their dress style for galas and important events? That's right: for those important red-carpet moments they copied the court culture of yesteryear, with its ball gowns, long trains, tiaras, expensive embroidery and fur (real or fake).

All of these royal dress codes are still observed by celebrities at society events, sometimes in unique ways, as recently at the Cannes Film Festival (2025) where, a day before the event, guests were urged to keep 'nudity' to a minimum, in response to the 'naked dress' trend at recent red-carpet events. Backpacks and sneakers were also explicitly forbidden on the red carpet, as well as gowns with trains that might form an obstacle to others. Of course some celebrities paid no heed whatsoever to these dress codes, and there were plenty of naked dresses and long trains at Cannes. Either you're a style icon, or you're not. Courtly imagery is still very much alive in pop culture, where the low-cut gown and long train will never go out of style. Even though, at the same time, many European monarchies are gradually modernising, and some have explicitly abolished dress codes. Modern royals increasingly dress like everyone else – their way of making a statement.

In short, this is a story that takes us from statement to style icon. Or, as designers Viktor & Rolf remarked in connection with their own *Royals* collection (2021), 'Everybody can be a queen, and everybody is his or her own creation'.

Paul Rem, senior curator at Paleis Het Loo
Madelief Hohé, curator of fashion and costume at Kunstmuseum Den Haag

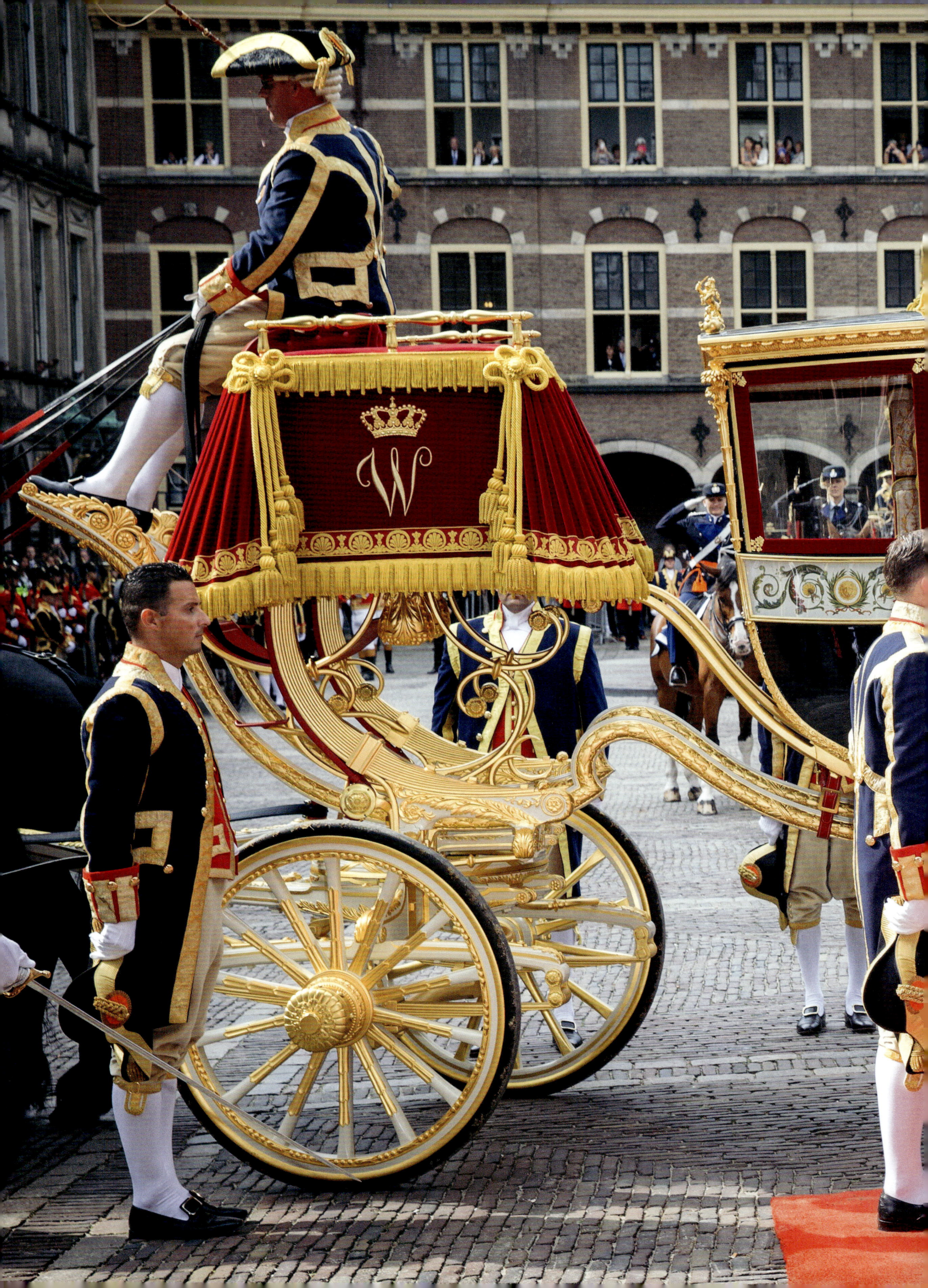

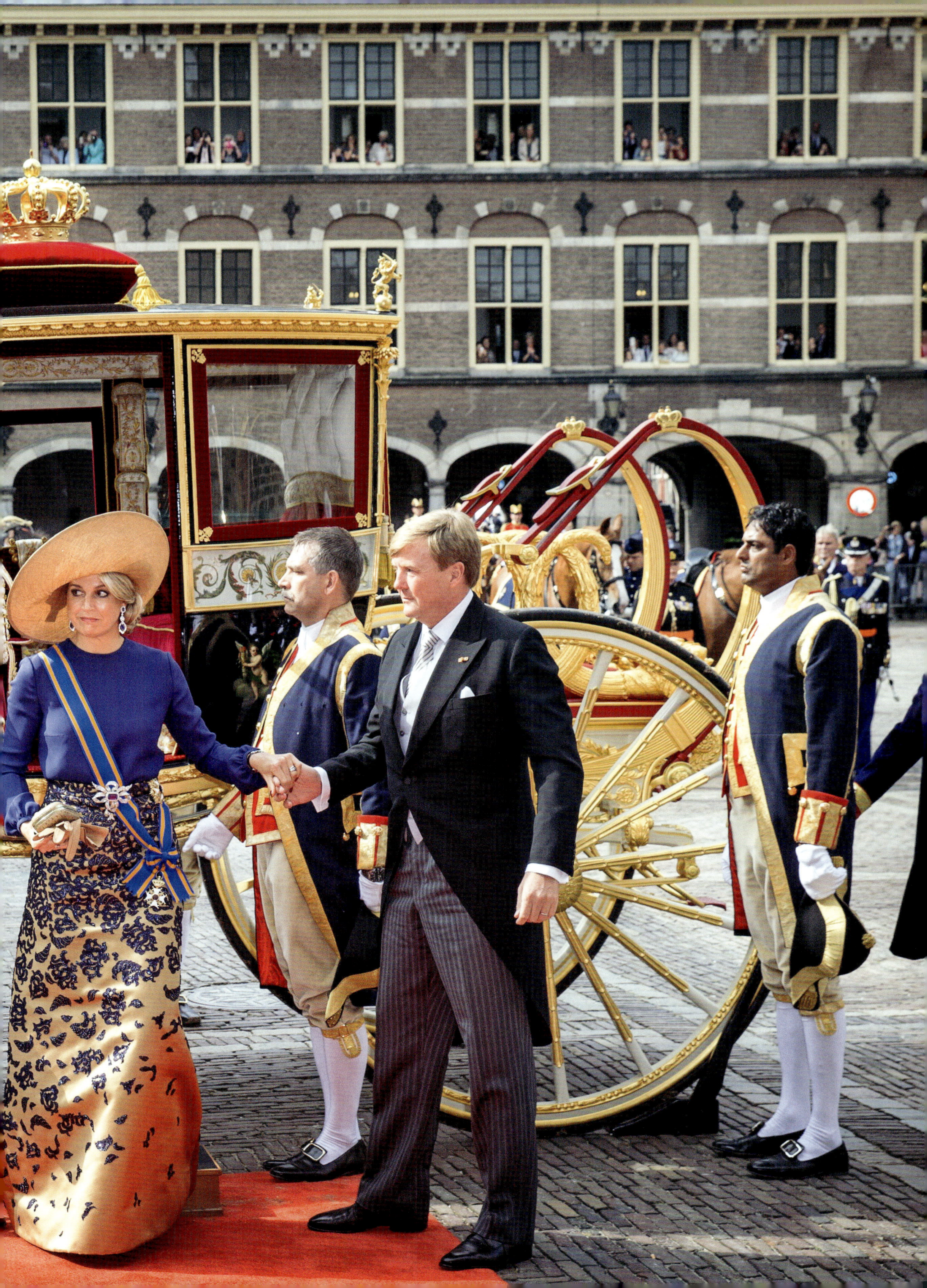

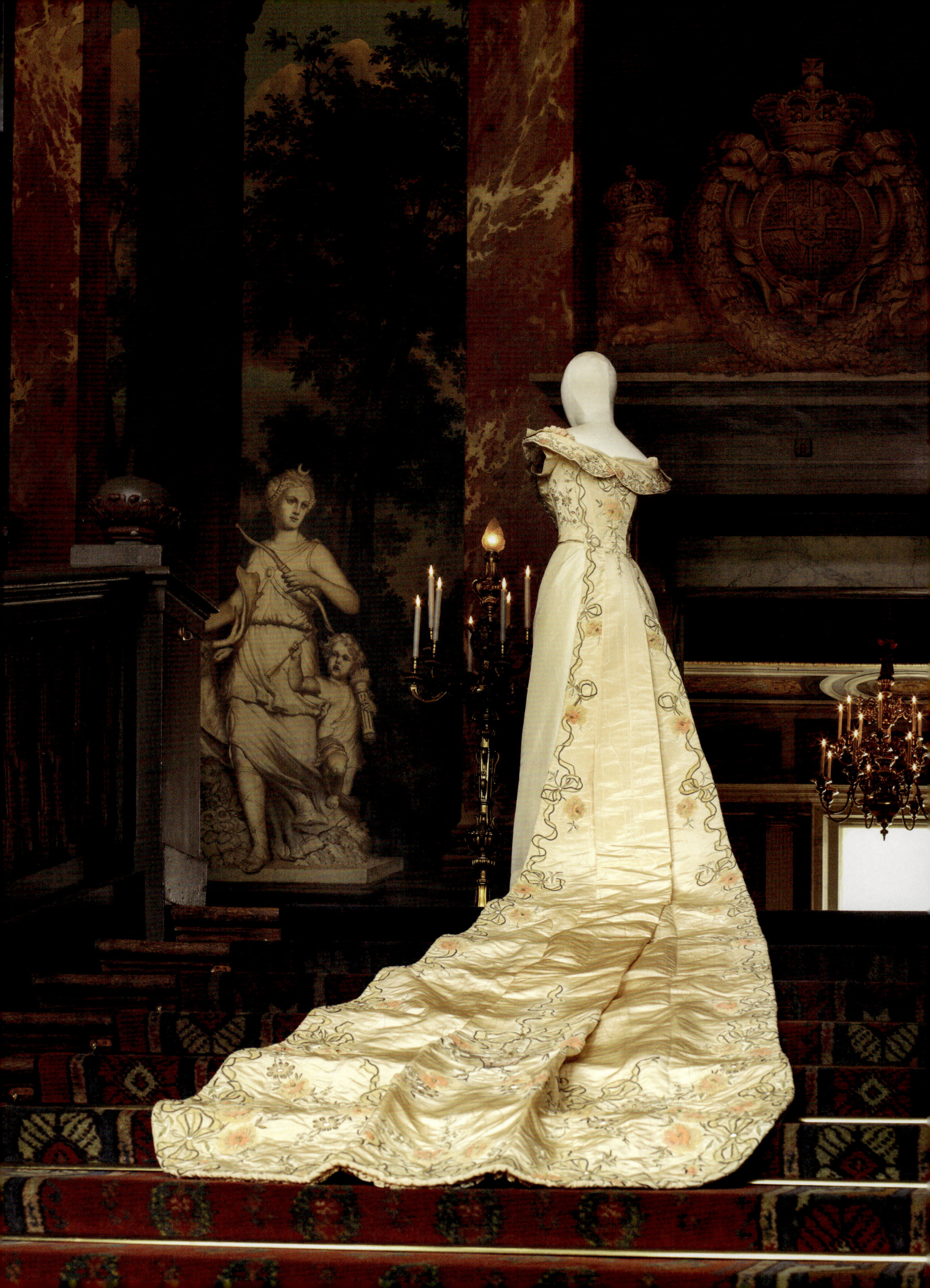

# DRESS CODES AT THE DUTCH COURT 1880–1940

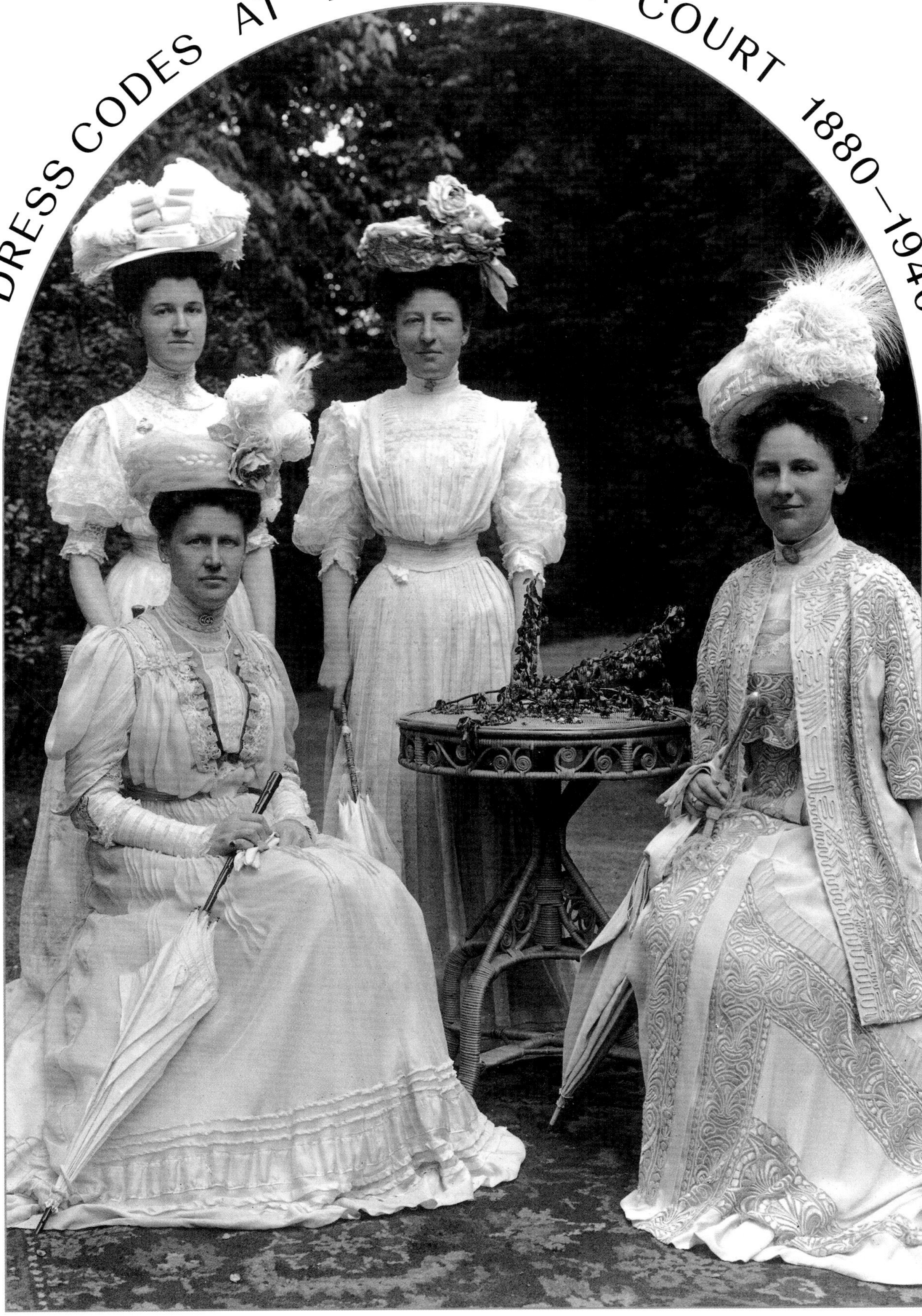

PAUL REM

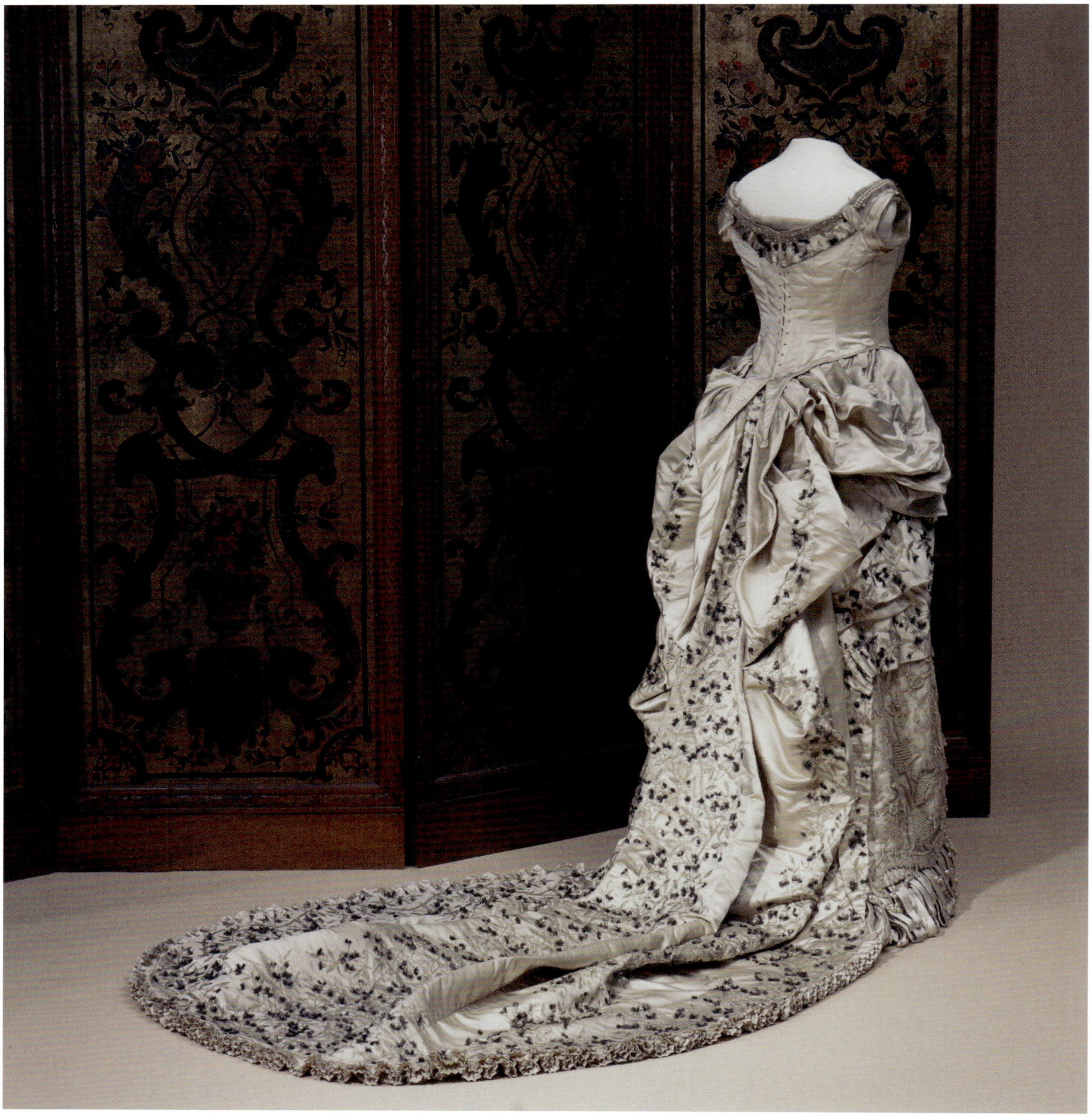

← Queen Wilhelmina and her ladies-in-waiting
Queen Wilhelmina (right) had her photograph taken with her ladies-in-waiting in the park behind Paleis Het Loo. From left to right, they are Anny Rengers (seated) and sisters Bella and Elisabeth Sloet van Marxveld. The queen is wearing a fashionable dress with a train. Her outfit is completed by a hat, parasol and gloves. The ladies-in-waiting followed the queen's example with their outfits, but it would have been inappropriate to appear better dressed.

Photo J.J.M. Guy de Coral, 1908
Royal Collections, The Hague

← ← Queen Wilhelmina's court train ◆
Paris, Nicaud Paris, circa 1900
Silk, silver thread, glass pearls
Paleis Het Loo, on long-term loan from the Royal Collections, The Hague

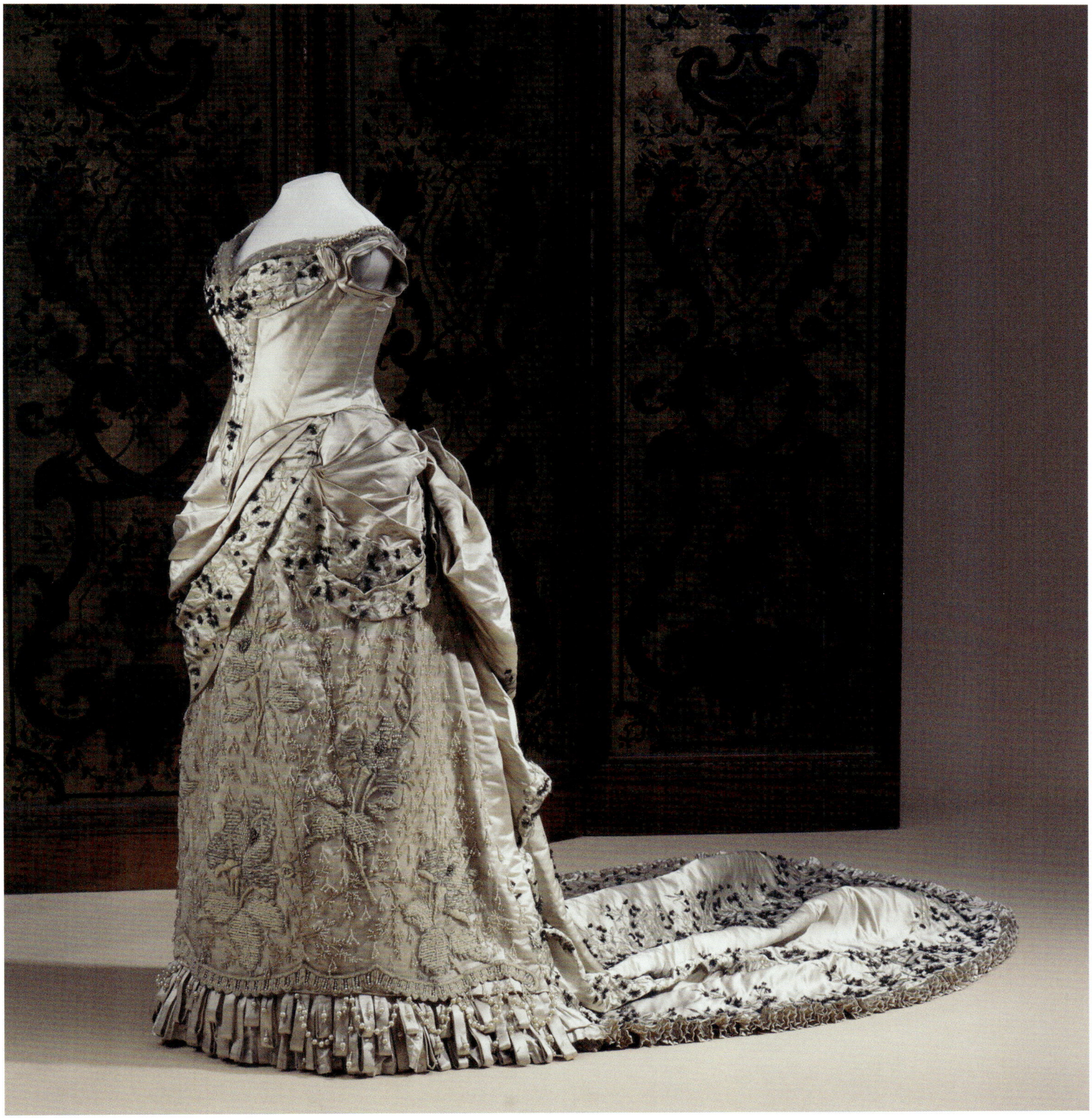

Queen Emma's wedding dress
On 10 January 1879, *the Opregte Haarlemsche Courant* newspaper described the new queen's wedding dress for its readers. 'The Bride's outfit consisted of a dress of white silk with silver embroidered flowers, and a royal ermine covered her shoulders.' The black specks on the dress are silver tassels that are now tarnished black.

Paris, Corbay-Wenzel, 1878
Silk, cotton, linen, silver thread, glass pearls
Paleis Het Loo. On long-term loan
from the Royal Collections, The Hague

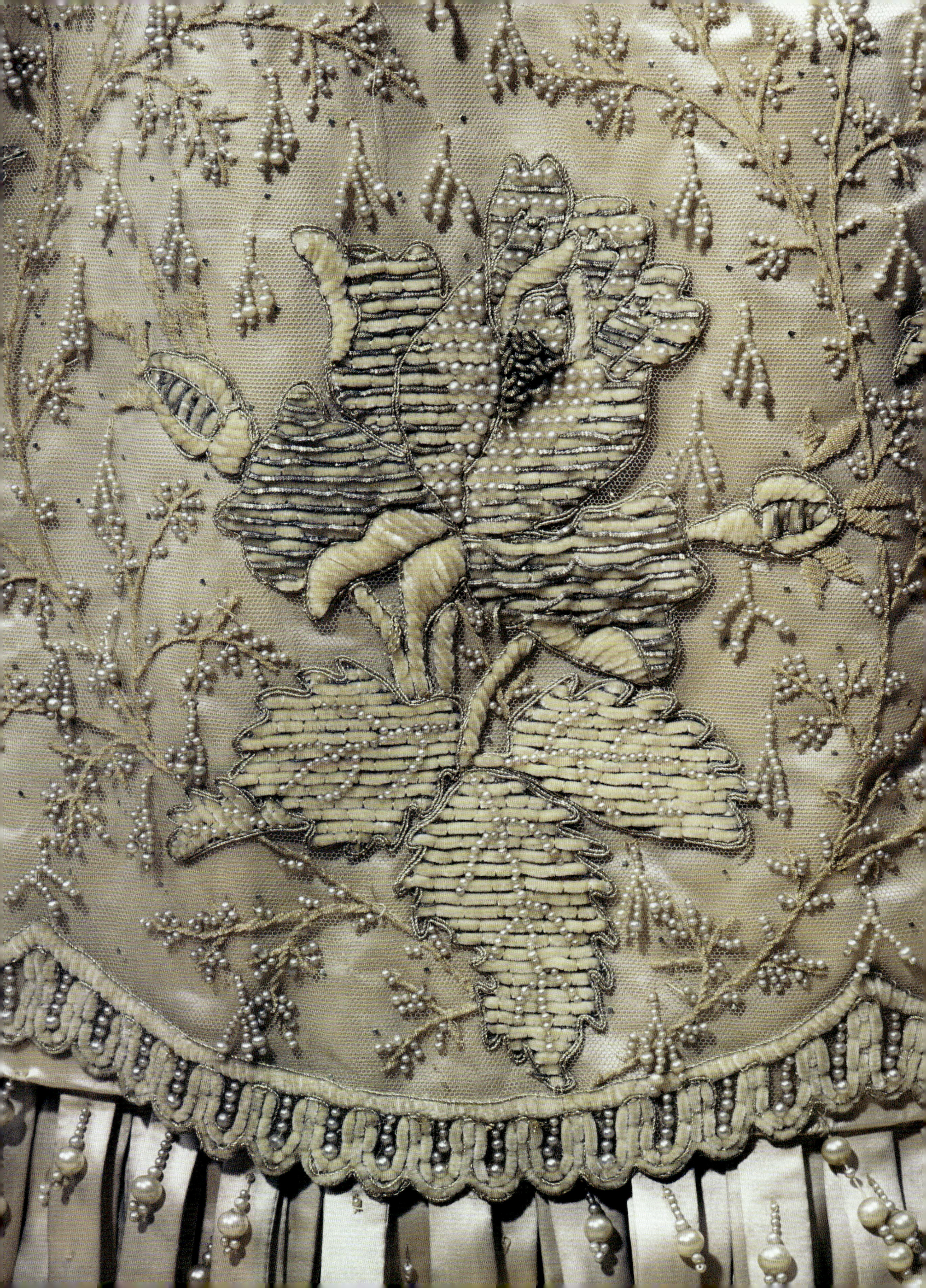

Queen Emma's (1858-1934) arrival in the Netherlands ushered in a revival of court life. King Willem III's first wife, Sophie of Württemberg, had performed her duties as queen to perfection, but in the final years of her life she was no longer a vibrant force at the centre of the Dutch court. This changed when Willem III remarried, taking the young German princess Emma of Waldeck and Pyrmont as his second wife. The royal wedding took place in the chapel of Emma's family castle in Arolsen on 7 January 1879. The king wore his Royal Navy admiral's uniform, with the insignia of his highest Dutch and Waldeck honours. Emma wore a white satin ballgown in the latest Paris fashion, with a train, a smooth bodice and short sleeves. She also wore an ermine cape in the cold chapel. The wedding ceremony was followed by three days of celebrations. The couple then left by train for the Netherlands, to spend their honeymoon at Paleis Het Loo. Emma's mother had spent a fortune on her trousseau, which travelled with her in trunks. Emma had barely set foot on Dutch soil when the sudden death of Prince Hendrik, the king's brother, brought the festive welcome to an abrupt end. A series of receptions, balls and dinners, carriage tours and theatre visits had to be postponed, as the chief master of ceremonies announced a period of court mourning on behalf of the king. For four weeks, the court would be in full mourning, followed by four weeks of half mourning and, finally, four weeks of light mourning. The notice was published in all newspapers, because although the pomp and circumstance was to be toned down for three months, some official receptions went ahead. Guests were expected to observe the dress codes for court mourning, published in the annual State Almanac.

## The splendour of court life

Guests were only too happy to conform to the rules of court. An invitation to a ceremony at the palace, in the radiant proximity of the royal family, was a privilege. The court was the epitome of civilisation in the age of King Willem III and Queen Emma, and later of Queen Wilhelmina, up to the outbreak of the Second World War in 1940. It was the diplomatic and cultural centre of The Hague, the monarch's official residence, and of the Netherlands itself – a European nation and colonial power. Protocol, formality, the glamour of expensive outfits, uniforms, jewellery, candlelight, music and footmen in livery reflected the grandeur of the reigning monarchy, which had a strong international orientation. European courts were in competition with each other, and to match their rivals, life at court had to be glamorous. Tradition and continuity have long been important aspects of monarchy. Receptions that proceeded according to fixed formulas, conforming to old rules, reaffirmed the allure of the royal family and its court.

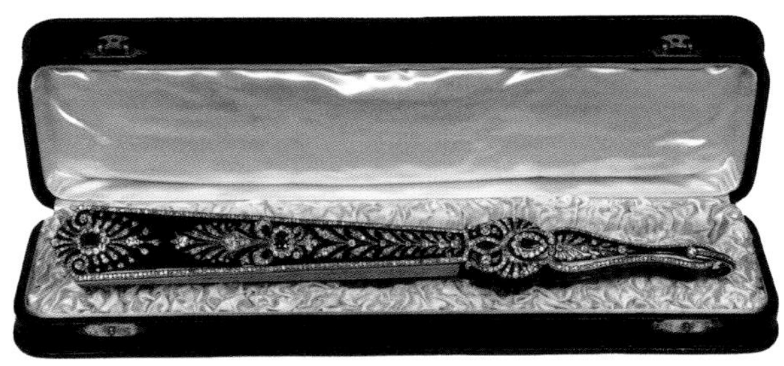

Emma's Mellerio fan ◆
Queen Emma owned many fans. One of the most costly was a painted fan with ribs of tortoiseshell decorated with diamonds and rubies, made by the Paris firm Mellerio dits Meller. It was part of a matching set of jewellery that also included a tiara, a choker, a breast ornament, a brooch, a bracelet and a pair of earrings.

Paris, Mellerio dits Meller, 1888
Tortoiseshell, gold, diamonds, paper
Royal Collections, The Hague

Detail of page 17

## Court ranks

A reception at court might have a particular dress code. It gave the court extra lustre. Dress codes ensured that people's rank at court and in society was instantly recognisable. At official receptions, male servants would wear their finest full dress livery. The gentlemen of the court and men who held public office wore their uniform. The ceremonial dress uniform would be expensive and, depending on the post held by the wearer, be embroidered with gold and silver and symbols referring to their post. Footmen had full dress livery. If a gentleman did not have a ceremonial dress uniform, he could wear a simple but elegant dress suit, with insignia and a sash making an impressive addition. Military personnel wore their dress uniform. Clothing therefore indicated rank at a quick glance.

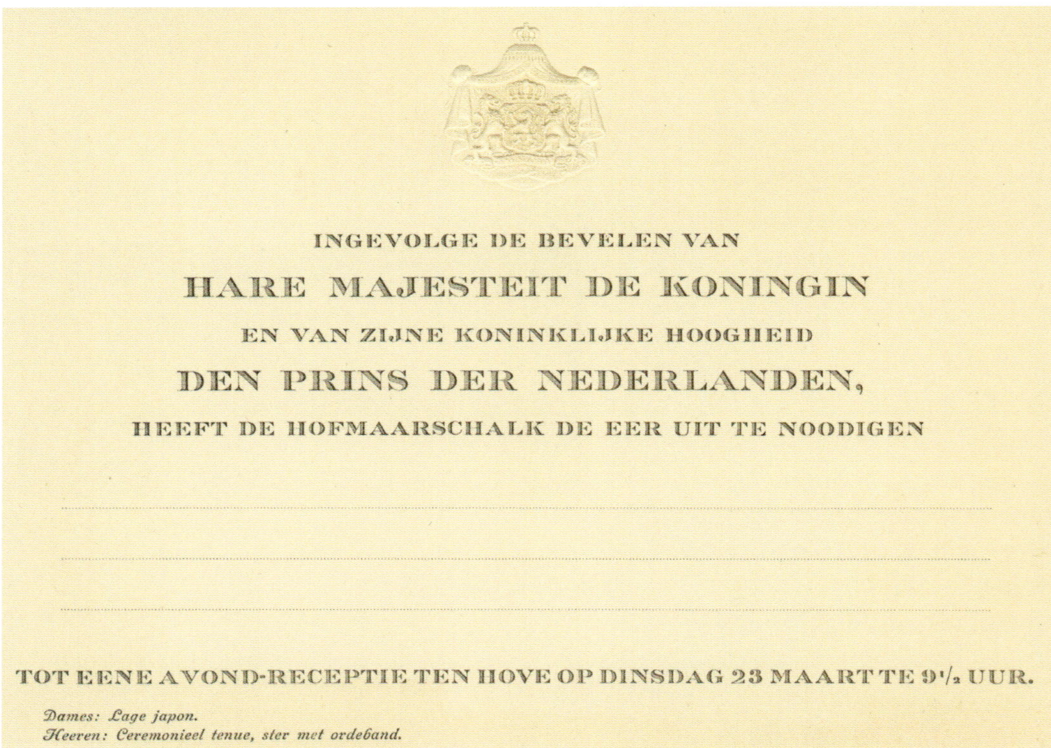

INGEVOLGE DE BEVELEN VAN

HARE MAJESTEIT DE KONINGIN

EN VAN ZIJNE KONINKLIJKE HOOGHEID

DEN PRINS DER NEDERLANDEN,

HEEFT DE HOFMAARSCHALK DE EER UIT TE NOODIGEN

TOT EENE AVOND-RECEPTIE TEN HOVE OP DINSDAG 23 MAART TE 9½ UUR.

*Dames: Lage japon.*
*Heeren: Ceremonieel tenue, ster met ordeband.*

**Invitation with dress code, 1926**
This invitation to a gala evening at the Royal Palace in Amsterdam requests that ladies wear a 'low-cut gown', a dress with décolletage, in other words. Gentlemen should wear their ceremonial uniform: a full dress uniform for military personnel, an official uniform for dignitaries, and a dress suit for other gentlemen. Invitations were still written in French in The Hague at the time.

Royal Collections, The Hague

**Three dignitaries in full regalia ◆**
From left to right: an envoy, Master of the Hunt and Grand Master of the Royal Hunt.

Wool, silk, leather, gilded metal, gold thread, cockerel feathers
Paleis Het Loo, on long-term loan from the Foundation for the Preservation of the Museum of the Chancery of the Netherlands Orders; Paleis Het Loo, on long-term loan from the Royal Collections, The Hague; Paleis Het Loo

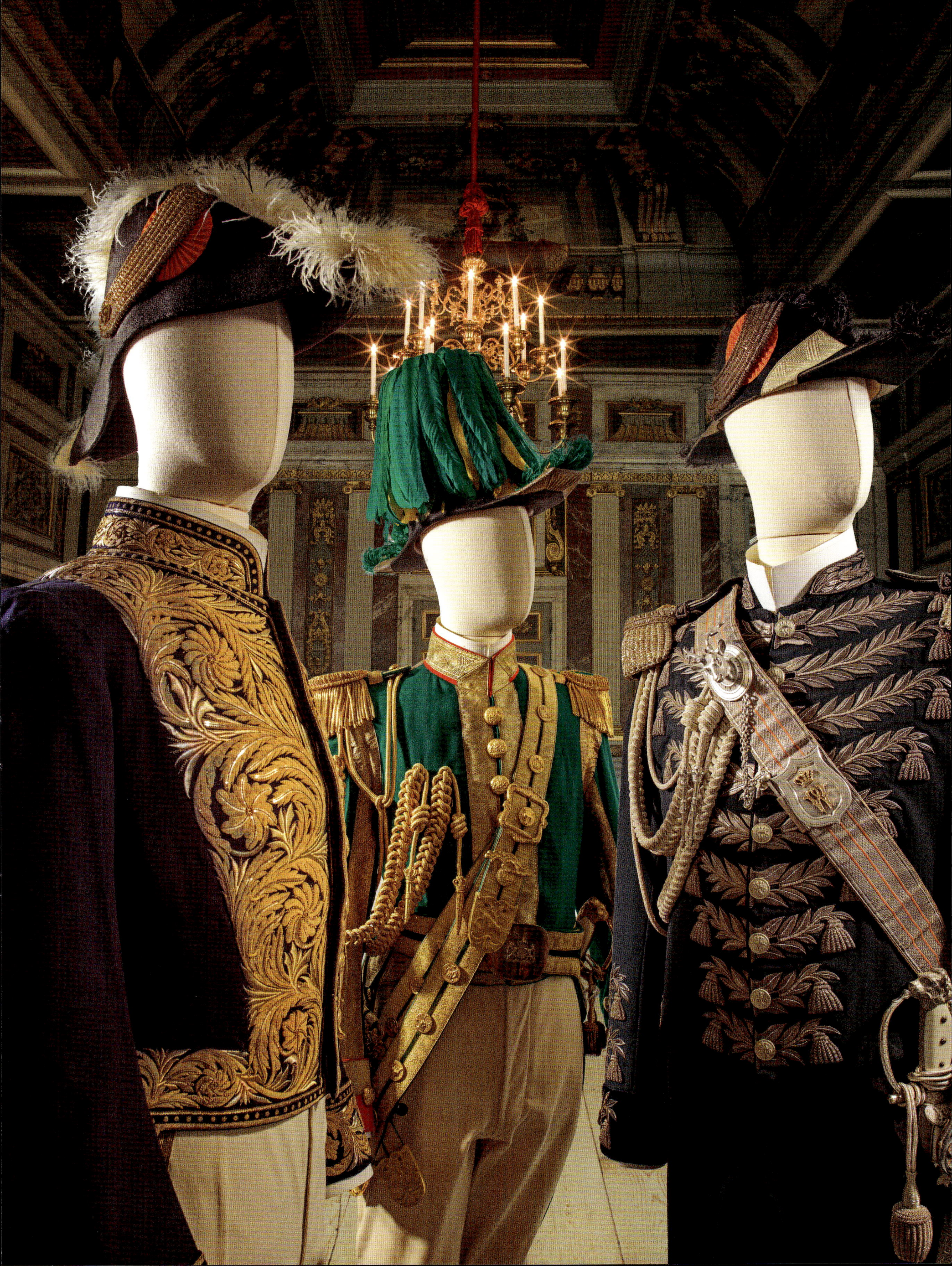

## Dress code: a perennial issue

The situation was more complex for women, because they did not wear a uniform dictated by regulations. Women at court were subject to the rules that Willem I had laid down by Royal Decree no. 20 of 17 March 1815. Roughly speaking, formal evening wear for a woman in the nineteenth and early to mid-20th century consisted of a white or coloured silk dress with a low neckline and short sleeves (or bare shoulders), long leather gloves and fabric-covered shoes. She would also be expected to carry a fan, and wear her hair up. In stipulating this official style of court dress for ladies, Willem I, King of the new United Kingdom of the Netherlands, conformed to tradition at the court of the King Louis XIV of France. In 1825 Willem I extended the rules to include a long court train, in addition to the train that was integral to the dress. The court, after all, set the tone in sophisticated official circles until 1940. It was vital to know how to behave and what to wear at royal receptions. A single mistake in terms of one's outfit could lead to disrepute, and prompt vicious gossip. There was a gala version of virtually every occasion at court, at which all the stops would be pulled out. But there were no fixed rules for the nature of the event. Each time, the appropriate dress code would be discussed, but it would not always be communicated. Families whose members were regularly invited to court had to be well prepared, so that they could comply with the wide range of dress codes. A young woman who lived in The Hague recalled in 1937 that her mother's parents gifted her a wardrobe that would enable her to accept invitations to court. 'My mother was given 3 gowns: a long white one with a train for the 'Raout', (the French name for the evening reception at which she would be presented to the Queen) and also 'formal evening', plus a short tulle dress for dances and a long dress for daytime receptions in light green broadcloth.. They were made by a Swiss seamstress called Heafeli, who also made gowns for Queen Emma.'[1]

**Gala dinner at Paleis Noordeinde, 1925**
At a gala dinner at Paleis Noordeinde on 26 February Prince Hendrik and most of the other male guests wore a dress suit, and the ladies wore low-cut ankle-length evening gowns with short sleeves, with the obligatory long gloves. Princess Juliana (seated, right) wore a ribbon round her head, in accordance with the fashion of the roaring twenties

Willem Coret
Paleis Het Loo

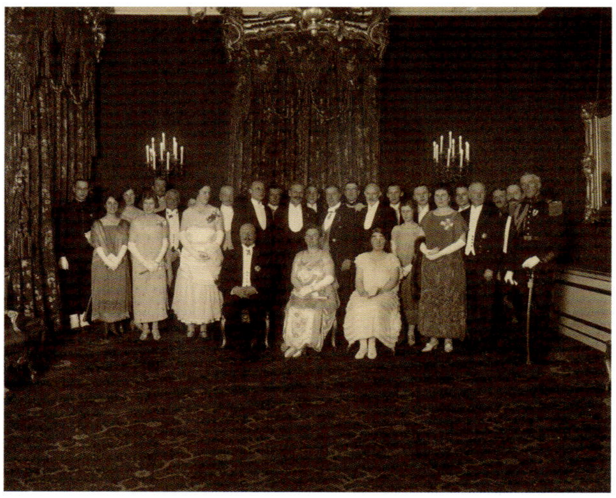

## So much choice

Besides the evening event, known as the *raout*, in the period 1879-1940 official court life included a whole range of receptions. Although they decreased in number during the reign of Queen Wilhelmina, official visits and audiences, receptions, dinners, special military dinners, balls and tea dances, plus small performances and concerts regularly took place within the palace walls from morning until deep into the night. Besides events at the palace, the royal family and their courtiers also attended important ceremonies such as weddings, investitures and jubilee celebrations, as well as many working visits, and ceremonies such as openings, unveilings and ship launches. All of these variations on themes could lead to confusion and uncertainty. Sometimes a dress code would be stipulated on the invitation. For women it would be one of three variations on the neckline: décolletage, semi low-cut or high. Sometimes, it was not clear which would be appropriate. King Willem III and Queen Emma were once about to attend a concert when the lady-in-waiting on duty became unsure as to whether she herself should wear a gown with décolletage, and so consulted another lady who was closer to the queen.[2] At court, there was always the danger of looking ridiculous by appearing in the wrong clothes. But there was plenty of opportunity to display one's own tastes, within the stipulated guidelines. For example, ladies-in-waiting attended evening festivities at Paleis Noordeinde in 1881 in safe white and cream dresses, while Queen Emma wore a light-blue satin dress decorated with black lace and dark-red roses, a gown that one lady-in-waiting described as a 'truly German' outfit.[3]

## No silk dresses at Het Loo

Dress codes reassured guests preparing to attend a reception at court, but the rules could be changed at the last moment. In September 1898 a series of gala dinners had been planned, for which invitations had been sent with the dress code 'gala' for ladies and gentlemen. A week before, the court announced in the newspaper that the 'gala' element had been scrapped. The marshal of the court had presumably realised that the dress code 'gala' would exclude gentlemen who did not have a military or civilian dress uniform. Abandoning the 'gala' aspect would allow these men to attend in the less formal 'frac', or white tie. Ceremonial receptions were held mainly at Paleis Noordeinde in The Hague, where the monarch resided, or at the Royal Palace in the capital Amsterdam. Court life at Het Loo, the summer palace, was much more informal. Queen Emma therefore requested that her ladies-in-waiting not bring any silk dresses or jewellery with them when they were working at Het Loo.

Costume party at Paleis Noordeinde, 1937
The dress code for the costume party was 'A Thousand and One Nights'. Prince Bernhard interpreted the theme in his own unique way.

Photo Erich Salomon, 1936
Royal Collections, The Hague

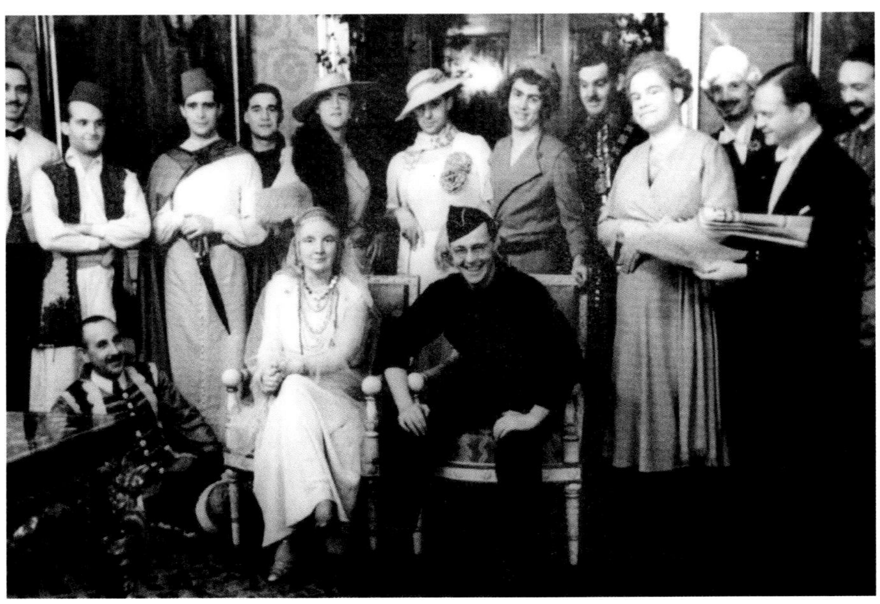

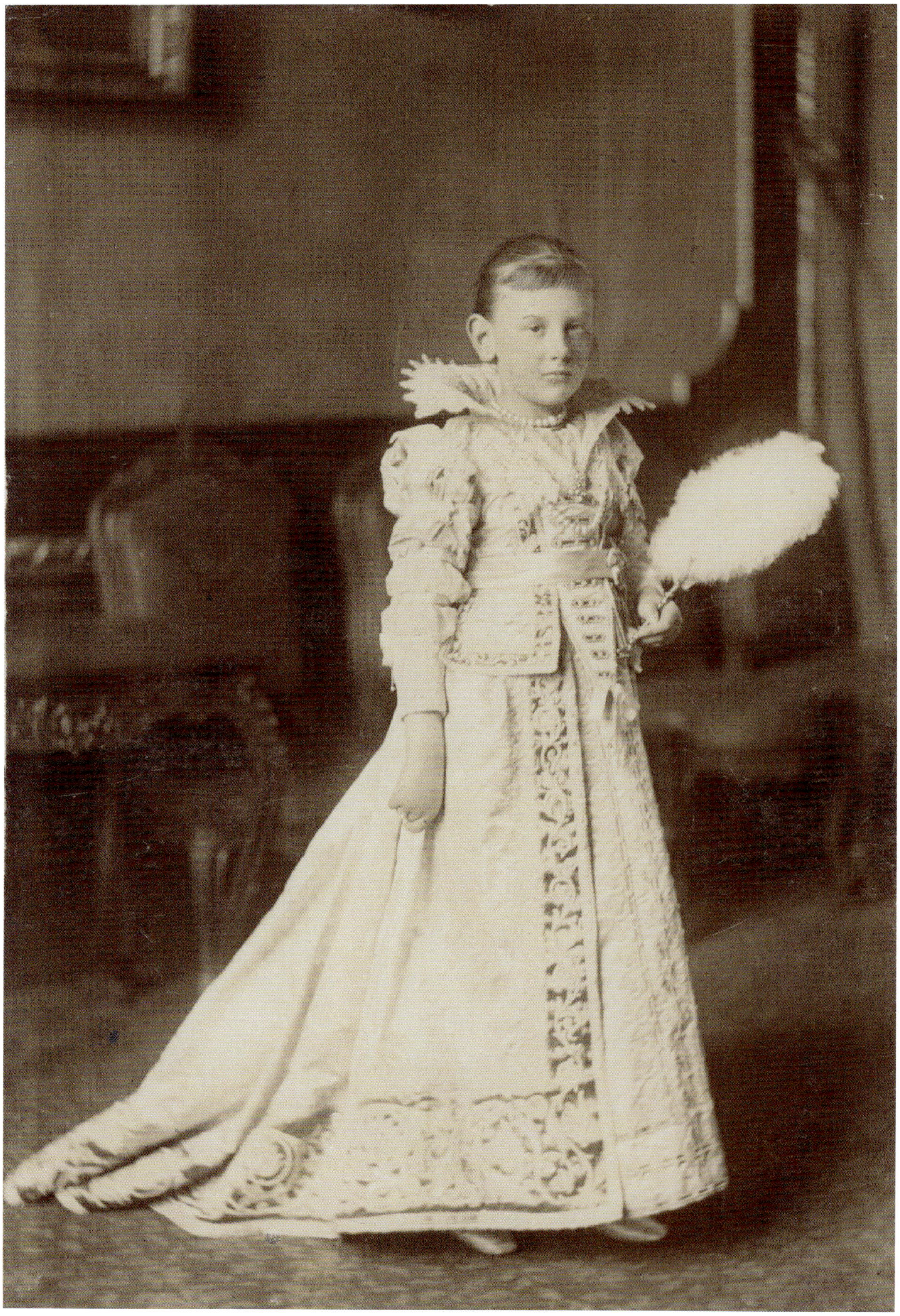

Queen Wilhelmina as Amalia von Solms-Braunfels ◆
Young Wilhelmina received this costume from her mother. It was inspired by the clothes worn in portraits of Amalia von Solms-Braunfels, wife of the stadtholder, in the 17th century. The costume was the work of a costume designer in Paris. It is not known whether Wilhelmina wore it at a children's ball, but she was photographed and also painted wearing it. The photograph was taken at Paleis Het Loo.

Photo Adolphe Zimmermans, 1891
Royal Collections, The Hague

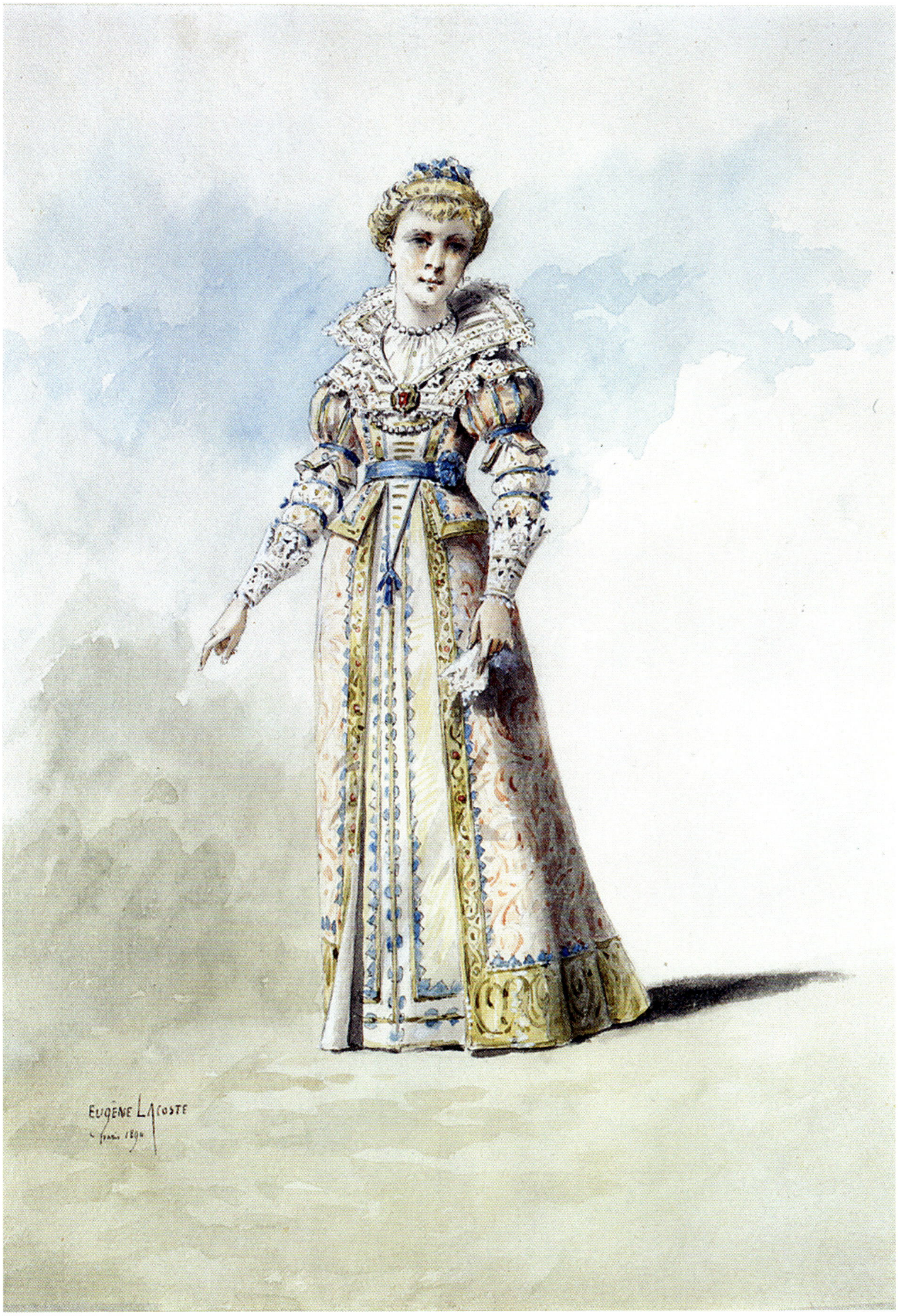


Design for the 'little Amalia von Solms-Braunfels costume'
Pierre-Eugène Lacoste, 1890
Watercolour
Royal Collections, The Hague

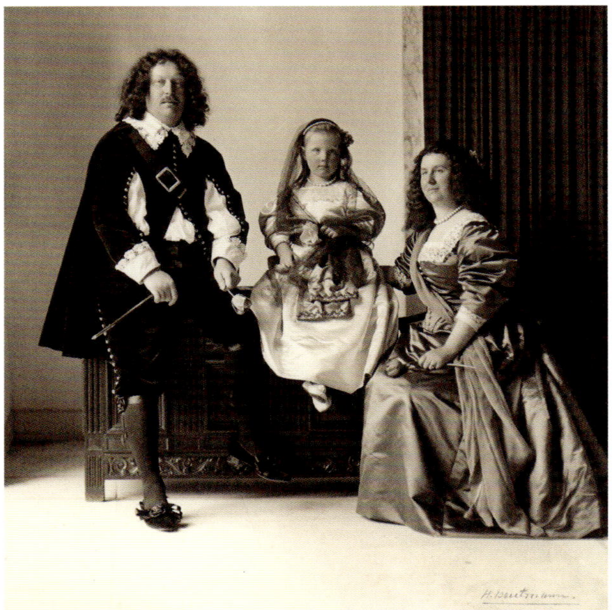

**Queen Wilhelmina, Prince Hendrik and Princess Juliana wearing 17th-century-style costumes ◆**
On Princess Juliana's fifth birthday celebration at Huis ten Bosch Palace the royal family wore costumes in the style of 17th-century stadtholder Frederik Hendrik and Amalia von Solms-Braunfels. Queen Wilhelmina and Prince Hendrik's costumes have survived.

Photo Herman Deutmann, 1914
Paleis Het Loo

## Sporty Wilhelmina

Alongside their mandatory duties, members of the royal family could indulge in sporting activities like skating and the more stylish tennis and rowing, which had originated in Britain. Each sport had its own dress code. Wilhelmina had a passion for driving and riding horses, ever since she had started riding lessons at the Royal Stables at the age of two. She liked to appear on horseback at the military parades she viewed during the First World War, wearing a riding outfit with a hat and long, full skirt, seated side-saddle, with both legs to one side of the horse, as was customary for women. This outfit enhanced the image of the heroic monarch descended directly from the princes of Orange, who had been military generals. She would also wear a special side-saddle outfit on her frequent horse rides in the vicinity of Paleis Het Loo, as it was the only option for a woman.

## Royal dress-up

The mandatory dress codes at court would be readily abandoned for costume parties. In this case, too, a pre-announced theme might provide guidance, but unlike formal balls, a costume ball allowed scope for one's own interpretation. At an event such as this, the differences between those attending – normally made clear by the rules concerning dress – would be blurred. Queen Wilhelmina and her husband Prince Hendrik loved fancy-dress parties. As a young queen, Wilhelmina had a book of masquerade costumes. There was great interest in historical styles during this period. A fancy-dress party was a serious matter. Lots of money would be spent on a costume, and people would make thorough preparations. At the age of nine, Wilhelmina posed in a costume in the style of Amalia von Solms-Braunfels, which had been made for her in Paris. At Paleis Het Loo there is a huge painting in which Wilhelmina, Hendrik and Juliana pose in historical costumes, dressed as residents of Huis ten Bosch in the time of Frederik Hendrik and Amalia von Solms-Braunfels. Princess Juliana gave a costume party at her student house, at which she briefly cast off her royal image, attending as a young lady from the time of Anna Pavlovna.[4] At the costume ball at Paleis Noordeinde on New Year's Eve 1936, just before Juliana and Bernhard's wedding, Juliana dressed as a harem girl. The bridegroom had the nerve to appear in the black uniform of a soldier in the army of General Franco, the fascist leader of Spain.

**Prince Hendrik in fancy dress ◆**
Prince Hendrik's jacket, waistcoat and calf-length breeches from a fancy dress costume in 18th-century style have survived. The prince also wore a white lace jabot and a white rococo wig with them. The costume was supplied in circa 1915 by Verch & Flothow, which also made theatre costumes for the imperial court in Berlin.

Paleis Het Loo. On long-term loan from the Royal Collections, The Hague

'Harlequin' costume ◆
Maker unknown, circa 1925-1930
Silk, cotton, metal
Kunstmuseum Den Haag

'Queen of Hearts' costume ◆
Maker unknown, circa 1930-1939
Silk, wool, synthetic fabric
Kunstmuseum Den Haag

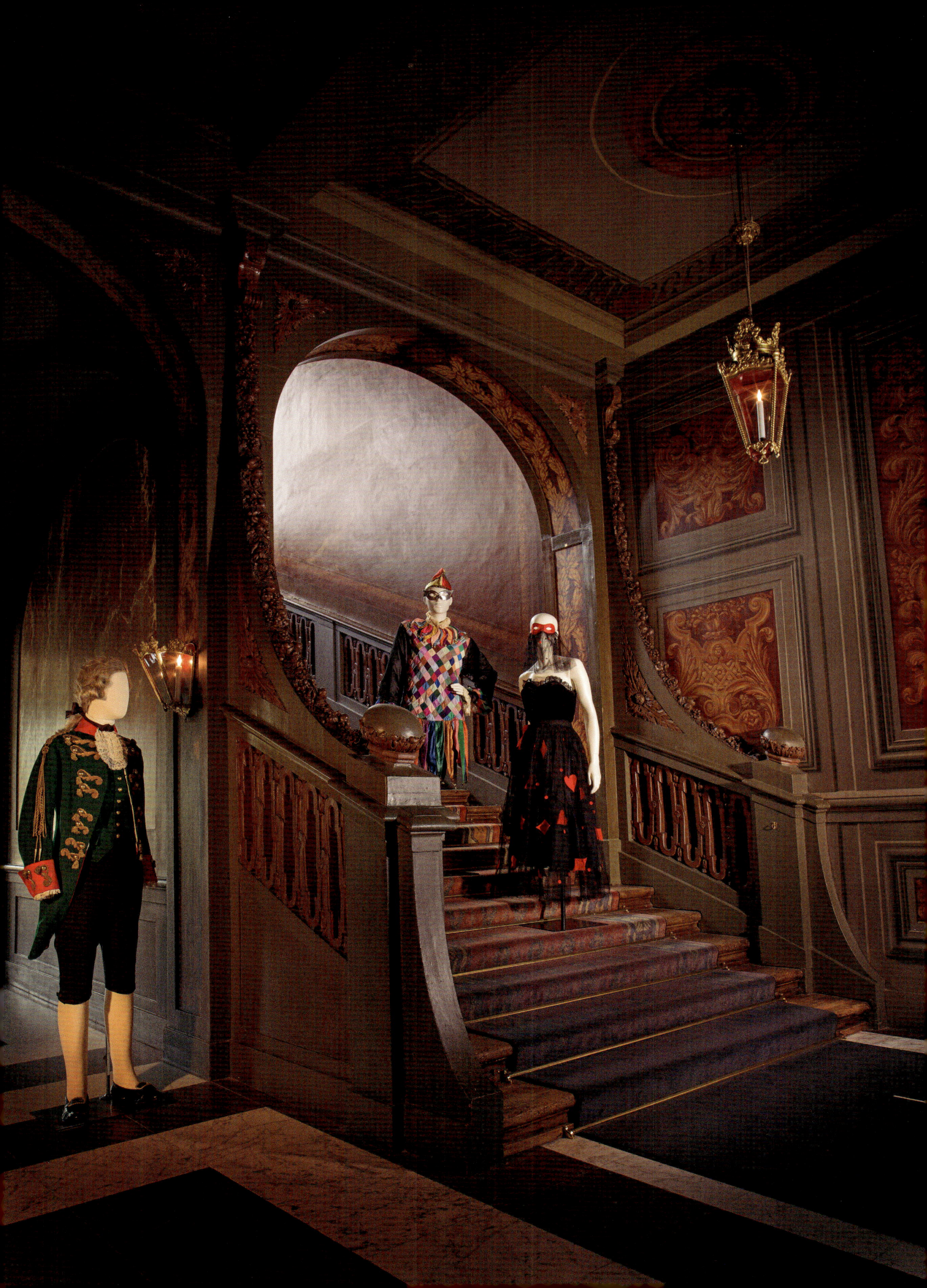

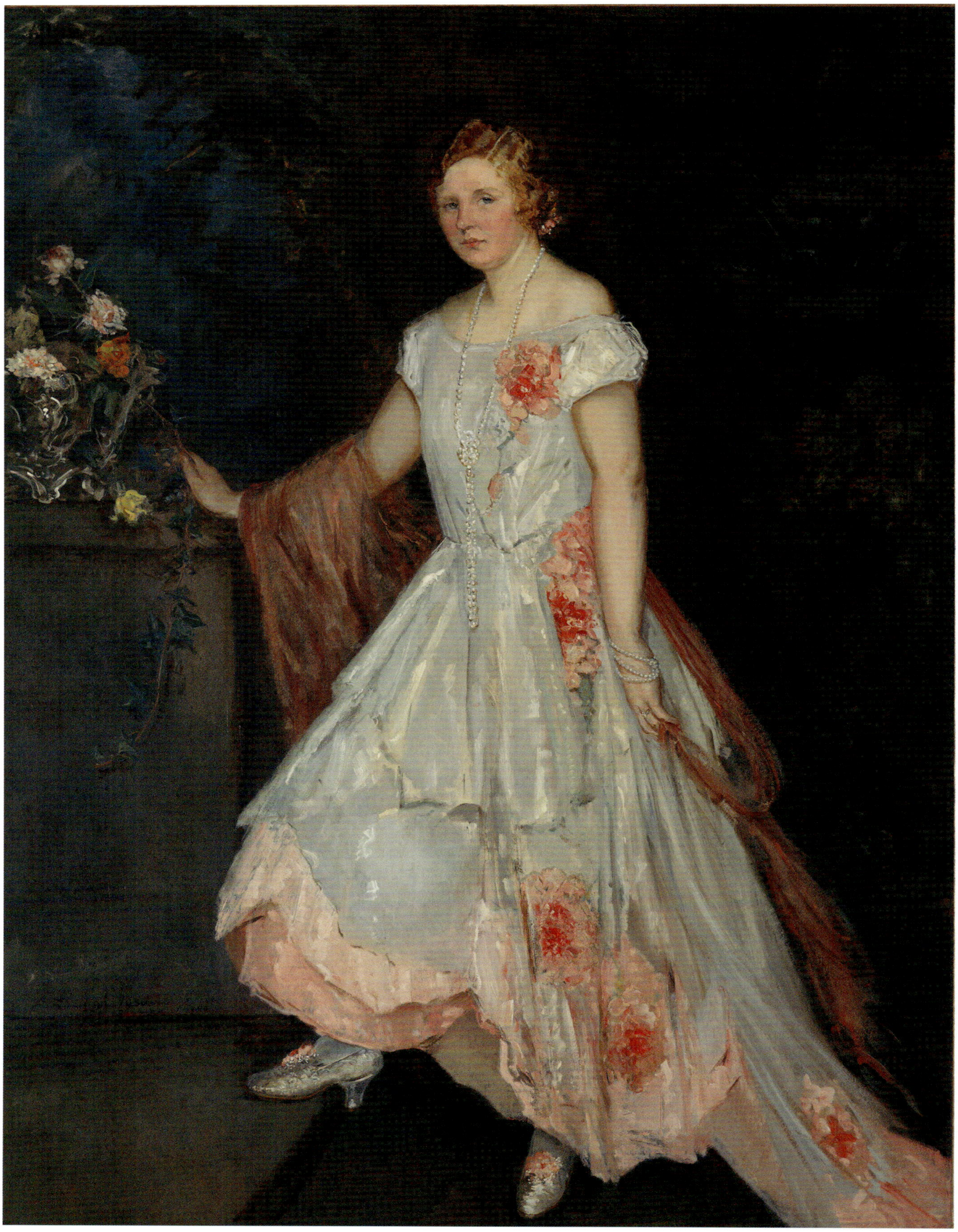

A graceful Princess Juliana, 1930
After studying in Leiden, Princess Juliana became more and more aware of her position as next in line to the throne. She also appeared to have a growing interest in fashion. Juliana posed for this portrait at Paleis Het Loo wearing a light, loose-fitting evening dress with pink roses.

Lizzy Ansingh
Oil on canvas, 212 x 168 cm
Paleis Het Loo, on long-term loan
from the Royal Collections, The Hague

## Juliana's dress code: bathing suit

The dress codes that applied when Queen Emma arrived in 1879 continued to apply, though to a lesser and lesser extent, until 1940. Fashions changed, and in response to the austerity measures Wilhelmina introduced at court at the start of the First World War and the economic crisis of the 1930s, the long train fell out of fashion at the palace. Young women in Princess Juliana's circle began to dread wearing the long gloves that were required at court. But during the last few years before the German invasion in 1940, the glamour of ceremonial life at court was spectacularly rekindled on a number of occasions, when Princess Juliana married Prince Bernhard of Lippe-Biesterfeld in 1937, and in 1938 when Queen Wilhelmina celebrated forty years on the throne. In that same year, Princess Beatrix was christened, and King Leopold II of Belgium made a state visit to the Netherlands. A year later, Wilhelmina made a return visit to Belgium. Participants required a suitable wardrobe for all these festive occasions, and for all the other receptions that went ahead as normal, and the public engagements of the royal family, such as the official opening of parliament, regional visits, openings, unveilings and launches.

The traditional court of the Orange dynasty had entered a new era. Princess Juliana and Prince Bernhard reshaped court life in the late 1930s in their modern home at Paleis Soestdijk. They enthusiastically broke with the formal conventions of the grand court in The Hague and Amsterdam. The young royal couple embraced the progress of the modern age. There were no balls or tea dances, no formal audiences and receptions at Soestdijk. Dress codes adapted to the unconventional receptions, which might mean that Princess Juliana invited her guests to an event with the explicit dress code 'Bring your bathing suit if the weather is fine!'[5] Dutch court life in the grand, 19th-century style had come to an end.

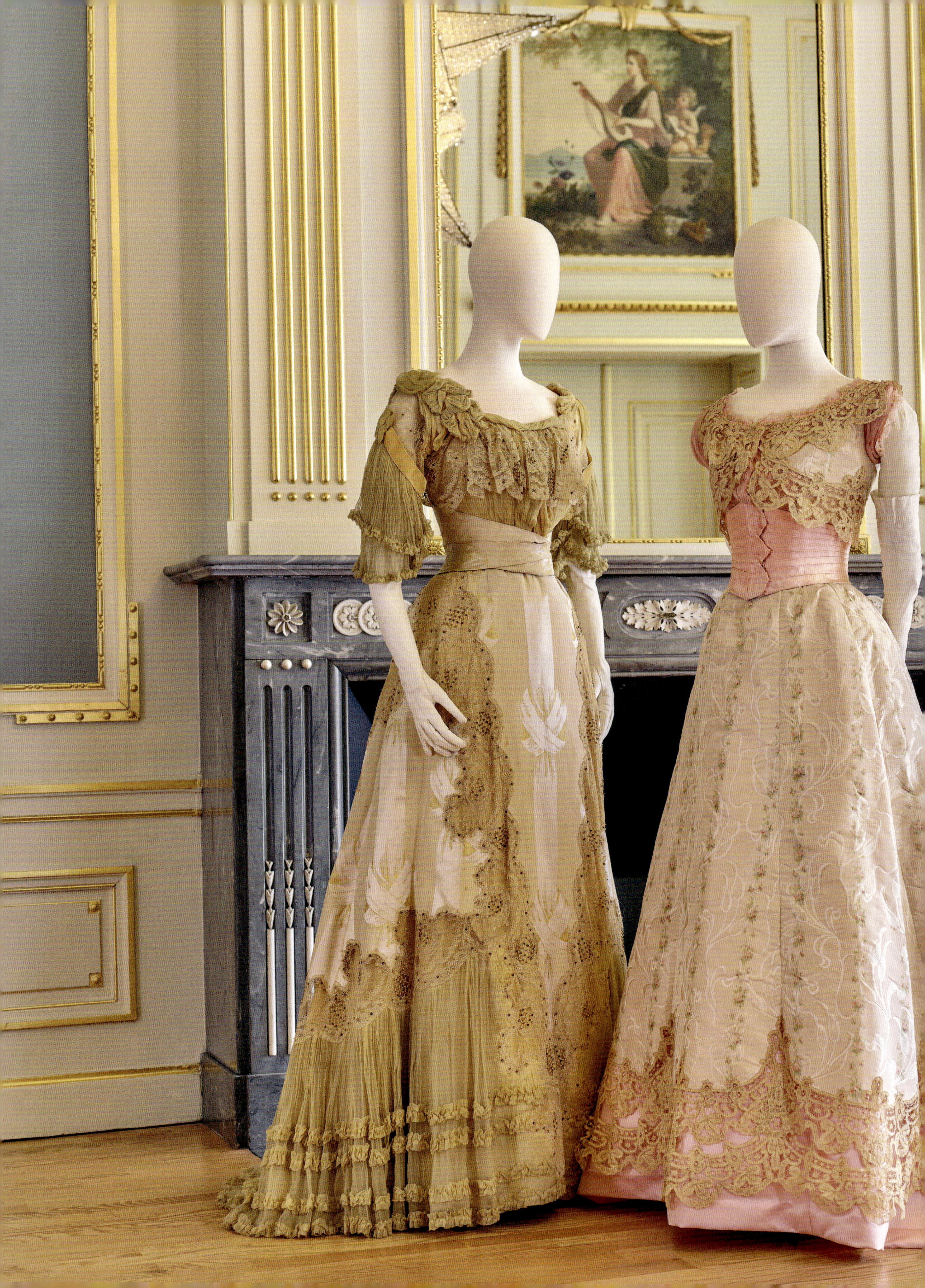

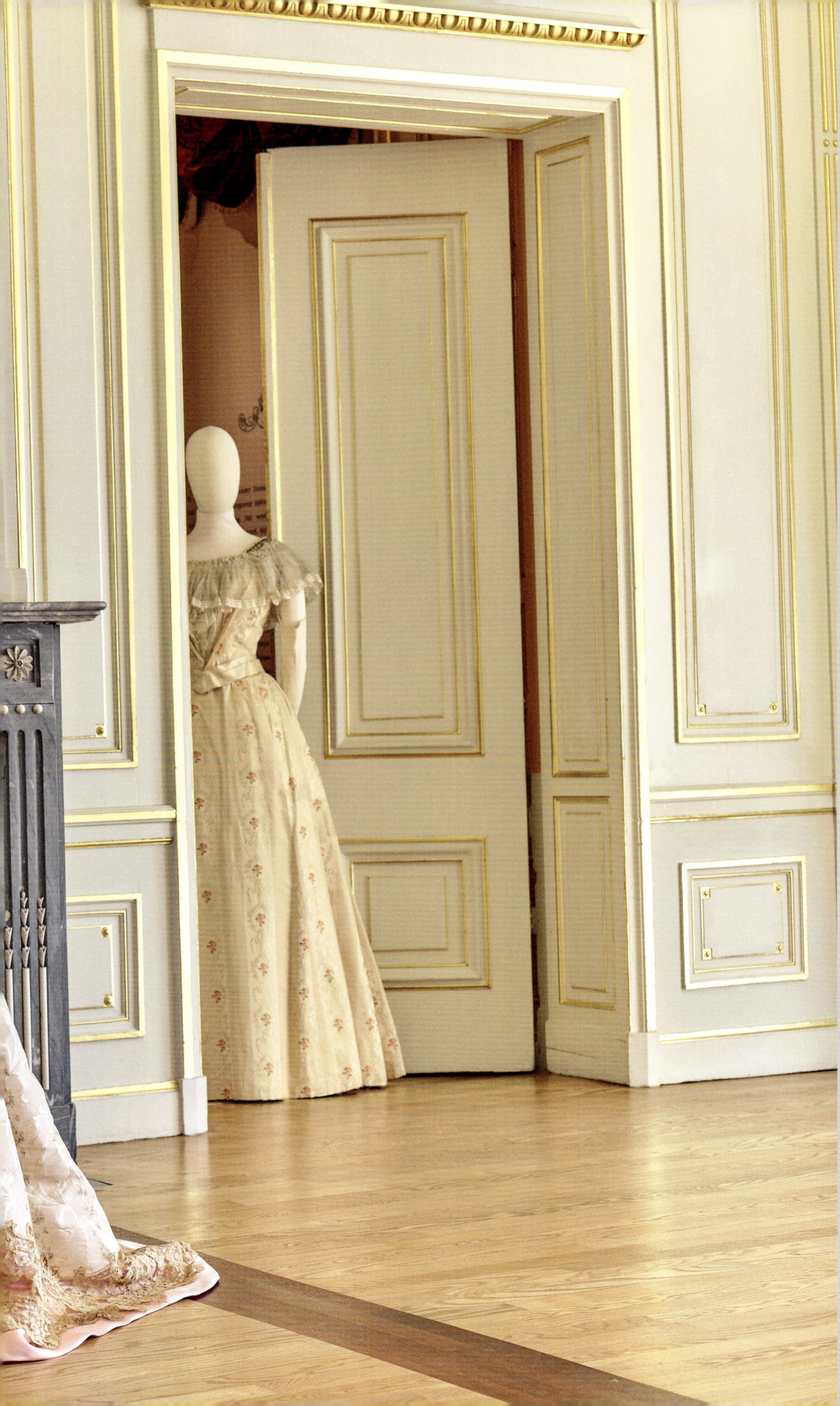

# DRESS CODES AT COURT

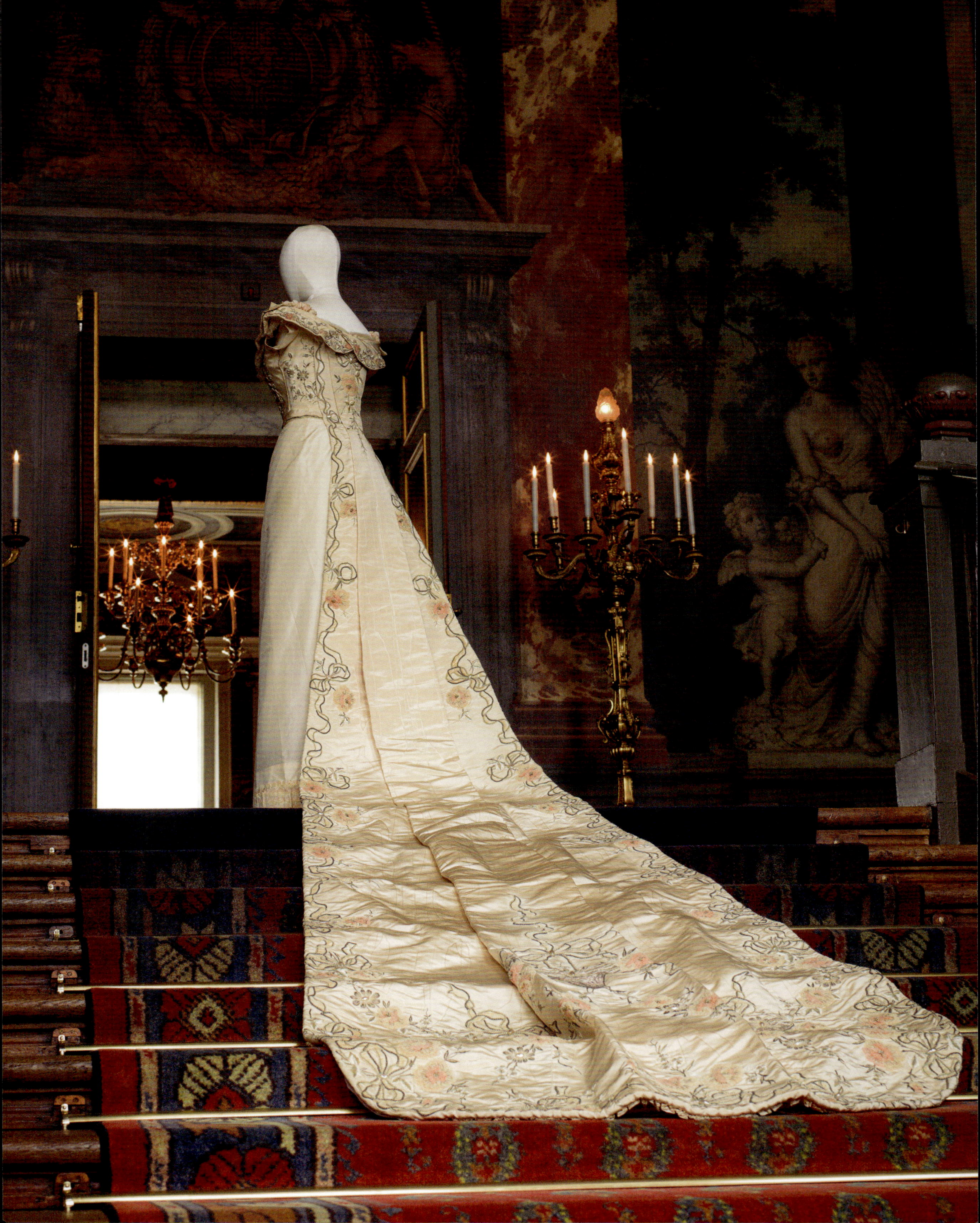

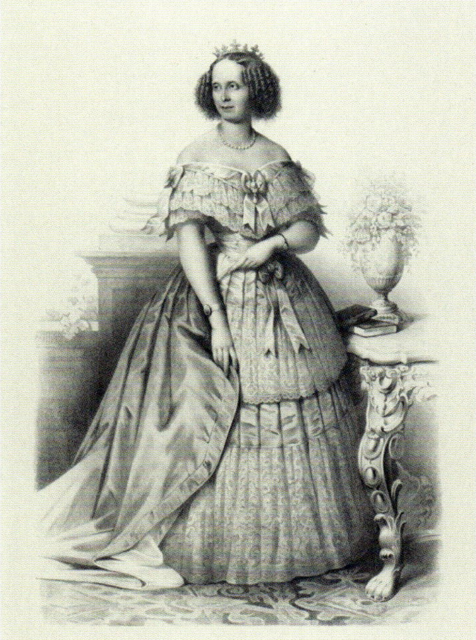

Queen Sophie wearing a court train
King Willem III's first wife Sophie wore a separate court train attached to the waist of her ballgown.

N.J.W. de Roode, circa 1865
Lithograph, 63.5 x 49.2 cm
Rijksmuseum, Amsterdam

# QUEEN WILHELMINA'S COURT TRAIN

Ladies were expected to wear a dress with a train at court receptions. But King Willem I issued a Royal Decree on 26 april 1825 requiring them to wear an additional train, known by the French term *manteau de cour*. This 'court cloak', or rather 'court train', was a separate piece that could be attached to the neckline or waist of a ballgown. It was used at the Dutch royal court until the early 20th century.

Queen Emma wore a red velvet court train, which was later used by Wilhelmina. It was probably made in 1882 for Emma to wear at Windsor Castle when her sister Helena married one of the sons of the British monarch, Queen Victoria. It was supplied by the renowned Paris fashion house Corbay-Wenzel, which was later taken over by the house of Nicaud, who made a *manteau de cour* for Queen Wilhelmina. The cream moire silk train was embroidered with baskets of flowers and bows in silver thread. The straight top section of the train covers the entire back; the end is rounded. Wilhelmina wore the train with a white silk and lace dress at a court ball in Schwerin, where her husband Prince Hendrik came from.

The advantage of a separate train was that it could be worn with different ballgowns. There were strict rules about the length of court trains at the European courts where were worn. Around 1900 the required length for queens was four metres; princesses and the ladies in their retinue would wear trains measuring 3.75 metres, and young unmarried women would wear a 3.25-metre train.[1] But these were only guidelines. Queen Wilhelmina's court train was 3.75 metres instead of four. And even a distinguished item like a court train was subject to change. Princess Marie, a cousin of Willem III who married the Prince of Wied in Wassenaar in 1871 had a separate train attached to the waist of her wedding dress. Newspaper journalists remarked that the princess was following the fashion of the Prussian court, rather than attaching the train at the neck, as was customary at the Dutch court.

A separate court train was the ultimate addition to a dress which, like every fashionable gown, would already have its own in-built train. Dresses with trains would therefore not only be worn at balls. At a formal evening ball or tea dance, where there would be dancing, it was not practical to wear a long train. Yet ladies would sometimes wear a dress with a substantial train, like Queen Emma at a ball at Paleis Noordeinde in 1882. It was no easy task to move gracefully in a dress with a train. Emma's lady-in-waiting felt that the queen took hold of her train in the wrong place when she was about to descend the stairs. Ladies who were presented to Queen Wilhelmina wrestled with the same problem. 'It [the train] required particular skill, particularly as one took three steps backwards when moving away from the queen. When walking, the train would be carried over the arm or, very elegantly, lifted with a little finger through a loop on the hem.'[2]
—PR

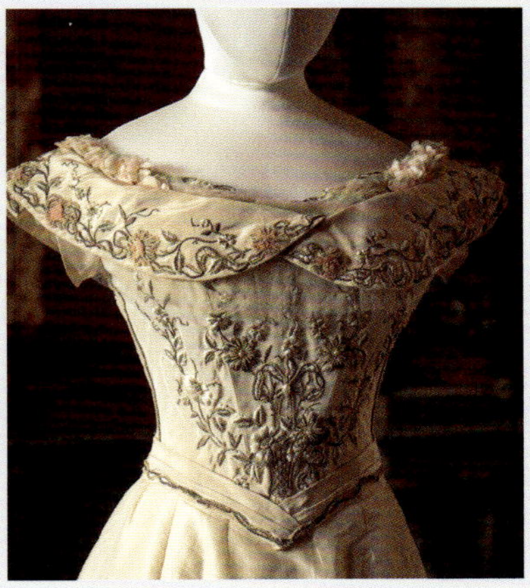

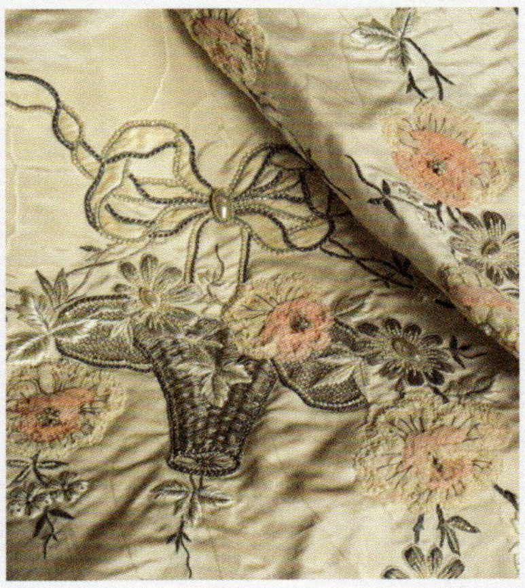

Queen Wilhelmina's court train ◆
Paris, Nicaud Paris, circa 1900
Silk, silver thread, glass pearls
Paleis Het Loo, on long-term loan from the Royal Collections, The Hague

**A court train from the time of Willem I**
King Louis Napoleon based his Dutch court on the example of the imperial court of France. Etiquette dictated that Queen Hortense, her ladies-in-waiting and all female guests must wear a court train. The lilac train embroidered with glass pearls was probably worn by a female guest at a formal reception at the court of King Willem I.

Centraal Museum Utrecht

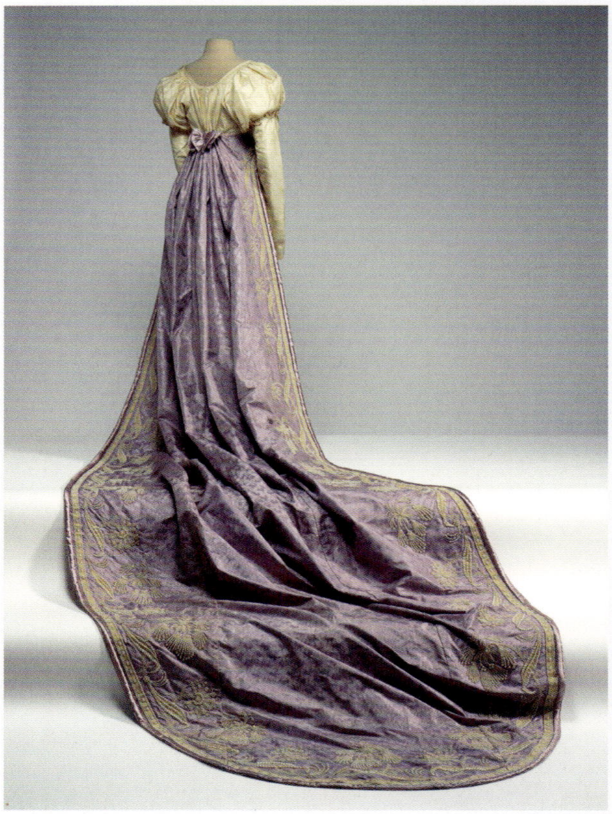

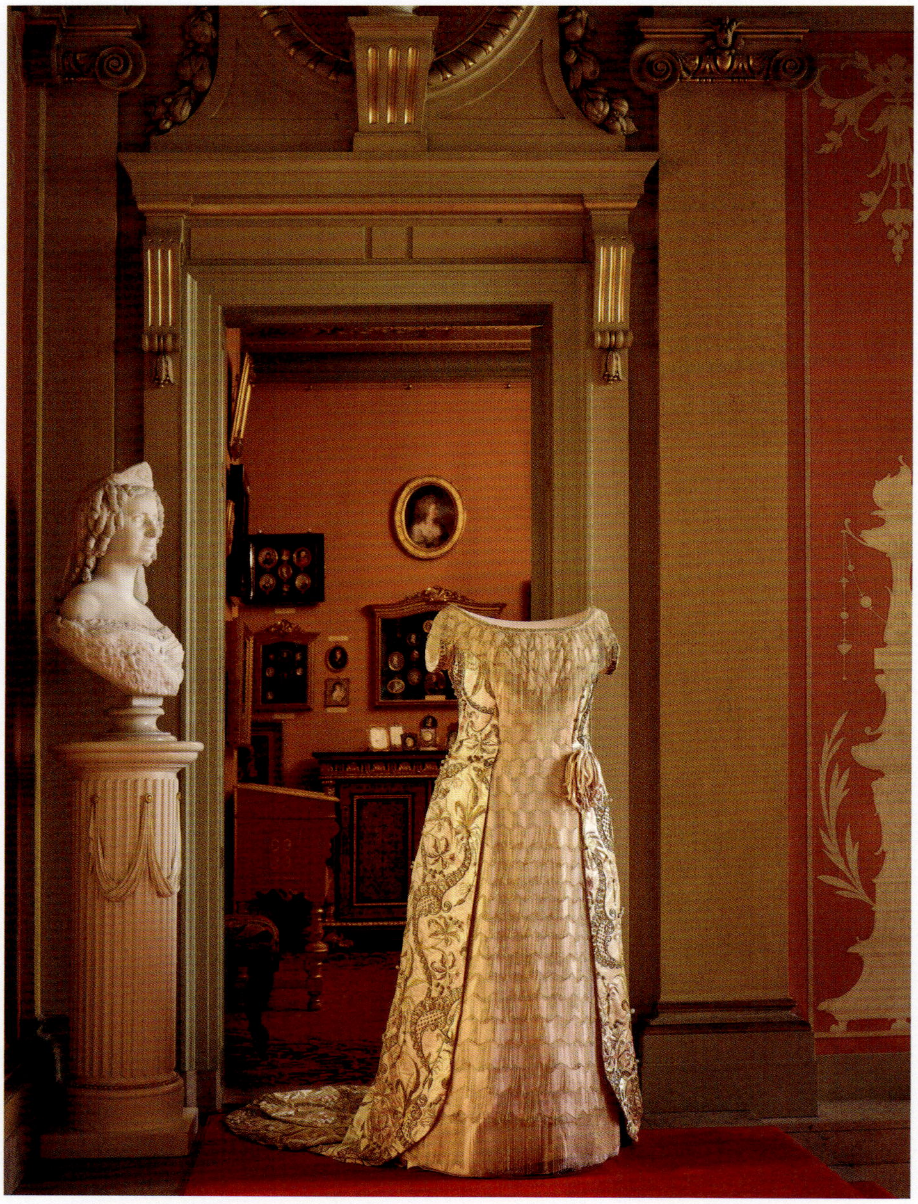

**Ballgown with train ◆**
Wilhelmina's ballgown is a single garment, but it is designed in such a way that it appears to have an over-dress with a court train. The dress was probably adapted to the queen's changing preferences around 1923.

Paris, Premet, circa 1910
Silk, gold thread, glass pearls, mother-of-pearl
Royal Collections, The Hague

**Emma's *manteau de cour* ◆**
A court train was worn for ceremonial occasions at court. Queen Emma's ladies-in-waiting assumed that they should dress formally for the baptism of Princess Wilhelmina at St. William's Church in The Hague, in a low-cut gown with a court train. But at the last moment, the Queen ordered them to wear a high-necked dress with a train and a hat.

Paris, Corbay-Wenzel, 1882
Silk, silver thread, glass pearls
Royal Collections, The Hague

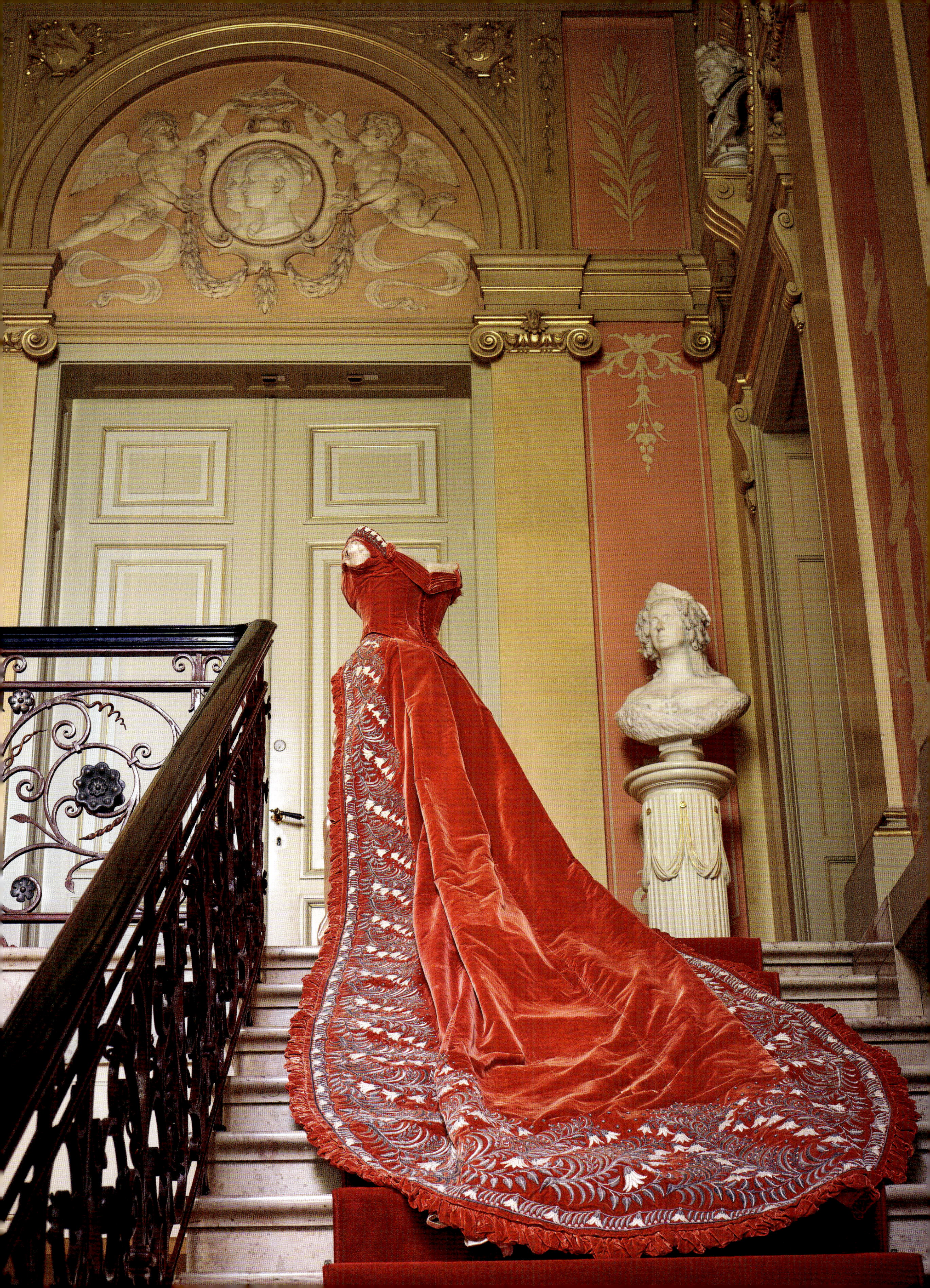

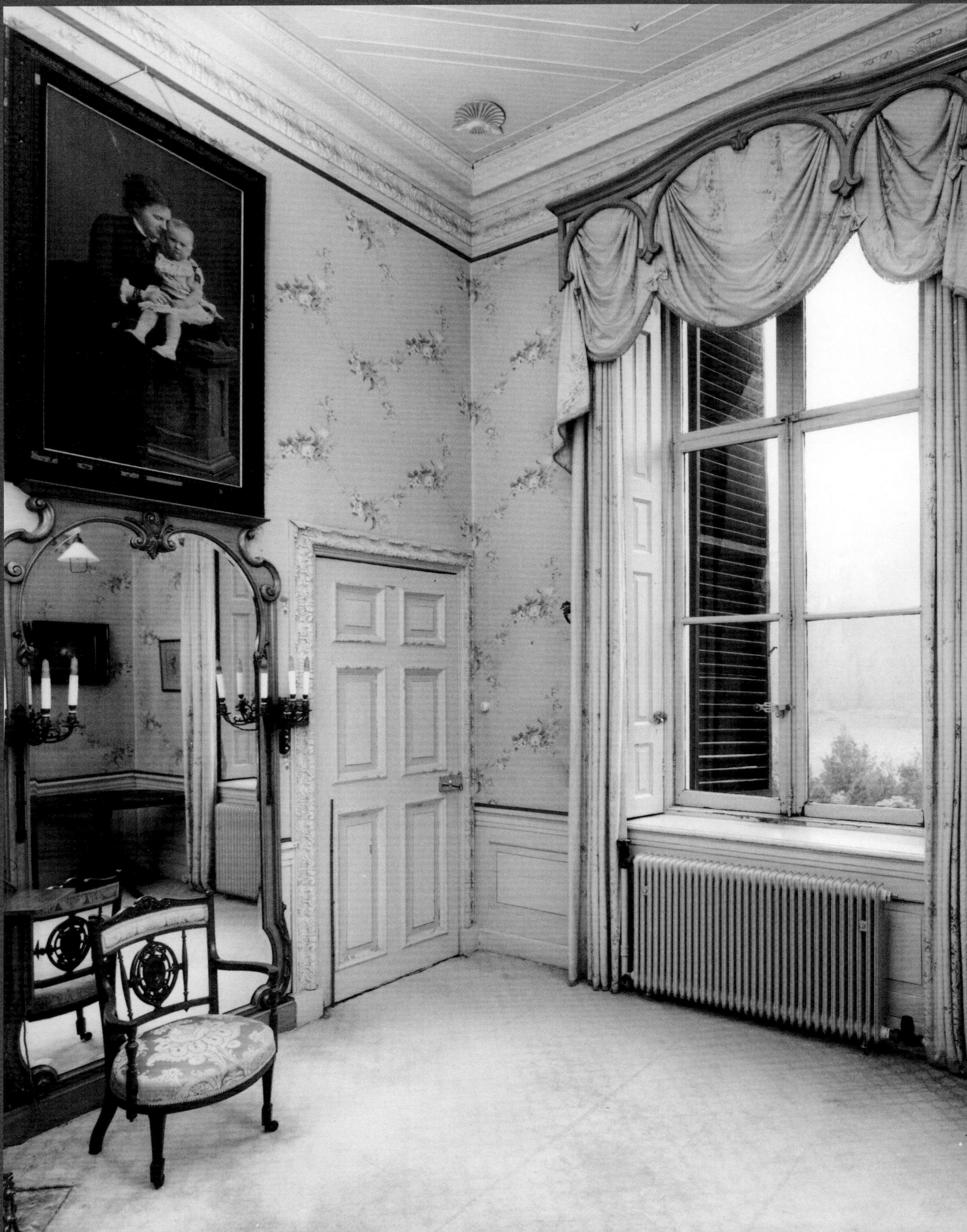

# THE DAILY CYCLE OF COSTUME CHANGES

'The afternoons were spent at audiences and getting dressed and undressed,' Queen Wilhelmina wrote to her former English governess in the month after her investiture.[1] A day at court was a day of costume changes for both men and women. This applied both to members of the royal family and to their courtiers and servants, such as footmen and equerries. Each individual reception often had its own dress code. Visits and private audiences in the morning required different clothes than lunches and afternoon receptions. Another change of clothes would be needed before dinner and the evening programme. If the day was to be spent on public duties, outfits would be chosen accordingly.

We have little information about the practice of constant costume changes. Dressing is an intimate act, few details of which have been recorded. It will have involved close contact with the man or woman responsible for the clothes. Kings and princes had a wardrobe master or valet and queens and princesses had a wardrobe mistress or dresser. These staff ensured that dresses and uniforms were in good condition and made simple repairs. They also set out the jewellery and insignia to be worn with the outfit. As a five-year-old princess, Wilhelmina was given her own dresser, who had a room at Paleis Noordeinde beside the princess's apartments. The dresser was also able to make clothes for the princess. The keeper of the royal wardrobe probably had a role in putting together suitable outfits for certain occasions. She would also help with dressing and undressing. When an outfit had to be changed quickly, the help of a dresser was vital.

In 1880, as an audience was about to begin Queen Emma was still not ready with her outfit. A lady-in-waiting who had been quickly summoned even saw the queen fastening the buttons on her dress in her dressing room, as her dresser threaded a medallion onto a chain.[2]

The help of a wardrobe mistress was essential for the fastening and unfastening of the hooks and eyes on evening gowns with separate bodices, skirts and trains. Corsets were always worn, until the early 20th century, even by young girls like Princess Wilhelmina. The corset supported the body and ensured that the tight bodice fitted correctly, keeping the dress in shape. Wearing a corset also produced a proud, elegant posture. Around 1905 there were calls for healthier fashions that would not require restrictive corsets. Up to that time, Wilhelmina had been slender, with an almost wasp waist. She too embraced the new fashion, which had a much more natural look although, like most ladies at the time, she continued to wear a figure-correcting corset.

The wardrobe was housed in the royal apartments. At Paleis Het Loo Queen Wilhelmina had a large oak cabinet. Prince Hendrik had a set of rooms on the ground floor. He had a built-in wardrobe in the doorway between his study and his dressing room. His dressing room will also have been used as a wardrobe, given the fact that the inventory lists a large oak three-door cabinet, with a large mirror in the middle door. A valet stand and a shaving mirror on a tall base were permanent features of the prince's dressing room.
—PR

**Wilhelmina's dressing room at Paleis Het Loo**
The queen would have her hair done in the dressing room, and her outfit would be completed with jewellery, plus a sash and breast star if the dress code required them. The door gives onto the small corridor that leads to her bedroom. Beside the door is a large mirror with lights on either side. Above it is a large photograph of Queen Emma with Wilhelmina as a child, taken in 1882.

Photo A. Meine Jansen, 1973
Paleis Het Loo

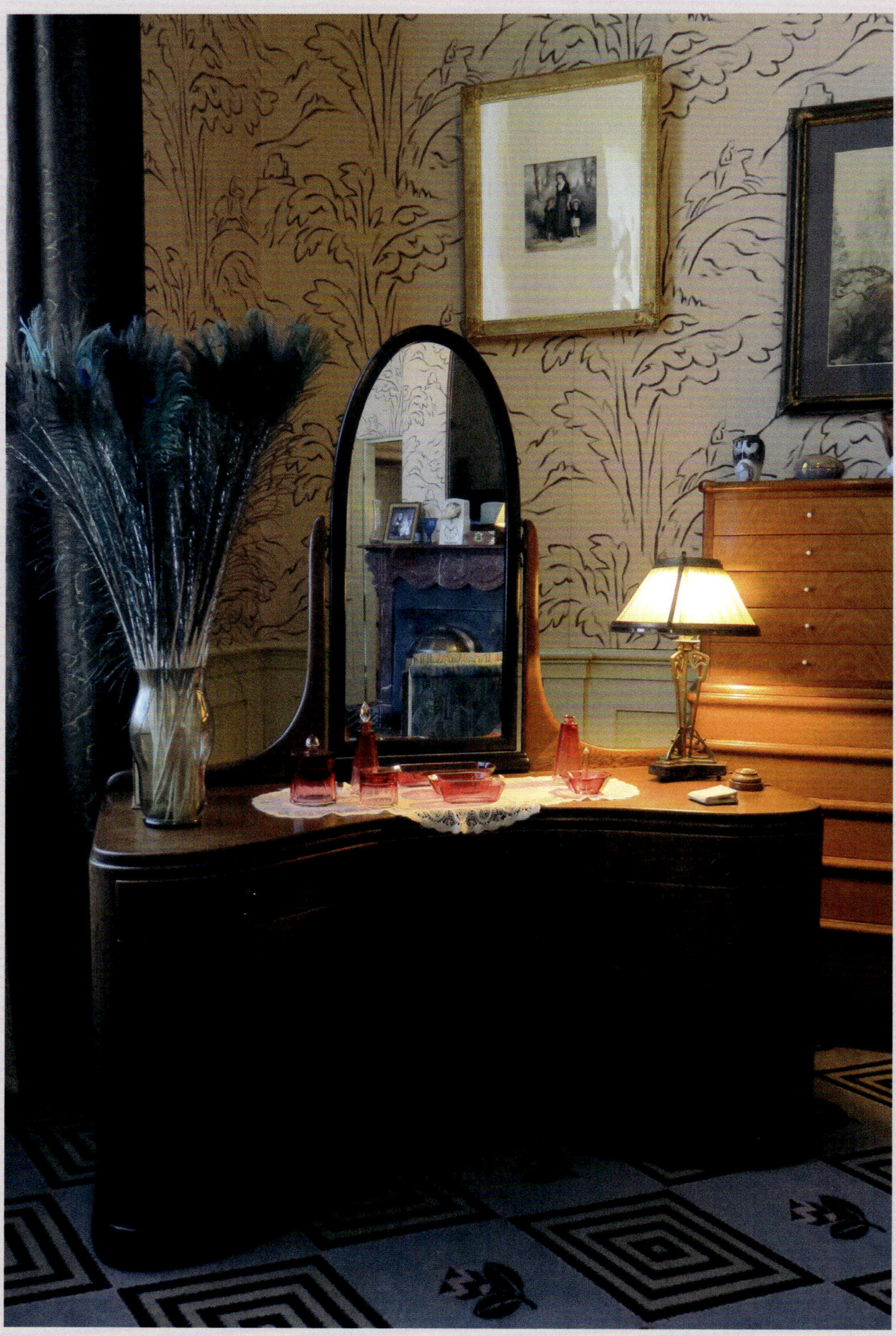

**Dressing table**
For her eighteenth birthday in 1927 Princess Juliana was allowed to have her room at Paleis Het Loo refurbished. She chose fittings in a contemporary Art Deco style from the catalogue of renowned furniture manufacturer Pander. The mirror is curved, as was typical of this style.

Rosewood, mirrored glass, circa 1925
Paleis Het Loo

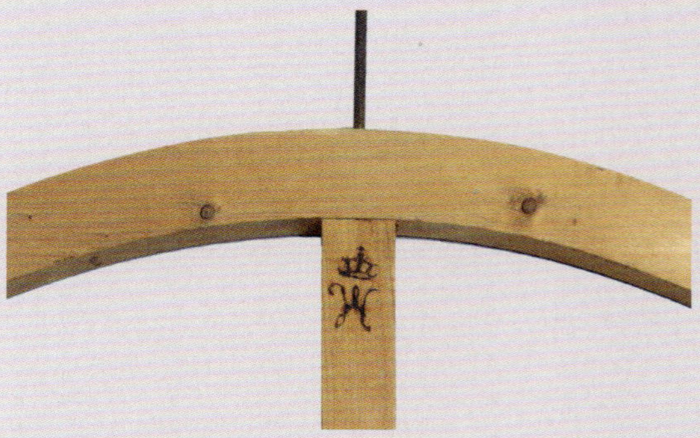

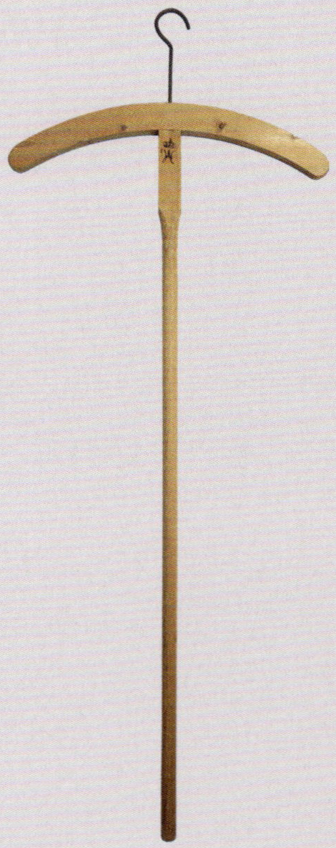

**Royal coat hangers**
Wilhelmina's wardrobes had coat hangers stamped with her crowned monogram. Her clothes for the day would be hung on copper coat hooks attached to the posts between the sliding doors.

Pine, circa 1880-1900
Paleis Het Loo

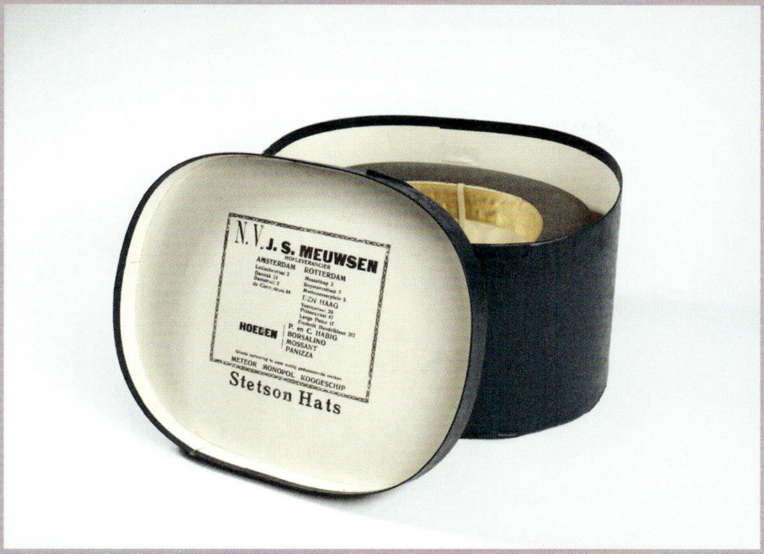


**Hat box belonging to Queen Wilhelmina**
Hats were kept in cabinets, but would be transported between palaces in hat boxes, such as those supplied by the hatmaker J.S. Meuwsen, purveyor to the royal court.

Paleis Het Loo, on long-term loan from the Royal Collections, The Hague

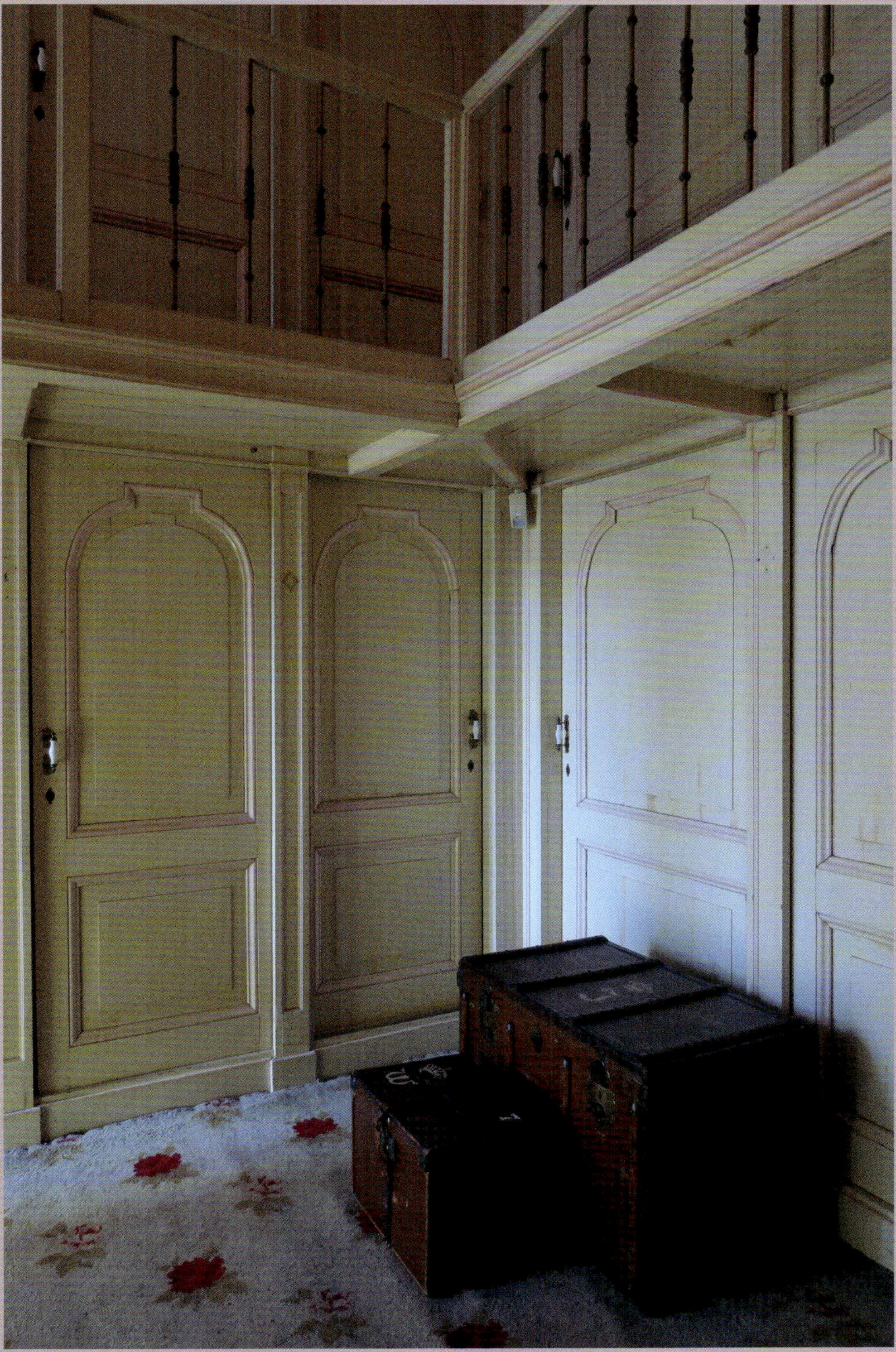

**A young queen's wardrobe**
The young Princess Wilhelmina's wardrobe at Paleis Het Loo was next to her bedroom on the ground floor. When she was fourteen, the high-ceilinged room was transformed into a walk-in closet, with built-in cabinets that had two layers of sliding doors. A generation later, Princess Juliana used the same wardrobe.

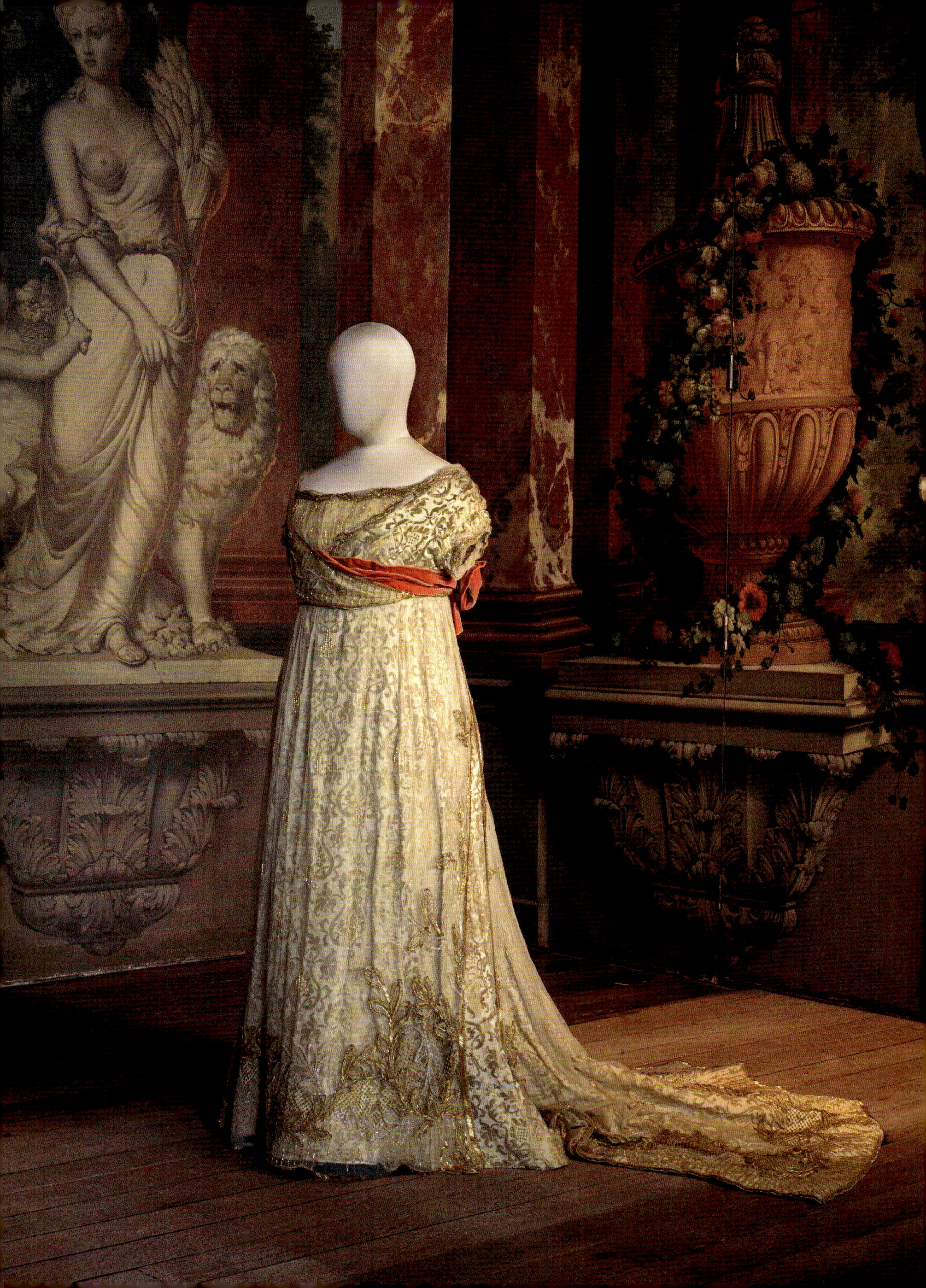

# QUEEN WILHELMINA'S EMPIRE WAIST BALLGOWN

The dress is made of gold brocade with floral motifs in gold thread and mother-of-pearl, and is entirely covered in silk tulle. The short bodice is made of cream silk, with two crossed strips of gold brocade and embroidered tulle applied over it, plus a third strip of pink silk velvet. The skirt is pleated and finishes in a straight train. The entire dress is covered with a front and back panel of tulle, embroidered with mother-of-pearl and glass beads in a scatter pattern. The edges are decorated with embroidered stylised laurel vines.

The design of the dress, which would be worn with long white gloves, was inspired by dresses from circa 1800, the late 18th century and the time of the Napoleonic 'empire'. In that period, a passion for classical antiquity, with its thin, draped garments and high waists, was reflected in women's fashions. Around 1910 there was a brief revival of this Empire style. Queen Wilhelmina's dress, with its low, straight neckline, high waist and Empire-style embroidery, is an example of this. Parisian designers' preference for supple fabrics was influenced by the dress reform movement. This international social movement campaigned, among other things, for women to have a full role in society. It also called for the abolition of the restrictive corset, which produced the S-line, with the bosom pushed forward and the hips back. Around 1910 the preference was for a slim, straight line, and corsets fell out of fashion. Most women started wearing less restrictive corsets. This was also true of Queen Wilhelmina. Though she followed the fashion trends from a distance, she did not go so far as to stop wearing a corset altogether. She did however benefit in informal settings from the more natural silhouette, accentuated by the use of supple fabrics.

The queen's choice of colour for this ballgown was remarkable. Though the Empire style is a quintessentially regal style, and the gold brocade goes well with the gold embroidered lions on the royal robe, the rose pink on the bodice and the orange of the sash of the Military Order of William are not a good colour combination.
—PR

**Wilhelmina's ballgown in Napoleonic 'empire' style ◆**
Unknown atelier, circa 1910
Silk, gold thread, mother-of-pearl, glass beads
Royal Collections, The Hague

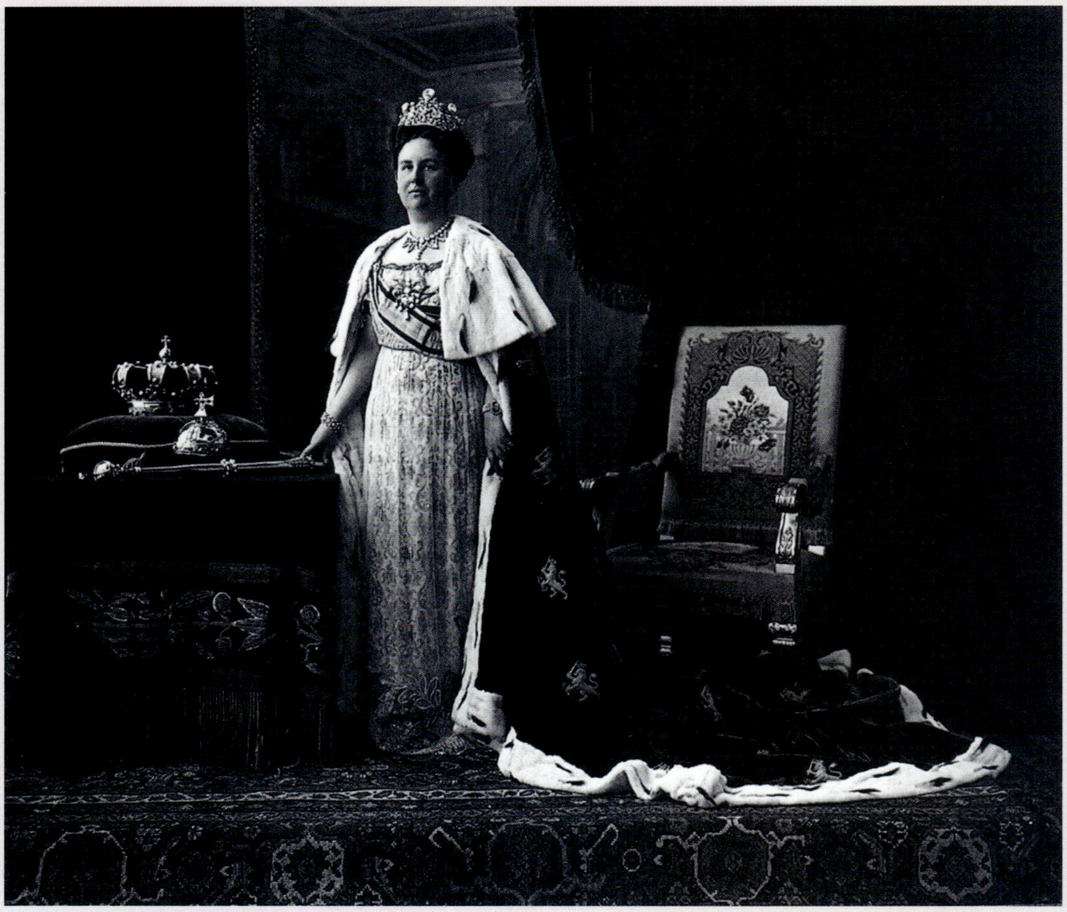

**Queen in full regalia**
The queen wore the dress in 1912, during a session in the photo studio at Paleis Het Loo, possibly to mark her copper jubilee. The royal robe and the table beside her with her regalia (crown, orb and sceptre) were transported from Paleis Noordeinde to Het Loo for the official photograph.

Photo J.J.M. Guy de Coral, 1912
Collection unknown

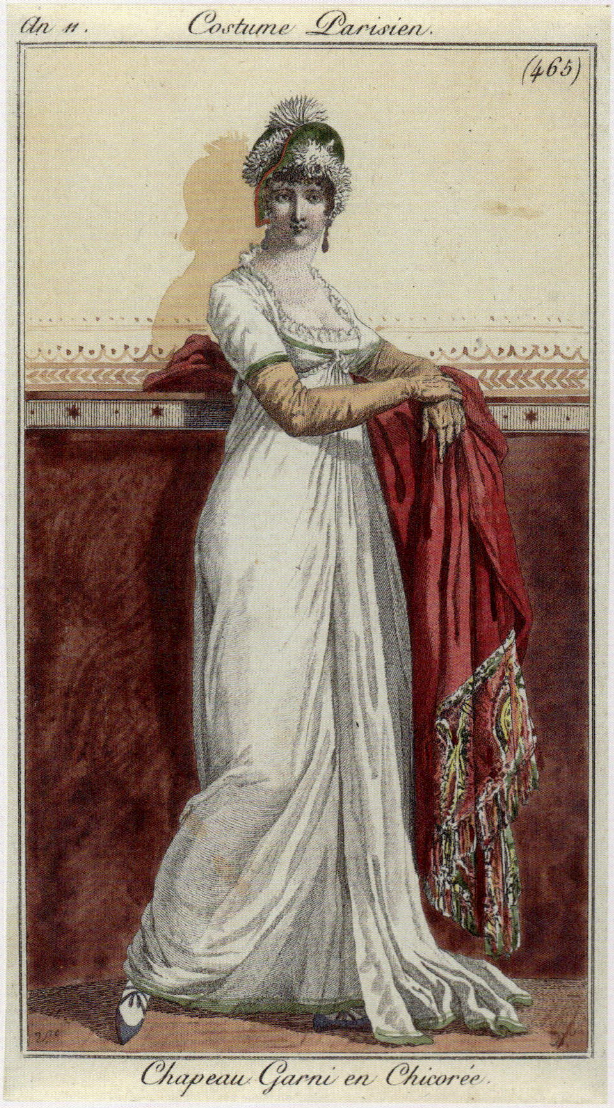


**Fashion plate from the Napoleonic era**
Paris fashion of 1803, a year before Napoleon Bonaparte established the empire, dictated lines reminiscent of the clothes worn in classical antiquity. The low-cut dress has short sleeves. It would be worn with long gloves. Print by P.C. Baquoy, from the fashion magazine *Journal des Dames et des Modes.*

Rijksmuseum, Amsterdam

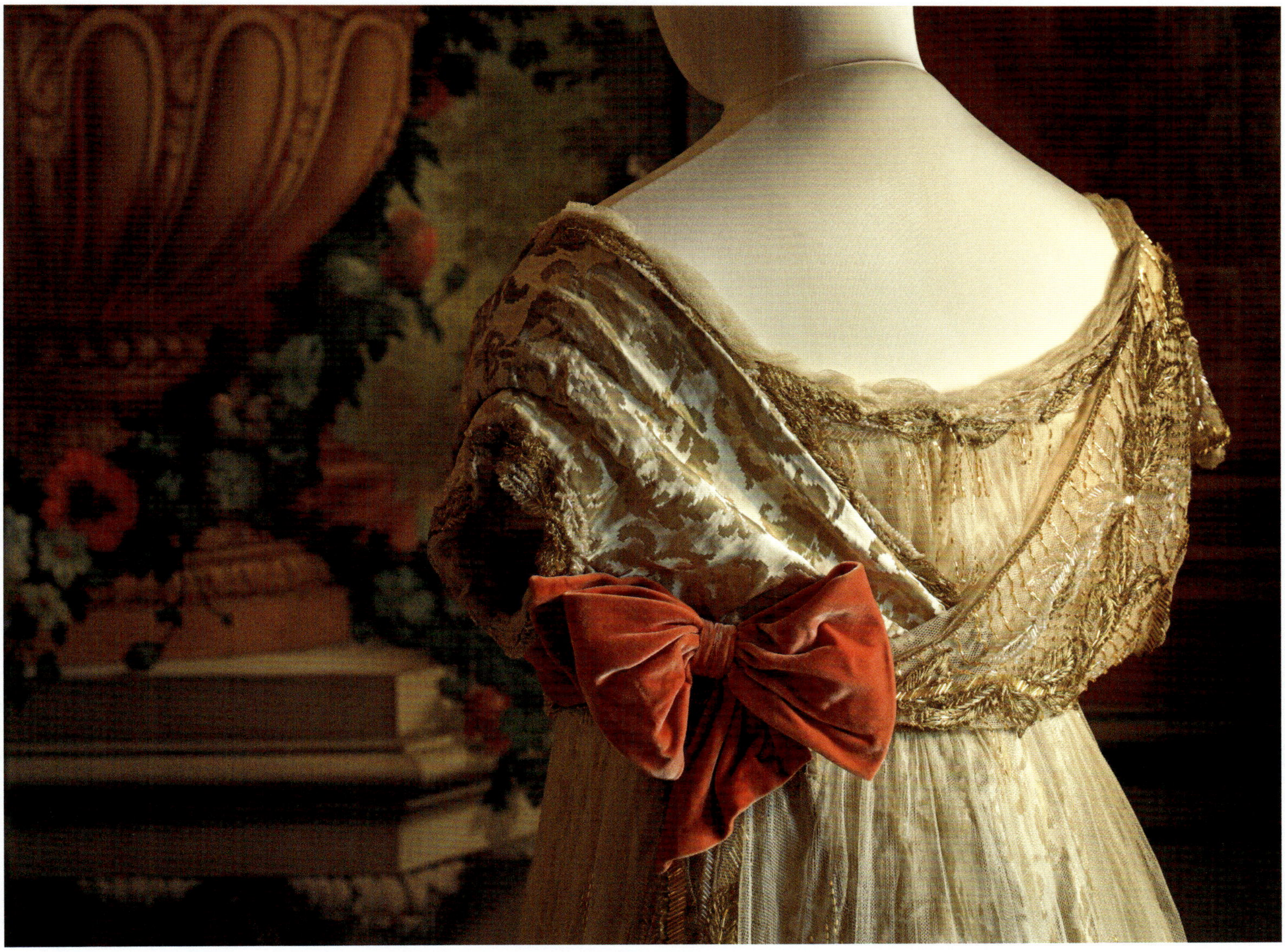

Details of Wilhelmina's ball gown

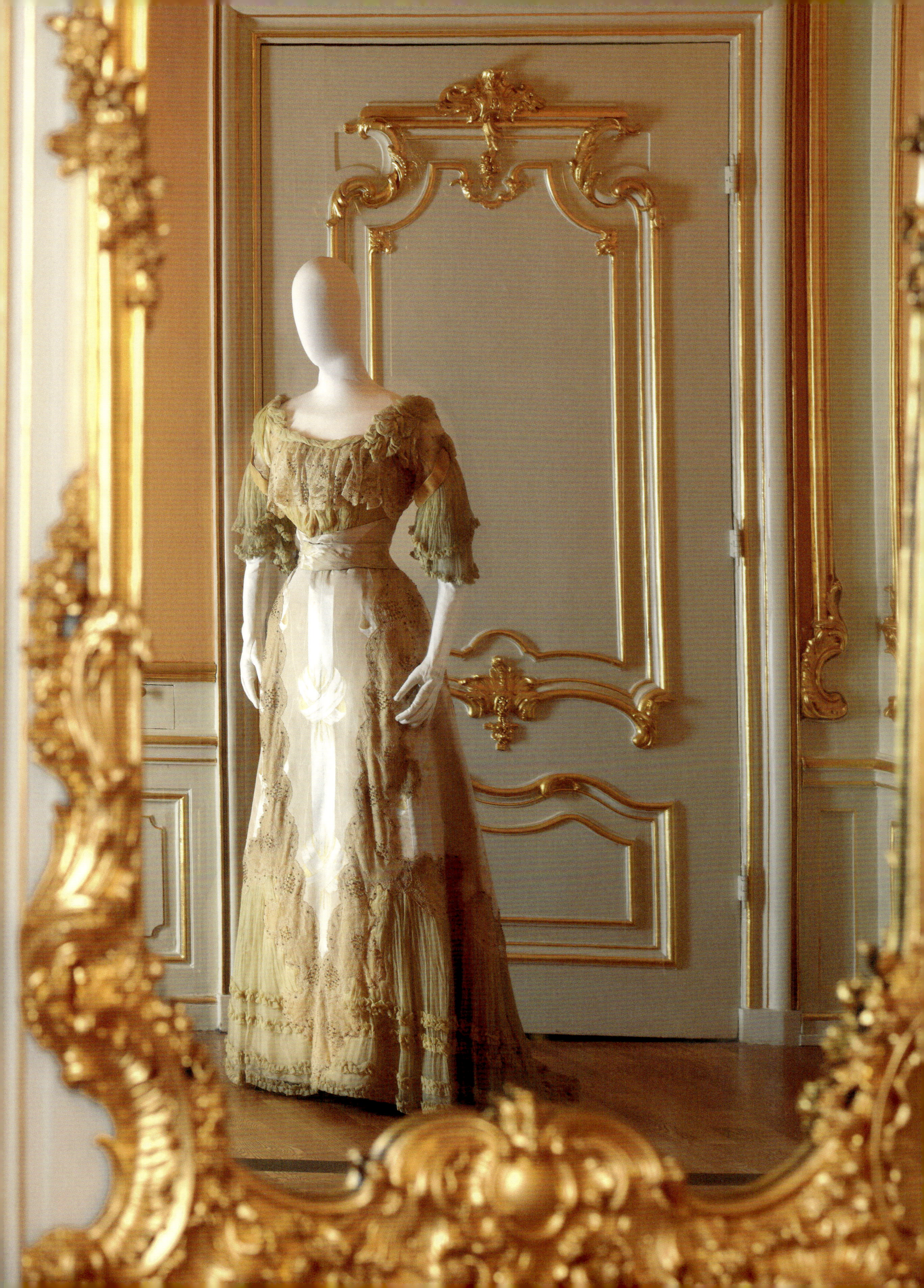

# DRESS CODES AT COURT

It must have been a relief for everyone concerned that dress codes were generally well communicated at court, so as a guest or courtier you knew exactly what was required of you. Most invitations for a reception at court, even a small reception like 'Au Thé' ('For Tea'), thus duly stated which 'attire' one was expected to don, often with separate stipulations for the 'Ladies' and the 'Gentlemen'. The invitations issued in The Hague were generally in French, as this was still the language of the elite in 'La Haye', even into the 20th century. The life of 'le monde' ('the world'), as the small world of the court was known at the time, consisted of many events at which fashionable attire must be worn. Several outfits a day, in fact, as each occasion had its own dress code. Any woman who wanted to be part of this world would need to have in their wardrobe a 'toilette de visite' (an visiting outfit, meaning a formal gown), a 'toilette de promenade' (walking costume, always with a hat), and outfits appropriate for the dress codes 'toilette décolleté' (low-cut gown), 'demi-décolleté (semi-low-cut gown), 'montante' (an outfit with a high neckline), 'gala' and 'grand gala'. Around 1900 many fashionable gowns consisted of a separate bodice and skirt. A 'robe à transformation', as it was known, was handy, as it allowed a high-necked bodice to be exchanged for a low-cut bodice, both of which were worn with the same skirt, so the wearer could quickly switch dress code when necessary for their busy social life.[1]

The festivities for the investiture (1898) and wedding (1901) of Queen Wilhelmina were high points in the dress code parade. In the runup to the investiture Henriette van de Poll, lady-in-waiting to Queen Regent Emma (Wilhelmina's mother) complained on 5 February 1901, two days before the event: 'All my clothes have come in; not everything has turned out to my taste, however, though I hope I shall not make too poor an impression among the others, and am remaining as calm as possible about the matter.'[2] This included two 'grand decolleté' evening gowns that Henriette had ordered from Madame Coche in Brussels and an afternoon dress with large velvet bows made by Madame Van der Taelen, also of Brussels.[3] All the dress codes were stipulated in the orders of ceremony for the wedding festivities. They give a nice insight into the range of outfits worn.[4] To start with, on Monday 4 February 1901 the 'Distinguished Royal Guests' were expected in their 'travelling outfits' on arrival at 9.15. This might be a tailor made or a practical dress for the women, while the men wore a fashionable frock coat or short jacket (lounge suit). Thus suitably attired, the guests attended a family supper at Paleis Noordeinde. This dress code only applied, incidentally, to 'newly arrived guests'; courtiers were expected to attend in gala attire.

The programme continued on Tuesday 5 February 1901 with a reception for 'the non-Royal Guests and Military Deputations' at midday. The dress code was formal suit or dress uniform. Afterwards, at 12.30, there was a 'Luncheon for the Distinguished Royal Guests', at which the ladies were received in 'walking costume, with or without hat. Gentlemen: uniform or frock coat'. Following the afternoon programme, which consisted of love songs performed by choral societies, there was a gala dinner at 18.30, after which the guests were treated to a concert in the Royal Theatre in The Hague, which began at 21.00; the ladies wore 'toilette décolletée', the gents 'gala'. The low-cut gown was a remnant of 17th- and 18th-century court culture, and it applied to women of all ages, from young to old. Adult women always wore their hair up at a gala. A gown of this type would be accessorised with long gloves and a fan.

Wednesday 6 February began with a déjeuner, again with the dress code 'Walking costume with or without hat', and 'morning coat or uniform' for the gentlemen. At the dinner which took place at 18.00 that evening, the ladies wore 'demi-montante', the men 'white tie and tailcoat or uniform.' The 'demi-montante', or 'demi-décolletée' (semi-low-cut) gown was an intermediate form between low-cut and high-necked. The guests had to change quickly in order to be ready by 21.00 for a 'Soirée at the Palace', which the ladies were required to attend in 'toilette décolletée', and the gentlemen in 'Demi-Gala, plaque en cordon.' A lady with two different bodices that went with the same skirt would thus be able to simply change her bodice. Thursday 7 February 1901 was the big day, when the wedding finally took place. The civil ceremony was at Paleis Noordeinde at 11.30, after which the procession 'immediately' (according to the order of the day) left for the church. Finally, there was a lunch at the palace for the guests. The clothes required for these ceremonies were 'toilette décolletée' for the ladies, and 'gala' for the gents. At the family dinner that evening, the ladies wore 'toilette demi-montante' and the gentlemen 'white tie and tailcoat or uniform'. The evening ended with a celebratory firework display, rounding off this sublime dress-coded fashion parade.

—MH

**Evening gown ◆**
Worn by Lady Henriette van de Poll (1853-1946), lady-in-waiting to Queen Emma
Brussels, Madame Coche, circa 1901
Silk, cotton
Kunstmuseum Den Haag

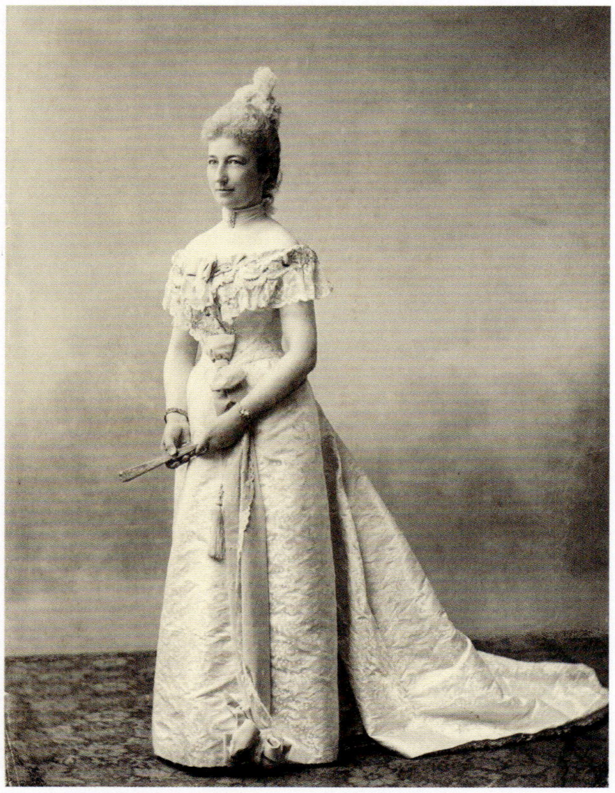

**Portrait of Frederika Louisa Henriëtte van de Poll, 1898**
Photographer unknown, RKD – Netherlands Institute for Art History, The Hague

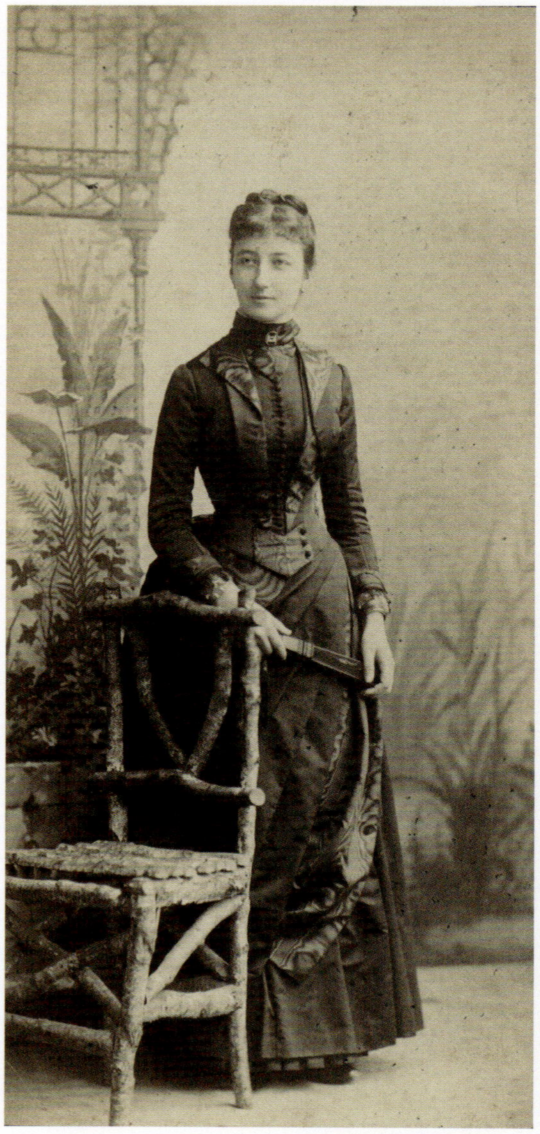

**Portrait of Frederika Louisa Henriette van de Poll (1853-1946), 1885**
Adolphe Zimmermans, RKD – Netherlands Institute for Art History, Den Haag

**Anna van Hannover, Princess of Orange-Nassau**
Studio of Johann Valentin Tischbein, 1752
Paleis Het Loo, on long-term loan from the Orange-Nassau Historical Society

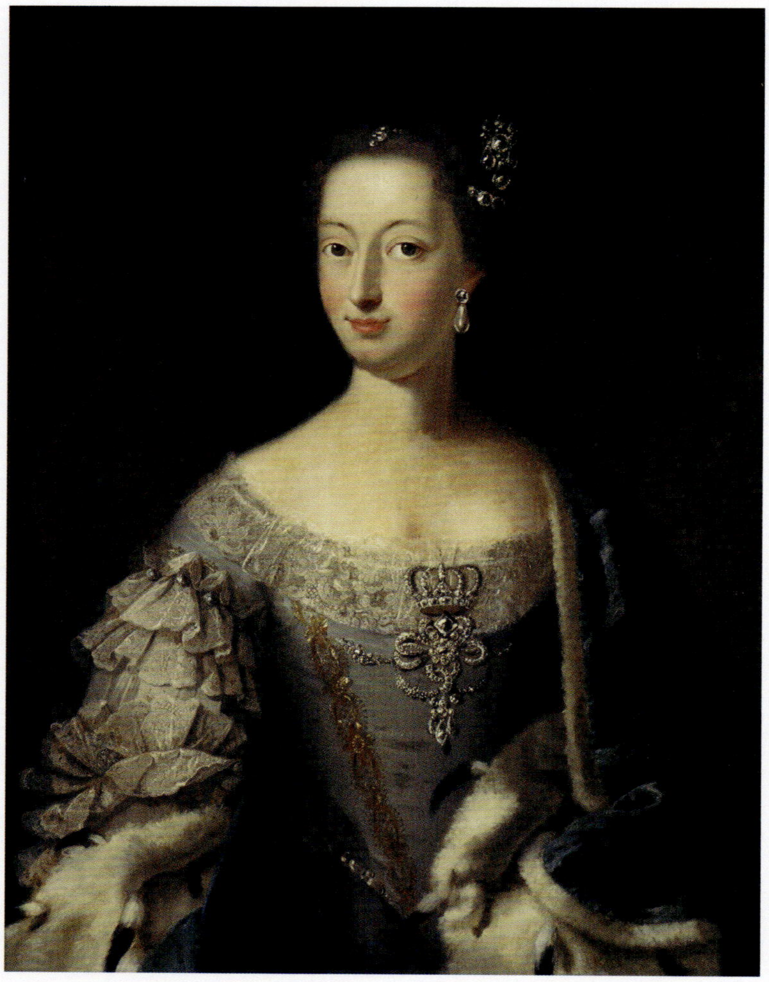

**Ball gown ◆**
Worn by Hillegonda van den Brandeler, Baroness van Randwijck (1880-1970)
Maker unknown, circa 1925
Liberty silk
Kunstmuseum Den Haag

**Evening dress ◆**
Worn by Baroness Marianne Jacqueline van Heemstra (1903-1991), lady-in-waiting to Princess Juliana
Maker unknown, circa 1937
Silk, metal, glass
Kunstmuseum Den Haag

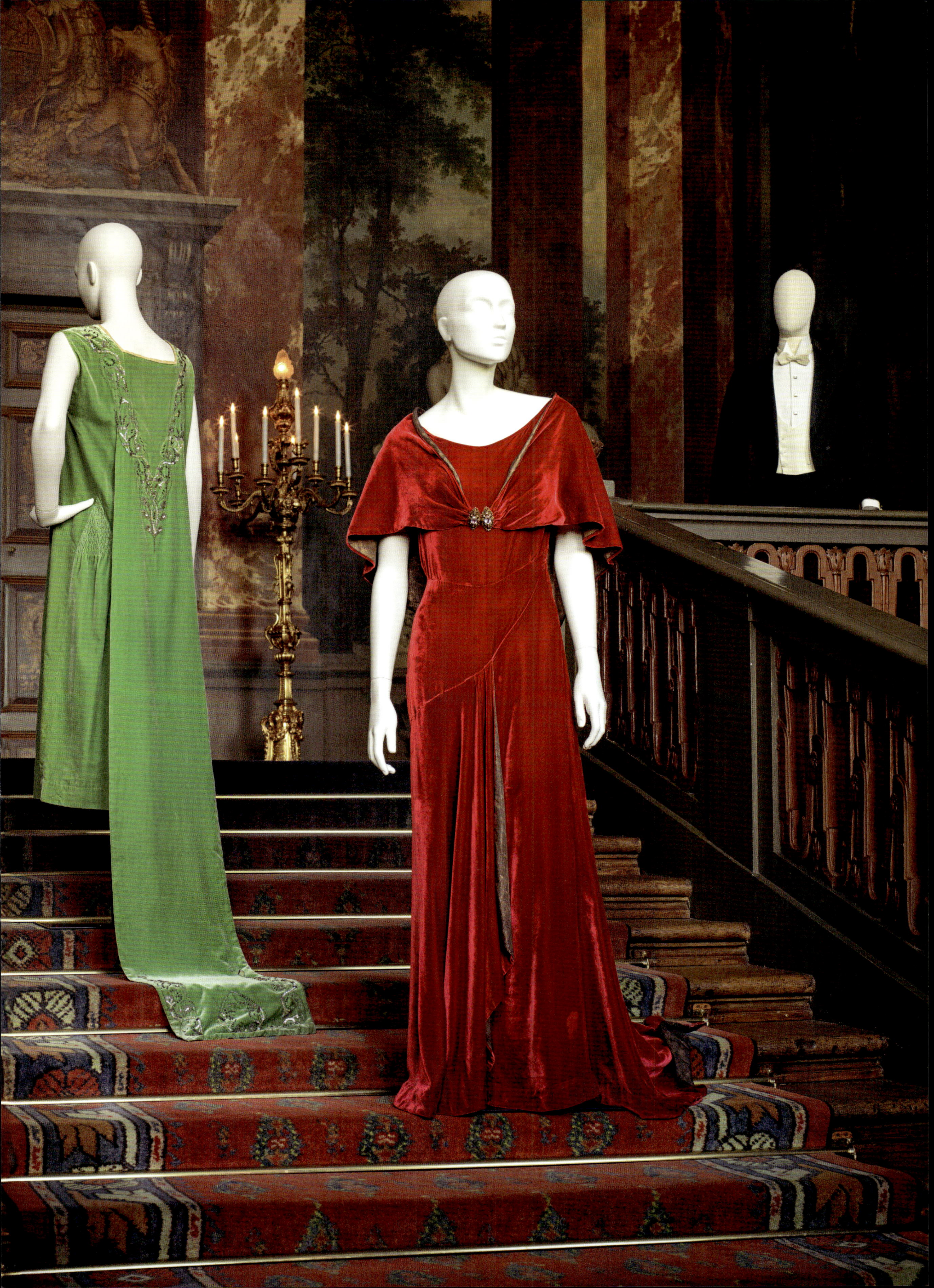

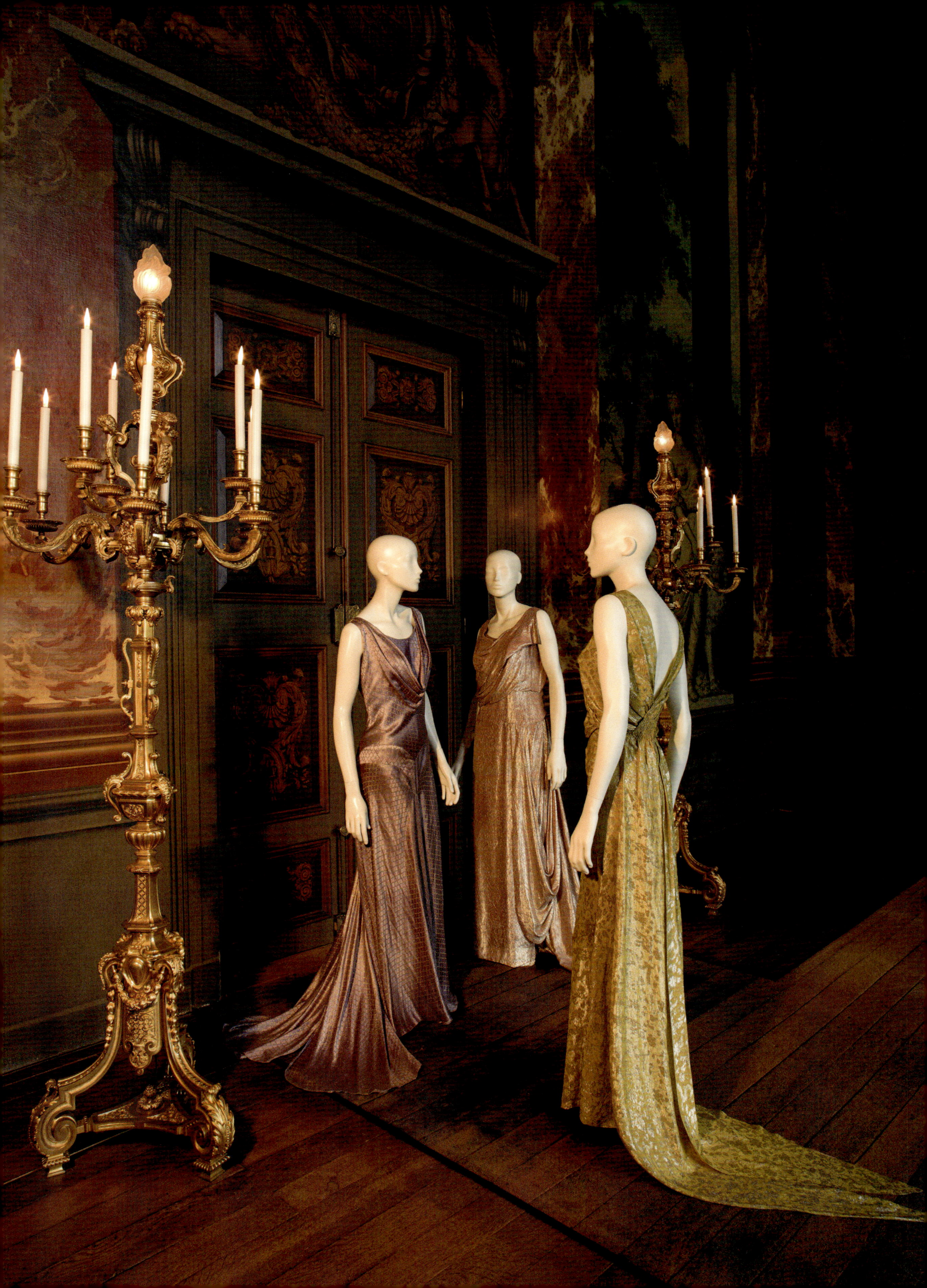

# DRESSED AS A COURTIER

For a courtier, participating in the various activities at court in the correct attire was an important part of the job. There was a clear ceremonial aspect to life at court, with everyone playing their part as if it were a stage play. Everything centred around the royals, dressed to reflect status, tradition and authority, with courtiers as the supporting cast. Courtiers' clothes had to be appropriate, as they formed the backdrop against which the monarch could shine. And a courtier must never, ever, be better dressed than the king or queen. This tended to be a little easier for the men at court than for the women. Since the French Revolution, the more imaginative aspects of the male wardrobe had fallen somewhat into decline. Men's clothes had become more restrained and uniform, with individuality expressed mainly in details like an embroidered waistcoat or tie. Most men's suits were a combination of long trousers, a jacket, waistcoat and tie. A fashionable man's wardrobe included a range of different suits, such as a frock coat, morning coat, dress suit and 'outdoor' attire. Anyone whose job allowed them to wear a civilian or military uniform had a relatively easy time with the dress codes. Everything was pre-defined, though there was a difference between 'gala' and 'grand gala'. For the latter, a gentleman would wear a 'ceremonial dress uniform' and for normal audiences, dinners, suppers, balls and concerts, they would wear their 'service uniform'.[1] Men who had no uniform would wear a fashionable suit, in compliance with the dress code stipulated. These included morning dress, frock coat or tailcoat with white tie, though a black tie would be worn at galas and less official occasions.[2]

It was considerably more difficult for the women, as so many variations were possible on the familiar types of dress, from walking costume to formal evening gown and everything in between. It was not the done thing to dress too ostentatiously at court. But nor could one keep appearing in the same outfit, so some variation was needed. Lady-in-waiting Henriette van de Poll was only too aware of all this. She worked for Queen Regent Emma from 1880 to 1934, along with her fellow lady-in-waiting Elise van Ittersum. She often discussed her wardrobe and that of the people around her in the letters she wrote to her mother and sisters. 'Concerns regarding outfits are most certainly the greatest difficulty in our position, but I always hope that we will grow accustomed to it in time, and that we will find it easier', Henriette wrote in a letter to her family on 28 May 1880.[3] As a lady-in-waiting, Henriette was continually concerned with keeping her wardrobe up-to-date, and having gowns altered and 'freshened up' in order to wear them again, without looking 'faded'. And preparing for important events by having fashionable – but not too fashionable – gowns made. Henriette was good at deciding what choice of outfit would be appropriate for her role, without being 'excessive'. She often received compliments about her attire.

Fortunately, Henriette had her own dresser, Cécile, to help her with her outfits. She also made a lot of the clothes she wore on a day-to-day basis.[4] A woman could not dress herself, so the dresser would help with this too, as her title suggests. The position of lady-in-waiting was an honorary one, with barely any remuneration, so Henriette's costly wardrobe was largely funded by her family. She therefore tried to be as economical as possible with her clothes, having several bodices made to go with the same skirt, for example. Queen Emma, the Queen Mother, sometimes helped her ladies-in-waiting Henriette and Elise when they were expected to make extraordinary purchases. She gave them beautiful expensive fabrics for gowns on a number of occasions, and gave each of them 500 guilders to have new gowns made for Queen Wilhelmina's wedding (see page 79).[5] Henriette was thus able to afford to order gowns from Brussels. Several of her gowns have survived and are now in Kunstmuseum Den Haag's collection. Some of the labels refer to fashion houses in Brussels, such as Madame Coche and Madame van der Taelen, V. François & Cie and Maison Divoire Bawin. In this respect, too, she had to differ from the royal women. While Henriette ordered her finest gowns from Brussels, Queen Regent Emma and Queen Wilhelmina ordered theirs from Paris for important festivities during that period, such as Wilhelmina's investiture in 1898 and her wedding in 1901. Never outdo the boss.

—MH

**Evening dress** ◆
Probably worn by Countess Marie Jacqueline van Lynden van Sandenburg (1903-1983)
Maker unknown, circa 1930
Silk
Kunstmuseum Den Haag

**Evening dress** ◆
Probably worn by Countess Marie Jacqueline van Lynden van Sandenburg (1903-1983)
Maker unknown, circa 1934
Artificial silk
Kunstmuseum Den Haag

**Evening dress** ◆
Worn by Agnes Margaretha van Beeck Calkoen, Baroness Schimmelpenninck van der Oije (1908-1991), lady-in-waiting to Queen Wilhelmina
Brussels, Mademoiselle Le Bel, circa 1937
Silk, artificial silk, metal
Kunstmuseum Den Haag

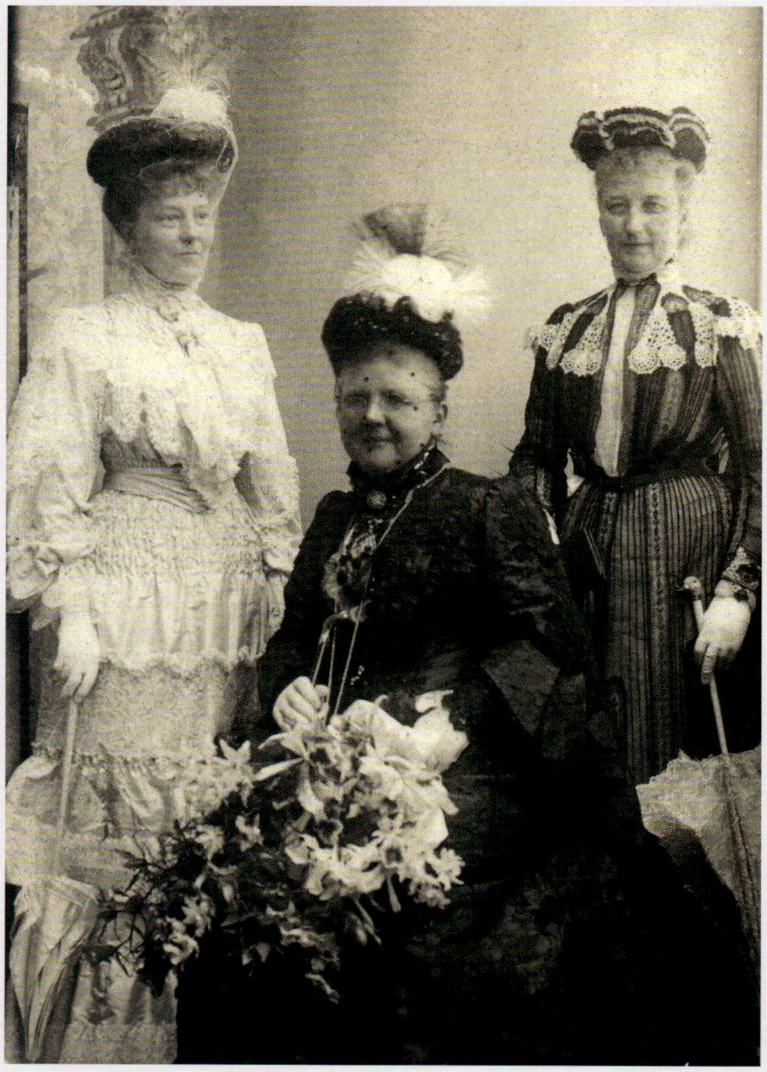

**Queen Emma with ladies-in-waiting**
Queen Emma was photographed with her ladies-in-waiting Baroness E.G. van Ittersum (1851-1936), on the left, and Lady F.L.H. van de Poll (1853-1936), on the right, at the summer fair at Buitenrust in The Hague, 1904

Photo C.J.L. Vermeulen, The Hague
Paleis Het Loo

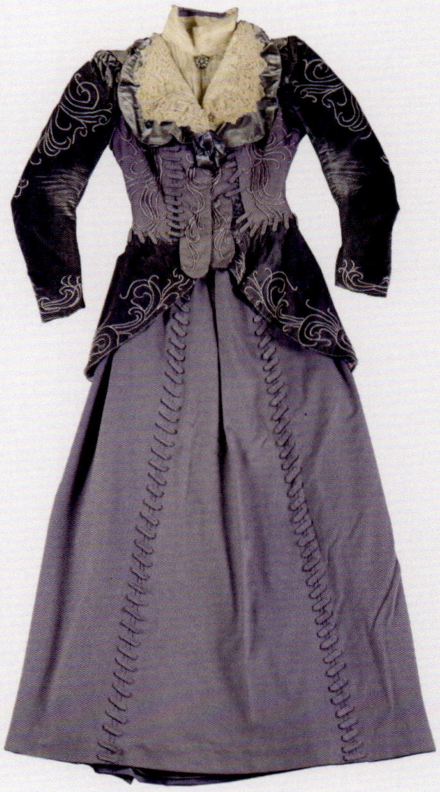

**Formal gown**
Worn by Lady Henriette van de Poll (1853-1946), lady-in-waiting to Queen Emma
Maker unknown, circa 1898
silk
Centraal Museum Utrecht

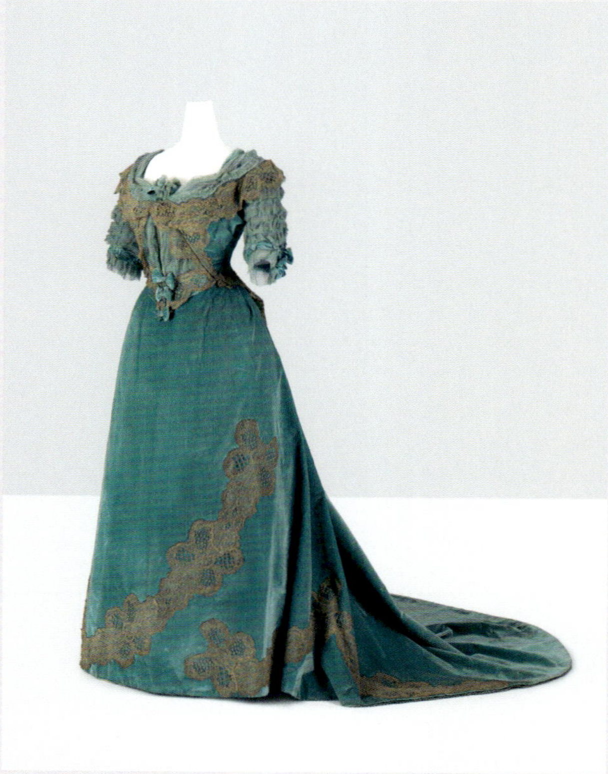

**Evening gown**
Worn by Lady Henriette van de Poll (1853-1946), lady-in-waiting to Queen Emma
Brussels, Mme. H. van der Taelen, circa 1905
Silk
Centraal Museum Utrecht

**Court train ◆**
Maker unknown, circa 1880-1890
Silk
Kunstmuseum Den Haag

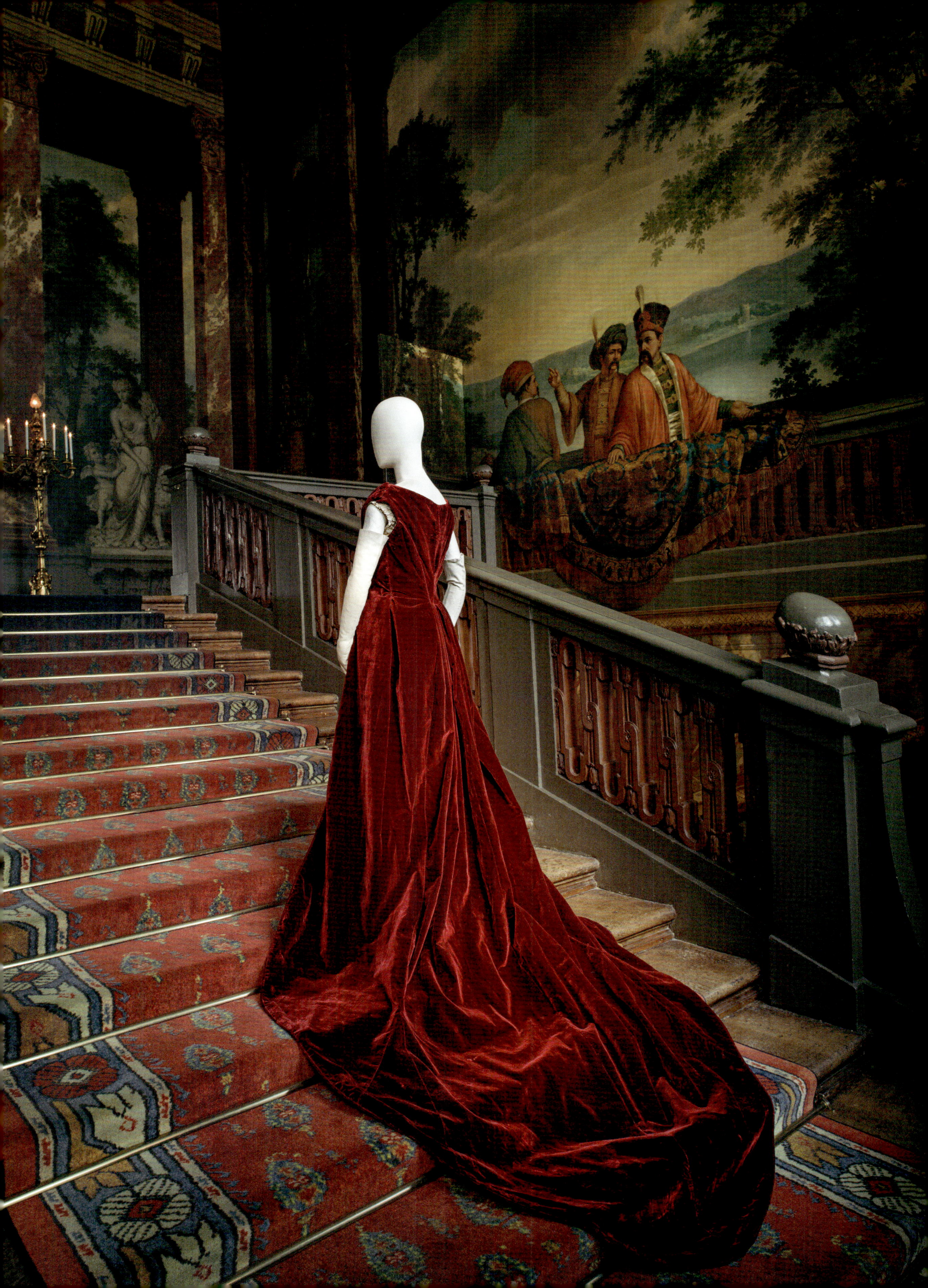

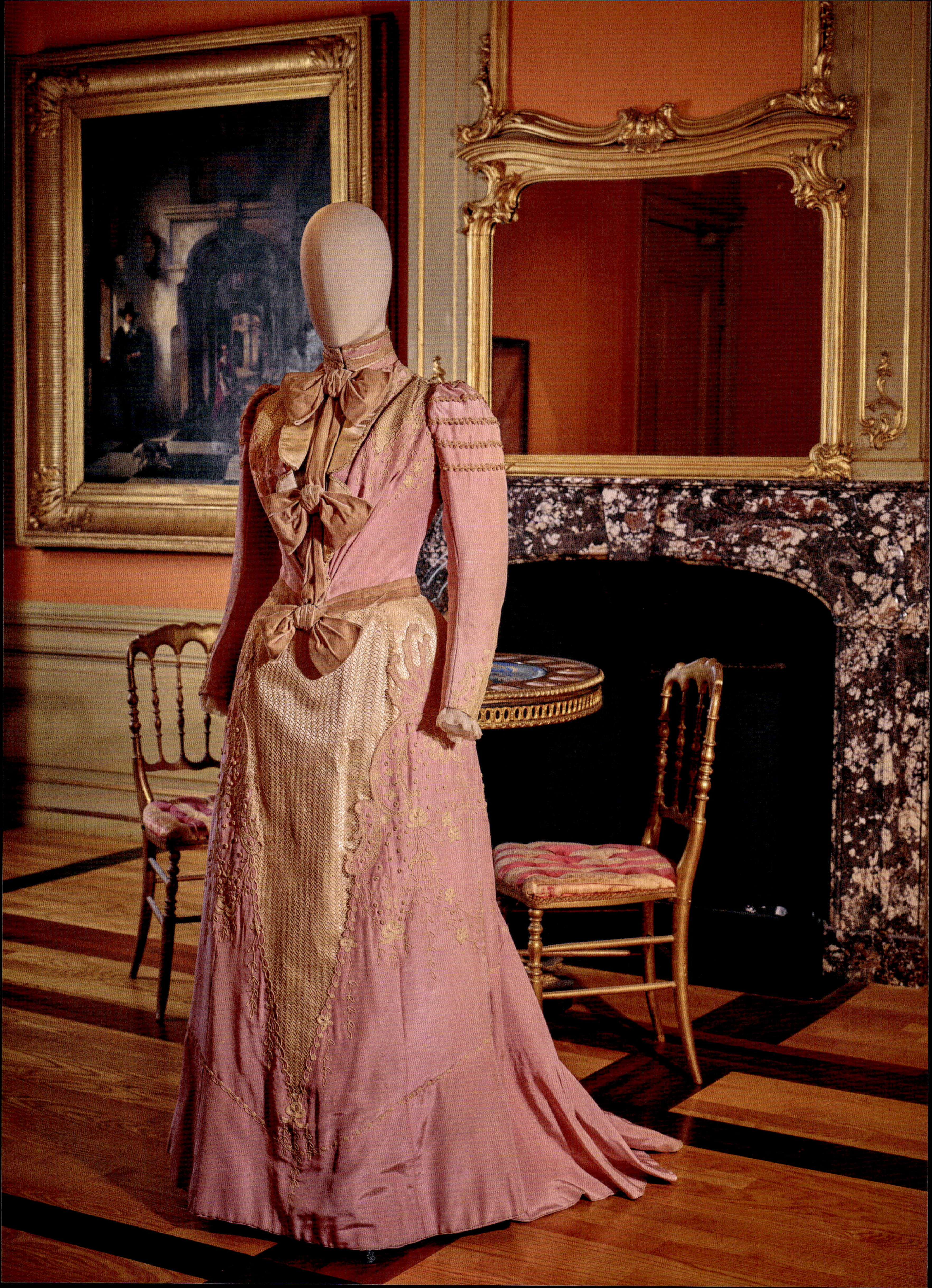

# FASHION FROM PARIS

Paris was the centre of fashion in court circles in the belle époque, too – the period around the turn of the 20th century. Queen Regent Emma and later also Queen Wilhelmina ordered clothes in Paris for important occasions. One of their favourite Parisian suppliers was Nicaud & Cie, of no. 2 Rue Cambon & 244 Rue de Rivoli. This Paris fashion house was a continuation of the former fashion house Corbay-Wenzel, as it was known from 1885, previously A. Corbay.[1] Queen Regent Emma was a client there in the 1880s and had purchased her wedding gown from Corbay in 1879 (as evidenced by the label A. Corbay), as well as a lavishly embroidered red velvet court train, which she wore at the wedding of her younger sister Helena of Waldeck and Pyrmont in 1882. Helena married Prince Leopold, Duke of Albany, the youngest son of Queen Victoria and Prince Albert of Great Britain. Like her sister Emma a few years later, she wore a fabulous bridal gown from Corbay-Wenzel in Paris. Queen Regent Emma introduced her daughter Wilhelmina to the successor to this fashion house, known as Nicaud, when she was 16. From 1896 onwards, more and more clothes were ordered from Nicaud in Paris for Princess Wilhelmina, including her investiture gown, court train and wedding dress (1901). A photograph from the belle époque shows the staff of Nicaud on the pavement before one of its two Paris branches, at no. 2 Rue Cambon, the same street where Gabrielle Chanel would open her first store in Paris a few years later. The Dutch queens did not have to travel to Paris themselves to place their orders, however. Staff from Nicaud would make several trisp from Paris to the Netherlands for fittings of the gowns ordered for the young Queen Wilhelmina.[2]

The embroidery on Wilhelmina's investiture gown and the court train she commissioned in 1898 strongly resembles designs from the fashion house Worth, established in Paris by an Englishman, Charles Frederick Worth. This house had grown into a real phenomenon, with a staff of more than 1200, who worked together almost like a conveyor belt producing couture for clients of the global 'beau monde', from monarchs to actresses, from the heart of Paris to Russia, Japan and America.[3] They also sold under licence to smaller fashion houses, which would then sell Worth designs under their own name. So might the investiture gown and train actually have been designed by Worth and made for the Dutch queen by Nicaud? It is known that Worth sold samples of dresses and patterns under licence to fashion houses and seamstresses both in France and elsewhere.[4] Charles Dickens commented on this in 1867: 'Milliners from every decent capital come to wait on Worth. They go away bearing a dress or a pattern, for which they pay fabulous prices.'[5] Worth would never dream of visiting his clients in their homes; in this sense, he himself behaved like a royal, expecting people to come to him. As a result, Dutch queens would clearly prefer to order from Nicaud, given that mademoiselle Nicaud would send her staff to the Netherlands for fittings.[6]

Dutch queens and their ladies-in-waiting regularly bought from certain suppliers in the Netherlands. In The Hague, which was known as a centre of fashion of international allure, given the presence of the court and the international nature of the diplomatic world, the favoured fashion houses were those run by M. Stuttman-Senault, F.K. Tripplevitz, A.M. Schelfhout-Picnot, fashion house Kühne & Sons and Maison de Paris. In Amsterdam, queens would buy outfits from Mrs A. van Scherpenzeel-Kahn on Keizersgracht and at Hirsch & Cie. The latter had opened in Amsterdam in 1882 and was a popular place to buy Paris fashions.[7]

Henriette and Elise also occasionally ordered clothes from Paris, but these would be ready-to-wear items from one of the modern department stores there, like Louvre or Bon Marché.[8] Their catalogues explained how to measure one's size and how to order, and then a parcel would duly arrive from Paris. Amsterdam lady-in-waiting Thora van Loon-Egidius had a larger budget and had a gown that was particularly expensive by Hague standards made by fashion house Paquin in Paris specially for Queen Wilhelmina's wedding.[9] 'Beautiful outfits had to be made once again, so my husband and I travelled to Paris in December 1900 and Maison Paquin once more made some lovely things', she wrote. She herself described the gown she wore at the investiture as follows: 'My outfit was fabulous, a warm pink full of different shades, entirely embroidered in Louis XIV style in grey, with small painted panels, truly a chef d'oeuvre (masterpiece).'[10] Let us hope that her contemporaries did not regard her gown as too fabulous.

—MH

**Formal gown ◆**
Worn by Lady Henriette van de Poll (1853-1946), lady-in-waiting to Queen Emma
Brussels, Madame van der Taelen, 1898
Silk, cotton, metal
Kunstmuseum Den Haag

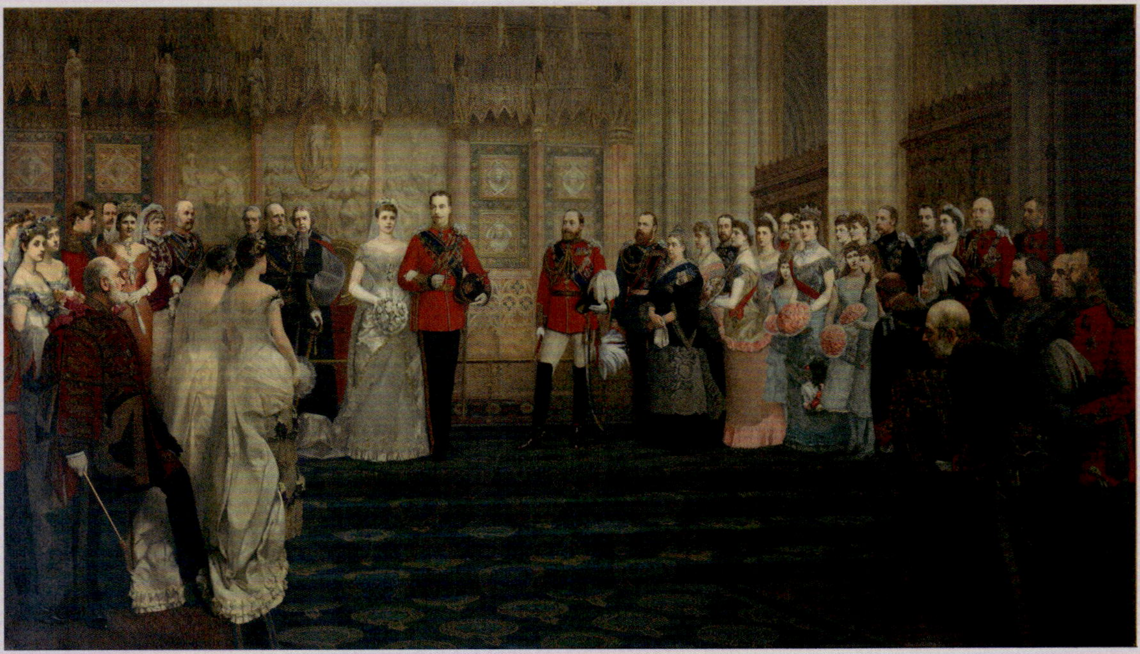

**Wedding of Princess Helena and Prince Leopold**
Sir James Dromgole Linton, 1885
Royal Collection Trust, ©His Majesty King Charles III, London

**'how to take measurements'**
Au Bon Marché price list
Kunstmuseum Den Haag

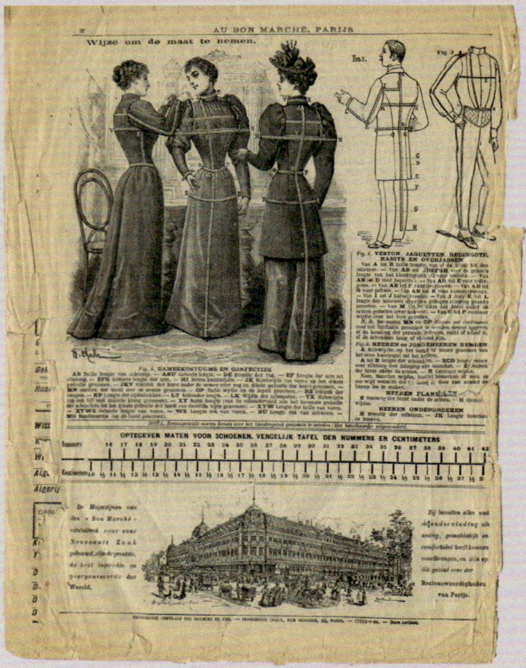


**Thora van Loon-Egidius, 1909**
Adolf Pirsch
Museum Van Loon, Amsterdam

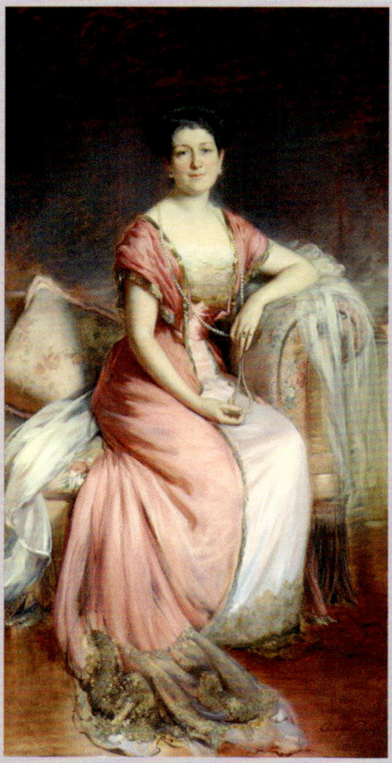

**Princess Helena van Waldeck and Pyrmont in her wedding dress, 1882**
Royal Collection Trust, ©His Majesty King Charles III, London

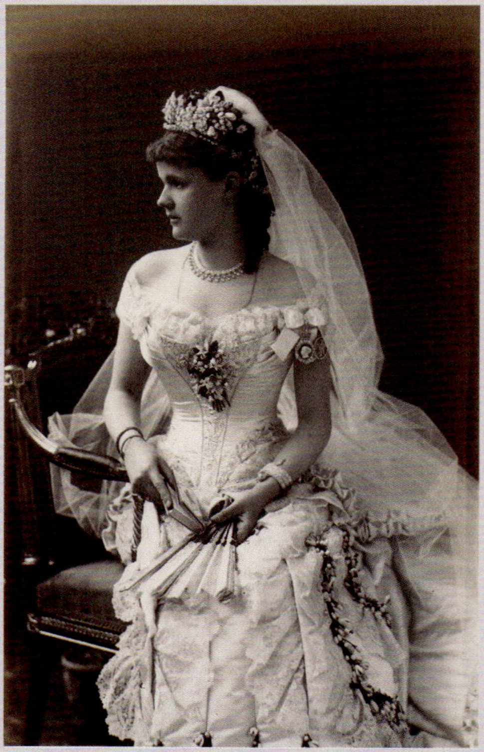

**Evening dress ◆**
Worn by Baroness Marianne Jacqueline van Heemstra (1903-1991), lady-in-waiting to Princess Juliana
Maker unknown, circa 1937
Silk, metal, glass
Kunstmuseum Den Haag

**Ballgown ◆**
Worn by Baroness Marianne Jacqueline van Heemstra (1903-1991), lady-in-waiting to Princess Juliana
Maker unknown, circa 1937-1938
Silk, metal
Kunstmuseum Den Haag

**Dress suit ◆**
Maker unkonwn, 1875-1899
Wool
Kunstmuseum Den Haag

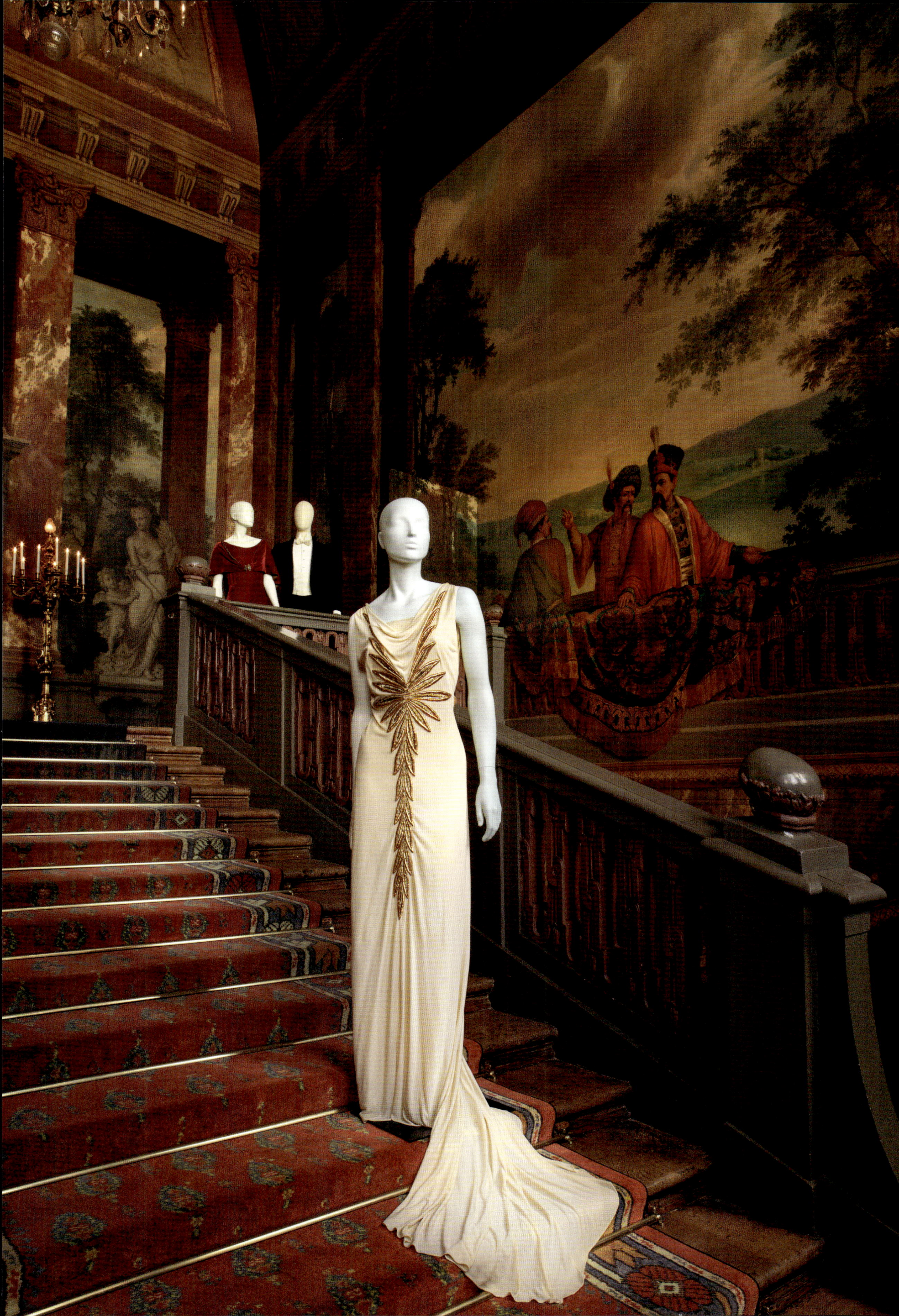

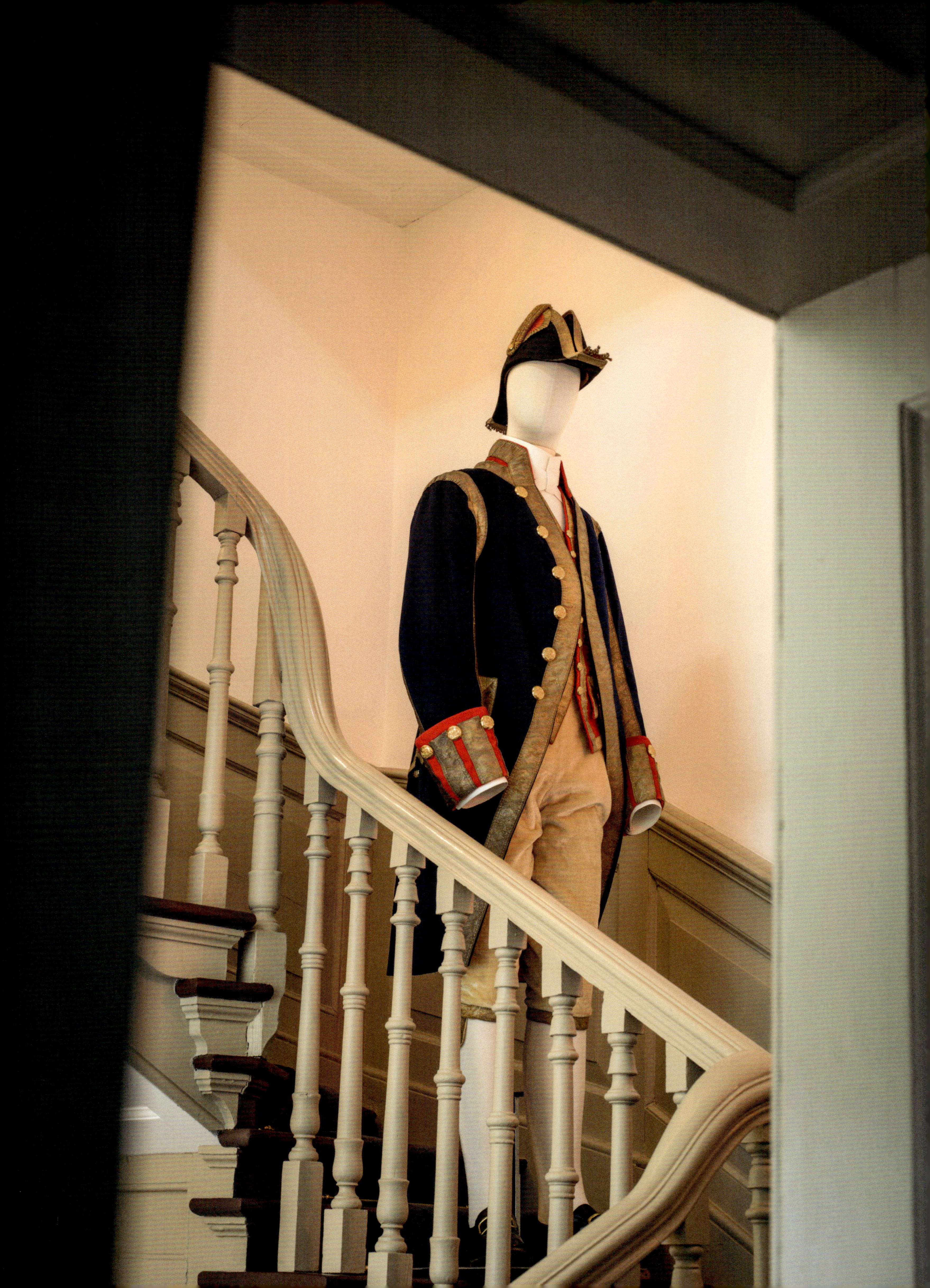

# FOOTMAN'S LIVERY

A footman, also known as an under-butler, is a servant at court. Women also work as under-butlers at the court of Willem-Alexander, but the job traditionally used to be the preserve of men. At the palace, a footman would be recognised by his livery (from the French *livré*), the uniform supplied by his high-ranking employer. As well as for purposes of recognition and ranking at court, livery was also a matter of prestige for the monarch. A footman in livery was a status symbol. Different liveries would be worn on different occasions. The more ceremonial the occasion, the more impressive the livery. While the day-to-day livery was fairly restrained, at a gala event a footman would wear his fabulous full dress uniform.

A footman at the court of Prince Willem V would wear livery in the family colours of the House of Orange-Nassau: gold for Orange and Nassau blue, in combination with red. King Willem I adopted more or less the same uniform when the Netherlands became a kingdom. Successive kings introduced changes to the livery from time to time, but Queen Wilhelmina left the restyling of the uniforms worn by court staff to Prince Hendrik, who loved military uniforms and theatre costumes. From 1903 onwards he introduced changes to the outfits worn by staff, including the footmen's uniforms. New liveries were introduced in 1907.

Livery is not a fashion item, and deliberately so. The reference to old family traditions and the use of family colours made a livery highly venerable, and this gave the court extra lustre. The new footman's livery introduced by Hendrik was therefore inspired by the outfits worn by servants in the 18th century, of which watercolour images have survived. Around 1770, Prince Willem V's footmen would wear a fashionable habit à la française, consisting of a long jacket with cut away front quarters, over a red waistcoat and red knee breeches with white stockings. The livery was trimmed with gold galloon and decorated with gilt buttons. One of the footmen who was issued with the new livery was Steven Eilander (1864-1927). His lavish full dress uniform – consisting of a jacket, waistcoat and breeches – has survived. Like the footmen of around 1770, at official court occasions Eilander would wear a blue jacket with a standing collar and red wool cuffs. There would be no economising on gold galloon at a gala event, as a full dress uniform was particularly impressive in candlelight. Though the jacket would not be fastened, it had a single row of gilt buttons featuring the royal crest. The red waistcoat decorated with gold galloon also referred to the livery of the 18th century, though the red knee breeches had been replaced by cream ones. As in Willem V's day, a footman wore white stockings and black slip-on shoes. Eilander wore white gloves, and he had a black bicorne hat decorated with gold galloon and an orange rosette for outdoors. These hats would generally be supplied by the firms Prinsen and Meuwsen, both of which were purveyors to the royal court. Clothes for court staff would often be made by Dutch tailors, though Prince Hendrik also ordered uniforms from purveyors to the imperial court in Berlin.
—PR

**Footman's dress uniform** ◆
Unknown atelier, early to mid-20th century
Cotton, wool, gilded copper, gold thread
Paleis Het Loo, on long-term loan
from the Royal Collections, The Hague

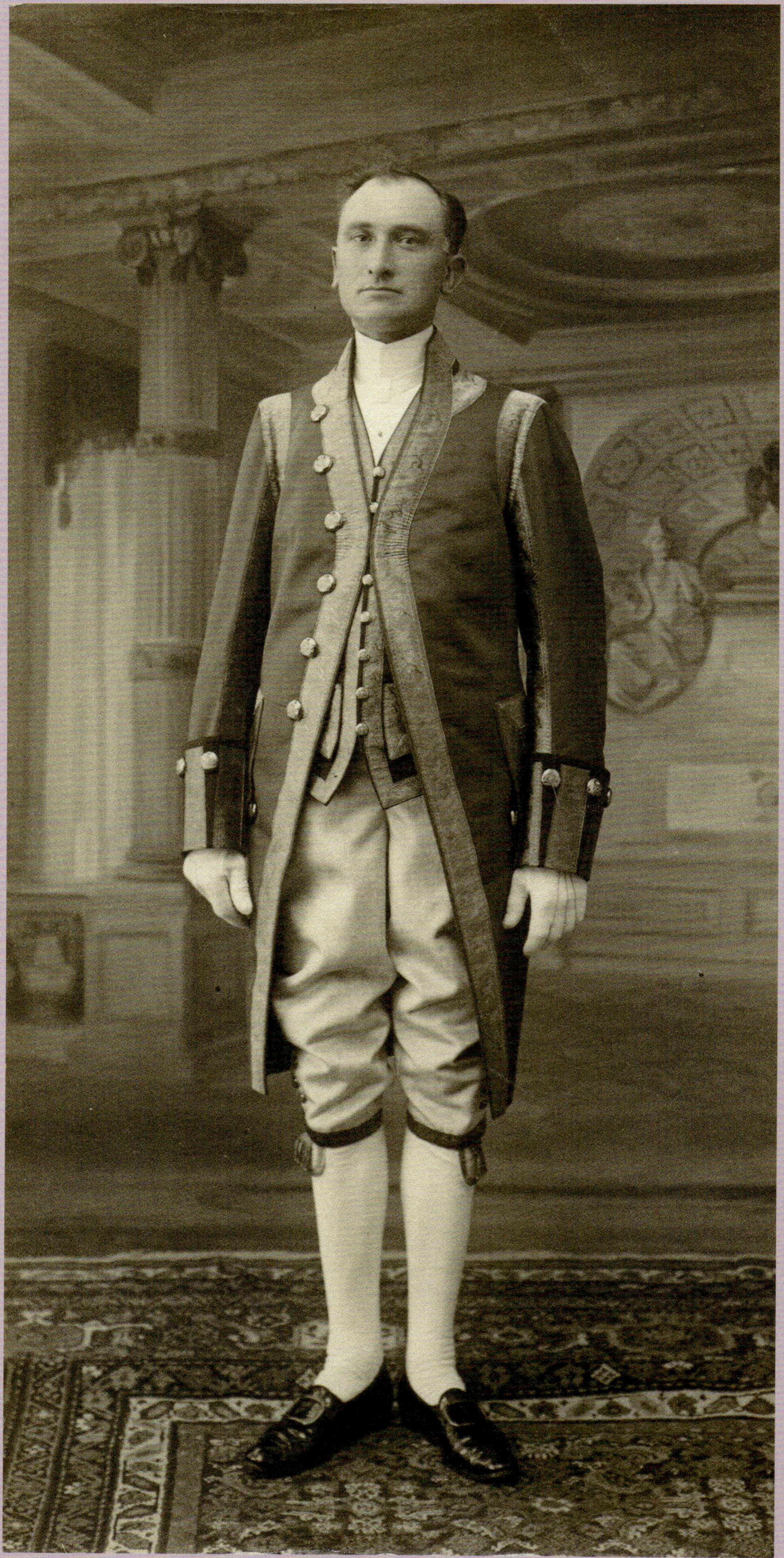

**Footman in full dress uniform**
Around 1920 several members of staff at court were photographed wearing their new outfits in a studio set up in the attic of a side wing at Paleis Het Loo. T he 'dining room' backdrop was used for the shoot with footman Isaac Verhoef.

Unknown photographer,
circa 1920
Paleis Het Loo

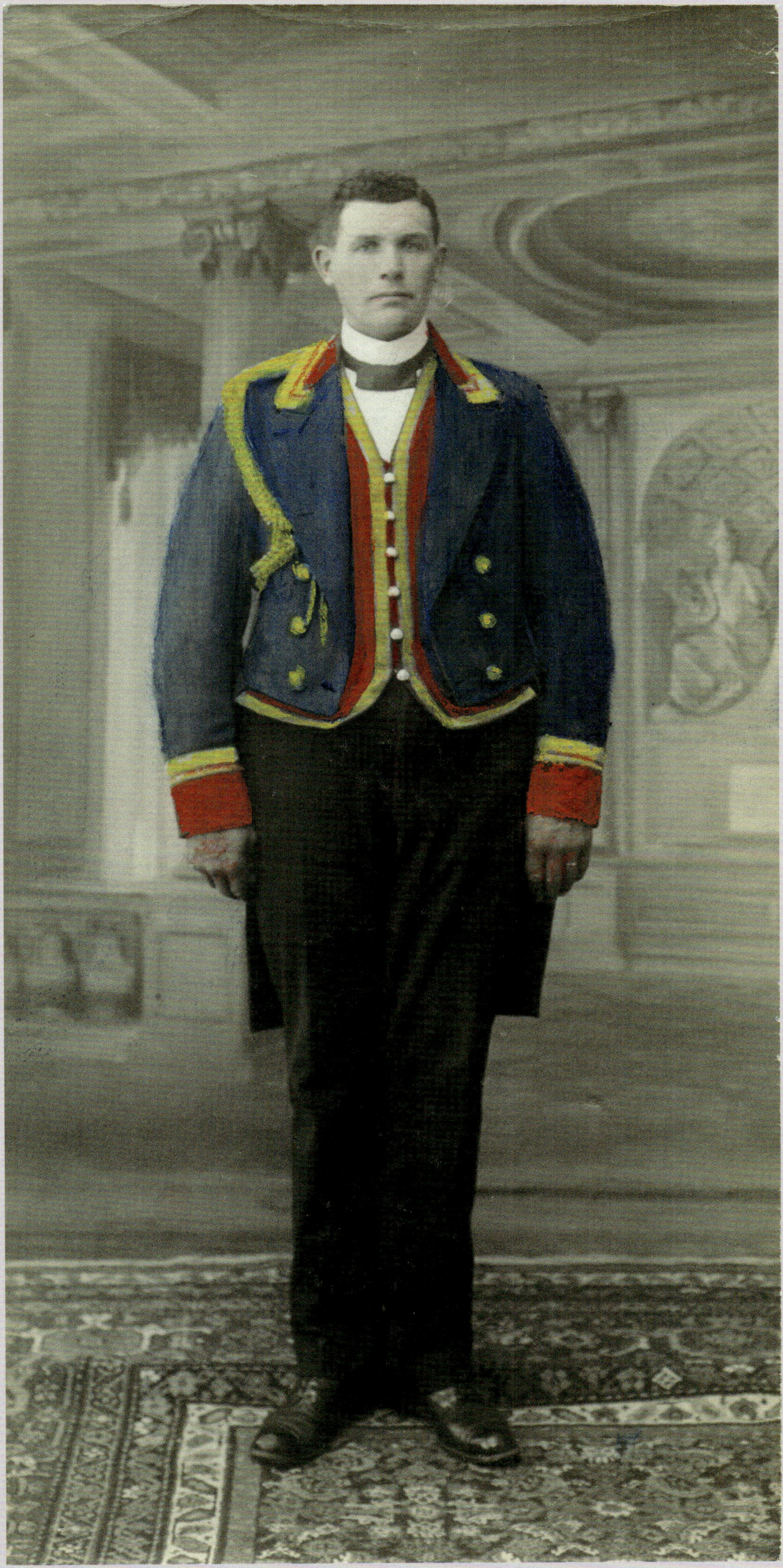

**Prince's valet**
F. Meijerink, who as Prince Hendrik's 'first footman-valet' was responsible for the prince's wardrobe, also posed for the photoshoot. The photograph was hand tinted to give an impression of the colours of the livery.

Unknown photographer
Paleis Het Loo

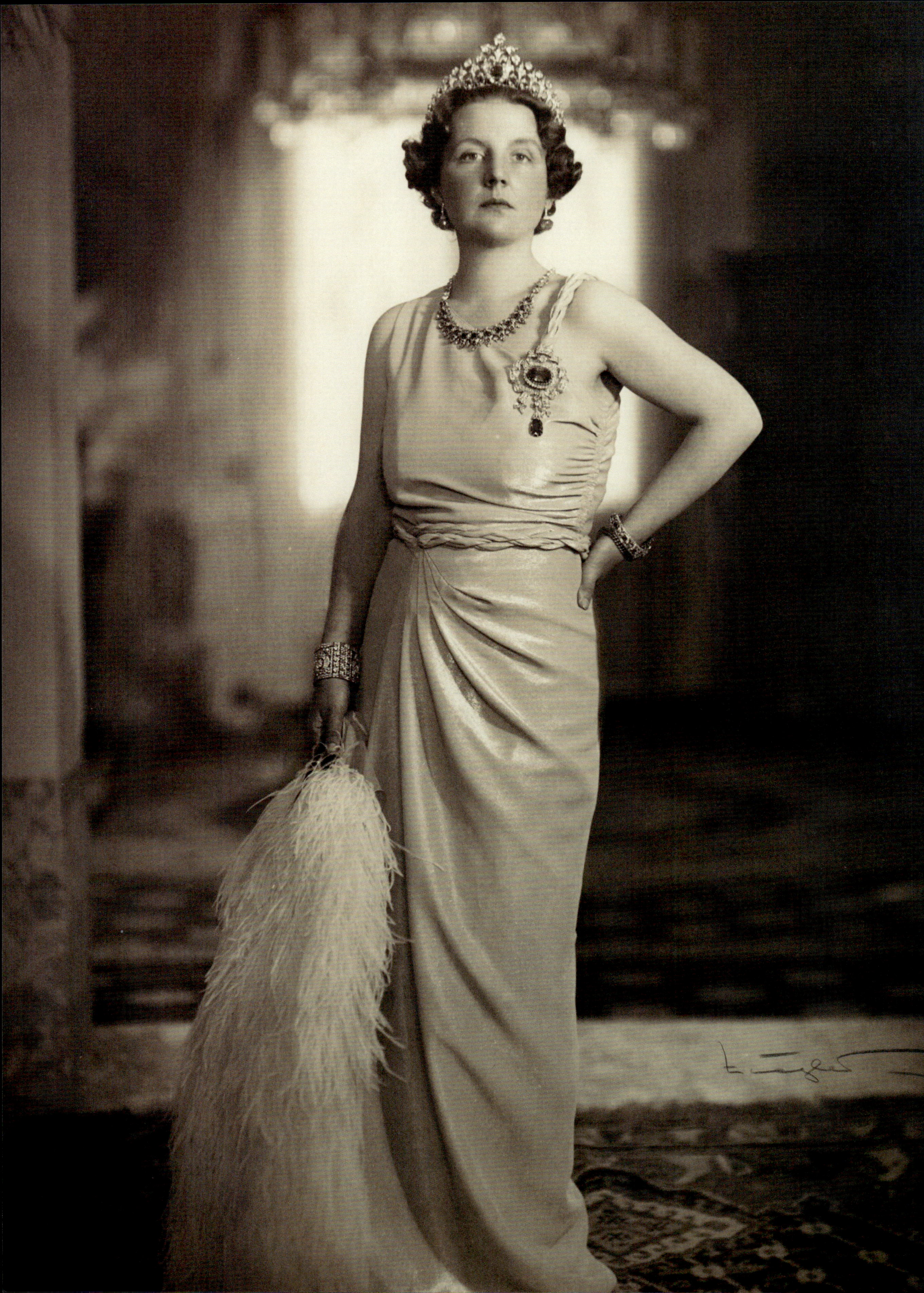

DRESS CODES

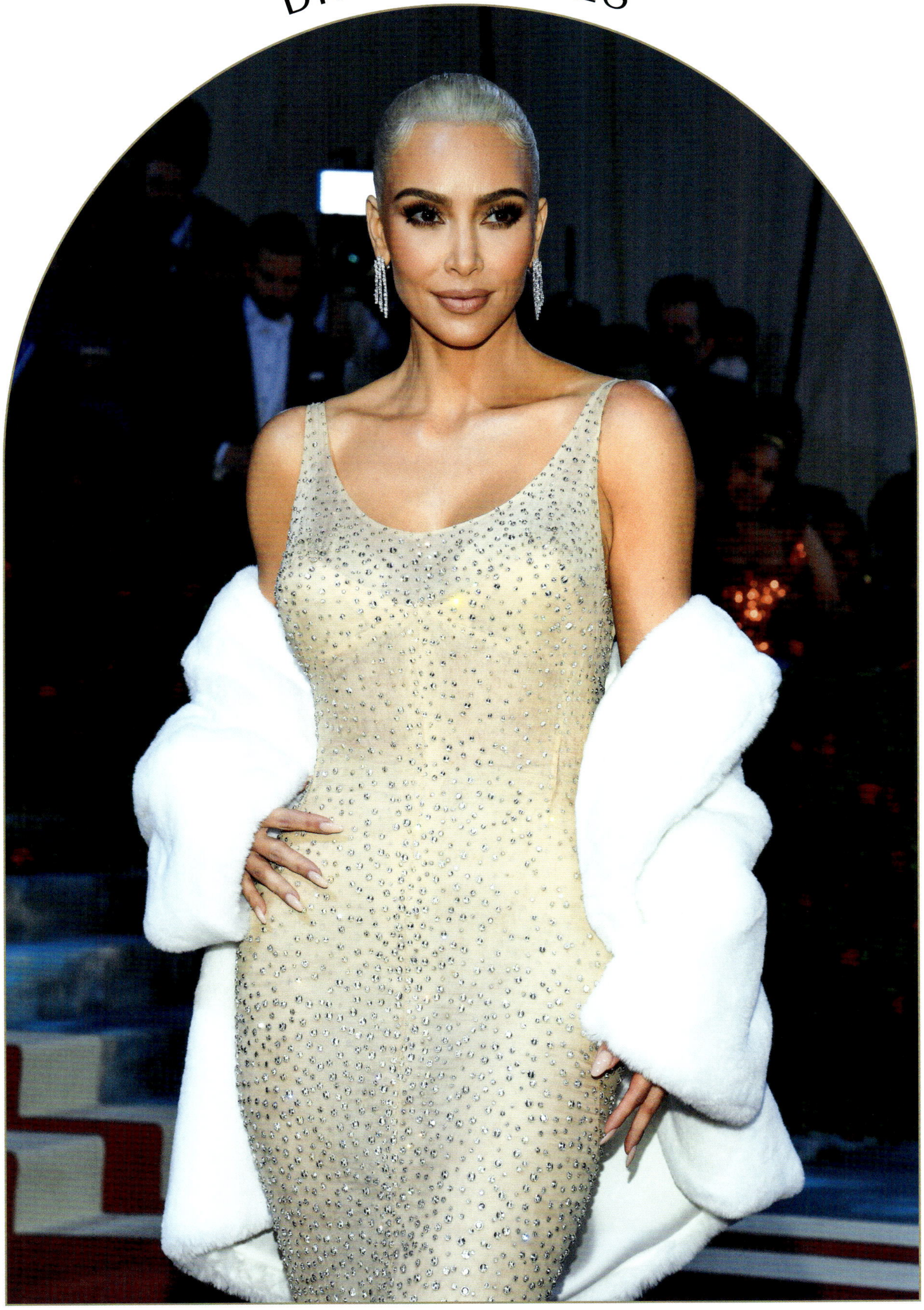

CÉCILE NARINX

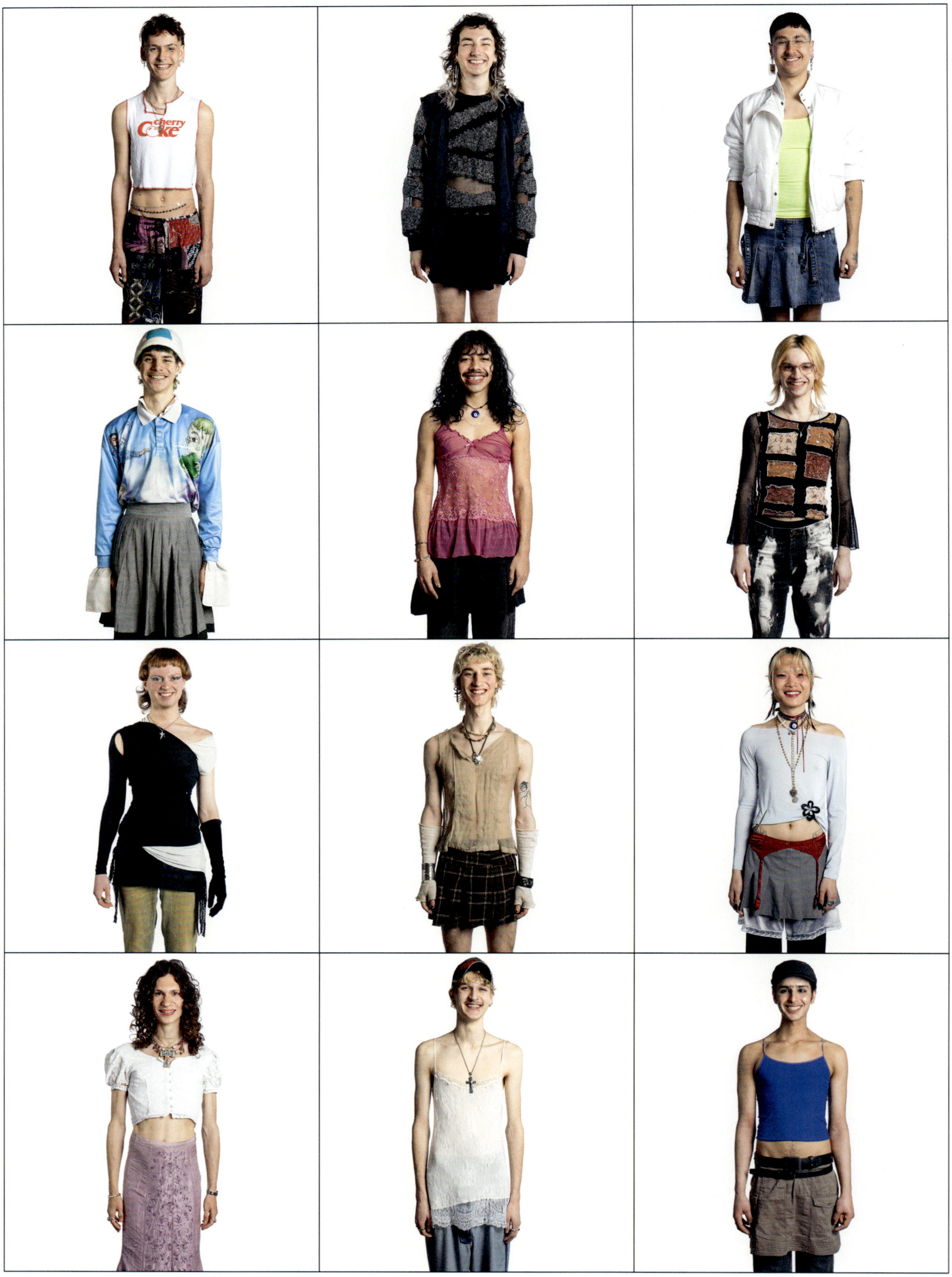


Exactitudes, 185, They ◆
Ari Versluis, Ellie Uyttenbroek, 2024
Rotterdam

It's an ideal game to play to stave off boredom while you're waiting: watching people and guessing their job or their story. The best places for a people safari are the railway station, a shopping centre or a pavement café at a busy spot. All you need, apart from as many people as possible to watch, is a comfortable bench or chair, eyes like a hawk, a good mood and a pinch of imagination. Someone with an orange jacket and a large, square rucksack in the same colour is easy: they are working for a takeout delivery service. Someone in a cornflower blue suit, white shirt and dark-blue scarf: KLM cabin crew. A man in black with a white square in the front of his collar has to be a man of the cloth. So far, so simple. So let's proceed to level 2. A man in his thirties wearing beige chinos, a smart jacket but no tie and suede shoes, making a phone call on a scooter: probably a real estate agent, or a lawyer. An older woman with an asymmetrical hairstyle, spectacles with a big, colourful frame, a wrist full of clinking bracelets and an artistic-looking robe: a gallery owner, or an artist. You know how it goes, and what fun it is to spot someone who has all the features of a particular archetype.

Admittedly, it is not very broad-minded to label people like this in an instant, and assumptions can always be premature, but they turn out to be true surprisingly often, especially when based on a person's clothes. I would be prepared to bet that the man on the nippy scooter does not work on a cargo ship, or as a tattoo artist, and that the woman in the robe is not a forest ranger or a pole dancer.

Whether we like it or not, what we wear reveals who we are, or who we would like to be. It shows which group we belong to, and which we don't. It indicates whether we are willing to conform to universal rules of decorum, or are more inclined to rebel against them. Whether we wish to appear politically neutral, or make a political statement. And in some cases it shows where we come from.

A brief history lesson: until well into the 20th century, where exactly a woman from Staphorst, Volendam, Hindeloopen or one of several other villages came from could easily be deduced from the fabrics and patterns in her traditional dress, and the size and shape of her bonnet, ear irons and breastcloth. Their husbands could be identified by the patterns in their knitted fisherman's sweaters, which differed from one village to another. The pattern of diamonds, cabling and other motifs in the sweater would therefore indicate whether a fisherman who drowned at sea came from Moddergat or Urk, for example. The gold earring worn by the unlucky chap, which might also indicate his origins, was intended to cover the costs of his funeral.

Now that few people wear traditional dress, it has been replaced by other common outfits, often chosen by the wearers themselves. Uniforms and work clothing, for example, as well as dress codes for entire neighbourhoods or population groups. Not so long ago, a woman from the Broekhoven neighbourhood in Tilburg would look just the part in pink velours homewear, a pair of Uggs and a head covered in tight curls. In the wealthy neighbourhoods of the Gooi region, women are more likely to walk around in ivory-coloured jeans tucked into faux riding boots. Their hair will likely

← ← Princess Juliana, 1937
Franz Ziegler
Royal Collections, The Hague

← Kim Kardashian, 2022
Kim Kardashian wearing Marilyn Monroe's 'Happy Birthday Mr. President' dress at The Met Gala 2022, New York. This caused a furore, particularly in the museum sector, in connection with the conservation of the dress.

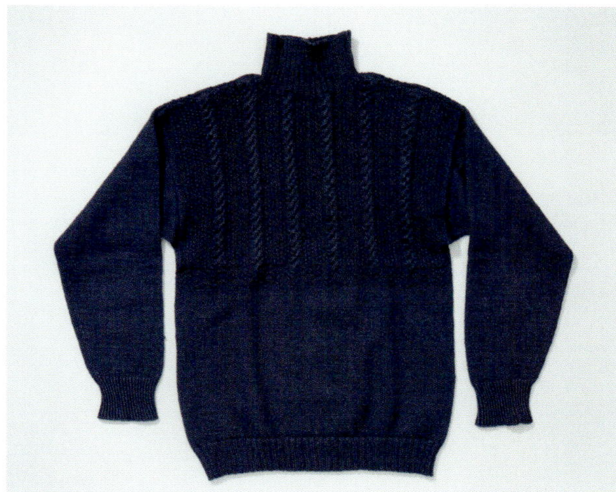

Scheveningen fisherman's sweater
Maker unknown, c. 1950
Wool
Dutch Open Air Museum, Arnhem, on long-term loan from the Royal Collections

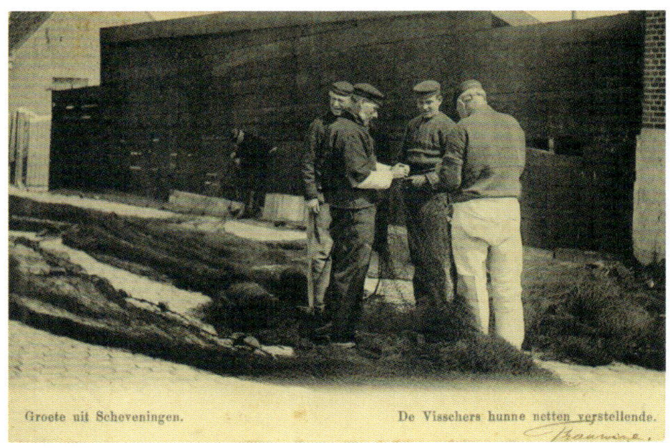


Fishermen in Scheveningen, 1912
picture postcard
Dutch Open Air Museum, Arnhem

be long, straight, subtly bleached, and possibly worn in a ponytail or hair clip.

If we zoom out a little more and consider all the kinds of groups there are in the Netherlands, we find that there are quite a lot of style tribes, people with a similar wardrobe and similar ways of spending their time. Just think of the countless men above the age of thirty with a job that does not require a suit, but who wear another kind of uniform: jeans, patterned shirt, dark-blue sweater and neat trainers with a white sole – guys like real estate agent Alex van Keulen and builder Bob Sikkes from a popular RTL 4 programme about buying and redesigning houses. Or women with practical short haircuts, generally dyed auburn, who go to ideal home and fashion and beauty shows wearing flowered tunics and cream cropped trousers. Think of young boys in bomber jackets, Dior sneakers and Gucci caps, carrying Louis Vuitton bags (or cheaper copies). Or older boys with beer bellies, in their brightly-coloured lycra cycling gear and supersonic helmets. Ladies in lamb's wool sweaters, pleated skirts and pearl necklaces. Old rockers in band T-shirts and jeans so tight they have to lie down and prise themselves into them with a shoehorn. You get the picture.

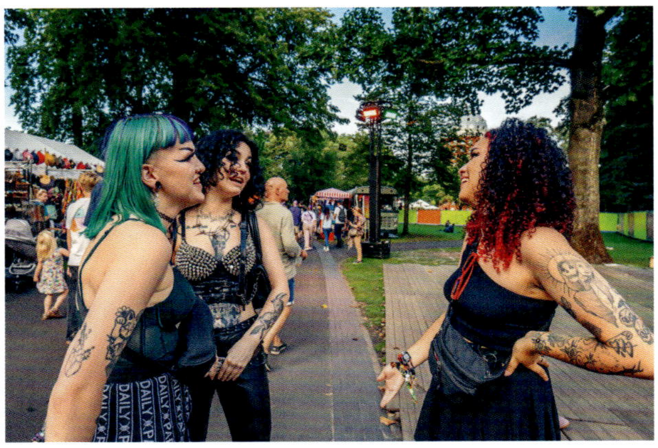

Gothic women
Breda Barst 2024, Breda

Anyone who has, or develops, an eye for it will find group style endlessly fascinating, and completely ubiquitous. In 1994 photographer Ari Versluis and stylist Ellie Uyttenbroek started categorising and documenting group style in an almost anthropological way. They began in Rotterdam and the first subculture they catalogued was the emerging gabber scene, followed by gays in checked shirts, gabber girls, skaters, football supporters, street dwellers, veiled Muslim women, women in fur coats – whatever you can think of, they have photographed it. The most recent group they documented – the 185th – as twelve non-binary youngsters in cropped tops with mullets and eye make-up. Uyttenbroek and Versluis call their project *Exactitudes* – a contraction of exact and attitudes – and it has attracted a great deal of attention and appreciation. They have now photographed people in many other cities and countries, and their work has appeared in books and exhibitions.

Louise Brooks, 1935
Photo: World History Archive

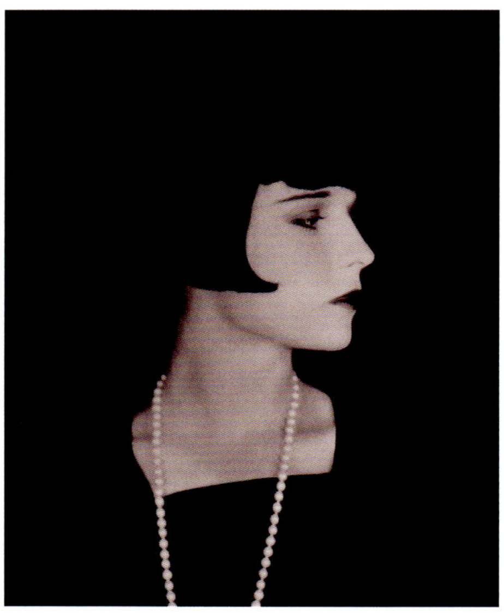

Seeing the *Exactitudes* pictures, we cannot help but ask ourselves, 'would I fit into such a group?' 'Which one?' 'So am I as unique as I thought I was?' And after pondering this for a moment, we would undoubtedly also wonder, 'How come people act like herd animals?'

The simplest answer is of course that people are born as herd animals. When we are at school, we want nothing more than to be part of the most popular group in the class. I was at a school full of posh kids in the 1980s, where everyone wore two polo shirts over each other, with checked trousers and a lamb's wool sweater knotted around their shoulders. I pestered my parents until they bought me a T-shirt with an MO'P logo on it, from the Marc O'Polo brand, regarded as supercool at the time. There was no way I would go to school in a sweater from the in-house brand of the Netherlands' most popular department store V&D, or something with the rearing horse of C&A's in-house Rodeo brand on it, as my mother suggested.

Gothic Lolitas at the Summer Darkness Festival, Utrecht

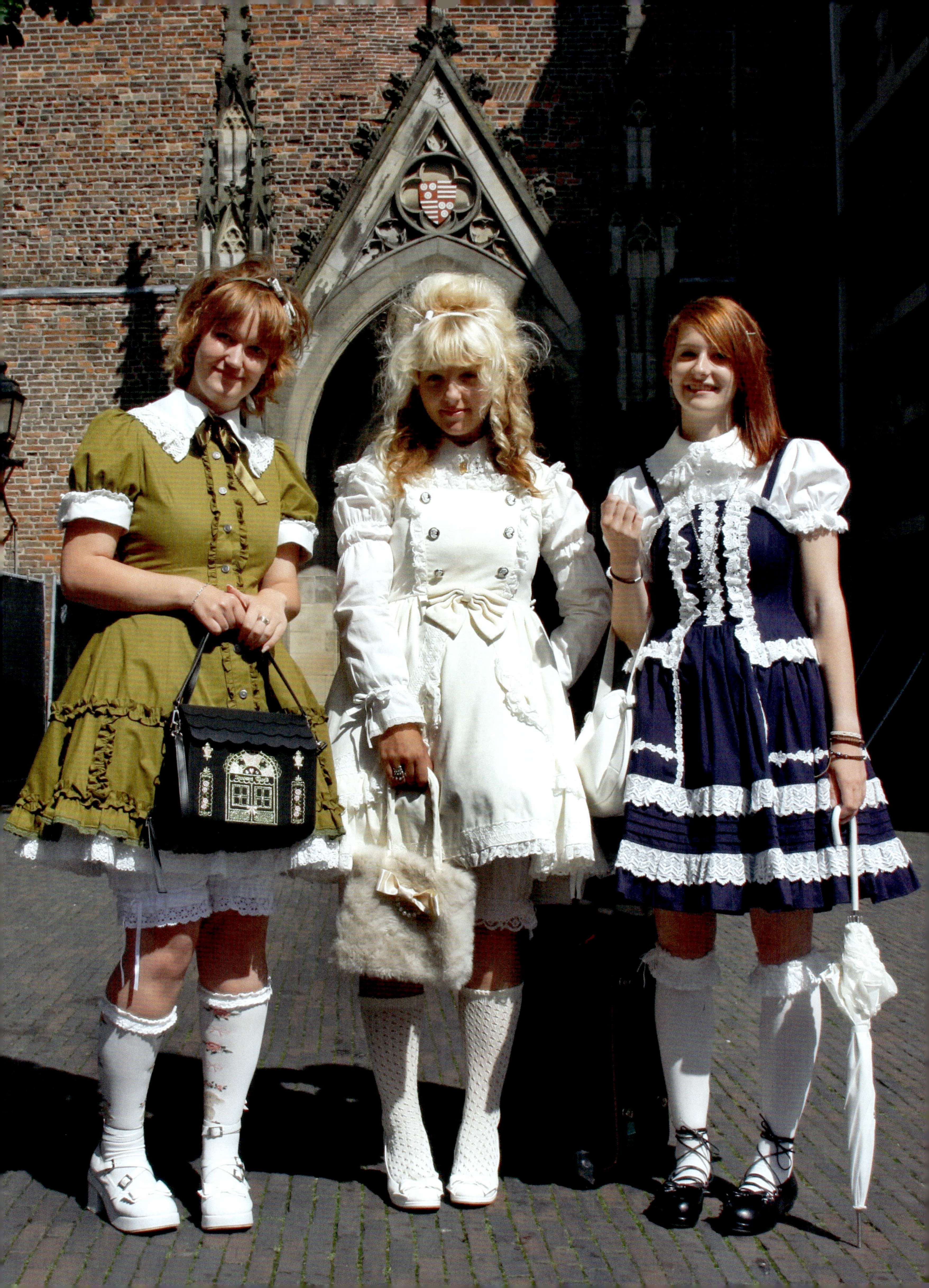

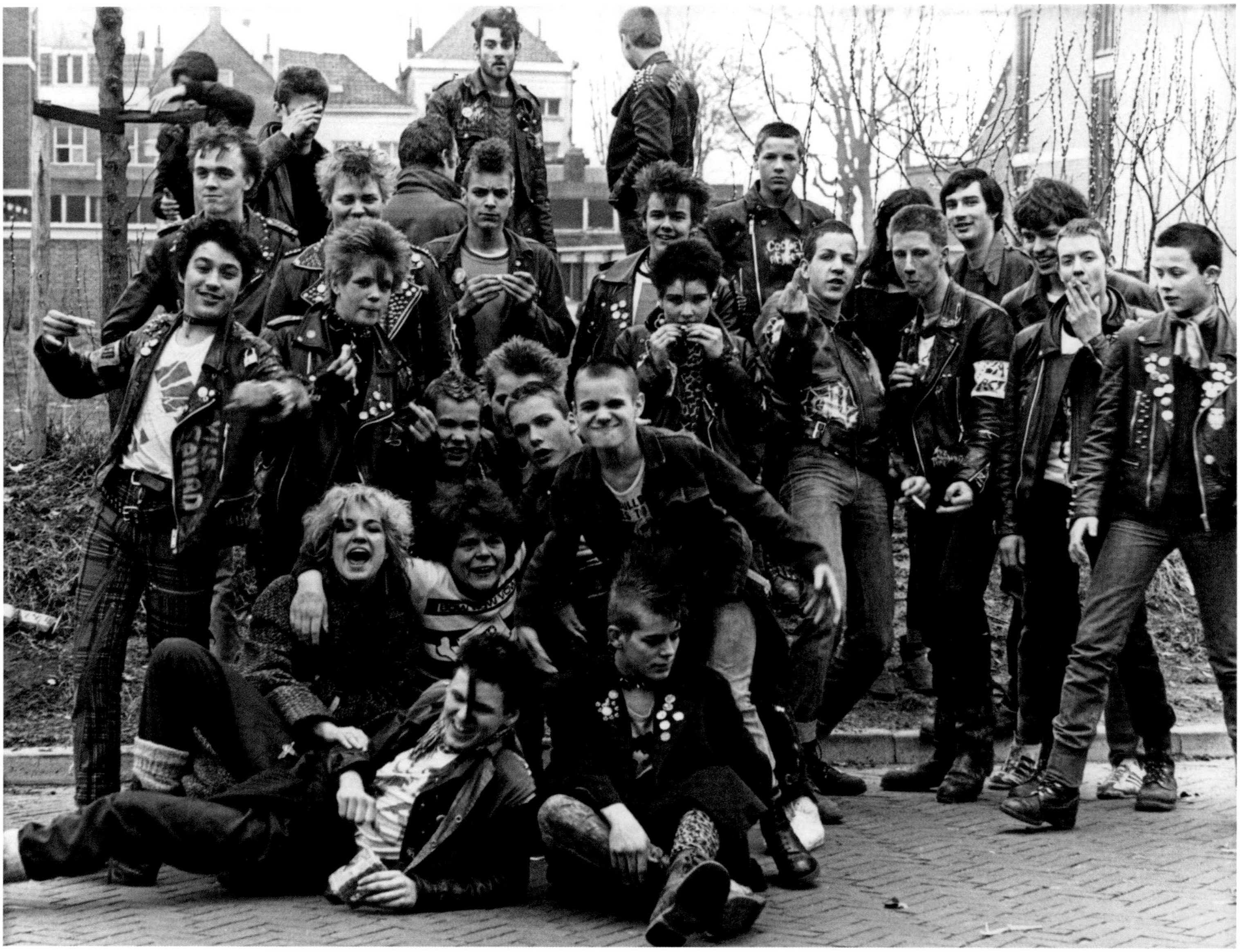

Punks at the Punk Festival, 21 March 1982, Stokvishal, Arnhem

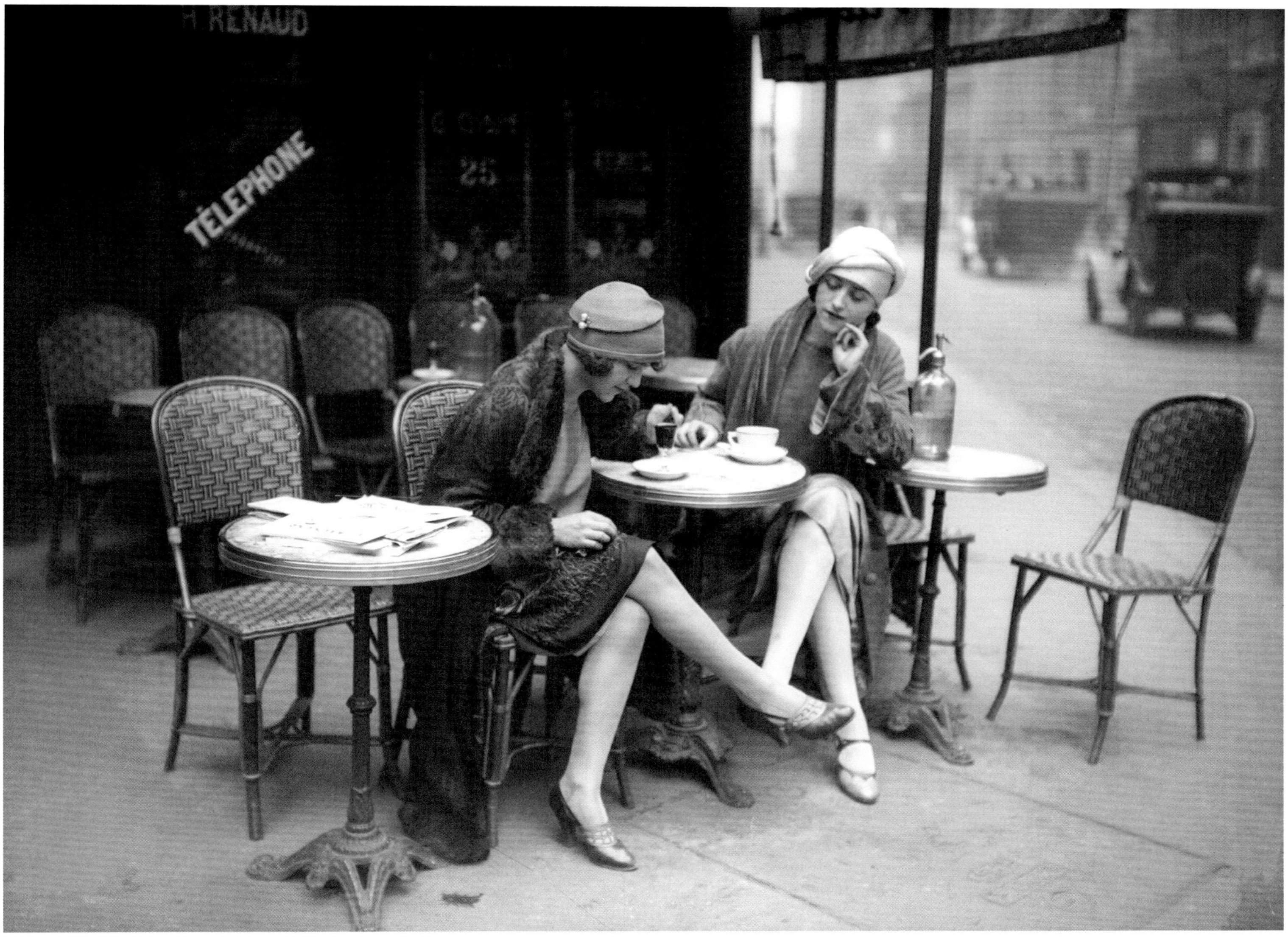


Women at a pavement café in Paris, 1925
Photo: Roger Viollet Agence Photographique, Maurice-Louis Branger

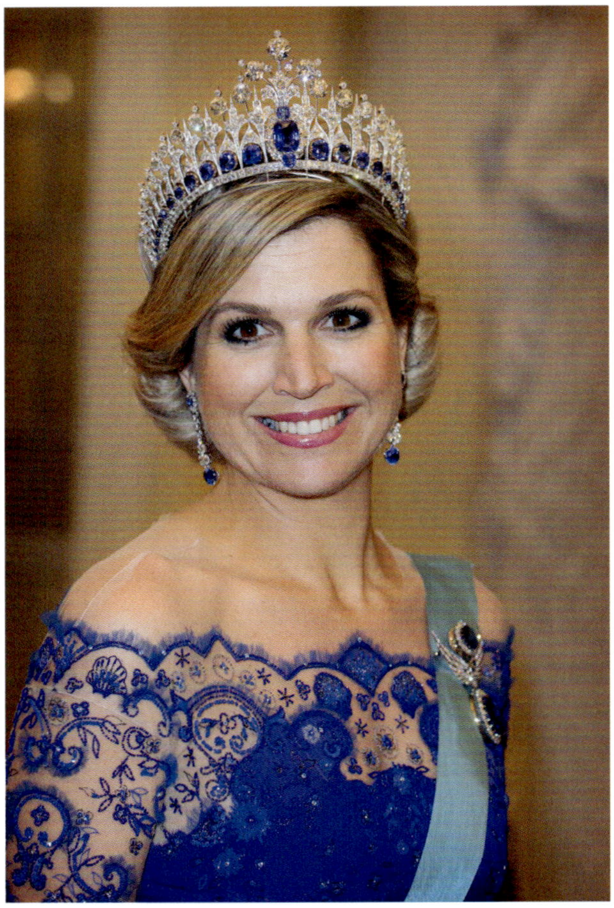

Queen Máxima at a state banquet in Copenhagen on 17 March 2015 Wearing her investiture gown from 2013, by Jan Taminiau.

In that respect, little has changed. A friend recently told me that her sixteen-year-old daughter, who likes to dress alternatively, Billie Eilish-style, didn't dare to wear her coveted Naked Wolfe boots with platformed soles and high heels – a gift from her mother – to school because they were too eccentric compared with what her conservative classmates were wearing. The style at school, her mother had observed, is fairly basic, as the students prefer to spend their money on vapes and mobile telephones than on clothes.

Snobs, normies and alternatives have existed for a long time, and they will still exist in forty years' time, alongside a few new subcultures. How these new subcultures emerge is a fascinating subject, and it has been explored in many thorough academic studies. In a nutshell, subcultures often begin among young people who decide they have had enough of their parents' boring habits, style of dress and music and go in search of a new way to shape their own identity. Think of the flapper girls of the 1920s, who cut their long hair short, discarded their corsets, let their waistlines drop and danced the Charleston while smoking like chimneys. Think of the rockers (and the nozems in the Netherlands) of the 1950s, with their quiffs, and the mods who rejected their parents' traditions and factory jobs. Then came the hippies with flowers in their long hair, wearing flapping robes and Afghan coats, who preached peace against the backdrop of the Vietnam war. A decade on, it was the punks, with their brightly-coloured mohicans, combat boots and torn clothes covered in safety pins, who rejected the political leaders they held responsible for unemployment and the economic crisis, followed by the black-clad, more morose goths.

The subcultures of the final decades of the twentieth century, like disco, new wave, hiphop, skater and grunge, were a little less rebellious, defined more by music and sport than by a rejection of the established order.

The most recent subcultures and the many niche cultures of this century – think hipsters, e-girls, Y2K, normcore, the oat milk elite – are less likely to be rooted in music than in gaming and social media. Some are no longer concerned with rebellion and innovation, but are purely about aesthetics and lifestyle, or even (completely non-counterculture) about a yearning for the past. The currently much-discussed 'tradwives' subculture – traditional housewives wearing aprons, baking cookies and buns for their kids while their husbands attempt to become as wealthy as their idol, influencer Andrew Tate – is in fact a bulwark of nostalgia and regression.
In a case like this, the word influencer perfectly encapsulates what happens when a large group of people are inspired or pushed to behave or dress like their idol. Kim Kardashian is another super-influencer who, along with her sisters, has prompted countless young women around the world to wear their hair long and straight (sometimes with extensions), stick on false eyelashes, shape their face with make-up, have their lips augmented and wear tight clothes that emphasise their buttocks and breasts.

Although we now used the word influencer mainly to refer to social media stars with a large band of followers, the concept is as old as the modern world. Almost all subcultures have their poster boys (from Elvis and The Beatles to Robert Smith and Kurt Cobain) and poster girls (Janis Joplin, Blondie, Madonna, Beyoncé). As well as musicians, actors like James Dean and models like Twiggy also inspired trends and subcultures. Artists and even philosophers have done the same. The existentialism of Jean Paul Sartre, Simone de Beauvoir and Albert Camus was discussed and adopted by groups of chain-smoking young intellectuals dressed in unisex black clothing. Fun fact for a dinner party: New Wave resulted from this philosophy.

Another unique group of historical influencers whom we cannot, of course, overlook in the context of this catalogue, is the royals. As long ago as ancient Rome, empresses determined the fashion in hairstyles, clothes and jewellery. Centuries later, it was France's last empress Eugénie, wife of Napoleon III, who set the tone for European fashion. Her hairstyle and the large crinolines she wore under her skirts were widely copied.

The last prominent royal influencer was Princess Diana. When the nineteen-year-old Lady Diana Spencer became engaged to Prince Charles, heir to the British throne, she enchanted the world with her shy smile and her prim wardrobe. She wore sailor dresses, bow blouses, sweaters, slipovers and calf-length pleated skirts, in a conservative, typically British upper-class style that suddenly became all the rage due to her influence. Diana's extravagant wedding dress with the hot-air-balloon-sized puffed sleeves and her short blond hair were imitated by many women in Europe. After her divorce from Charles her outfits became shorter, tighter and more daring, and Diana – dressed in couture by Versace and Dior – evolved into a global style icon.

So are there no more royal influencers these days? Yes and no. Yes, in the sense that there are plenty of online content creators with royal blood, like Countess Eloise of Orange-Nassau, the Maharaja of Jaipur and Princess Stéphanie of Monaco's jetsetting daughters. But they do not have any real influence over the behaviour and dress style of their followers. Nor do Queen Máxima and Catherine, Princess of Wales, have even half the impact that Diana had, however well-dressed they may be. They are more trend followers than trendsetters, and as well as wearing couture, they are also regularly spotted in jeans and off-the-peg items from Zara and H&M.

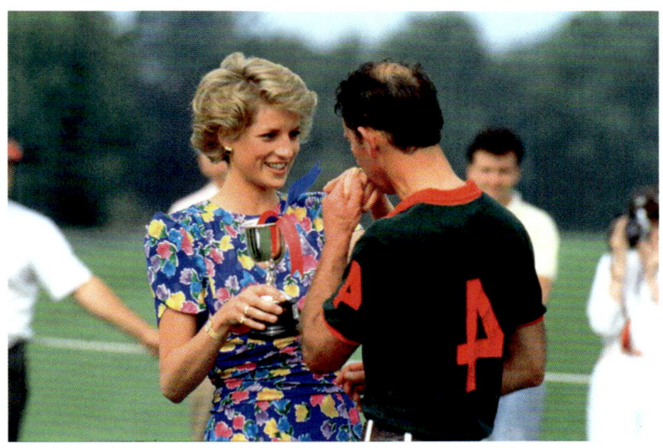

Princess Diana at a polo match, 1988

Times have changed, hierarchy and royal aloofness have become hopelessly old-fashioned. Nowadays, the royals want to belong with the people. When Máxima poses with her family for the annual summer shoot on the beach or in the gardens of Huis ten Bosch palace, she looks just like her wealthy peers from Wassenaar or the Gooi region, with her long blonde hair worn loose, her big earrings and ivory outfits. Which might well earn her a place in one of Uyttenbroek and Versluis' *Exactitudes* photo galleries.

So what I'm trying to say is that everyone's identity is shaped by outside influences, whether consciously or otherwise. And ultimately everyone belongs to a group of some size or other, one that feels comfortable and familiar. Have you worked out which style tribe or subculture you belong to? Not yet? Well I have: you are part of a small but perfect sub-club of culture vultures. People who like carefully curated fashion exhibitions and the catalogues that go with them. People who read them with interest, cover to cover. Which happens to be one of my favourite subcultures ;-).

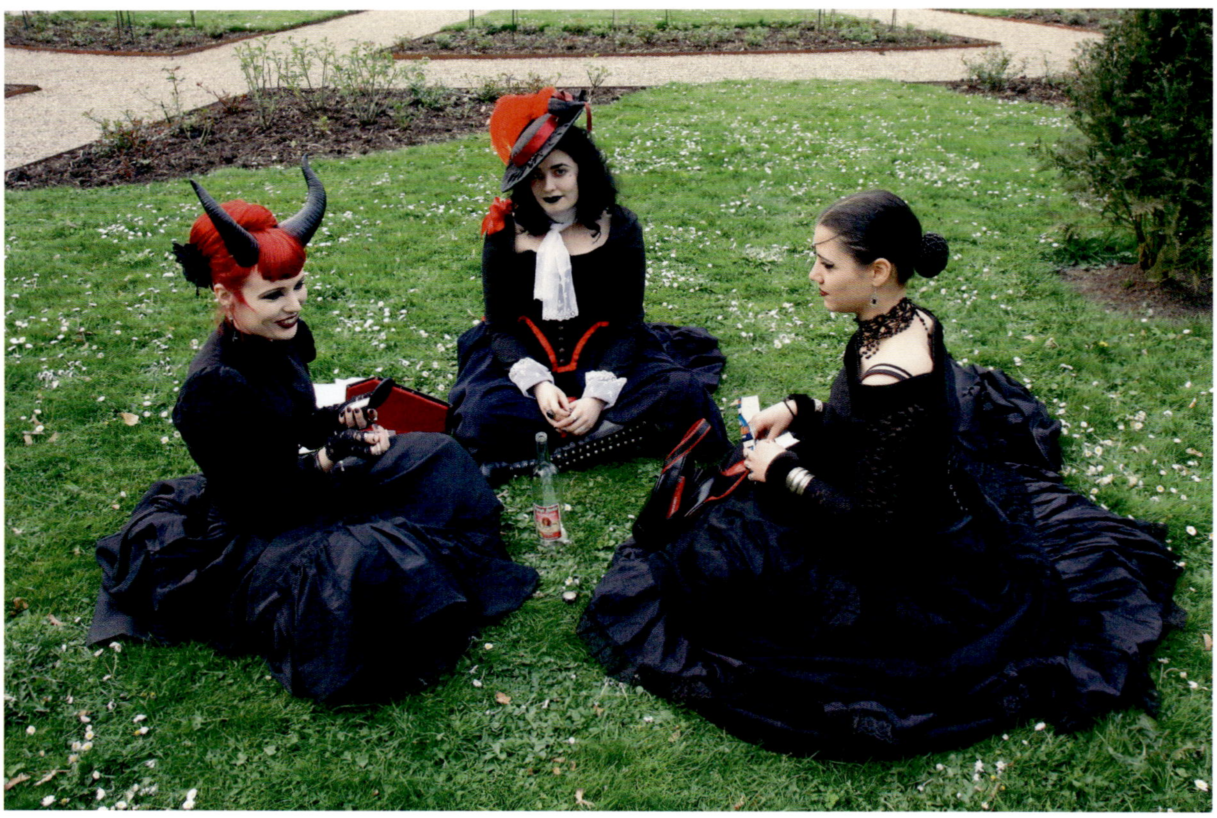

Elf Fantasy Fair at Kasteel de Haar, 16 April 2011

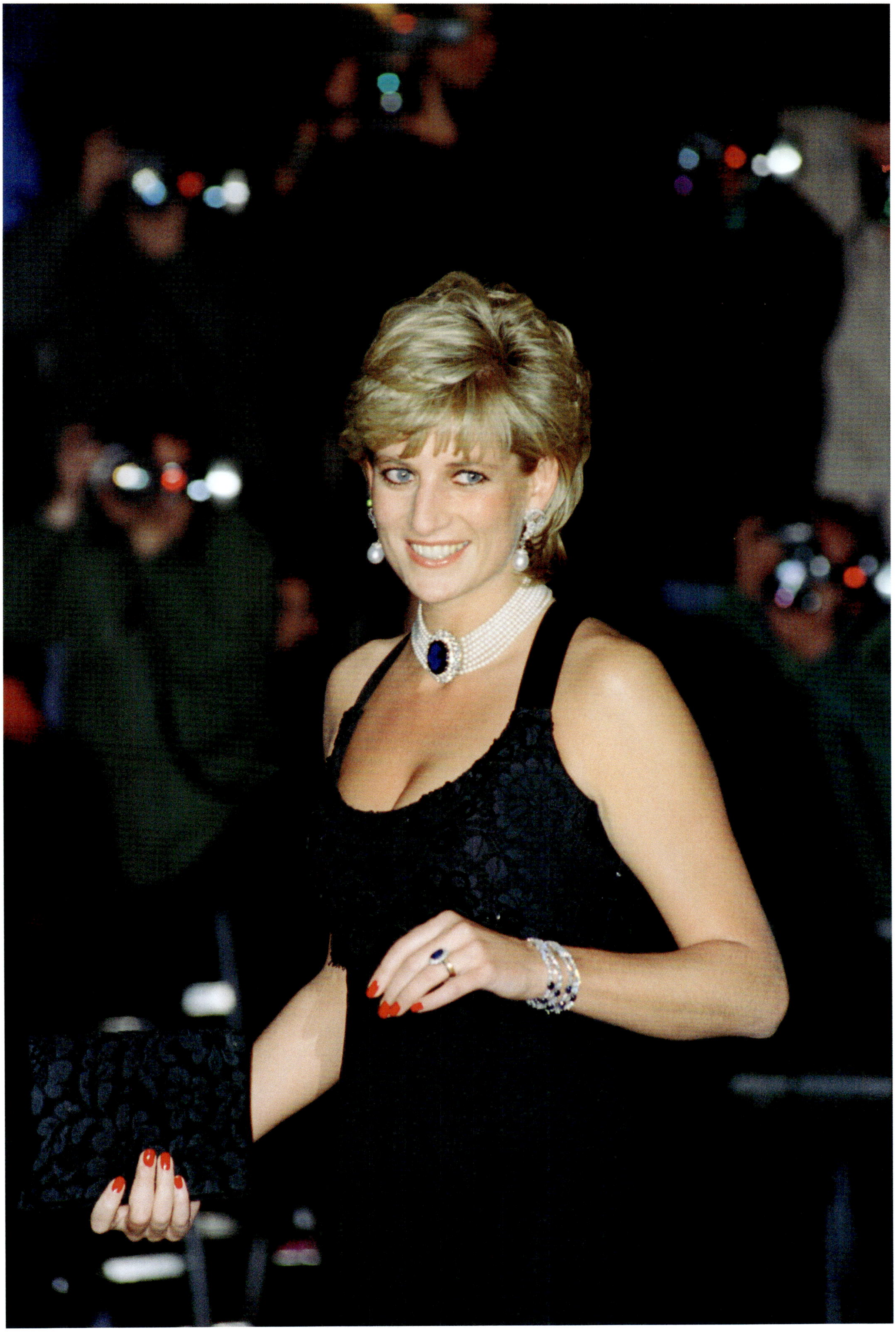

Princess Diana wearing an evening dress by Jacques Azagury on a visit to the Tate Gallery in London, 1 July 1997 ◆
On loan from the Princess Diana Museum Los Angeles

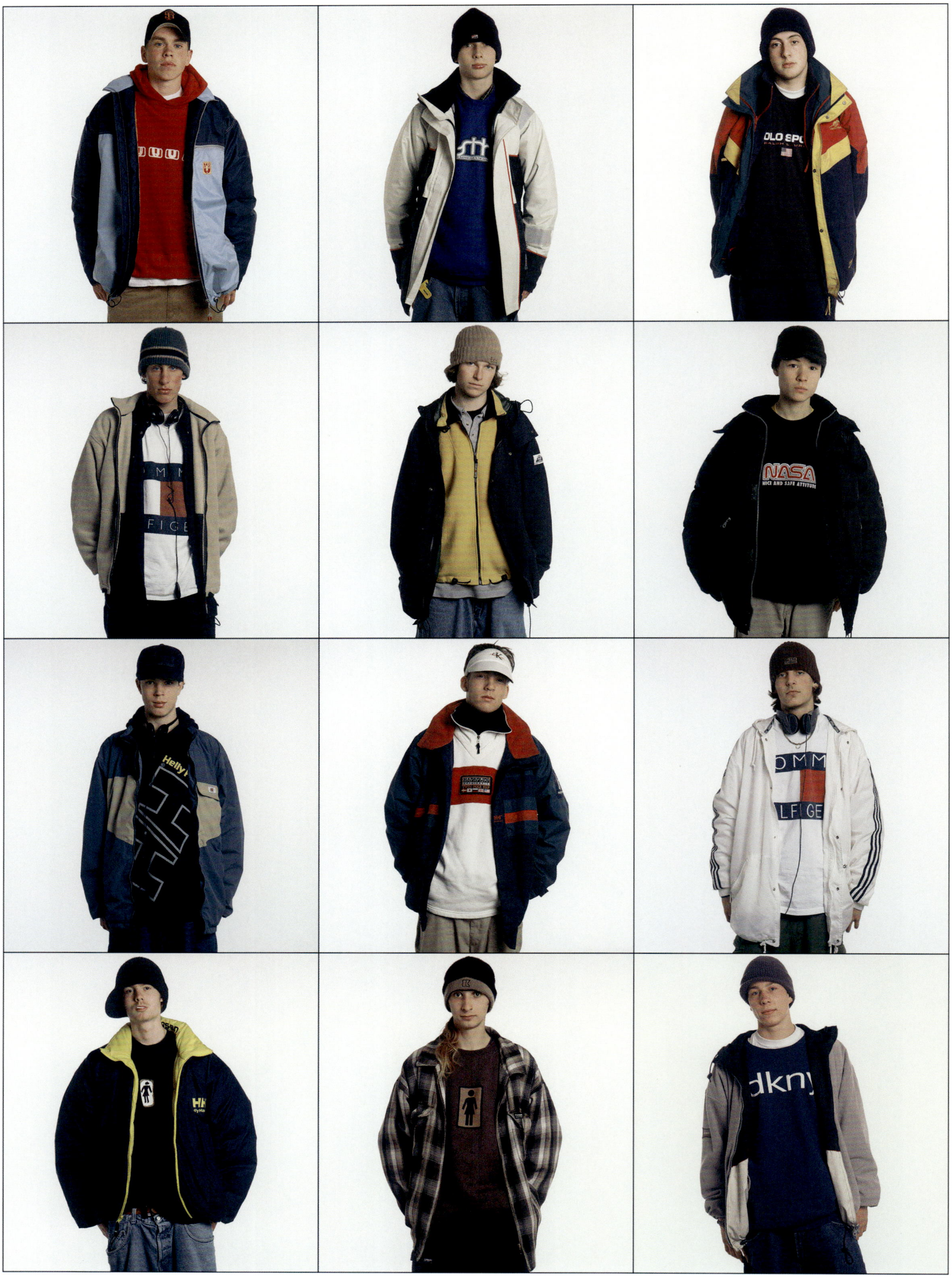

Exactitudes, 010, Skaters ◆
Ari Versluis, Ellie Uyttenbroek, 1997
Rotterdam

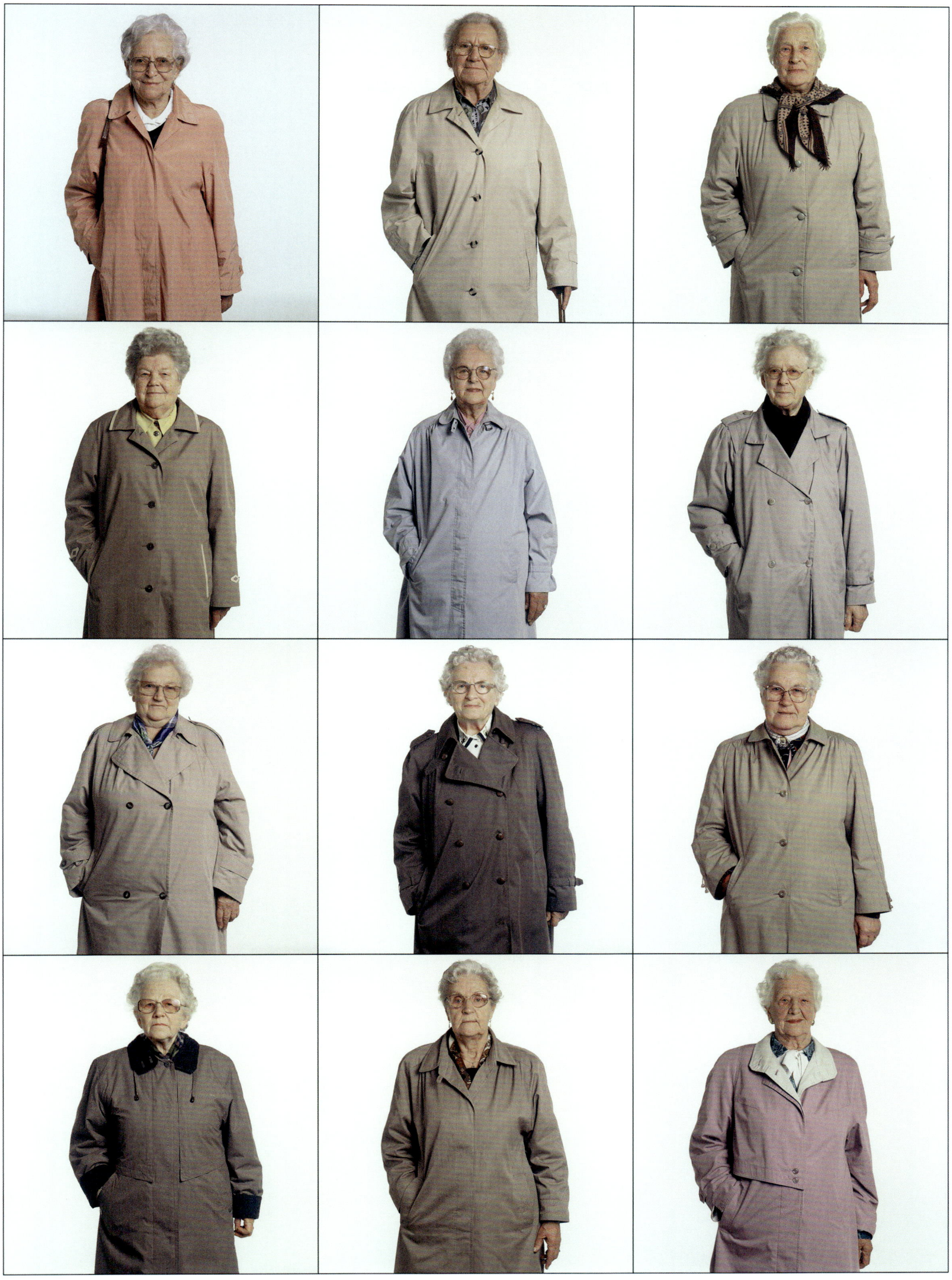

Exactitudes, 025, Grannies ◆
Ari Versluis, Ellie Uyttenbroek, 1997
Rotterdam

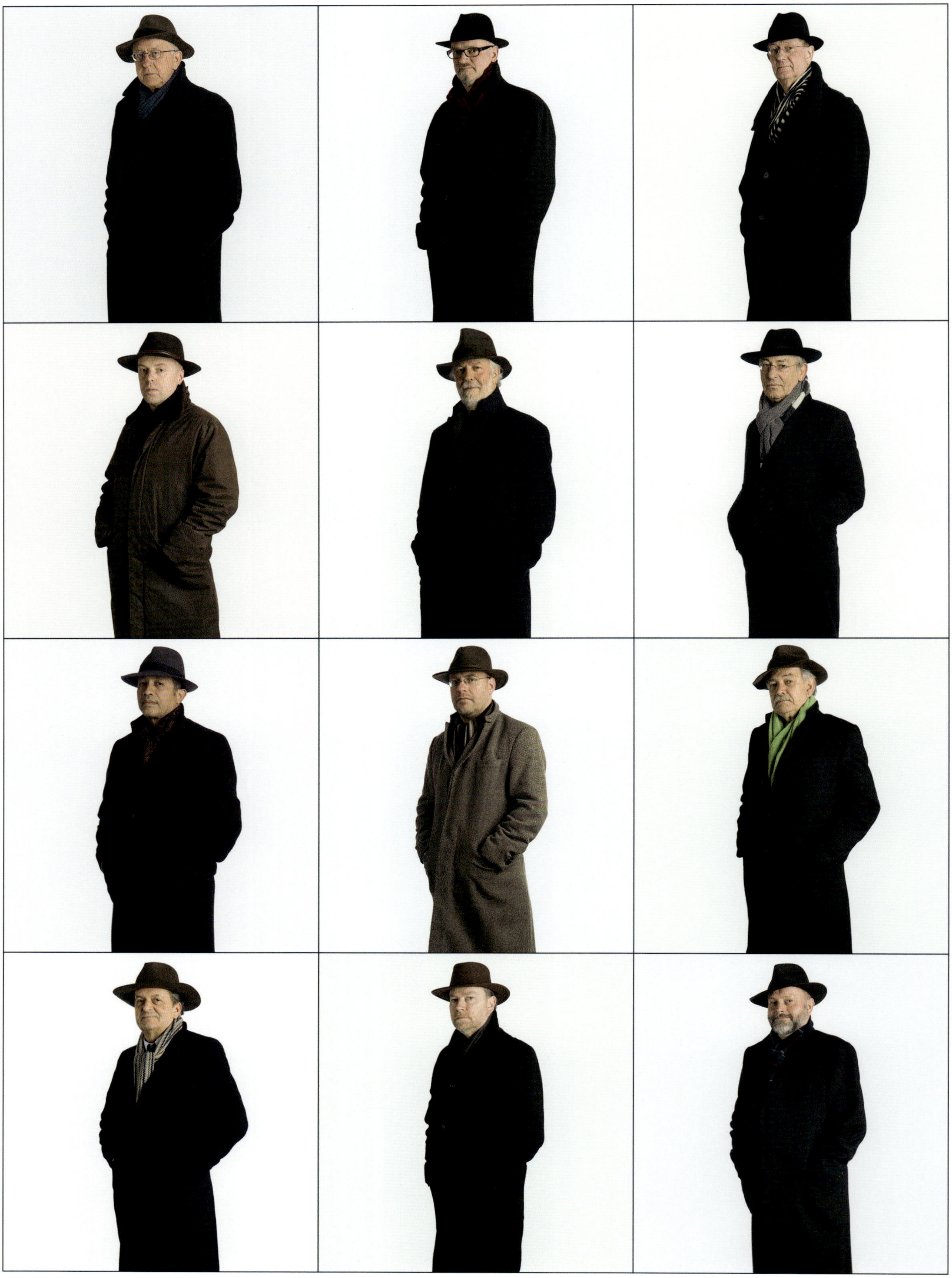

**Exactitudes, 119, Intellectuals ◆**
Ari Versluis, Ellie Uyttenbroek, 2009
Limburg

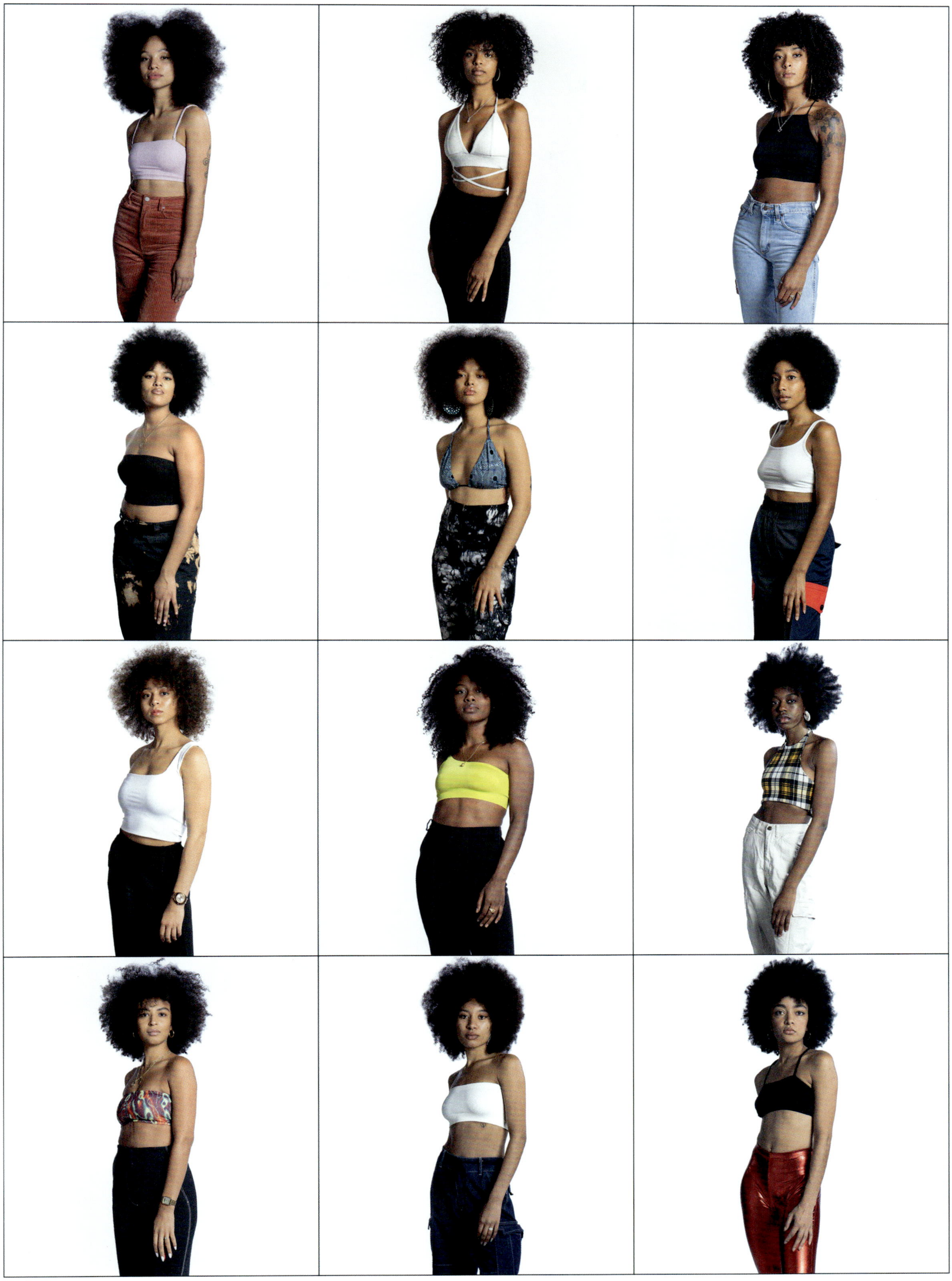

Exactitudes, 159, Originals ◆
Ari Versluis, Ellie Uyttenbroek, 2018
Rotterdam

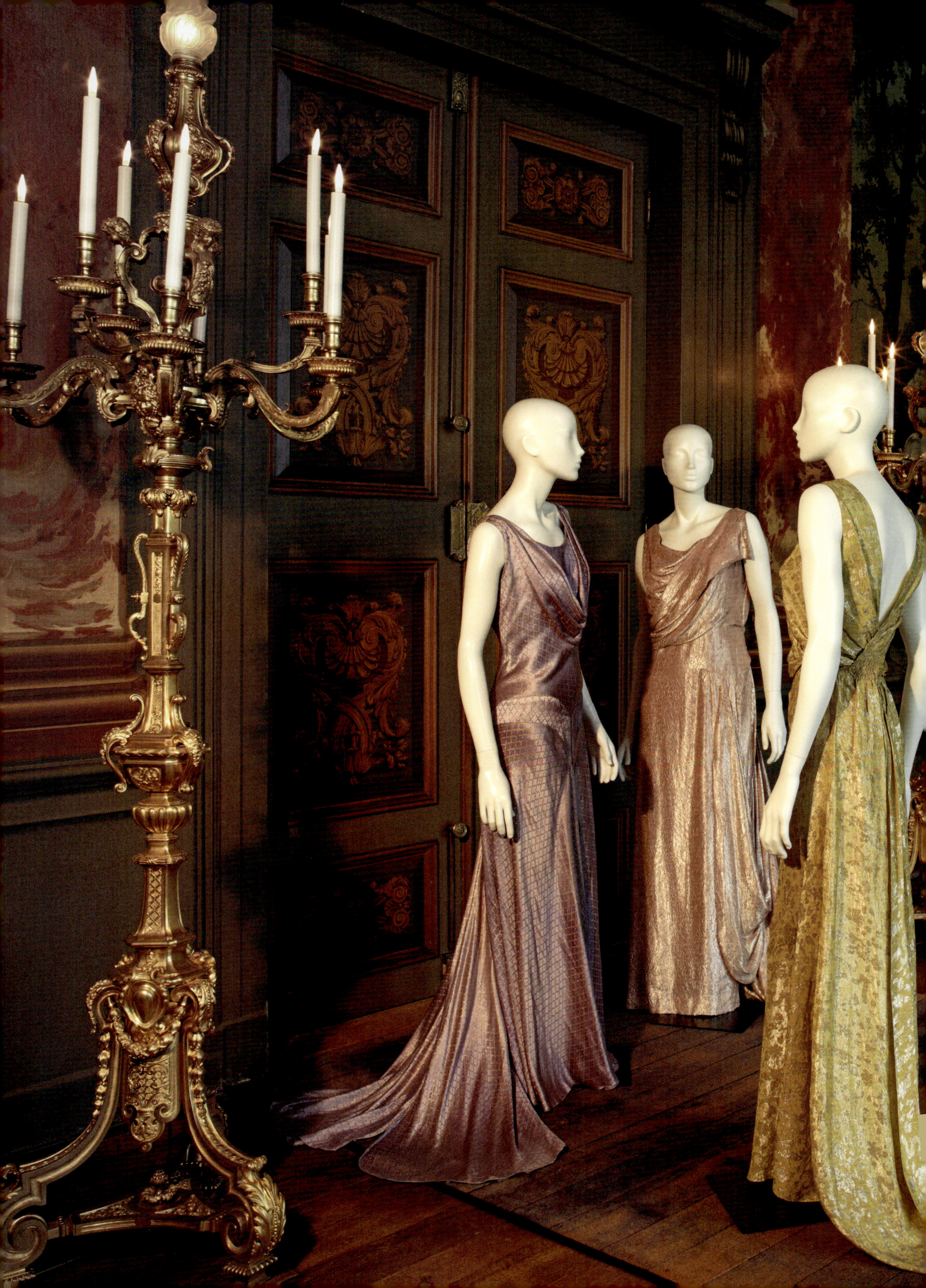

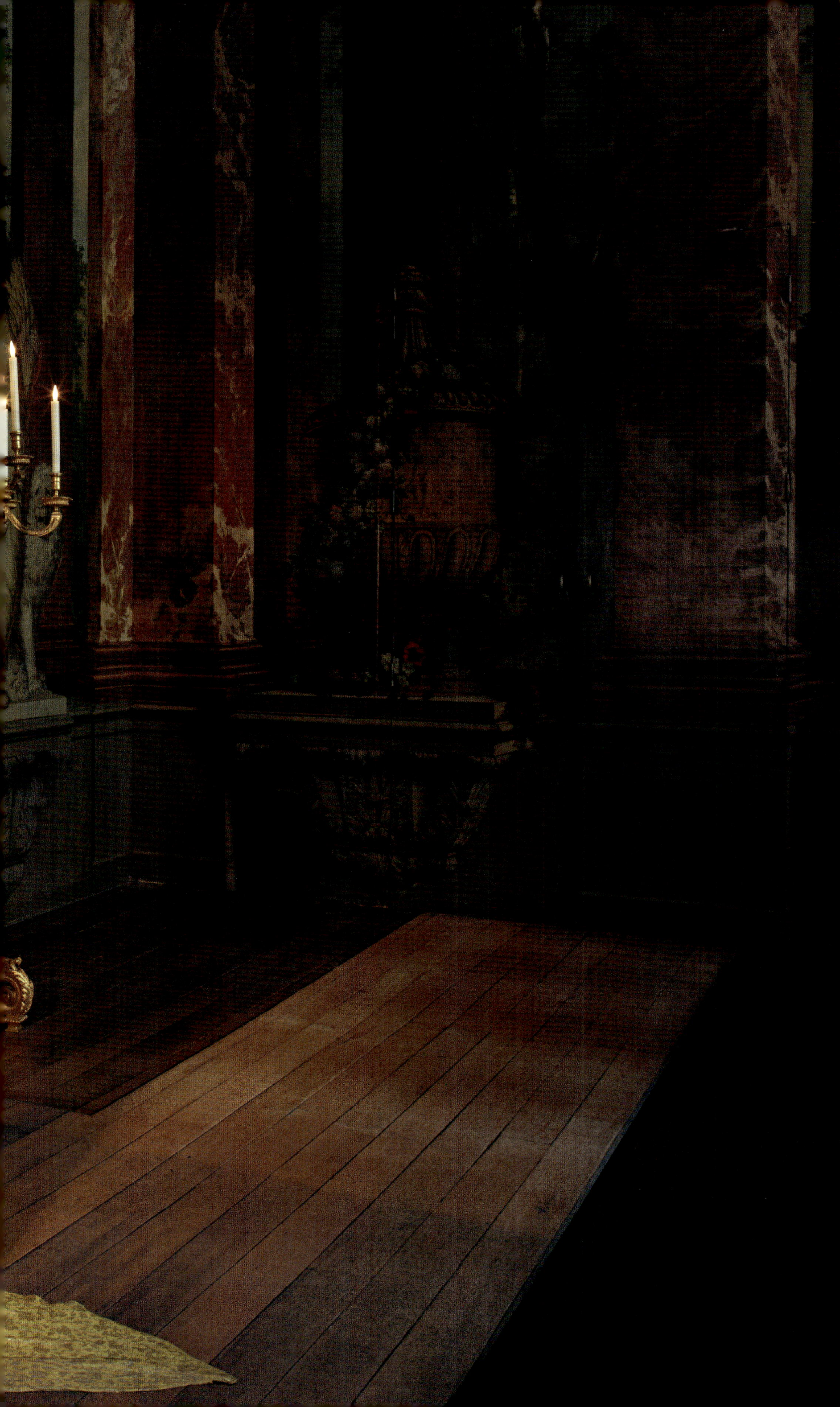

# GRAND GALA DRESS CODE

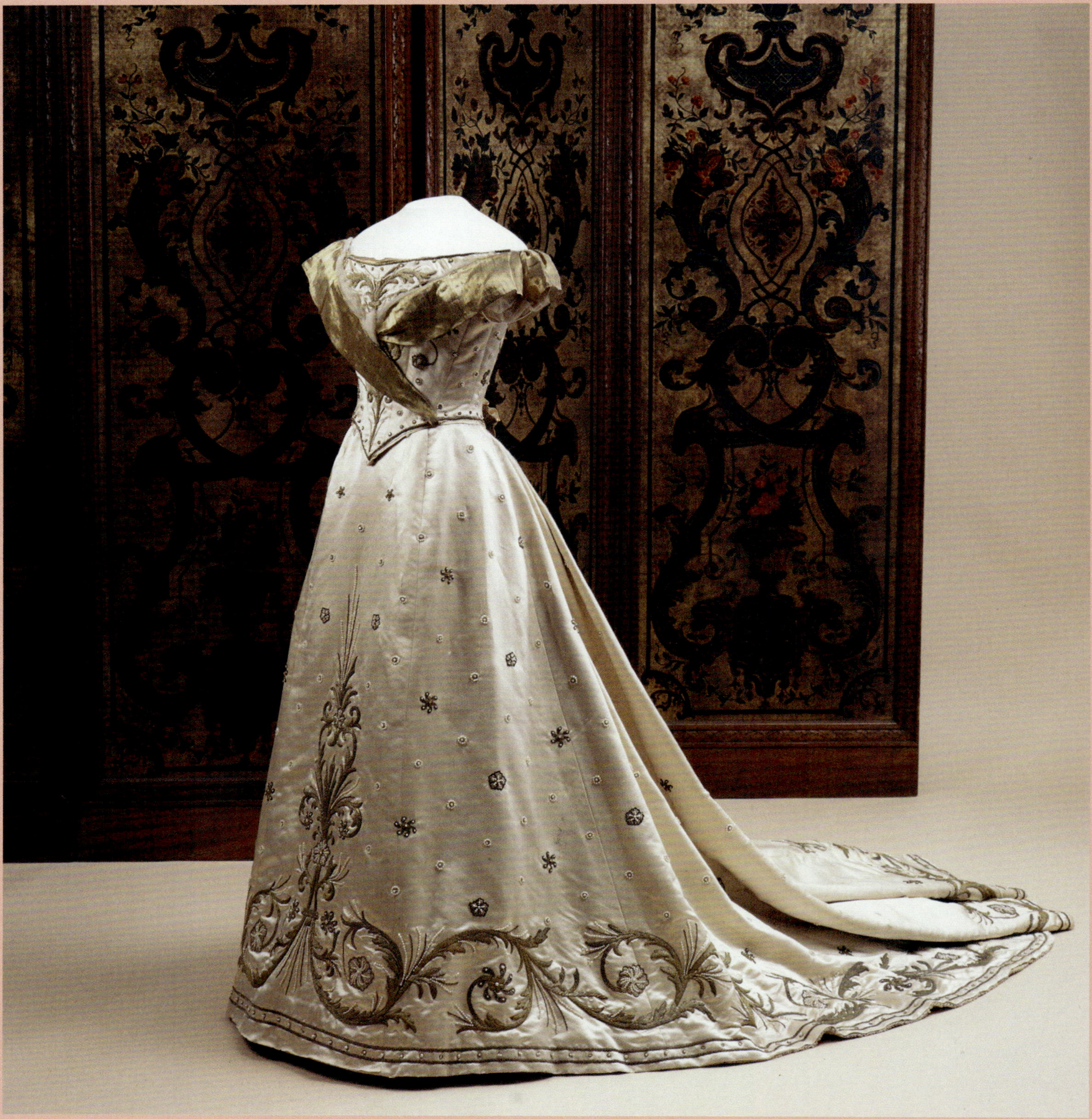

**Wilhelmina's investiture gown**
Paris, Nicaud & Cie, 1898
Silk, gold and silver thread, gold lamé, glass pearls
Paleis Het Loo, on long-term loan
from the Royal Collections, The Hague

# WILHELMINA'S INVESTITURE GOWN

Queen Wilhelmina's cream satin investiture gown consists of a separate bodice and skirt that extends into a long train with a rounded end. The front panel of the skirt is decorated with a symmetrical renaissance motif of acanthus vines and rosettes of glass pearls. The motif continues along the edges of the train. The gold lamé revers may originally have been covered with lace. The gown was designed by Nicaud and was made in Paris, but the embroidery was the work of the artistic needlework department of the National College of Decorative Arts in Amsterdam, overseen by two associations: Tesselschade and 'Arbeid Adelt'. This meant that the gown was also a national product. Wilhelmina wore the sash of the Military Order of William, the oldest and highest royal honour in the Netherlands, of which, as reigning monarch, she was grandmaster. She also wore long white gloves.

The day of the investiture, 6 September 1898, had been preceded by a summer of preparations. Ten days before Wilhelmina's eighteenth birthday, the day on which, under constitutional law, she would reach the age of majority and ascend the throne, the Nicaud gown she would wear at her investiture was delivered to Paleis Soestdijk, where she spent the hot summer of 1898. 'Tomorrow my people from Paris will come for a fitting; I hope it will be pleasant in these temperatures! Then I will have to have my hair dressed with tiaras a number of times & I will have to practise wearing the robe with the four aide-de-camps. Quite some tasks in this heat!', Wilhelmina wrote to her former English governess in a letter of 21 August.[1] Wilhelmina was the first reigning queen of the Netherlands, the first woman on the throne, following a series of male monarchs. Her predecessors Willem I, Willem II and Willem III had worn a uniform under the historic royal robe at their investitures. An official gown had to be designed for Wilhelmina that would reflect her central role in one of the most important ceremonies in the kingdom. Queen Emma may have asked Nicaud to take inspiration from the white satin dress suit embroidered with gold which was believed at court to have been worn by Willem I at his investiture as King of the United Kingdom of the Netherlands in Brussels. This was not so much out of veneration for the first king from the House of Orange, but perhaps merely to provide some basis for a female version of an investiture outfit.

In some of the photographs that were taken in the runup to Wilhelmina's investiture, she wore a ballgown – white, low-cut, with a train and short sleeves – under the royal robe. A dress like this was suitable for the photographs, as the investiture was also a gala occasion. But more pomp would be needed for the actual ceremony, hence the heavy fabric and grand gold embroidery, which matched the gold embroidered lions on the royal robe. It was all about that one dramatic moment when Wilhelmina took the oath. All eyes would be on the queen as she raised her right hand, causing the robe to fall open to reveal most of the gown. Queen Wilhelmina wore her investiture gown one more time, at the New Year's ball at Paleis Noordeinde, in January 1899.[2]
—PR

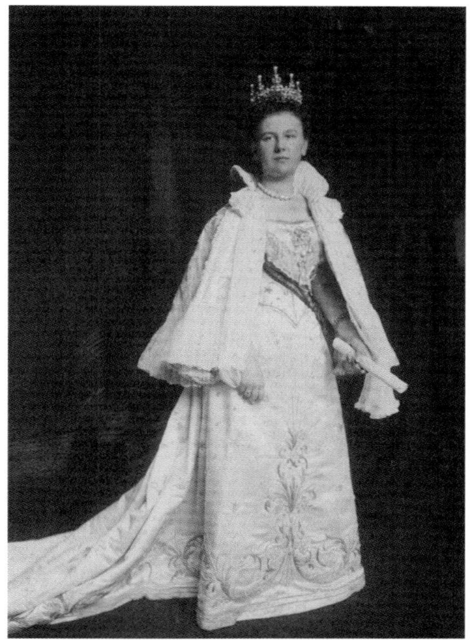

**Rehearsing for the big day**
During one of the rehearsals for the investiture, Wilhelmina was photographed wearing her investiture gown. A short cape stood in for the royal robe, and she was trying out the Württemberg tiara here, which had been specially assembled for the event. She would ultimately choose the Stuart tiara, however, which included the famous jewels of the House of Orange.

Unknown photographer, 1898
Royal Collections, The Hague

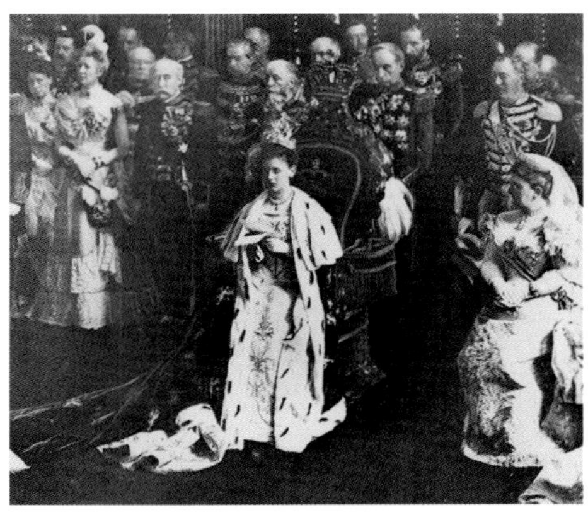

**The queen gives her investiture speech**
Just before taking the oath, Queen Wilhelmina gave her investiture speech, in the presence of her mother Emma and members of the royal household. The ladies are wearing evening gowns, the gentlemen are in their ceremonial court uniforms or full dress uniforms. The embroidery on Wilhelmina's dress can clearly be seen.

Photo F.R. Ebner (fragment)
Paleis Het Loo

**Wilhelmina takes the oath**
Artist Nicolaas van der Waay was commissioned by Queen Emma to capture in a large oil painting the moment that her daughter Wilhelmina took the oath. A preliminary pencil study in a sketchbook includes a meticulous depiction of the investiture gown.

Atlas van Stolk, Rotterdam

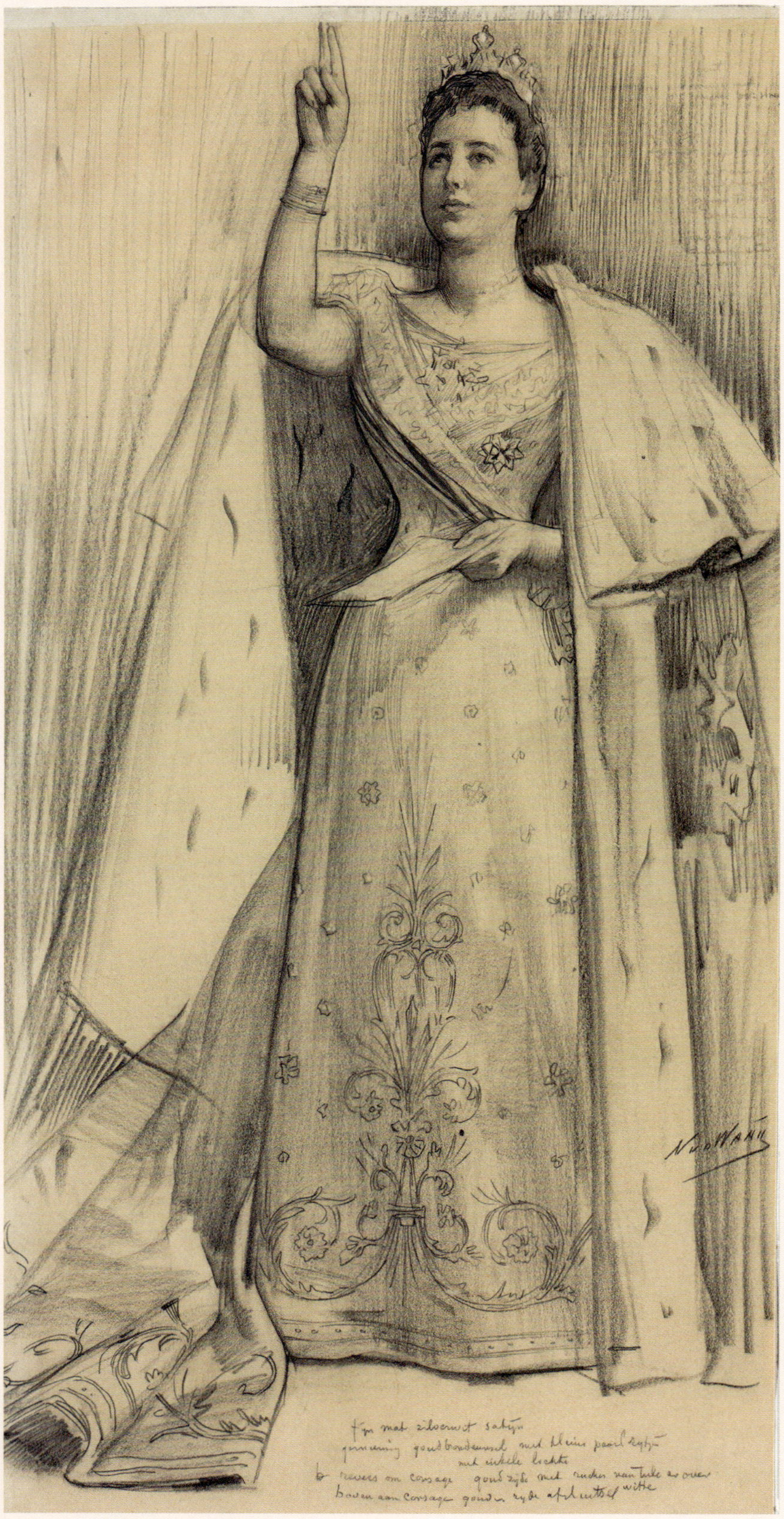

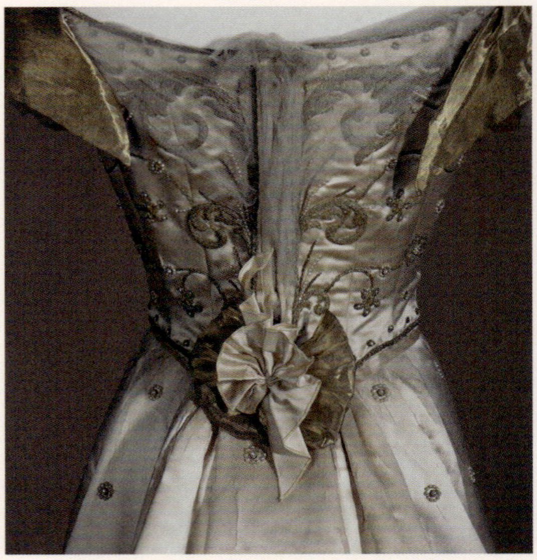

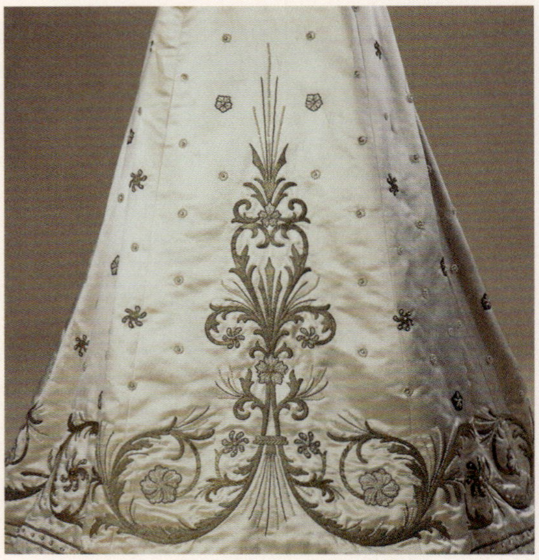

Details of Wilhelmina's investiture gown

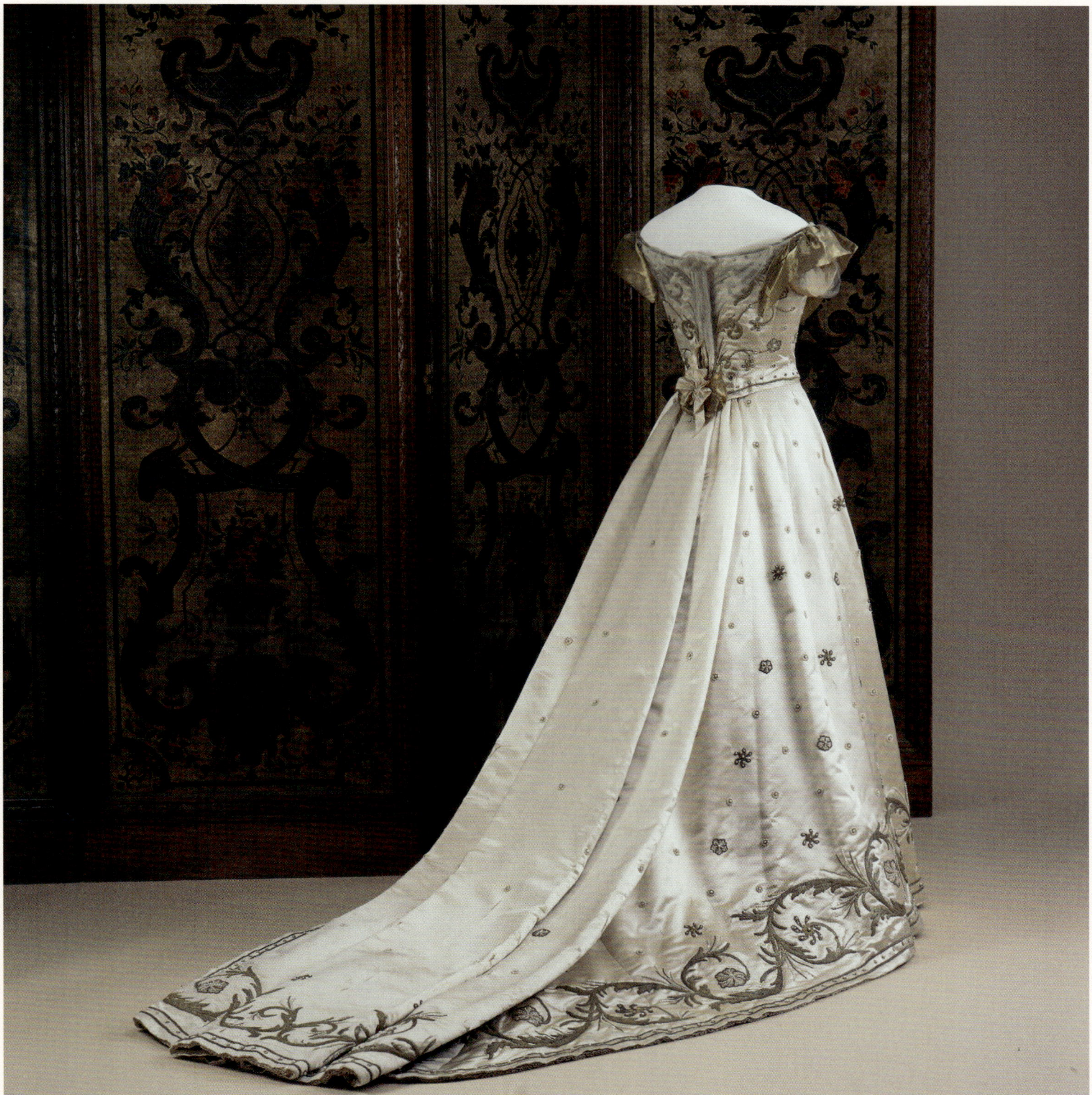

**Wilhelmina's investiture gown**
Paris, Nicaud & Cie, 1898
Silk, gold and silver thread, gold lamé, glass pearls
Paleis Het Loo, on long-term loan
from the Royal Collections, The Hague

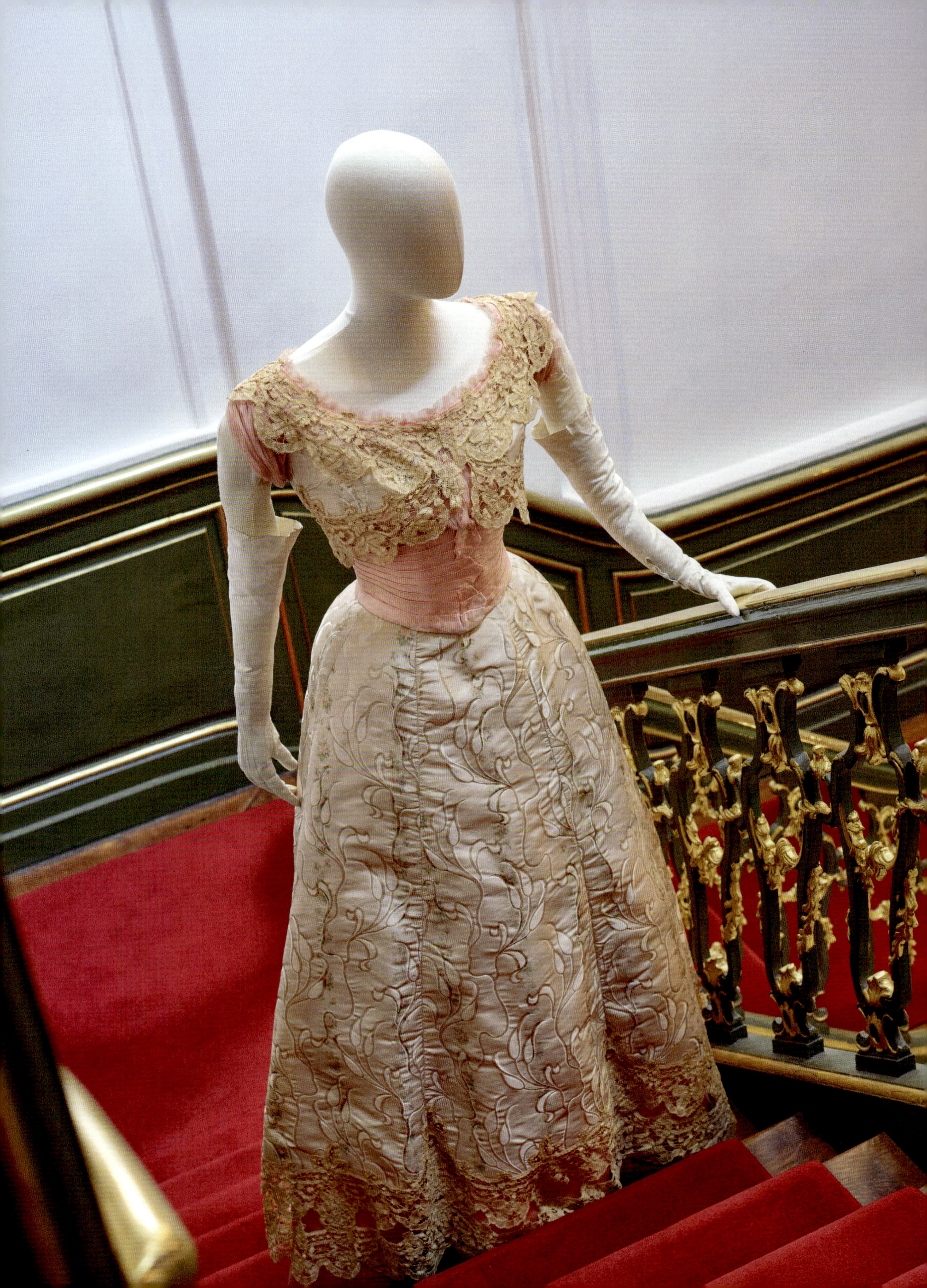

# LADY-IN-WAITING AT A ROYAL WEDDING

When the engagement of Queen Wilhelmina and Prince Hendrik was announced on 12 October 1900, it was not only the bride-to-be who was concerned about what she would wear. Henriette van de Poll, lady-in-waiting to Queen Emma, the Queen Mother, wrote in a letter to her mother that she was constantly receiving 'outfit queries'. Apparently, her parents consulted her, too. She advised her father to wear the uniform of his office which he had had made for the investiture, and she thought the 'new blue and red gown' would be suitable for her younger sister. When her brother Frits asked what would be the normal thing to do with gloves, Henriette admitted that she did not know, but concluded after making enquiries that the men should probably carry them in their hand.[1]

The guests' uncertainties and doubts were not unfounded. Appearing in an inappropriate outfit could be fatal for one's social standing. Newcomers at court were subjected to particularly close scrutiny. Take Baroness Catherina Elisabeth Boudewina Sloet van Marxveld (known as Elisabeth), who became lady-in-waiting to the new Queen Wilhelmina in 1898, at the age of 27, for example. In January 1899, the seasoned lady-in-waiting Henriette van de Poll wrote of her, 'the Honourable Miss Sloet still bears and dresses herself a little stiffly, but things will get better.' Van de Poll was instructed to ensure that Miss Sloet was 'dressed nicely' for a trip to Potsdam later that year.[2]

At Queen Wilhelmina's wedding on 7 February 1901 Miss Sloet wore a low-cut gown that is now in Kunstmuseum Den Haag's collection. The gown is made of cream silk faille with flower and twig motifs woven into the fabric. In the bodice, the fabric falls in the form of a short vest over a pink satin waistband with wide pleats. The neckline and armholes are trimmed with pink voile. Like the short vest, the skirt is trimmed with lace, and ends just above the floor. A skirt with a train (probably pink) would have been worn under this skirt, though it has not survived, unfortunately. Needlemarks in the fabric suggest that this gown was made from an older one.

The gown is well documented. Elisabeth appears, for example, in photographs taken at the Grote Kerk church in The Hague, where the wedding took place. As a lady-in-waiting, she occupied a prominent position in the row behind the royal party. If one looks closely, she can also be discerned in Otto Eerelman's painting of the event, although the gown appears pinker, possibly as a result of an artistic choice. The church ceremony was also depicted in an etching after a painting by Mari ten Kate, in which the gown is shown in fine detail. The whereabouts of the painting on which the etching is based are unknown, unfortunately.

Interestingly, the images of the church ceremony show that several dress codes applied at the event. The queen and her entourage are, for example, dressed in low-cut gowns, with tiaras or feathers in their hair, while the other ladies are dressed in high-necked gowns and are wearing hats. This difference in dress codes caused a practical problem. For fear that 'all the older ladies would contract bronchitis' the church was specially heated for this winter wedding, so 'for people not wearing low-cut gowns it must in fact have been oppressively warm', as Henriette van de Poll remarked.[3]

Three years after the queen's wedding, Elisabeth herself got married, to Dr. Willem Frederik Röell Esq.[4] The marriage meant the end of her career. Her younger sister Isabella Geertruida followed in her footsteps as a lady-in-waiting, and one of her dresses is also in the collection at Kunstmuseum Den Haag. She wore the purple velours and satin gown at Princess Juliana's wedding celebrations in 1937.[5]
—TW

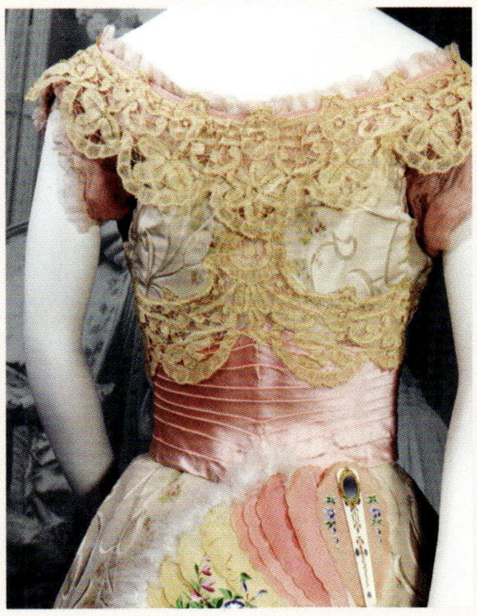

**Ballgown ◆**
Worn by Baroness Sloet van Marxveld (1871-1941) when, as lady-in-waiting, she joined Queen Wilhelmina's wedding procession.
Maker unknown, 1901
Silk
Kunstmuseum Den Haag

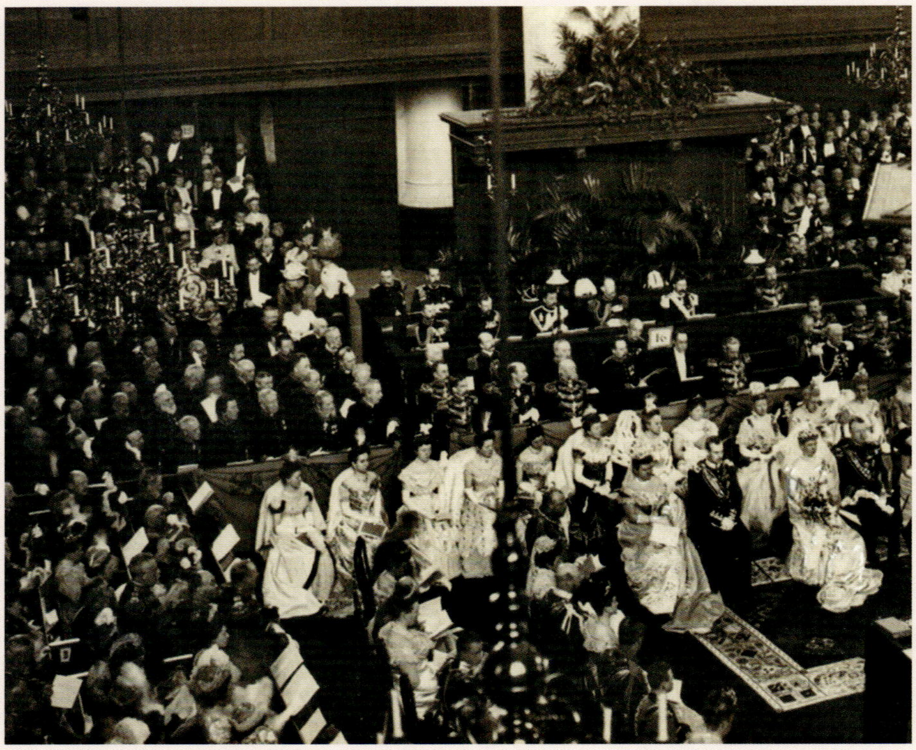

The Wedding of Wilhelmina and Hendrik, 1901 ◆
Otto Eerelman
Royal Collections, The Hague

Royal wedding at the Grote Kerk church in The Hague, 1901
Hermanus Deutmann
Royal Collections, The Hague

Portrait of Catharina Elizabeth Boudewina Sloet van Marxveld (1871-1941), c. 1885
Georg Rothe
RKD – Netherlands Institute for Art History, The Hague

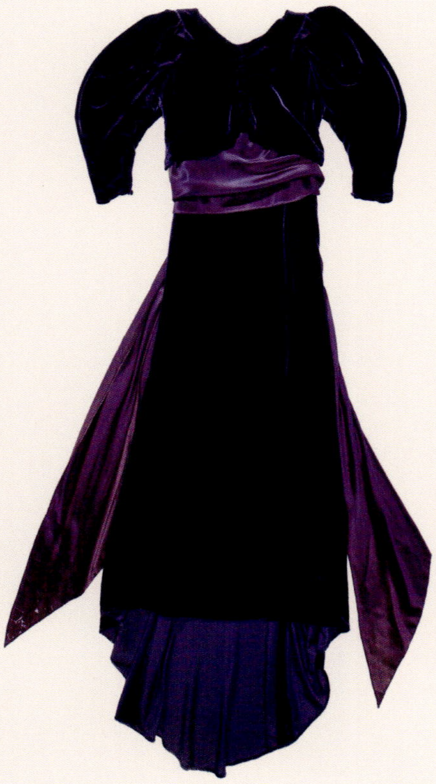

Evening dress
Worn by Lady Isabella Geertruida Sloet van Marxveld, lady-in-waiting to Queen Wilhelmina and Queen Juliana, at the wedding celebrations of Princess Juliana and Prince Bernhard in 1937.
Maker unknown, circa 1937
Silk
Kunstmuseum Den Haag

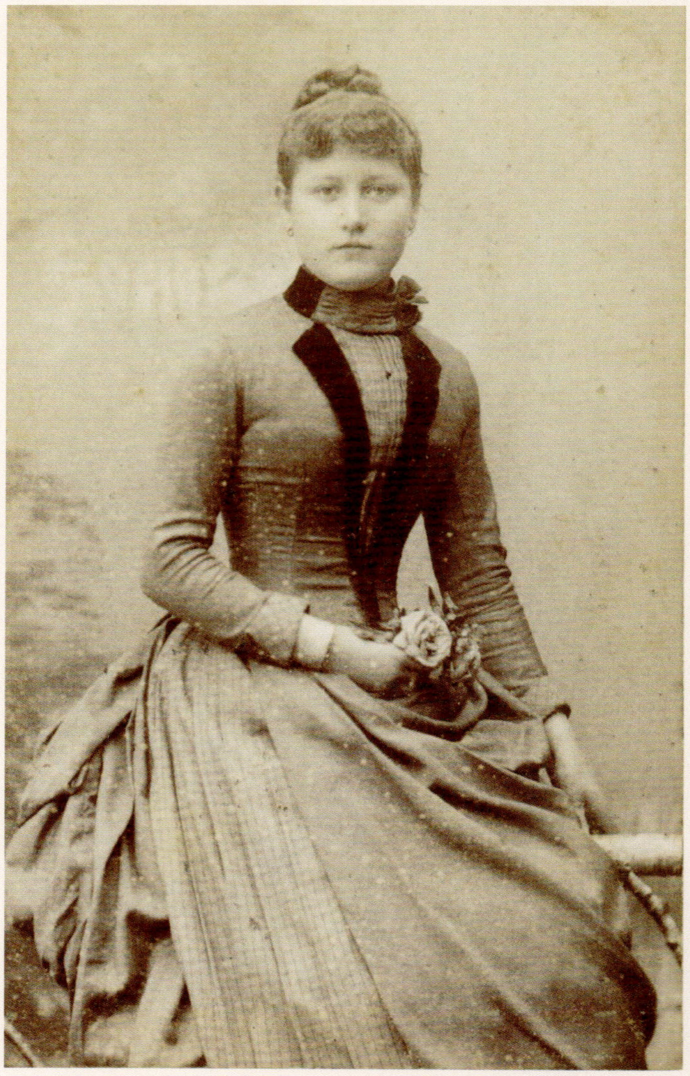

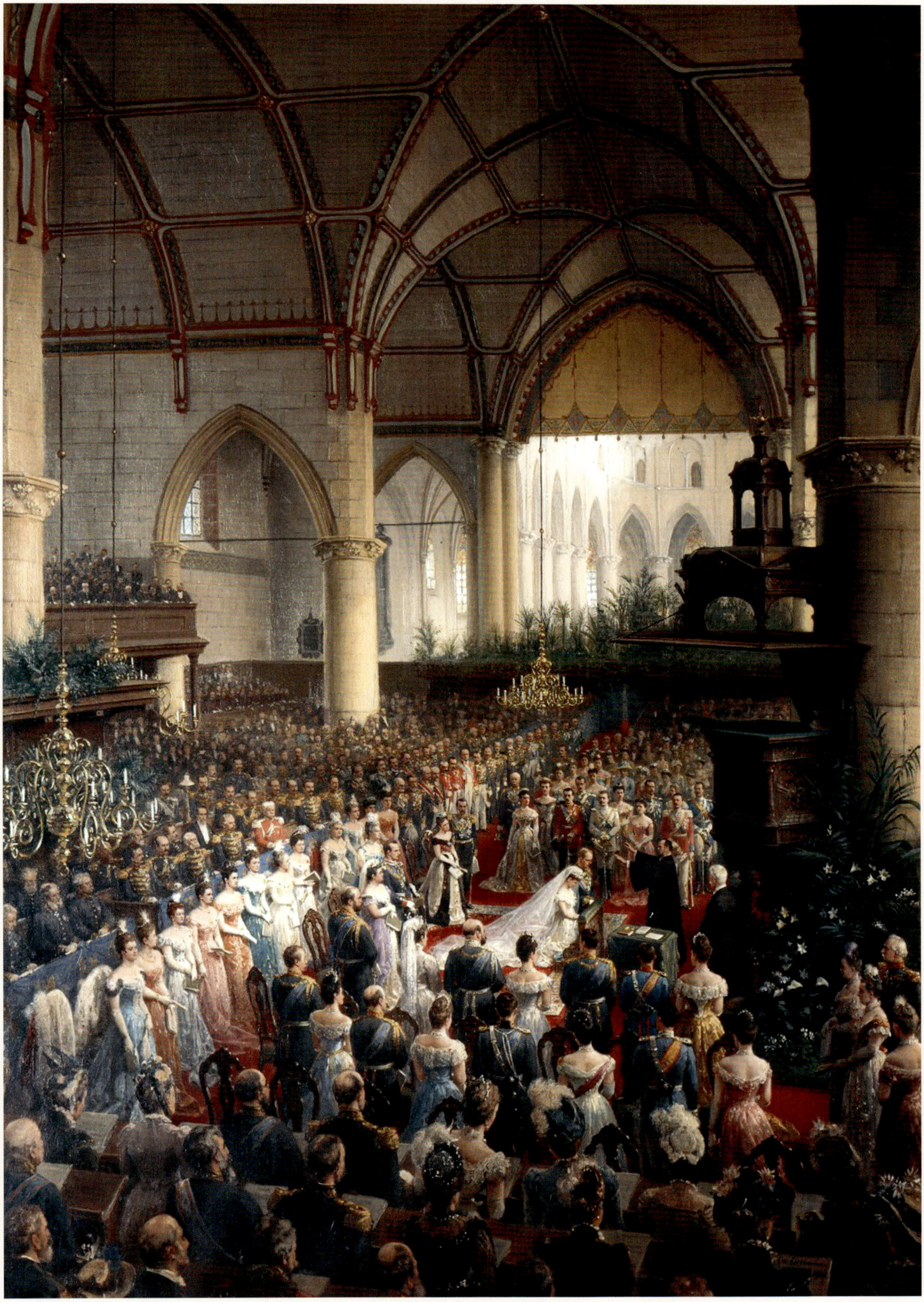

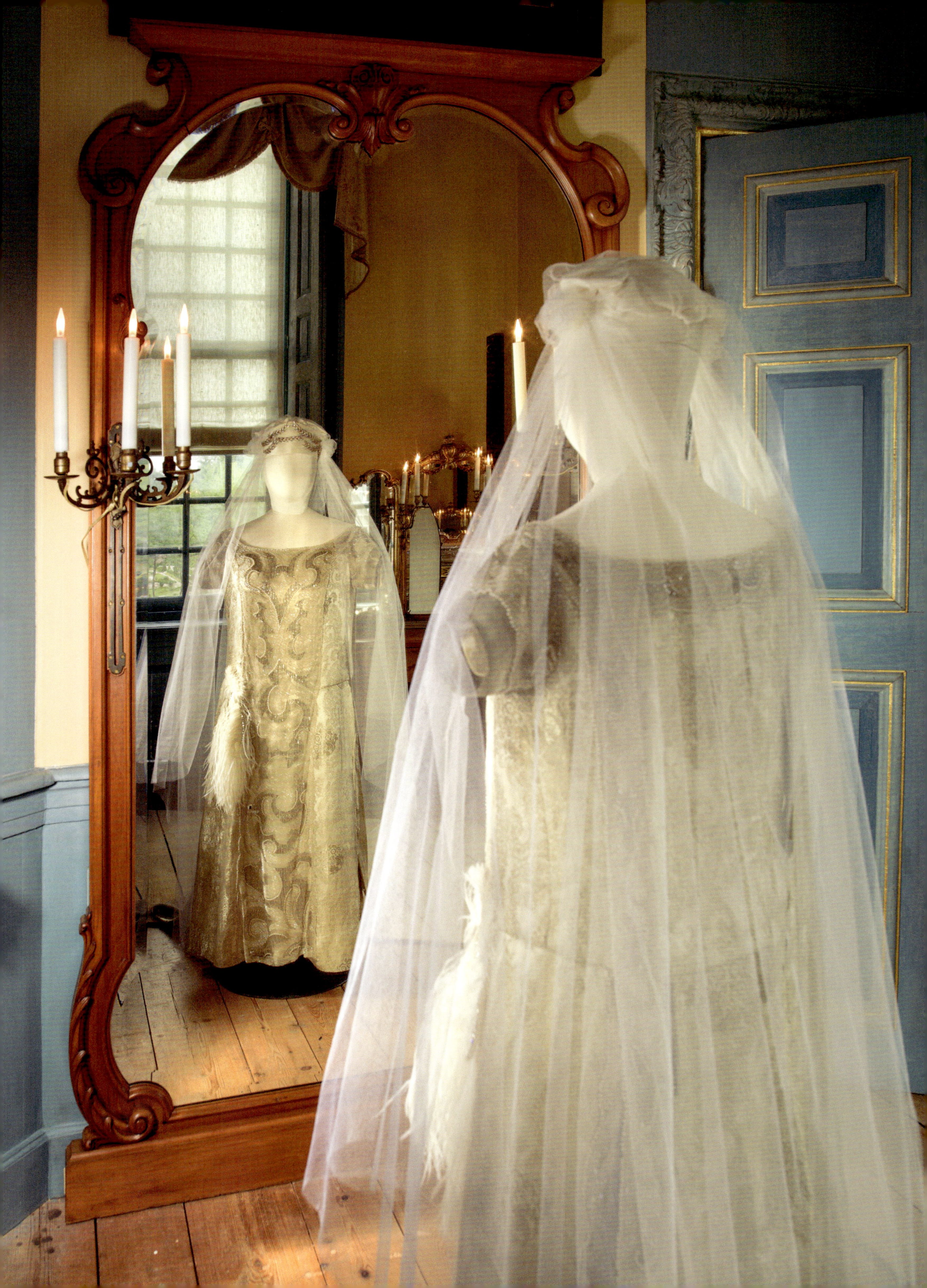

# SILVER WEDDING IN CHARLESTON STYLE

Fashion house Premet had designed a formal silver brocade court dress for Queen Wilhelmina in 1923. She wore it at a photoshoot to mark her silver jubilee that same year. The brocade dress had a long straight train and very short sleeves in silver lamé. The front middle panel was decorated with striking embroidered stylised vines in silver, with glass pearls and mother-of-pearl beads. Her status as queen meant Wilhelmina also wore a sash and star, plus expensive diamond and sapphire jewellery. She carried an ostrich feather fan. Premet, established in 1909, with its premises on Place Vendôme in Paris, had its heyday in the 1920s. It was popular with both aristocratic French ladies and with the Dutch female royals Emma, Wilhelmina and Juliana.

Two years later, in 1926, there was another royal anniversary. Wilhelmina and Hendrik had been married 25 years, and they gave a big party for friends and family at Paleis Het Loo on Saturday 6 February. The queen decided to wear the Premet dress again. She had it altered, however, transforming this ever stately monarch into a queen of the roaring twenties. Premet's traditional court dress was radically recut to conform to the fashion of the 1920s by shortening the skirt, so her shoes were visible. The straight train became a diagonal train that finished in a point to one side. A great example of repurposing an expensive dress. Since she was celebrating her wedding anniversary, Wilhelmina dressed as a bride, wearing a long tulle veil. Rather than the traditional tiara, she wore a band around her forehead, as was fashionable at parties and festive occasions in the 1920s. Parts of the diamond ears of wheat tiara were attached to the pointed headband covered in white silk.

The guests at this grand family celebration were not expected to wear 'gala' attire. The dress code was 'evening wear', so the ladies wore low-cut evening gowns. Some ladies wore a tiara, including Queen Emma, the Queen Mother. Sixteen-year-old Juliana and her friends wore evening dresses in soft, light fabrics with short skirts and a low waist. The anniversary medal handed out to the guests added an official-looking element to the party outfits. The gentlemen, including Prince Hendrik, were in 'civvies', or 'frac, cravatte blanche' (white tie). This dress code specified on the invitation referred to the black wool dress suit, the outfit worn by men on festive ceremonial occasions. It consists of a long jacket with sharply cut body panels, a waistcoat and trousers with satin piping, and a white dress shirt that has a standing collar with two wingtips. The tie had to be white, so the outfit is now known as 'white tie'. At court, insignia and sashes would be worn with the dress suit.
—PR

**Wilhelmina's ballgown in 'roaring twenties' style ◆**
Paris, Premet, 1923/1926
Silk, glass, mother-of-pearl, ostrich feathers
Paleis Het Loo, on long-term loan from the Royal Collections, The Hague

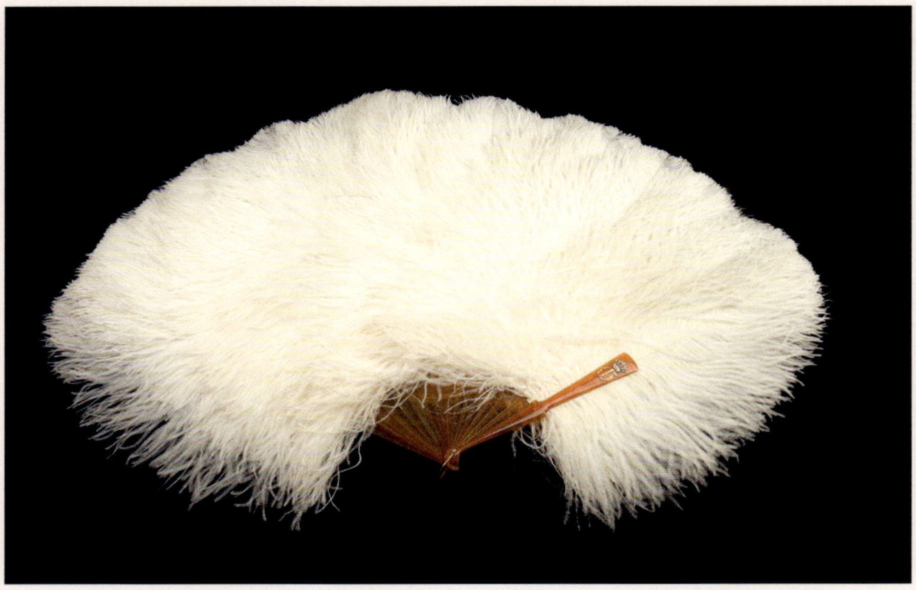

**Official portrait in French formal gown**
Queen Wilhelmina posed for a photographer, both seated and standing, on the occasion of her silver jubilee. The dress designed by Premet had a long straight train. The queen wore the jewellery she had received as a gift from the nation on her marriage.

Photo H.F.J.M. Deutmann, 1923
Royal Collections, The Hague

**Ostrich feather fan ◆**
Queen Wilhelmina liked to carry a fan made of white ostrich feathers at gala events. In 1920 the Association of Ostrich Farmers gave her a large folding feather fan. It is believed to have been made in London, using feathers from South Africa. The ribs, made of bone, are decorated with the queen's monogram in gold. The crown is made of platinum set with diamonds.

Ostrich feathers, bone, gold, platinum, diamonds, circa 1920; span when open 90 cm
Royal Collections, The Hague

**Royal family in festive spirit ◆**
Before the silver wedding party got going at Paleis Het Loo, the royal couple posed for a photographer with their daughter Juliana. Wilhelmina is dressed as a bride. Juliana is wearing a knee-length evening dress in accordance with the latest fashion.

Photo H.F.J.M. Deutmann, 1926
Paleis Het Loo

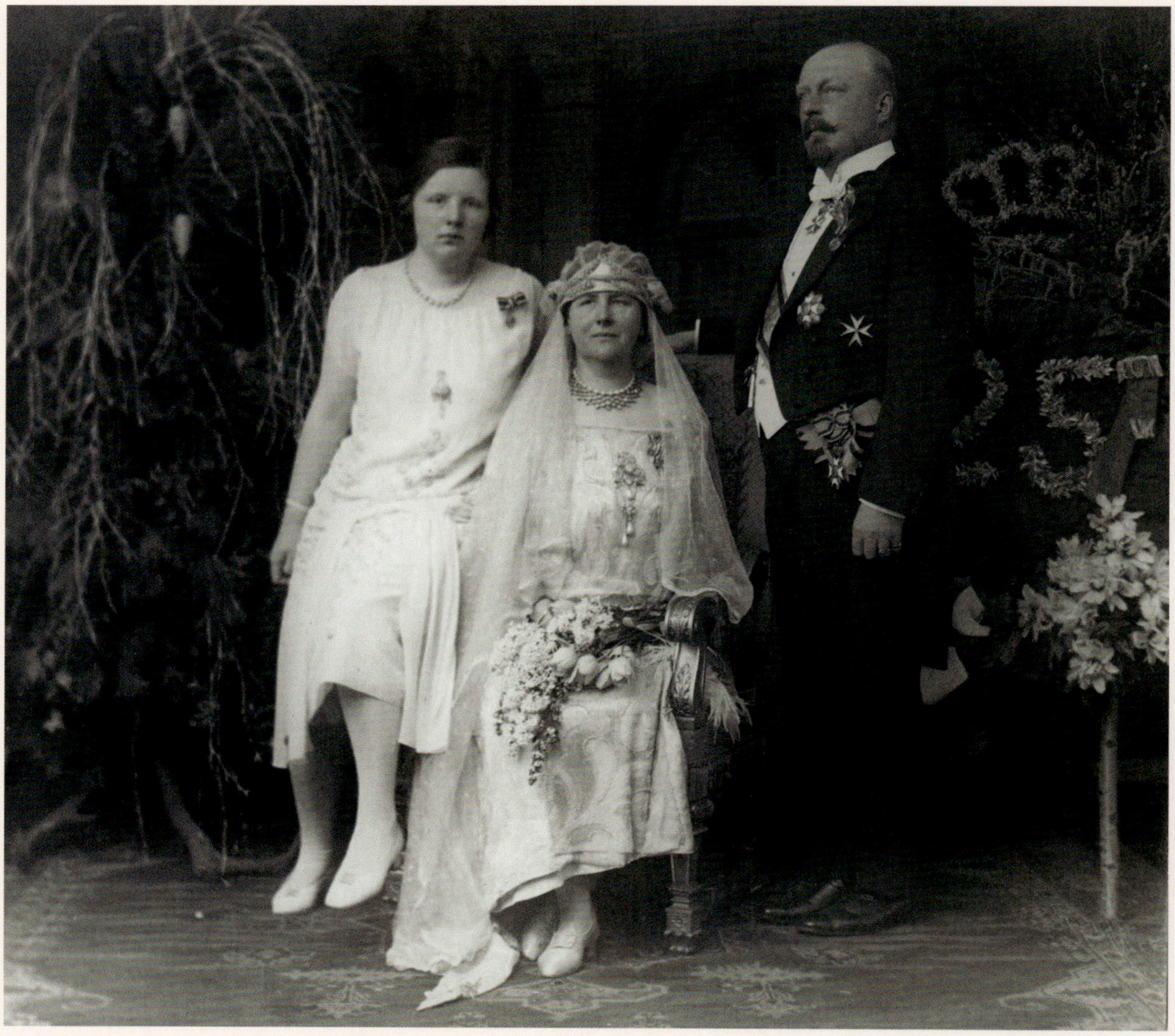

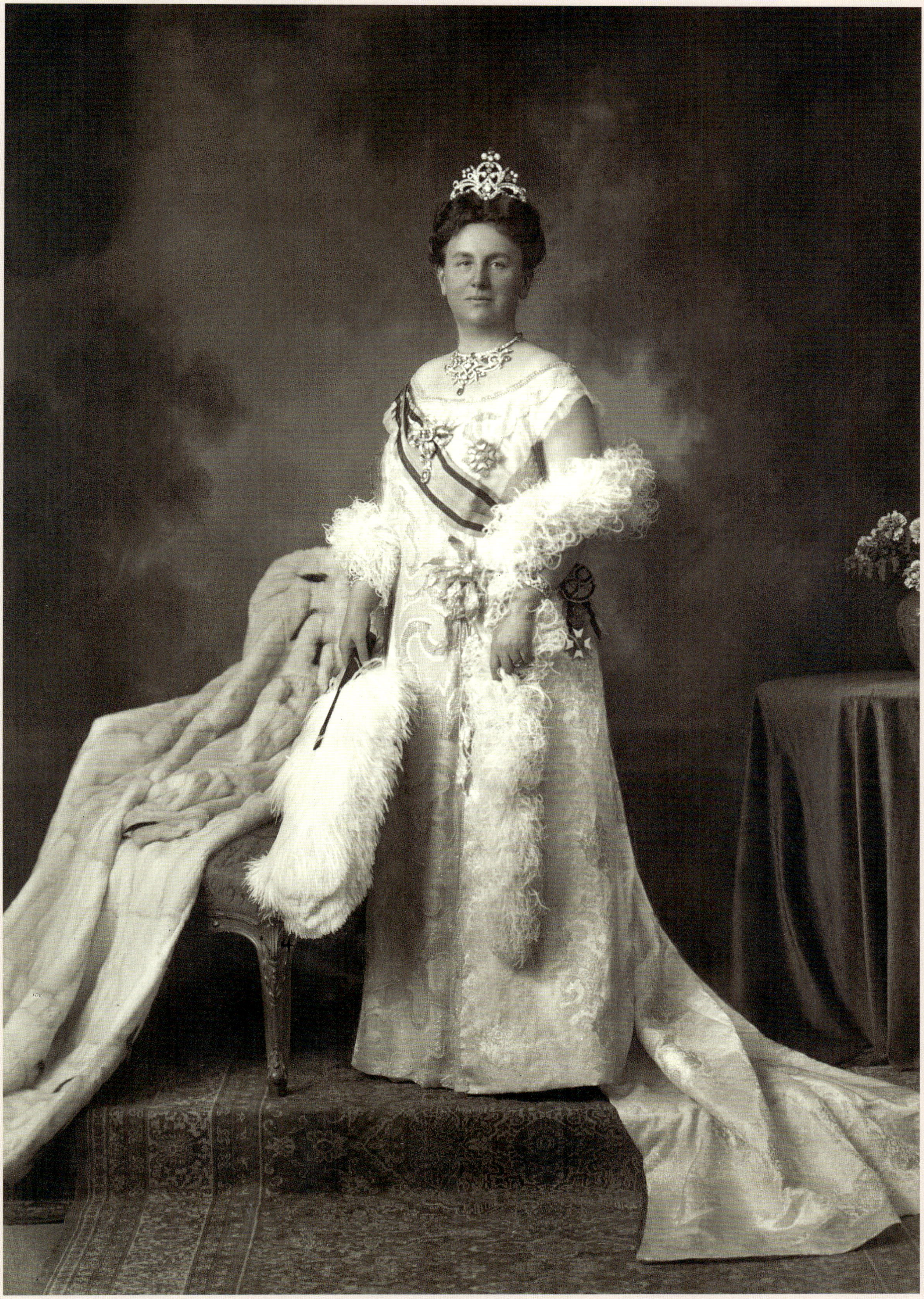

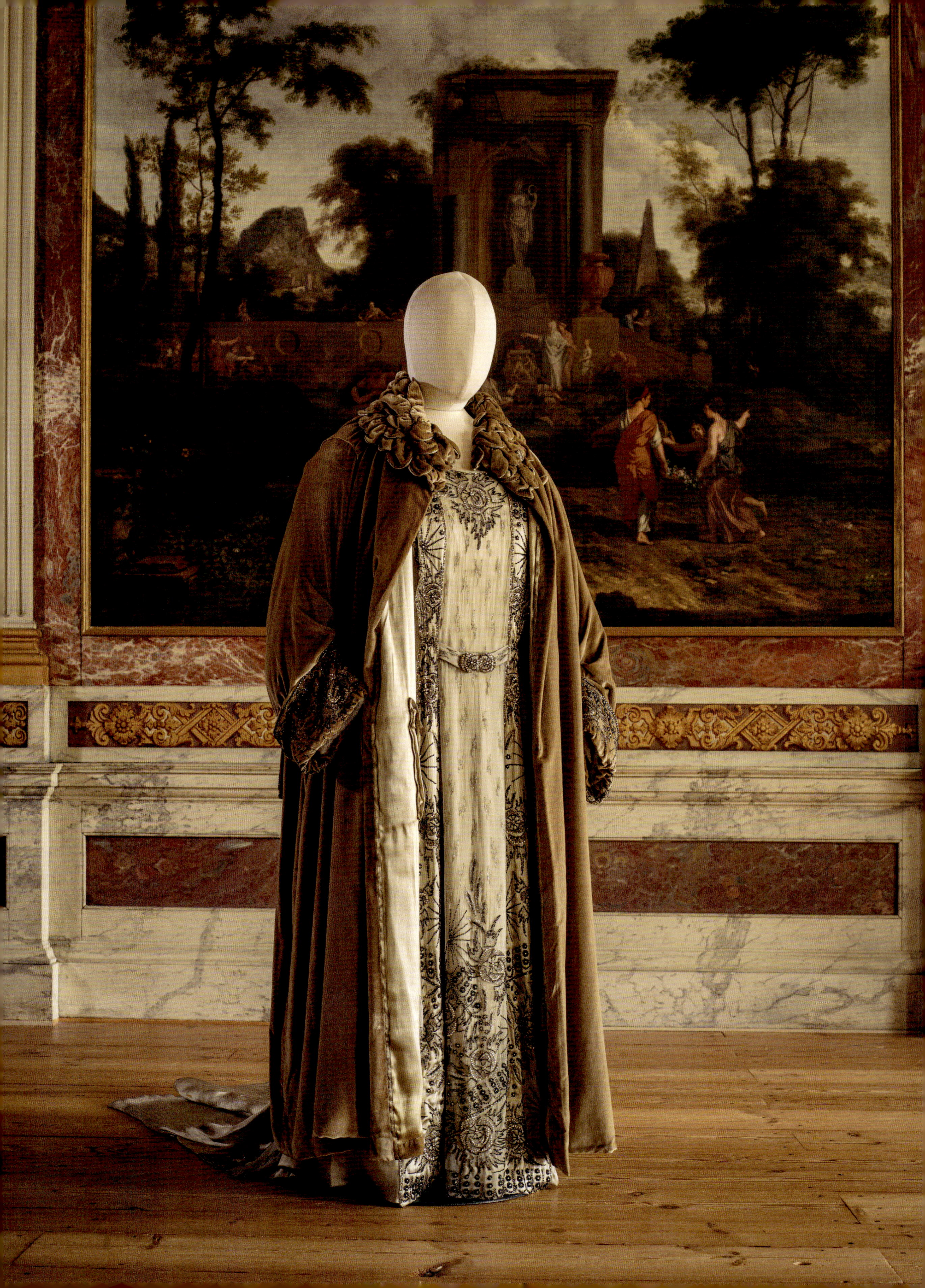

# QUEEN EMMA'S GALA DRESS AND COAT

When she was to attend a gala, Queen Emma, the Queen Mother, could have her wardrobe mistress, who was responsible for her clothes, hang a pearl-grey silk satin gown ready for her. For the drive to the festivities, she would wear a coat of bruin silk velours. Both garments were from the Paris fashion house Premet, which often supplied Emma and Wilhelmina's gala outfits in the 1920s. Both the dress and the coat have a label that reads 'Premet 8. Place Vendôme. Paris' sewn into them. This was used by Premet until it moved to its new premises in 1929. The house of Premet was popular with the French nobility and aristocracy because of its indisputable craftsmanship. Premet's creations were fashionable but safe, as they were never 'over the top'. The most successful design produced by this company – which employed only female designers – was 'La Garçonne', a black dress in two parts, with a low waist and white detailing on the cuffs and collar, launched in 1923. Emma and Wilhelmina will not have worn this exceedingly 'young' precursor to Chanel's 'little black dress'.

Emma's dress – which was adapted to her changing tastes over the years – complied with the dress code for a gala dress worn by a slightly older queen, with its train, modest decolletage and expensive embroidery. The grey satin gala dress has a striking front panel in thin crêpe, which fans out over the shoulder into a broad central back panel. Strips embroidered with sequins, silver thread, beads and glittering ornamental gems, stylised flowers and spiderweb motifs are attached on either side. The neckline and the bottom of the central panel are also embroidered. A shorter layer of tulle lies over the satin underskirt. The three-quarter length crêpe sleeves are embroidered with the same scatter motif in silver thread as the front panel.

When she travelled to attend a gala elsewhere, Queen Emma would wear an ankle-length coat of brown velours, decorated with the same embroidery as the grey gala dress. One unusual detail is the high rolled collar made of three overlapping semicircular bands of fabric, with white silk on the bottom and brown velours on top. Emma could fasten the collar up to the neck with a large button and loop. The sleeves end in large embroidered cuffs. Queen Emma wore the coat on one of the carriage tours she made during a visit to Amsterdam in 1929. In June of that year, there were celebrations to mark her arrival in the Netherlands fifty years previously, following her marriage to King Willem III.

Queen Emma was in the habit of wearing a long lace veil for gala events, out of respect for an old European custom of attaching a veil to a tiara worn with a ceremonial court dress. The veil should not be confused with the white lace widow's veil in which the Queen Mother was often photographed. As well as ready-made bonnets with an attached veil, Emma also had a veil made from a long, wide strip of lace, which was folded on the head and attached to the hair with decorative pins. Emma loved her lace, most of which she bought herself with the intention of wearing it.[1] She bought antique and new bobbin and needle lace from the leading European lace-making centres Brussels, Venice and Alençon. It would take the form of individual strips, veils, handkerchiefs, shawls and lace for fans and parasols. Emma accessorised the dark-coloured dresses with a train that she wore at home with white lace collars and strips of lace attached to the panels of the dress and along the sleeves. Strips of black lace were used on mourning dresses.
——PR

**Ballgown belonging to Queen Emma ◆**
Paris, Premet, circa 1929
Silk, silver thread, decorative gemstones
Paleis Het Loo, on long-term loan
from the Royal Collections, The Hague

**Coat belonging to Queen Emma ◆**
Paris, Premet, 1929-1934
Wool, cotton, silk, silver thread
Paleis Het Loo, on long-term loan
from the Royal Collections, The Hague

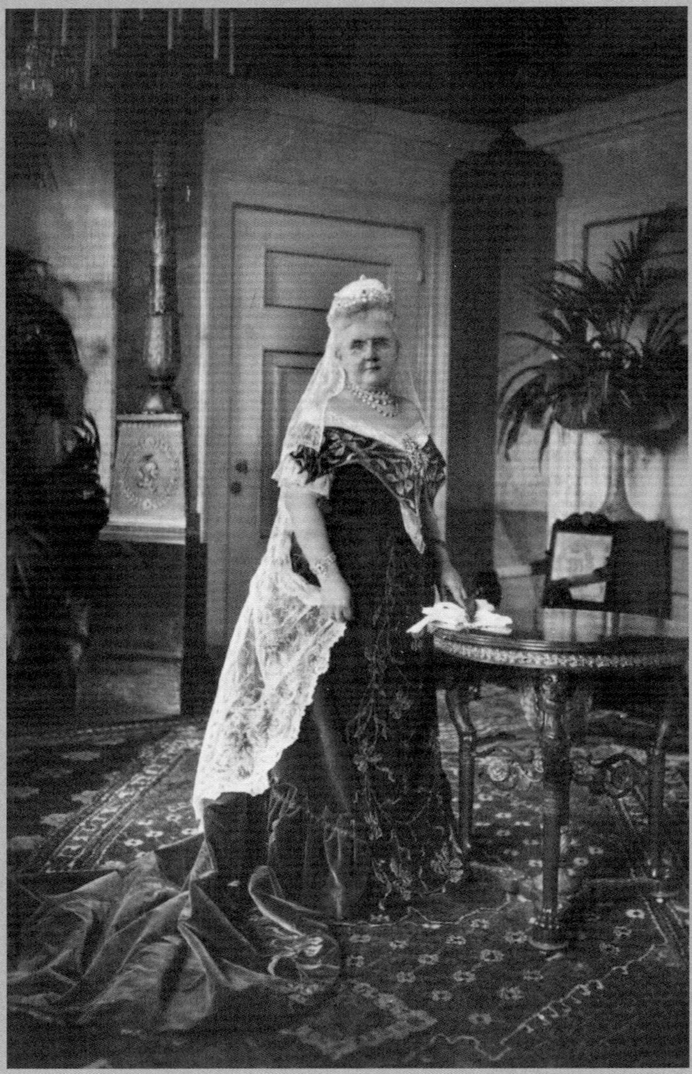

Ballgown belonging to Queen Emma ◆
Paris, Premet, circa 1929
Silk, silver thread, decorative gemstones
Paleis Het Loo, on long-term loan
from the Royal Collections, The Hague

Emma in full formal dress at Soestdijk
Around 1920 Queen Emma posed in the stucco room of her summer residence, Paleis Soestdijk. Her velvet ballgown has a traditional design, with a bodice ending in a point and a long train. A long lace veil hangs from the tiara that was part of the jewellery set made by the Paris firm Mellerio.

Photo A. Boer, circa 1920
Rijksmuseum, Amsterdam

Carriage tour in Amsterdam ◆
Sunday 9 June 1929, Amsterdam. Queen Emma is seated on the right in the back of the open caleche – the most important position in a carriage. Queen Wilhelmina is seated beside her, and Princess Juliana sits opposite, in a light-blue summer dress, according to press reports. Prince Hendrik, dressed in uniform, was the fourth passenger. He is not visible in the photograph.

Photographer unknown
Paleis Het Loo, on long-term loan f
rom the Orange-Nassau Historical Society

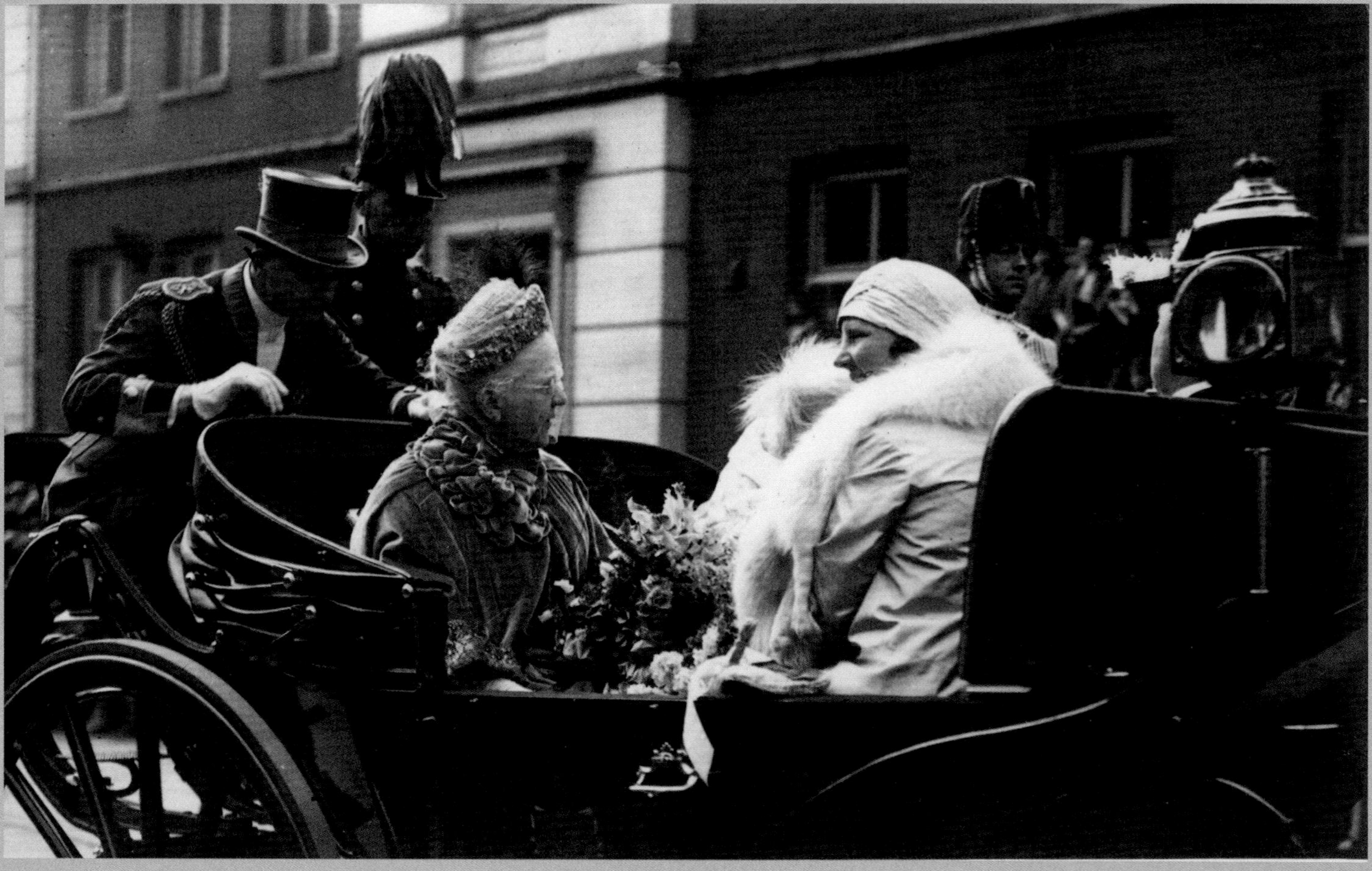

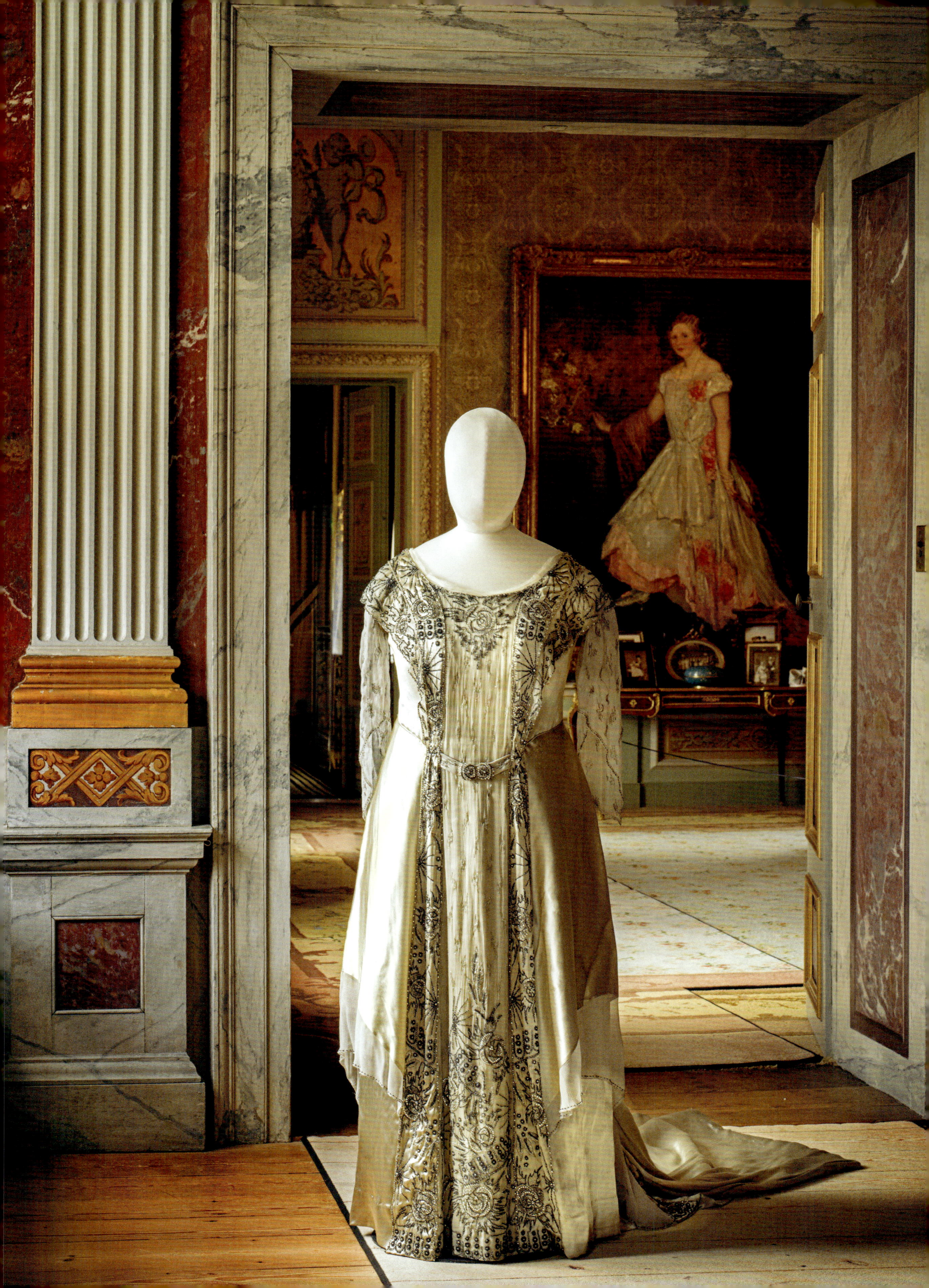

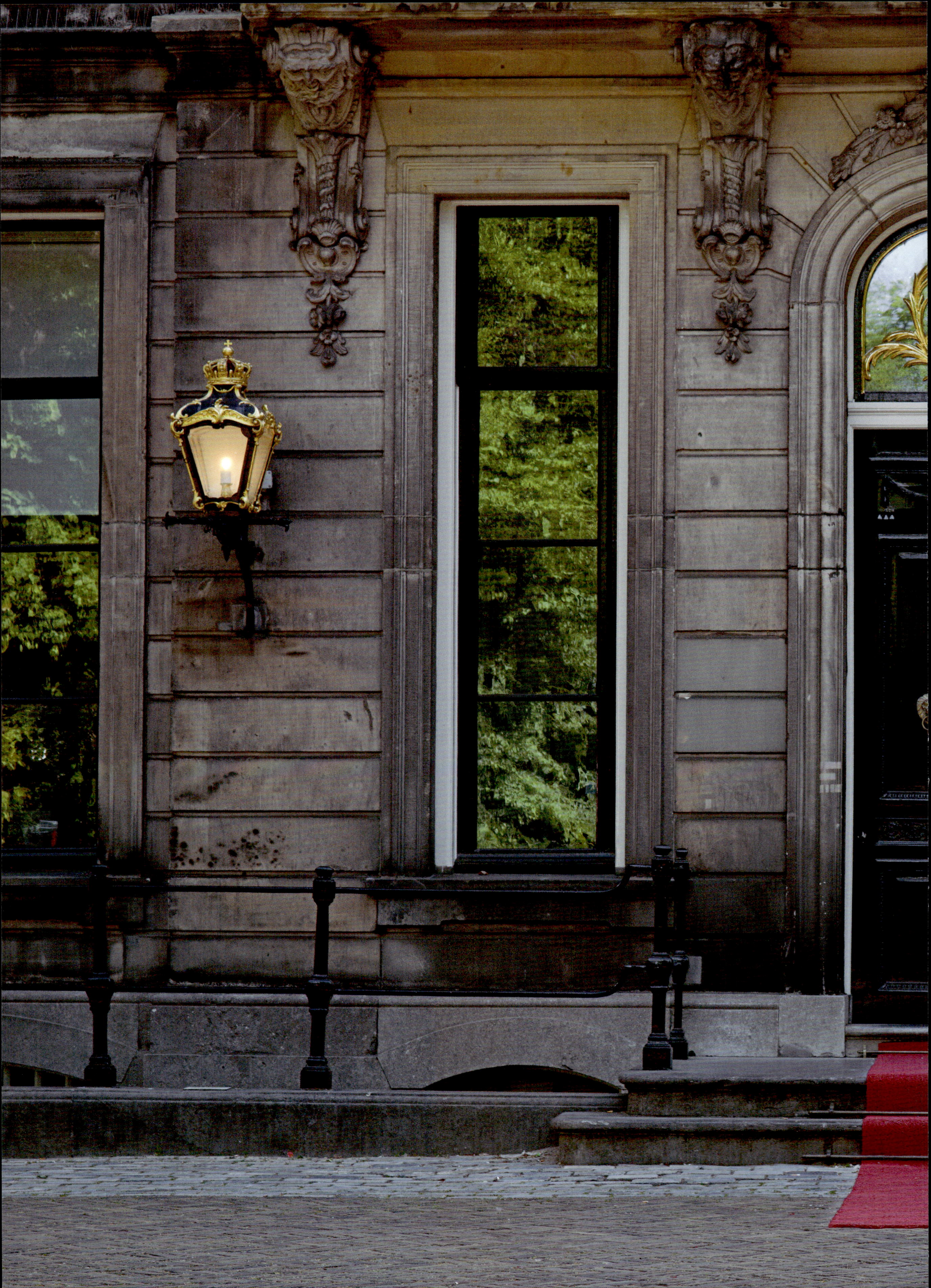

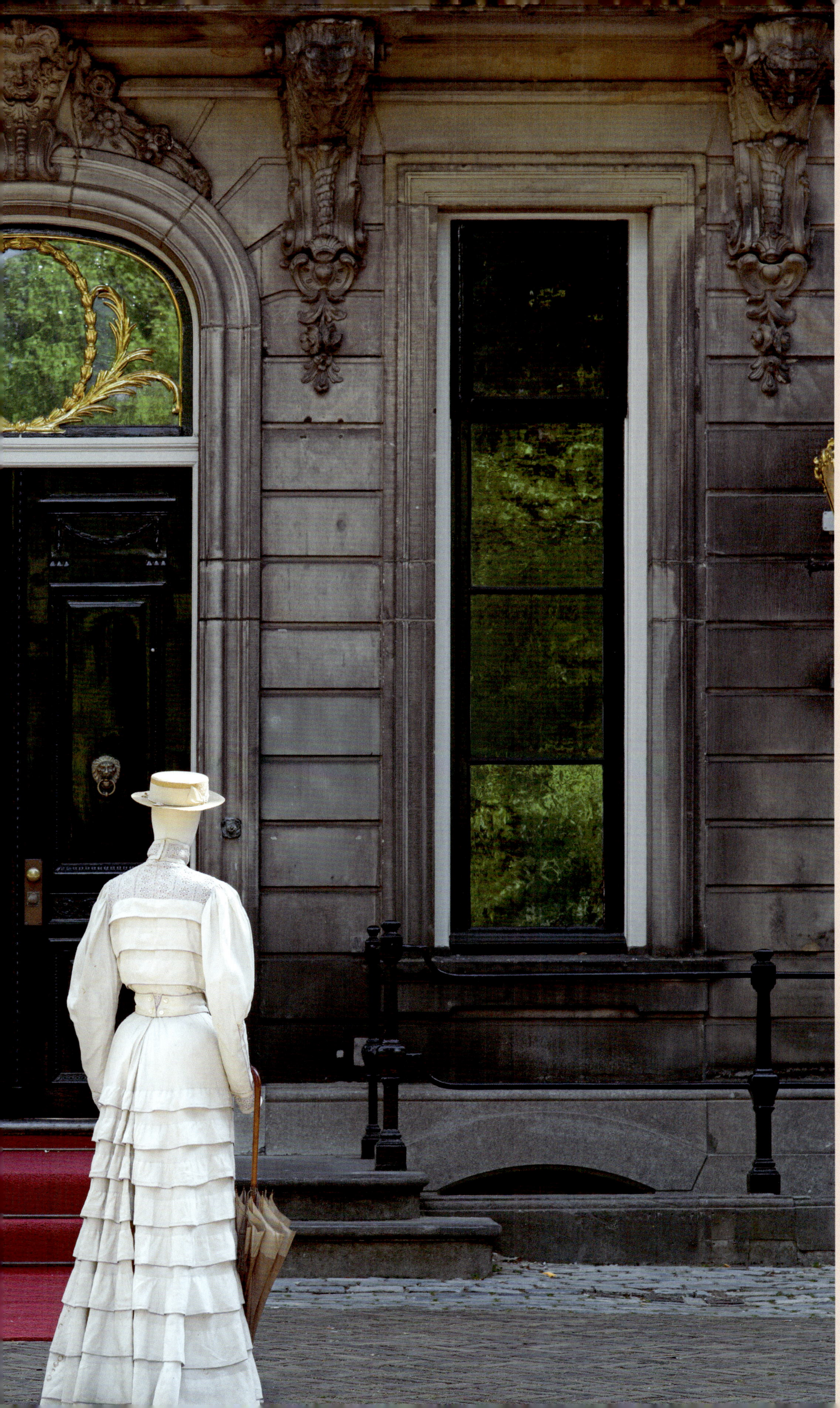

# OUTDOOR DRESS CODE

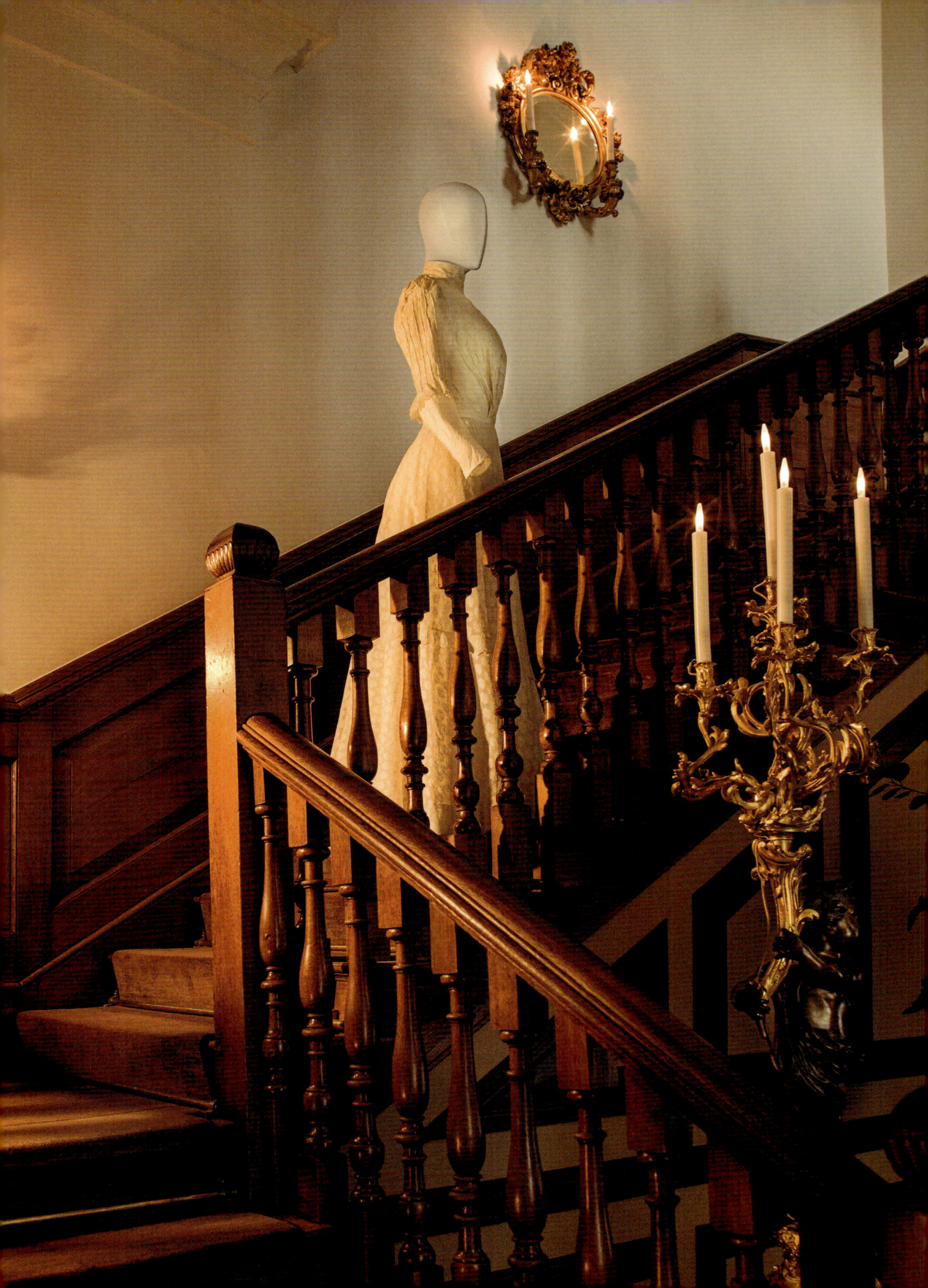

# SIMPLE OUTDOOR DRESSES

In 1898 the Ministry of Colonies commissioned artist Willy Martens to paint a portrait of Queen Wilhelmina in her 'coronation robes'.[1] The portrait, which was initially exhibited at Pulchri Studio in The Hague and was intended for one of the palaces in the Dutch East Indies, shows the queen beside a throne seat, wearing a white silk gown with gold embroidery and an ermine mantle.[2] Several months later Martens painted the queen again. This time, she is shown in the garden of Paleis Soestdijk, wearing a simple-looking white dress and a hat decorated with daisies.[3] The queen, free of her regalia, is dressed for a walk in the garden. The contrast with the official portrait could not be greater. Rank versus recreation, indoors versus outdoors.

Just as there were dress codes for indoor occasions, so too were there dress codes for outdoor activities. Even a simple walk in the garden required a suitable outfit. A white dress like the one in Martens' painting was a good choice for light exercise such as a short walk, or a garden party or picnic.[4] Unfortunately, the dress in the picture has not survived, but Paleis Het Loo's collection includes several similar white cotton dresses that were worn by the queen. White cotton clothes, unlike those made of wool or silk, were easy to wash, and were therefore ideal for warm summer days and for sporting activities. The absence of a label, combined with the simplicity of the dresses, suggests that they were not from a well-known fashion house, but may have been made by the palace seamstress.[5]

Besides simple cotton dresses of this type, Wilhelmina also owned a number of skilfully made walking costumes. The inventory of her trousseau in 1901 includes no fewer than five 'simple walking dresses', all of them from the leading fashion store Hirsch & Cie. It is noted that two of the costumes, both of them a moss green colour, are specifically intended for 'walking in the woods', one for winter (with an extra skirt) and the other for summer.[6] The fabric is not mentioned, but the winter costume will certainly have been made of some heavy quality material. Following English fashions, fabrics like tweed were very popular for long walks.[7] Although the queen was perfectly aware of the importance of suitable clothing, things did go wrong on occasion. In 1896, for example, Wilhelmina wrote in a letter to her former *surintendante* Henriette van de Poll of a trip up a mountain in France. 'You will understand that my clothes tore dreadfully', she said.[8]

Besides sporty walking costumes, the queen's wardrobe also had to include riding habits. Wilhelmina had ridden since the age of two. For horseriding, ladies would wear a jacket inspired by men's fashions, which would originally also have been made by a tailor. The accompanying skirt was cut in such a way that the legs remained neatly covered while the lady rode side-saddle (with both legs on one side of the horse). When walking, the extra fabric could be pulled up and fastened with a button. Wilhelmina also enjoyed playing tennis. All her ladies-in-waiting were expected to be able to ride, skate and play tennis.[9] Specific outfits for tennis were not common around 1900, so ladies would often simply play in a sporty, washable white cotton dress.[10]

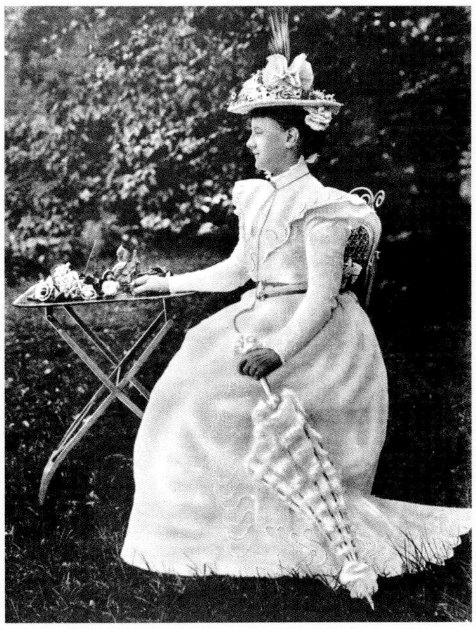

**Queen Wilhelmina in the garden of Paleis Soestdijk, 16 July 1898**
Photo: Rousel, J.M.
National Archives/ RVD – National Institute for Art History Royal Family

**Gown, circa 1900 ◆**
Paleis Het Loo's collection includes several white cotton worn by Queen Wilhelmina, including this one in white openwork cotton from circa 1900. The lace has been removed from the lower sleeves and reused.

Paleis Het Loo, on long-term loan from the Royal Collections, The Hague

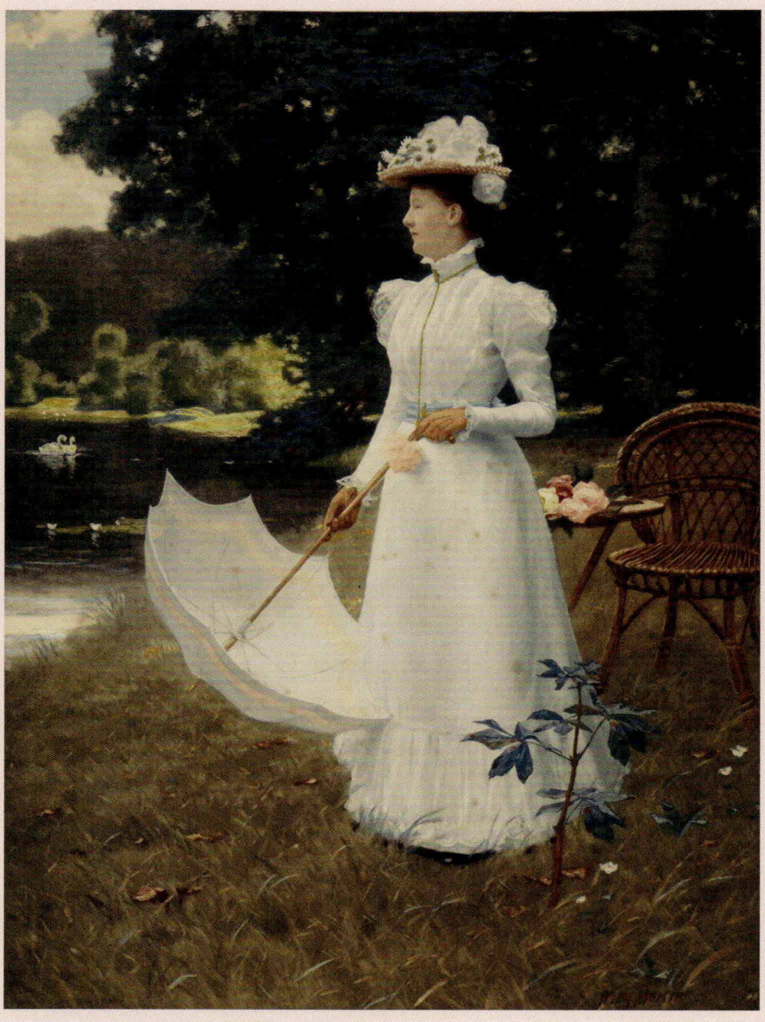

**Gown ◆**
This white gown, worn by Lady Anna Mathilde Meteler-kamp-den Tex, who was frequently attended the Dutch royal court, is in the collection of Kunstmuseum Den Haag. Like Wilhelmina's gown, this one is made of light white cotton, though in this case the fabroc os also robust. Interestingly, this one does not have whalebone supports in the bodice, as is usual, which suggests that it was worn specifically for sporting activities.

Gown, circa 1900-1905
Kunstmuseum Den Haag

**Queen Wilhelmina in the garden of Paleis Soestdijk**
Willy Martens, 1898
Paleis Het Loo, on long-term loan
from the Orange-Nassau Historical Society

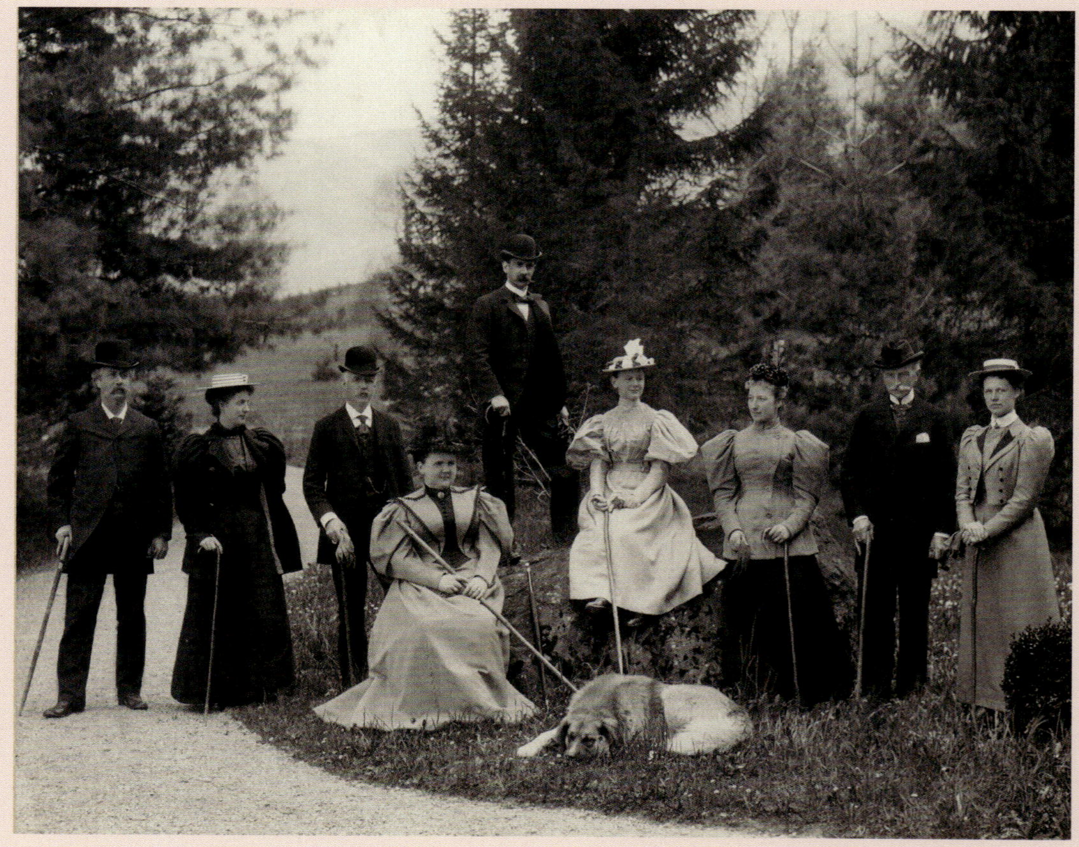

**Queen Emma and Queen Wilhelmina and company out walking in Switzerland, 1896**
Photo J. Moegle.
Royal Collections, The Hague

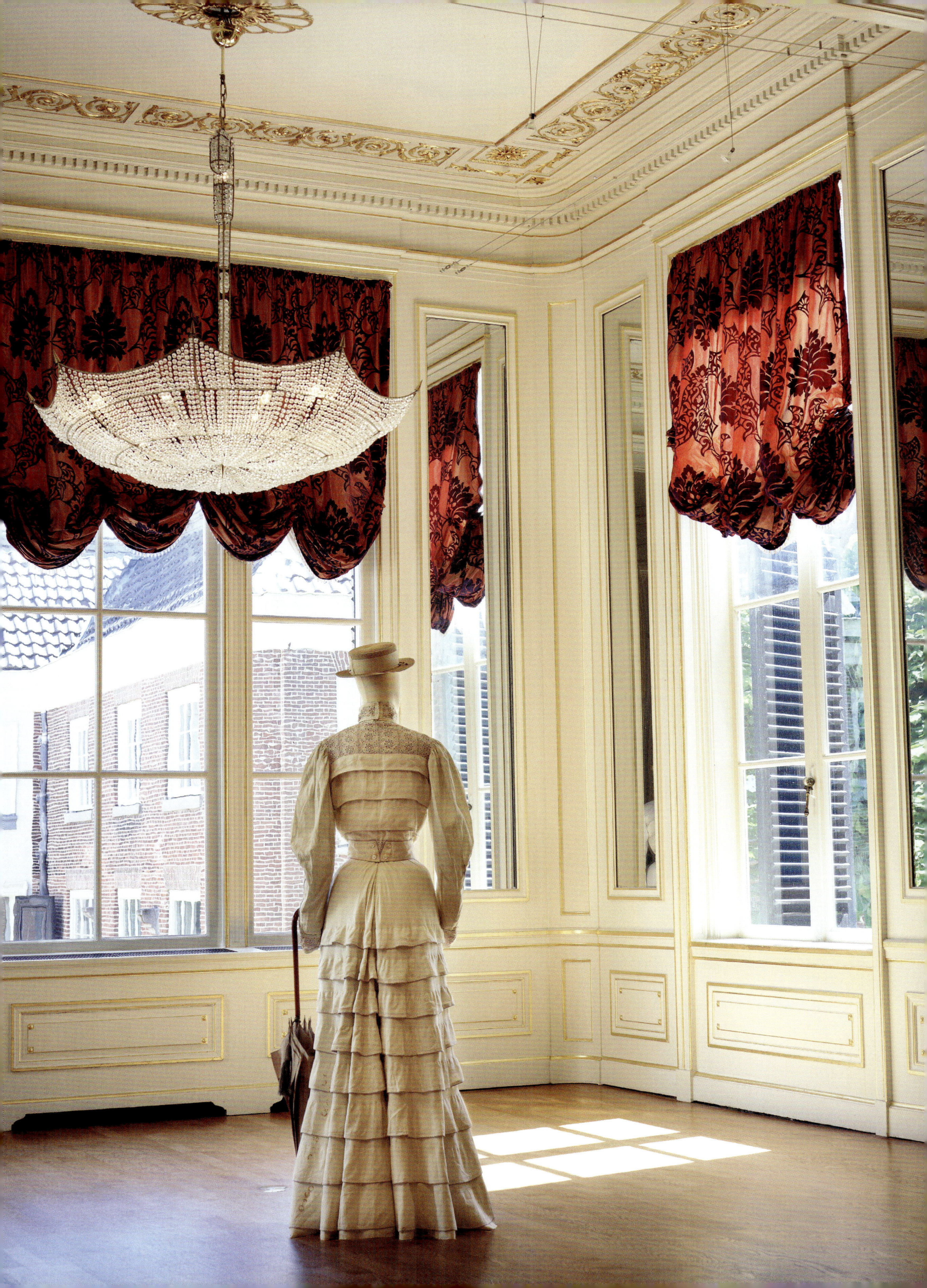

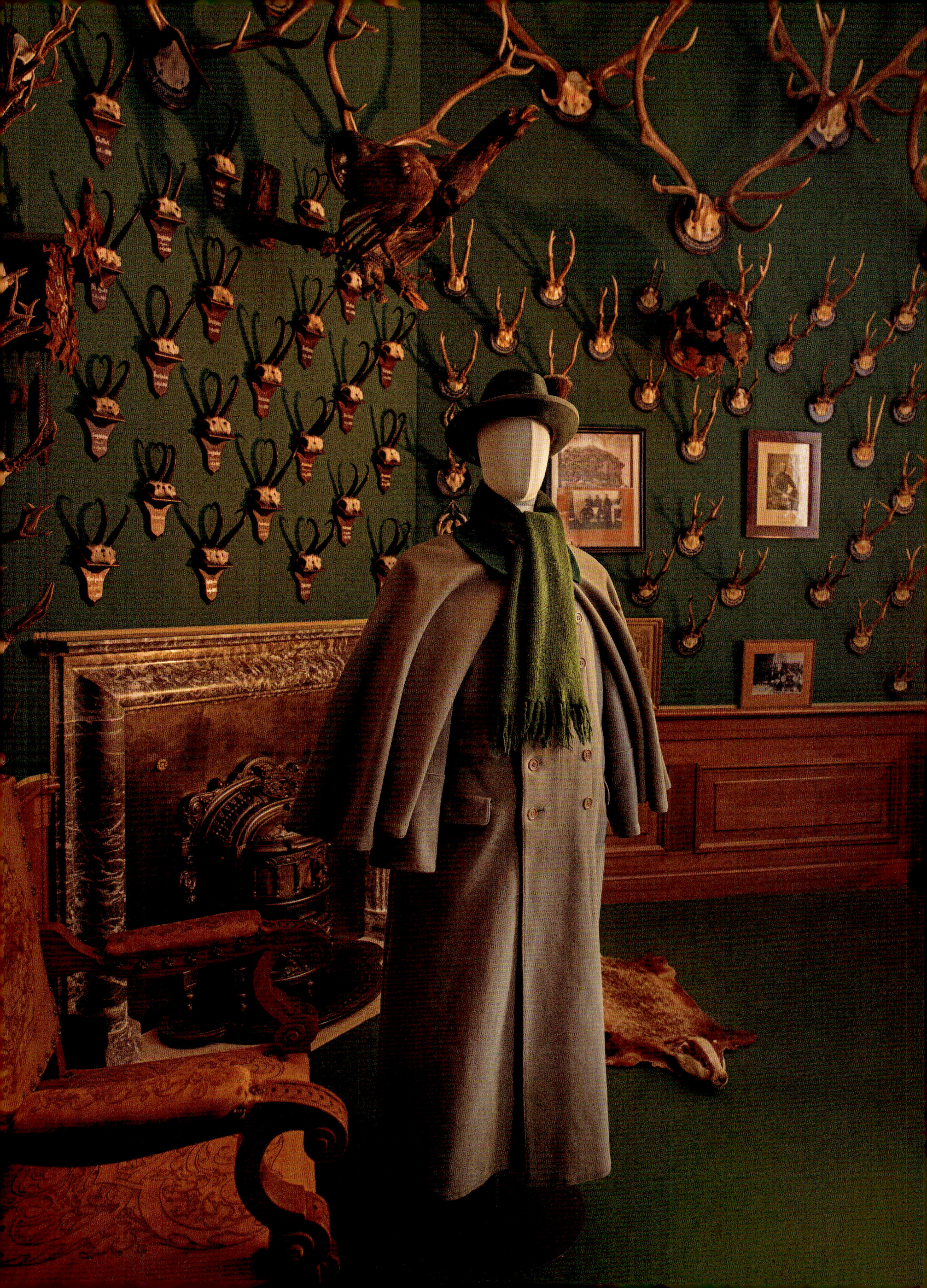

# PRINCE HENDRIK'S HUNTING OUTFIT

Prince Hendrik's long wool hunting coat is of very heavy quality. In the cold hunting season, a hunter would have to remain motionless observing game for long periods of time, so a warm coat was no excessive luxury. The coat is also wool-lined. A cape or pelerine (from the French *pèlerin*, which refers to the cloak worn by medieval pilgrims) is attached to the coat to give extra protection. The coat was worn over the matching hunting suit, consisting of trousers, boots and a short double-breasted jacket. Prince Hendrik wore a green wool scarf with the coat. The dark-green felt hunting hat is the most striking item in the prince's hunting outfit. The rosette on the side is made of folded silk in blue, red and yellow, the colours of Mecklenburg, the line from which Prince Hendrik was descended. A brass crown with a plume made from wild boar hairs and grouse tail feathers is attached to the rosette. The portrait of the prince which Jan Kleintjes painted in 1917 shows Hendrik in his hunting suit, with his hunting hat. A painting of the prince with his hunting party on Soeren Heath, near Paleis Het Loo, dates from 1901, the year he married Queen Wilhelmina. The prince is seen in his hunting carriage, dressed in his hunting coat with pelerine.

The queen and the prince frequently bought pieces of land to extend Het Loo Royal Estate, which became one of the largest game reserves in the Netherlands. The prince worked to improve the local wildlife on the Veluwe heathland by releasing high-quality red deer, wild boar and mouflons. Hendrik's proposal for the reclamation of heath in the Veluwe region and the gradual planting of woodland transformed the Veluwe into the wooded recreational area and nature reserve we know today. The couple not only spent the period of their engagement, but also their honeymoon in the Veluwe region. During his first few months as a married man, Prince Hendrik would go out at night to shoot black grouse, hence the feathers on his hunting hat.

Prince Hendrik was a great lover of the outdoors. Having been born and raised in the Grand Duchy of Mecklenburg-Schwerin in northern Germany, he became accustomed to dogs, horses, hunting, game management and forestry at a young age. He accompanied the queen in public dressed, depending on the occasion, in a day suit with a hat, a tailcoat, a scout uniform, or even military uniform. Hendrik was above all a man who enjoyed the outdoor life, who was not comfortable with the restrictions of the protocol that applied within the walls of the palace. Rather than associating with critical courtiers who ridiculed the prince for his lack of flair, he preferred to go out with his hunting friends. The hunting grounds that surrounded Paleis Het Loo provided the best hunting around. In fact he shot his first stag there during his engagement, which was announced at Het Loo on 16 October 1900. A sign mounted with the antlers reads: 'Erlegt am 22 October 1900 von Herzog Heinrich in het Loo' (Shot by Duke Henry at Het Loo on 22 October 1900).
—PR

**Hunting coat with Prince Hendrik's scarf** ◆
unknown atelier, circa 1900
Wool

**Prince Hendrik's hunting hat** ◆
Kehl am Rhein, Rehfus & Co., circa 1900
Wool, leather, brass, silk, wild boar hair, black grouse feathers

Paleis Het Loo, on long-term loan
from the Royal Collections, The Hague

**Prince Hendrik Dressed for Hunting**
In the year of his wedding, Prince Hendrik posed in a corner of the armoury at Paleis Het Loo beside a grandfather clock which he had probably brought with him from Germany. The prince wears his hunting suit; the matching hat is in his hand.

Photo F.R. Ebner, 1901
Paleis Het Loo

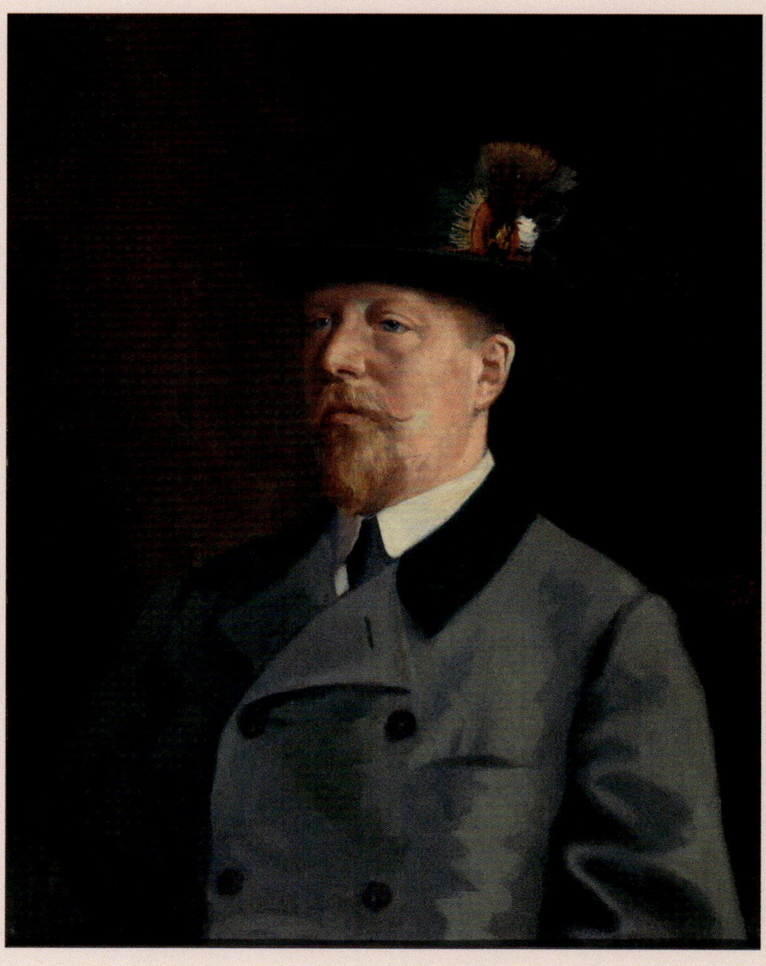

**Prince Hendrik Dressed for Hunting**
J. Kleintjes, 1917
Oil on canvas, 81 x 65.3 cm
Paleis Het Loo, on long-term loan
from the Royal Collections, The Hague

**The Prince on Soeren Heath**
E. von Stenglin, 1901
Oil on canvas, 107.5 x 148 cm (fragment)
Paleis Het Loo, on long-term loan
from the Royal Collections, The Hague

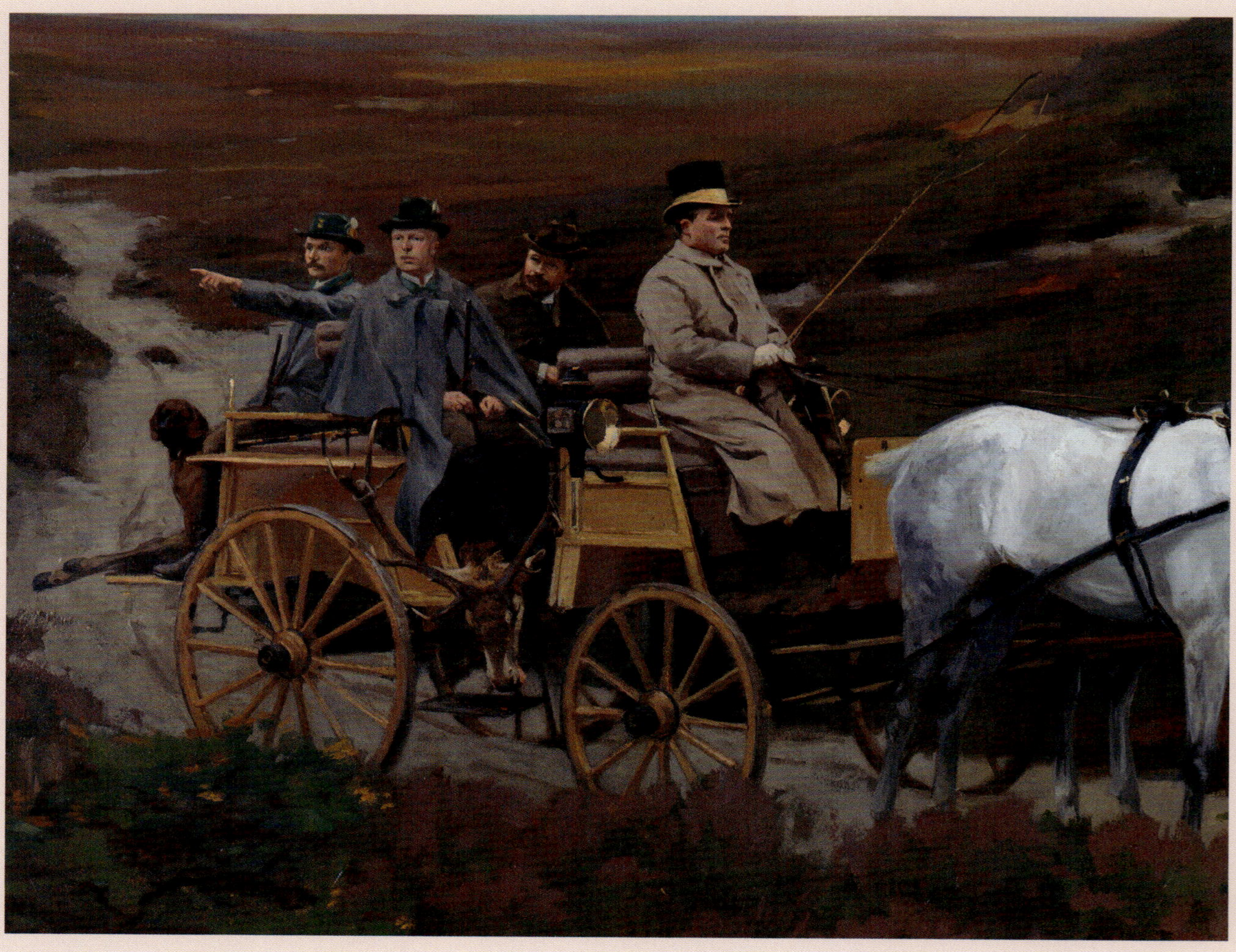

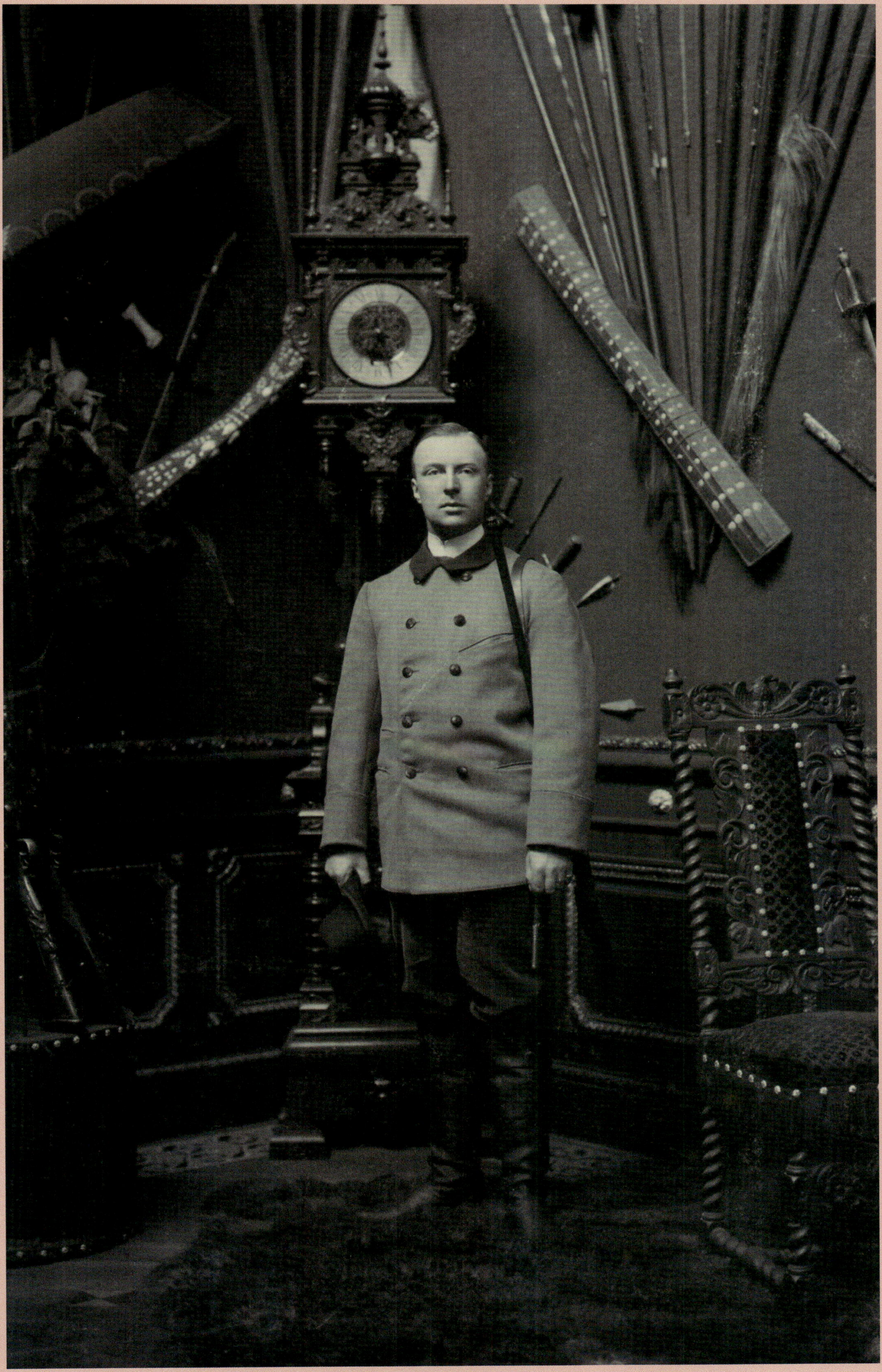

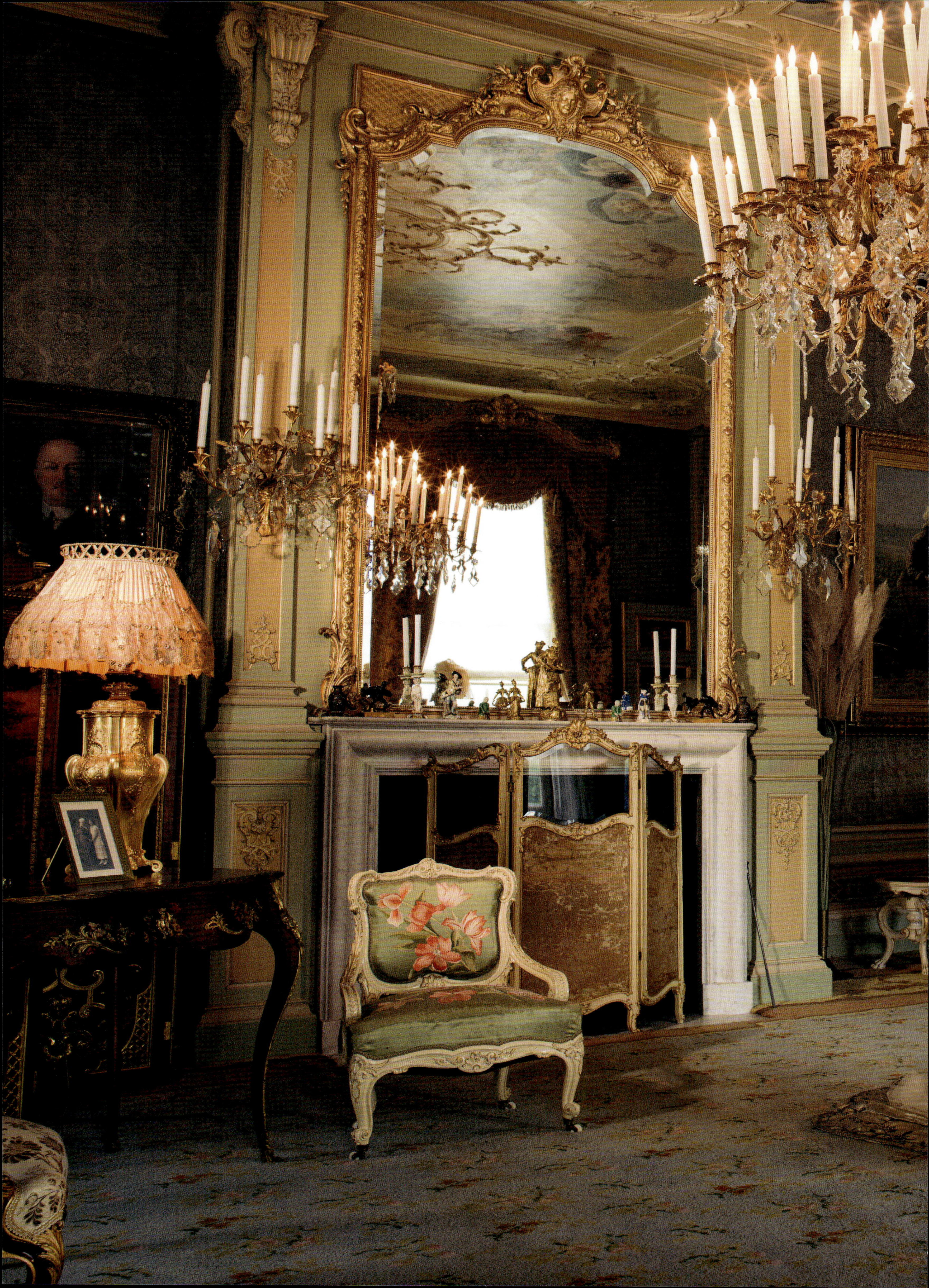

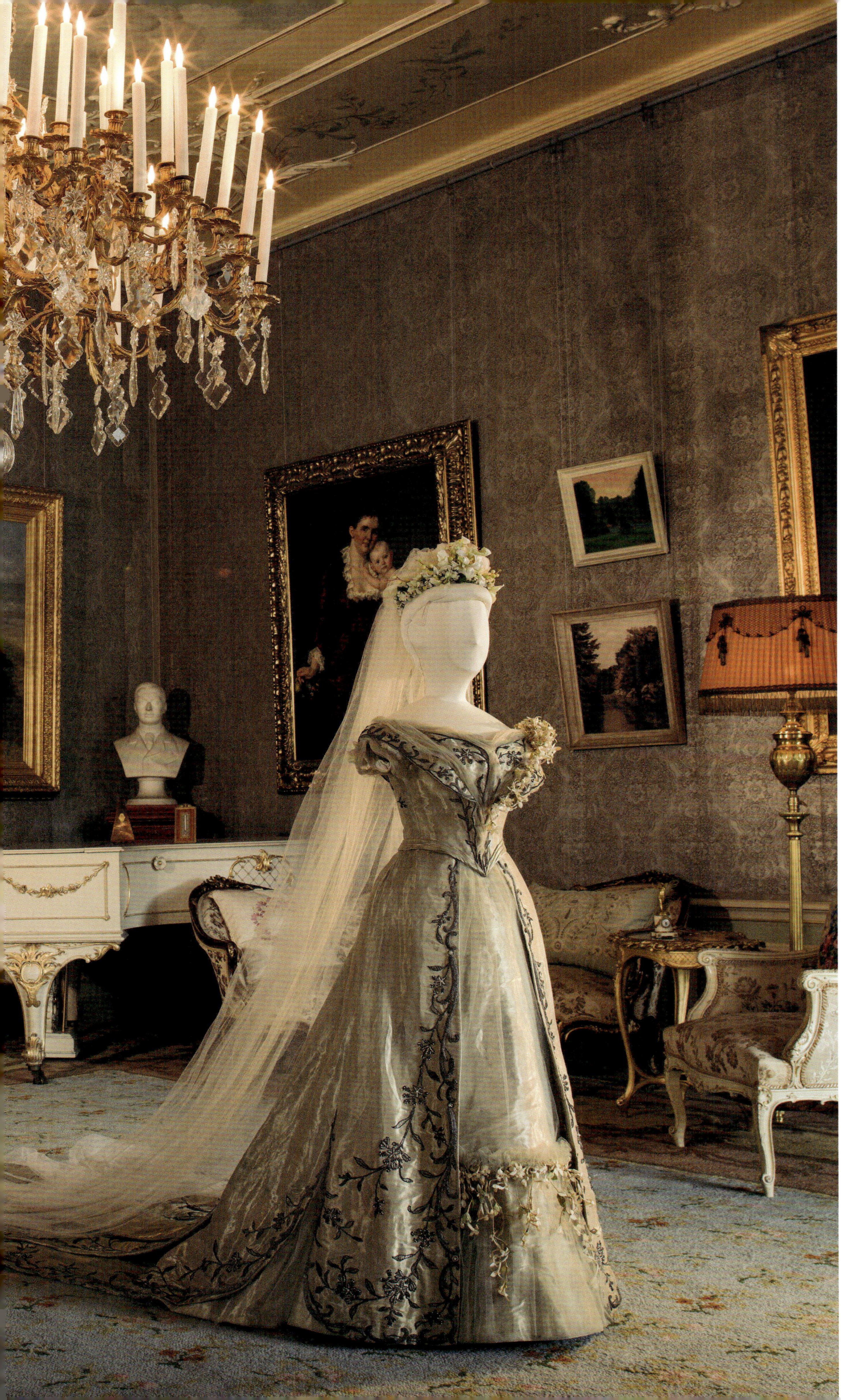

# WEDDINGS & MOURNING

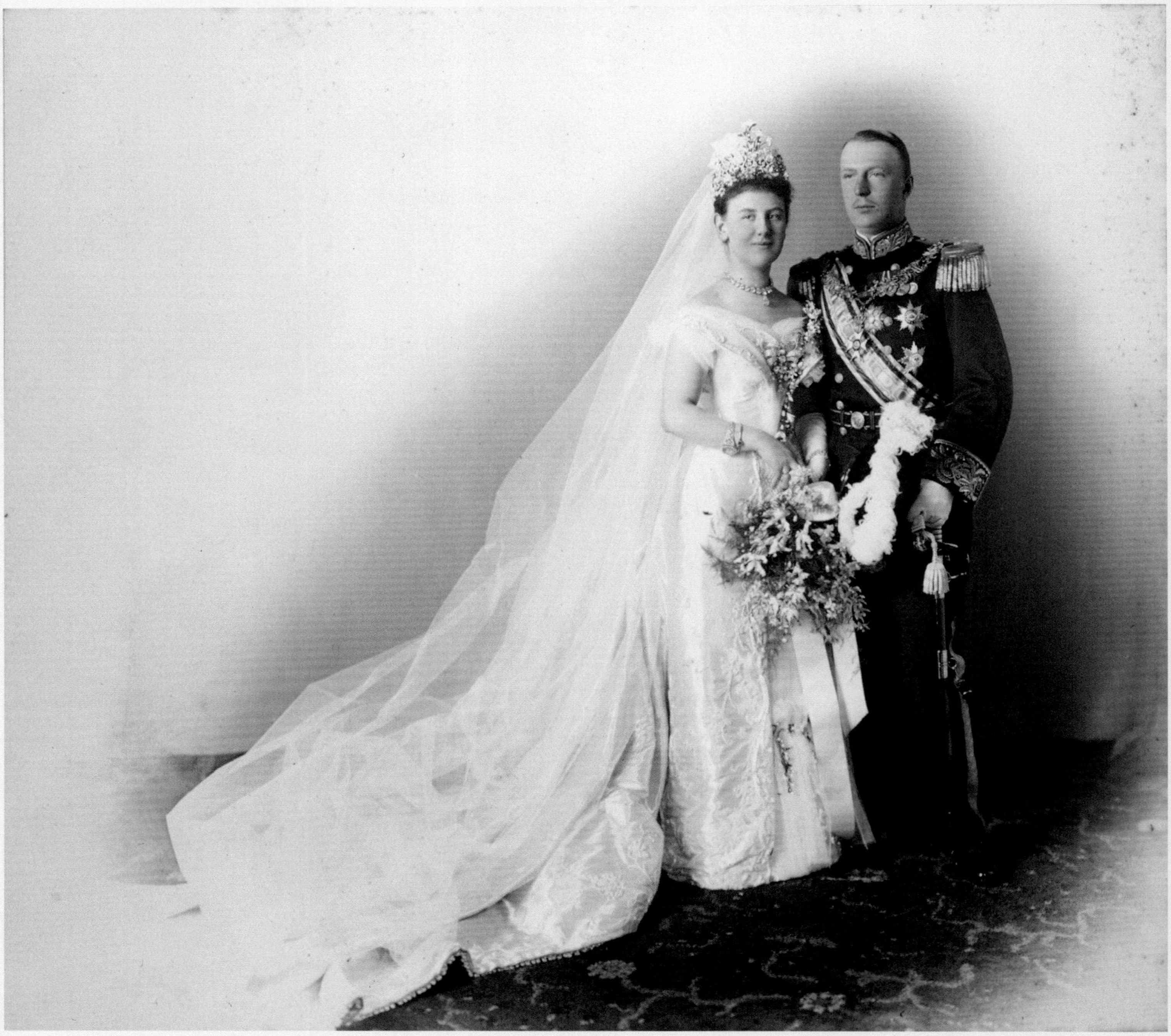

# QUEEN WILHELMINA'S WEDDING DRESS

Brides in the Dutch royal family traditionally married in the city where they lived, The Hague. The same was true of twenty-year-old Queen Wilhelmina, when she married Prince Hendrik on Thursday 7 February 1901. This was the first time a reigning queen had married in the city of the royal court. The dress code for the bride, her family, the royal guests and the royal household was therefore 'grand gala'. The queen and female guests wore low-cut gowns with a train and short sleeves. The bride, her mother Emma and female members of the royal family also wore a tiara. The gentlemen wore full dress uniform, either military or civilian, or a dress suit.

The silver lamé on Wilhelmina's wedding dress now looks somewhat somber, as the shine of the silver thread has dulled. Silver can be polished, but not if it has been woven into fabric. Like most dresses from that time, Wilhelmina's wedding dress was in two parts: a close-fitting bodice and a separate skirt. The skirt falls open in the middle of the waistline and extends into a long train. The bodice, the edges of the overskirt and the pleats in the train are decorated with relief embroidery of silver thread, sequins and glass pearls in the form of vines, curlicued Cs in 18th-century style and orange blossom. Like Wilhelmina's investiture gown of two years earlier, the wedding dress was designed and made by the Paris fashion house Nicaud. It was then embroidered in Amsterdam by the artistic needlework department of the National College of Decorative Arts. This averted any criticism that the wedding dress, to be worn at a national ceremony, had been made in another country. A prominent member of the royal household, Wilhelmina's critical *dame du palais* (her lady-in-waiting in Amsterdam) Thora van Loon, who was in close proximity to the bride, noted later in her diary: 'The Queen's wedding dress was made entirely of silver fabric, which was opulent but I believe that heavy white satin would have had more impact, particularly since the embroidery that took so much work and time (needlework school in Amsterdam) did not stand out sufficiently, or in fact not at all, against the silver, as the embroidery was in silver with pearls.'[1]

Orange blossom was an apt motif for a wedding dress. In the Netherlands, and at the British court too, for example, it was regarded as a symbol of fertility. A not unimportant consideration in a marriage which, though entered into out of deep affection, was also expected to carry on the dynasty. Wilhelmina's German mother had worn myrtle, as was common in Germany, but as the head of the House of Orange, Wilhelmina may also have been swayed by the association with her family's name. Orange blossom made of wax was therefore woven into her diamond tiara. Orange blossom of silk and metal wire was also attached to the bodice and the visible front panel of the skirt. The queen wore embroidered stockings and her shoes were covered with embroidered silver lamé.

Long white gloves completed Wilhelmina's gala outfit. The wedding of a head of state was first and foremost a formal state occasion, not a festive family gathering, but Wilhelmina chose not to wear the insignia of her Dutch honours. Queen Emma had already had a say on her daughter's bridal outfit even before there was any talk of engagement. She had discussed with her ladies-in-waiting whether Wilhelmina should wear a veil made of lace or of tulle. Eventually, she wore a cloud of tulle that almost entirely covered the long train. Wilhelmina was a winter bride, and there were freezing temperatures on her wedding day. She therefore wore a silver lamé 'sortie' cape over her bare shoulders during the cold ride to and from the church. This too had been supplied by Nicaud. Hendrik, made a Prince of the Netherlands the day before his wedding, wore his brand-new rear admiral's dress uniform.

——PR

**Royal couple ◆**
Queen Wilhelmina and Prince Hendrik on their wedding day, 7 February 1901. The prince wore the insignia of his Mecklenburg honours, combined with the sash and breast star of a Knight Grand Cross in the Order of Orange-Nassau on his uniform, which he had also worn at the gala soirée the evening before.

Photo H.F.J.M. Deutmann
Royal Collections, The Hague

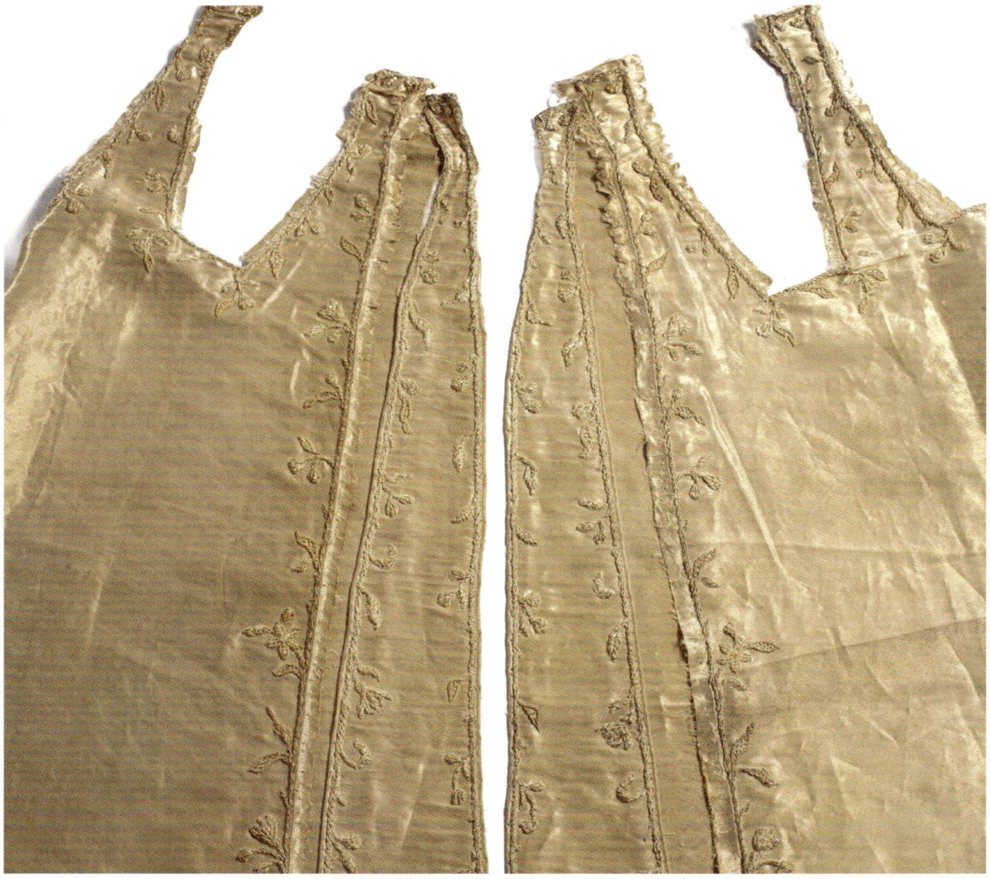

Fragments of the cape belonging to Wilhelmina's wedding dress
Possibly Nicaud Paris, 1900-1901
Silver lamé, silk, silver thread, mother-of-pearl, glass pearls
Paleis Het Loo, on long-term loan
from the Royal Collections, The Hague

Shoes worn with Wilhelmina's wedding dress
Nicaud Paris, 1900-1901
Leather, silk, silver thread, glass pearls
Paleis Het Loo, on long-term loan
from the Royal Collections, The Hague

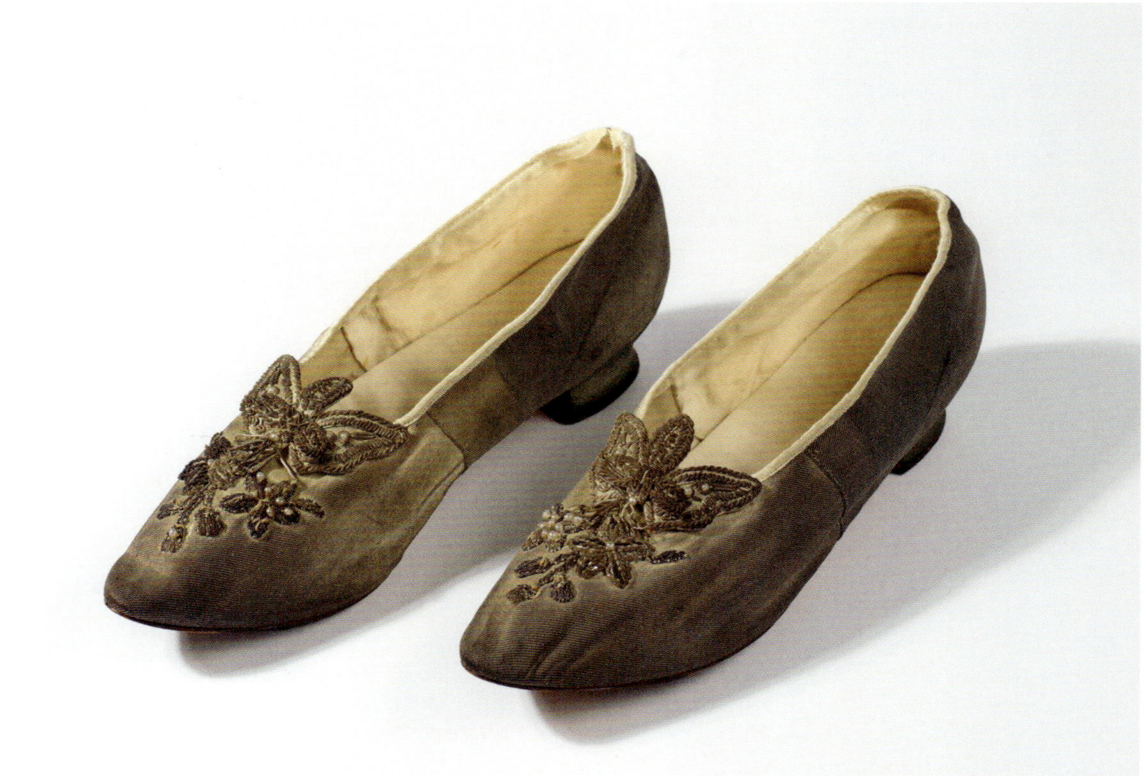

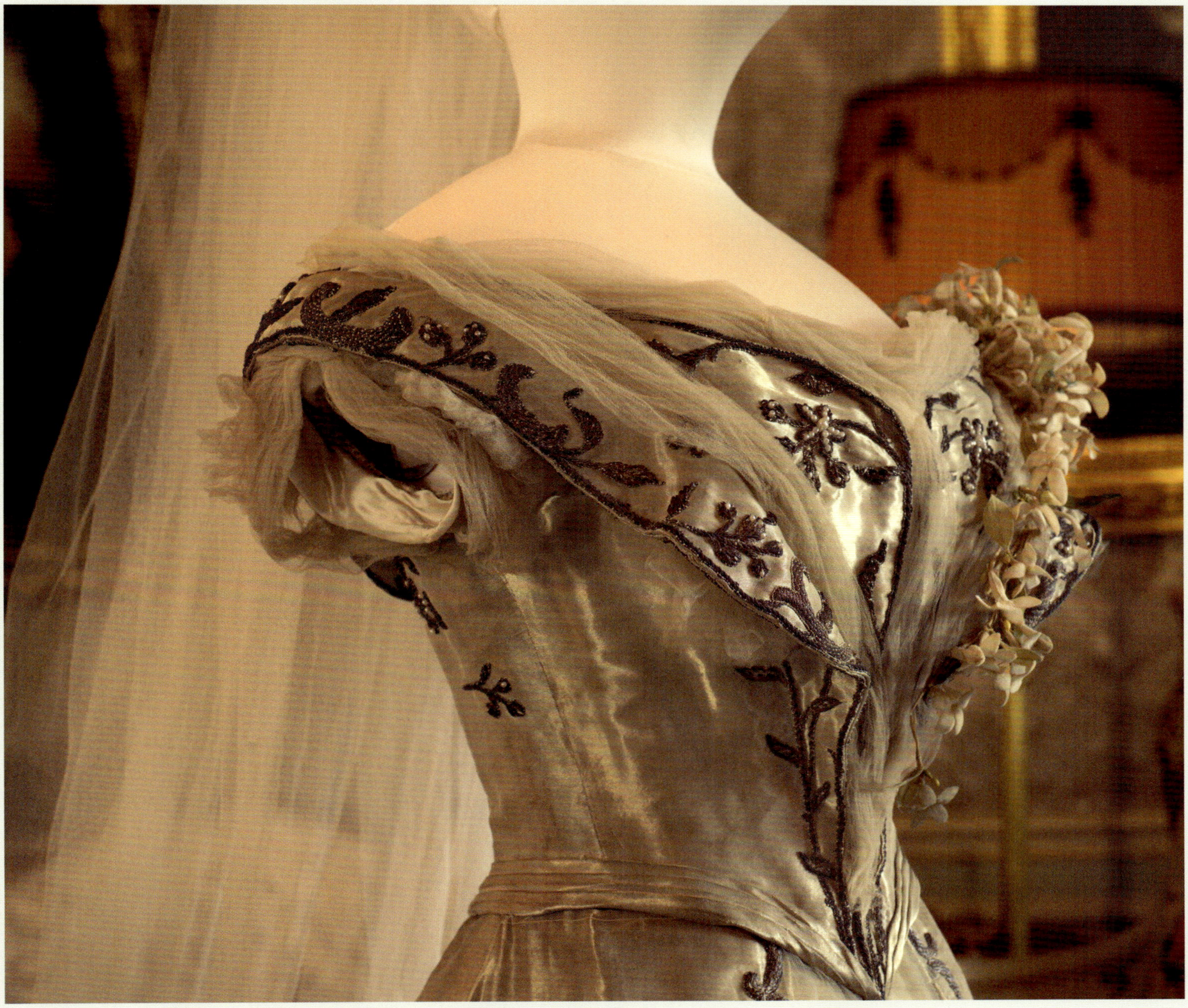

Bodice of Wilhelmina's wedding dress ◆
Nicaud Paris, 1900-1901
Silk, silver thread, cotton, glass pearls
Paleis Het Loo, on long-term loan
from the Royal Collections, The Hague

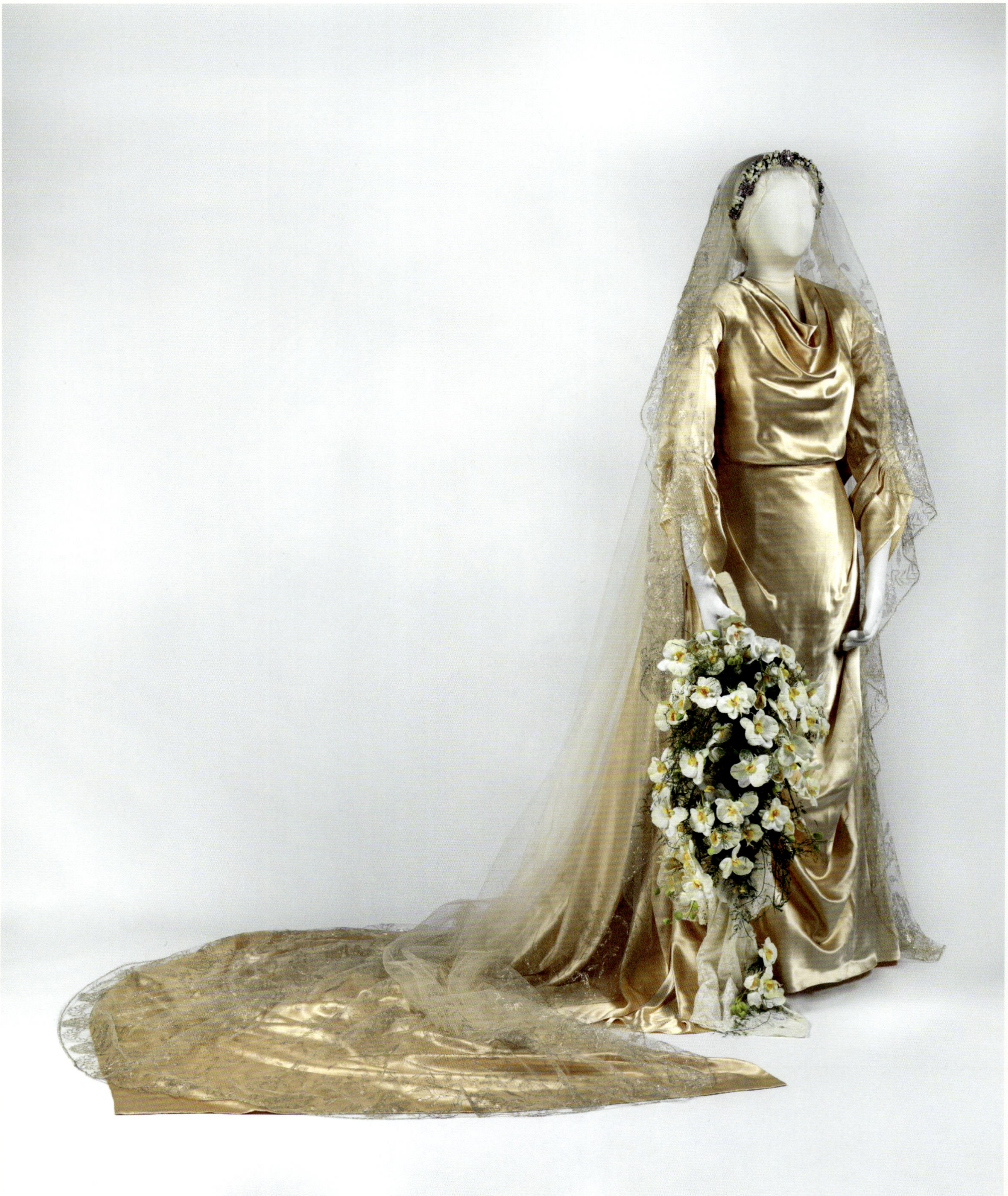

# PRINCESS JULIANA'S WEDDING DRESS

Like her mother Wilhelmina before her, Princess Juliana was a winter bride. She married Prince Bernhard in The Hague on 7 January 1937. No wedding dress with an uncomfortable low neckline and short sleeves for Juliana, however, but a fashionable modern dress of ivory satin, with long sleeves and a high neckline. And a woollen underskirt, on the orders of the mother of the bride. The newspapers, including *De Volkskrant*, shared information on the dress with their readers. 'The bridal outfit in ivory satin peplum was, in consultation with Her Royal Highness, made in a simple but tastefully draped design, whose elegant lines were reminiscent of a Greek robe, with a *manteau de cour*'. The supple satin had been made by French fabric manufacturer Bianchini. Mrs Strauss, one of the directors of Hague fashion house C.H. Kühne & Zonen, made several trips between The Hague, Paleis Het Loo and Paris so that the princess could have two fittings for her wedding dress.

Juliana ordered her bridal outfit, and the outfits of the pages and bridesmaids, from Kühne of The Hague. Maison Kühne, established in 1842, and Maison Hirsch & Cie of Amsterdam, were the main Dutch suppliers of clothing to Queen Wilhelmina. The commission to supply Juliana's wedding dress was a highpoint in the history of fashion house Kühne. It used a Parisian designer, Maggy Rouff, to design the gown. Her label is sewn into the dress. Juliana's wedding dress is an example of a couture gown ordered in the Netherlands that was made here under licence. Maggy Rouff, born Marguerite de Wagner, and known since her marriage 1917 as Mrs Bescanson de Wagner, was a Belgian designer with a business on the renowned Avenue des Champs Elysées in Paris. The Dutch firm Hirsch had taken over the Parisian fashion house Drecoll, which had belonged to Rouff's parents. Their daughter worked there until she opened her own house in Paris in 1929, under the name Maggy Rouff. Her royal clientèle included Princess Marina, Duchess of Kent and the Queen of Albania, as well as Queen Wilhelmina. For several seasons, Maggy Rouff came to The Hague with her head of atelier and a model to show the queen her latest designs.[1] Wilhelmina ordered an evening dress from Rouff in 1936 and a year later she ordered a gold lamé ballgown decorated with antique lace from her own collection.[2]

The bridal veil covered the entire five-metre train of the *manteau de cour*. The tulle was embroidered with orange blossom and rose motifs in glittering silver thread. The orange blossom was a universal, traditional bridal motif, but it also referred to the House of Orange. The roses were a reference to the emblems in the prince's coat of arms. The veil was held in place by a crown of real orange blossom and five roses made of diamonds. The waistband was also decorated with real orange blossom from the ancient orange trees at Paleis Het Loo. Juliana's train was carried in the procession by four young bridesmaids and pages. The couple were preceded by twelve adult bridesmaids and groomsmen. Juliana had ensured that the twelve bridesmaids wore dresses in pastel shades that together formed a rainbow, to symbolise the Biblical connection between heaven and earth. In short, this was a dress code with a personal touch. Like Juliana's wedding dress, these silk dresses with train, made by Kühne, had distinct draping. The velvet waistbands and hairbands, and also the silk covering the shoes and the long leather gloves were dyed the same colour as the dress, only a shade darker. The twelve groomsmen wore tailcoats, civilian dress uniform or military uniform, depending on their position. Prince Bernhard wore the blue uniform of a cavalry captain of the hussars, plus the grand cross of the Order of the Netherlands Lion and the Cross of Merit First Class, of the Princely House of Lippe. The other guests had been instructed to wear a long gown ('visite toilet') with a hat, and black tie for the gentlemen.[3]
—PR

**Princess Juliana's wedding dress** ◆
Paris, Maggy Rouff; The Hague, C.H. Kühne & Zonen, 1936-1937
Silk
Paleis Het Loo, on long-term loan from the Royal Collections, The Hague

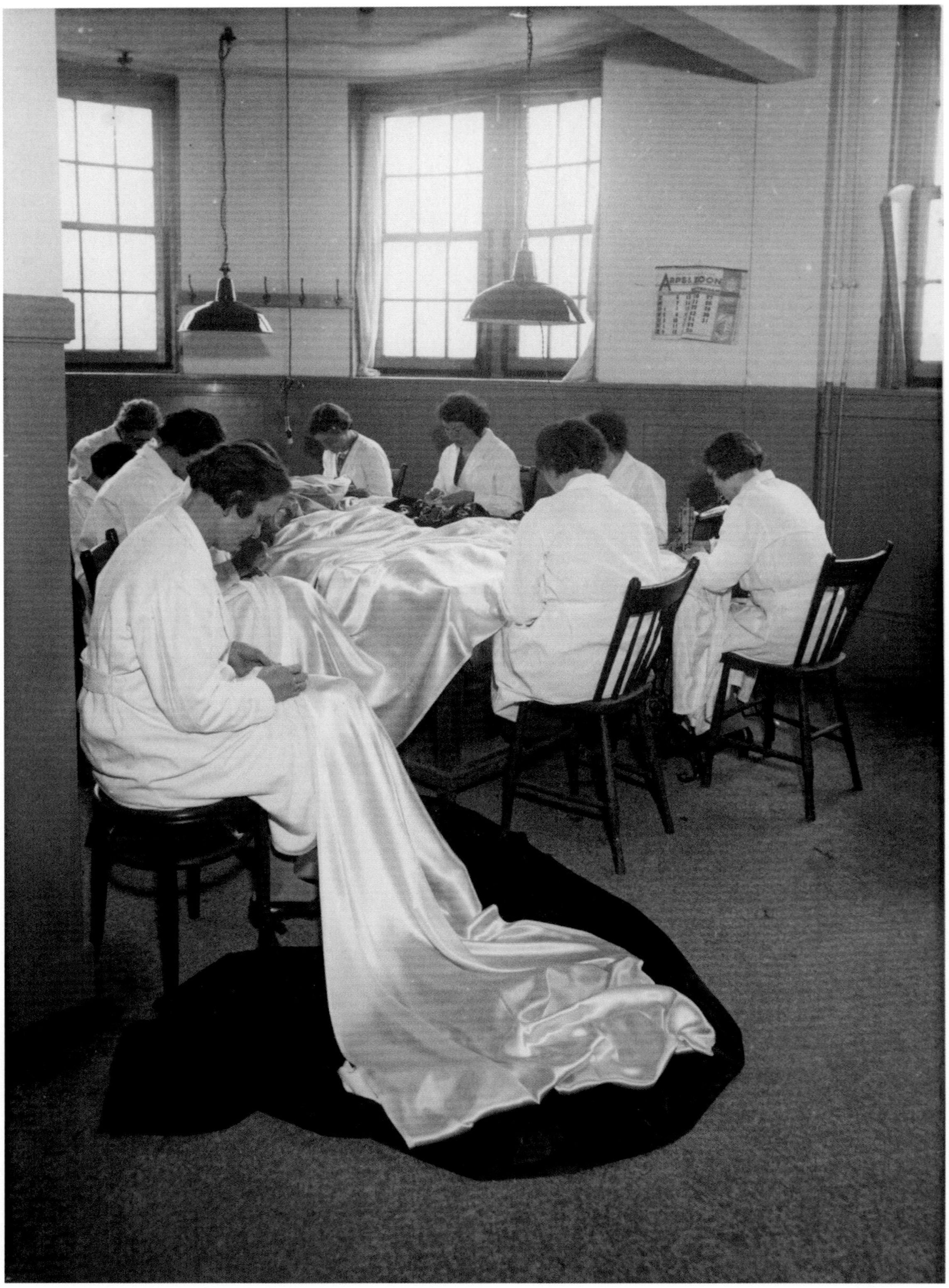

**Juliana's wedding dress is assembled**
Nine seamstresses from fashion house Kühne assembled Juliana's satin wedding dress in December 1936. In the weeks leading up to the marriage, Kühne worked with double staff, not least because the festivities at court had prompted a rise in the demand for evening dresses.

Photo N.V. Polygoon
National Archives,
Elsevier Domestic photography collection

**Juliana and Prince Bernhard's wedding photo, Paleis Noordeinde**
Franz Ziegler, 1937
Jos-Pé tri-colour print
Paleis Het Loo, on long-term loan
from the Orange-Nassau Historical Society

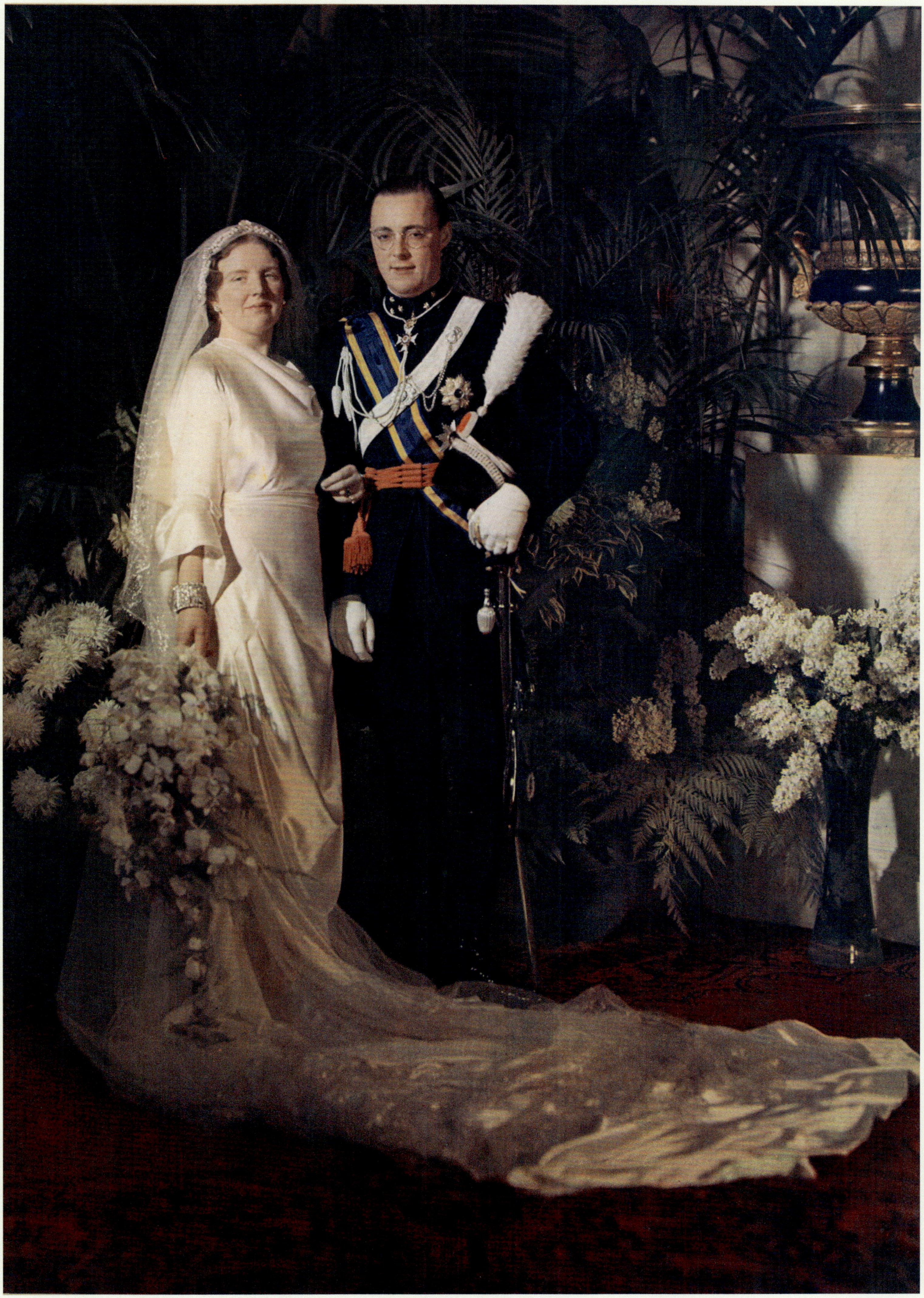

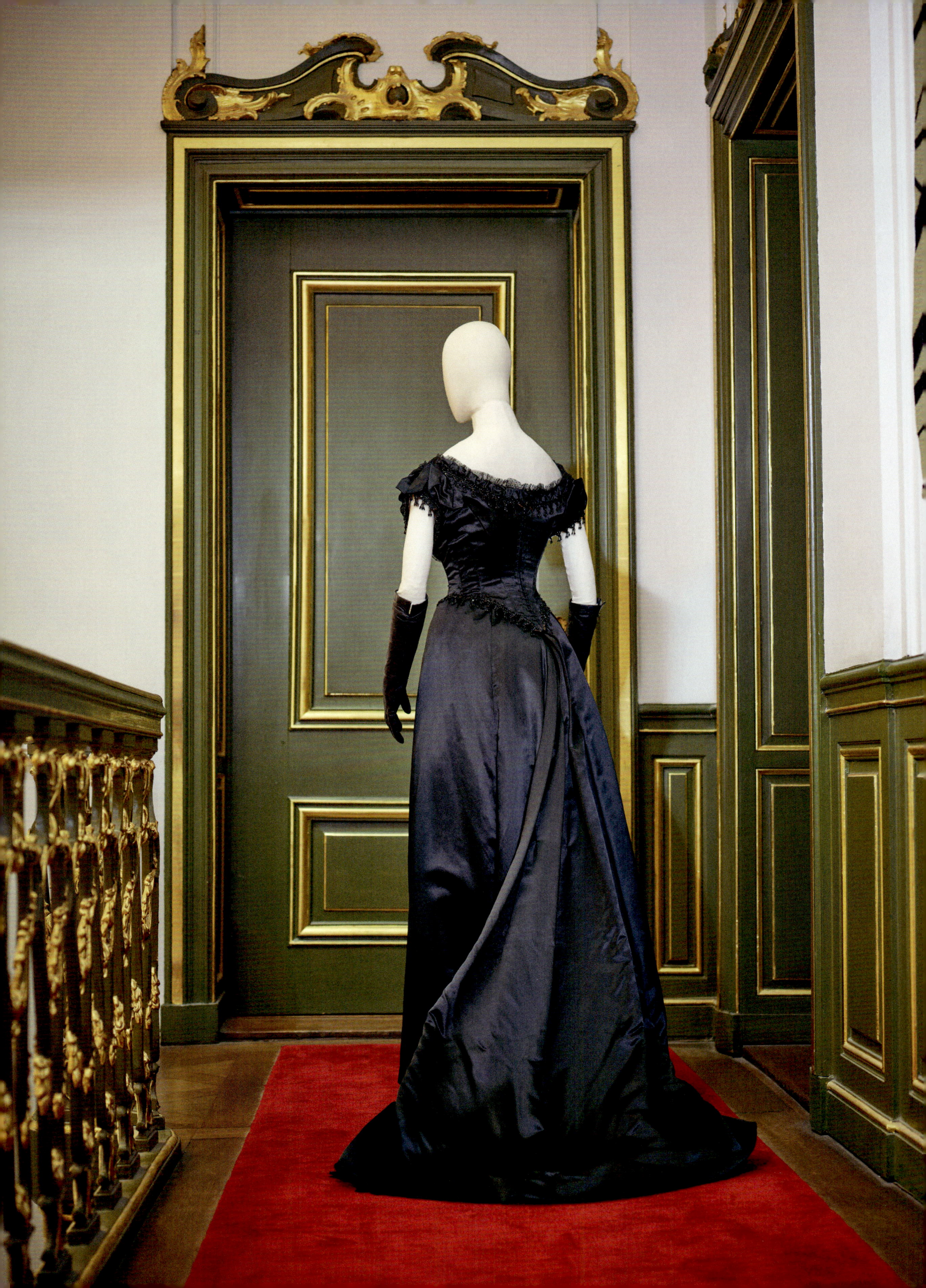

# IN MOURNING

'The mourning is somewhat inconvenient for me, as I had hoped to have a frugal autumn and now I shall have to buy all kinds of things, here at Het Loo we can adapt things a little, but in The Hague we have to look just right',[1] lady-in-waiting Henriette van de Poll complained in 1881, when court mourning had just been announced again. The court would regularly go into mourning, whether in response to the death of a closely acquainted or related monarch, or the passing of a distant friend or relative of the royal family. This often happened unexpectedly, of course, prompting both improvisation and worries about appropriate attire. The rules for court mourning had been laid down in 1815 in the 'Bepalingen omtrent de Hof-Costumes' ('Regulations concerning Court Outfits'), and had been amended a number of times since.[2] There were several stages of mourning, from full mourning to half mourning and light mourning. Each stage had different dress codes for different occasions, from mourning clothes worn at home in the morning (casual dress, or 'negligé', in white, without decoration and not in silk, with black accessories) to mourning dresses, and even gala evening gowns in mourning style. Shiny satin and decorations on black gowns were covered with mourning crêpe during heavy mourning, as was the trim on the liveries worn at court (see page 125).

When the death of Prince Frederik, second son of King Willem I, became imminent in September 1881, Queen Emma advised Henriette to start readying her mourning clothes. 'We received the death announcement yesterday morning and I have been terribly busy, while Cécile (the dresser) covered all the satin on my black gown with crêpe (mourning crêpe), I applied crêpe to my satin hat, the Queen loaned me a scarf, and by the time the extra train arrived at 1:25 I was completely in mourning.' Henriette travelled to Wassenaar to give her condolences, where 'Everyone at the Paauw [the country house where Prince Frederik lived] was very surprised that I already had such a complete mourning outfit; of course I did not say how I had come by the scarf. We must remain in mourning for 3 months, one full with scarf and a half bonnet. This morning we sent Cécile to The Hague to buy fabric for mourning dresses, since we also need to be in cashmere for the dinner, this was the simplest and surest way to be supplied quickly, as all seamstresses are of course terribly busy. I slept poorly last night what with all this expense, fuss and agitation…'[3]

In order to reduce costs, Henriette had some old mourning clothes altered when Prince Alexander, the youngest son of King Willem III, died in 1884. 'I am having Cécile make a new bodice for my old black gown, it is shiny with age and in the heat is even filthy. I will have her modernise the long black one.'[4] An announcement of mourning could completely disrupt plans for a festive wardrobe, as Mrs Van Loon-Egidius, dame-du-palais (an unpaid lady-in-waiting) in Amsterdam, discovered. On one occasion when mourning was announced, she lamented, 'This has thrown a spanner in the works and – such a shame – all those beautiful gowns will now have to stay in the wardrobe, for the entire court is to go into mourning'.[5] Dinners and receptions went ahead at court, even during times of mourning, so low-cut mourning gowns were nothing unusual. Several mourning bodices and matching skirts from Henriette van de Poll's wardrobe have survived. They are decorated with gleaming black beads in attractive patterns. Henriette referred to occasions such as these on 23 September 1881, when the court was in mourning. 'Tomorrow there is cour (reception), Sunday a gala dinner, which we will attend in high-necked black gowns with crêpe voiles on our heads.'[6]

A period of mourning at court would be announced by postcard. The duration of the different stages of mourning would be stipulated, along with the dress code applying in each stage. When the court was in mourning, a lady-in-waiting would adhere to the type of mourning that 'her' royal adopted. It could therefore be that Henriette van de Poll, who as well as being lady-in-waiting was also head governess to the young Princess Wilhelmina for a number of years, went into paternal mourning along with the princess when King Willem III died. At the same time the other lady-in-waiting, Elise van Ittersum, adhered to the same type of mourning as Queen Regent Emma who, as the king's widow, was in heavier mourning than her young daughter, and for a longer period.[7] Mourning bonnets and veils were important during full mourning. These too were made of black crêpe, and the letters of Henriette van de Poll suggest that they were not pleasant to wear: '… the church, where I almost suffocated under that thick crêpe voile…'.[8] Queen Wilhelmina and Princess Juliana wore them in 1934 when Queen Emma, the Queen Mother died.

—MH

**Mourning gown ◆**
Worn by Lady Henriette van de Poll (1853-1946), lady-in-waiting to Queen Emma
Brussels, Maison Veuve Divoire, 1890
Silk, cotton
Kunstmuseum Den Haag

Mourning gown ◆
Worn by Lady Anna Mathilda Metelerkamp-den Tex (1861-1944)
Amsterdam, Van Scherpenzeel Kahn, circa 1891-1893
Silk, cotton, metal
Kunstmuseum Den Haag

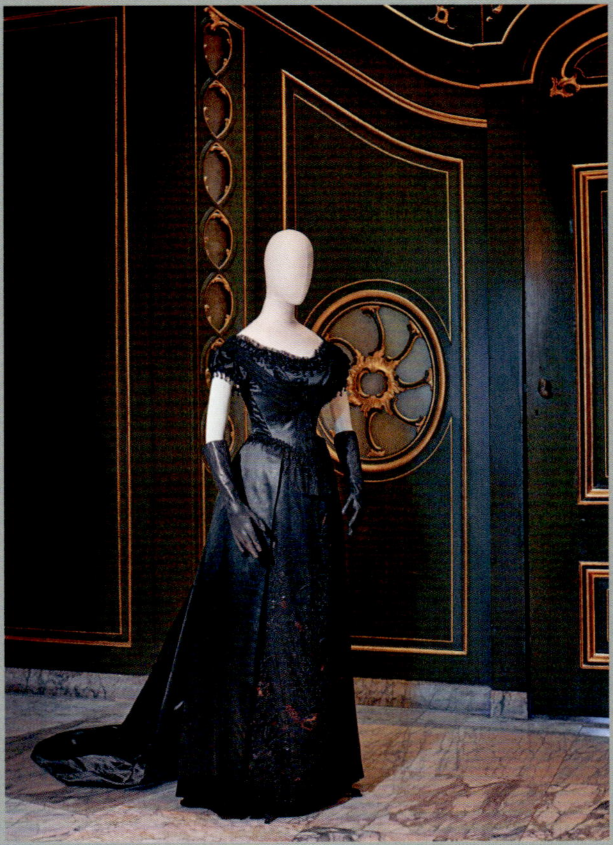

Mourning gown ◆
Worn by Lady Henriette van de Poll (1853-1946),
lady-in-waiting to Queen Emma
Brussels, Maison Veuve Divoire, 1890
Silk, cotton
Kunstmuseum Den Haag

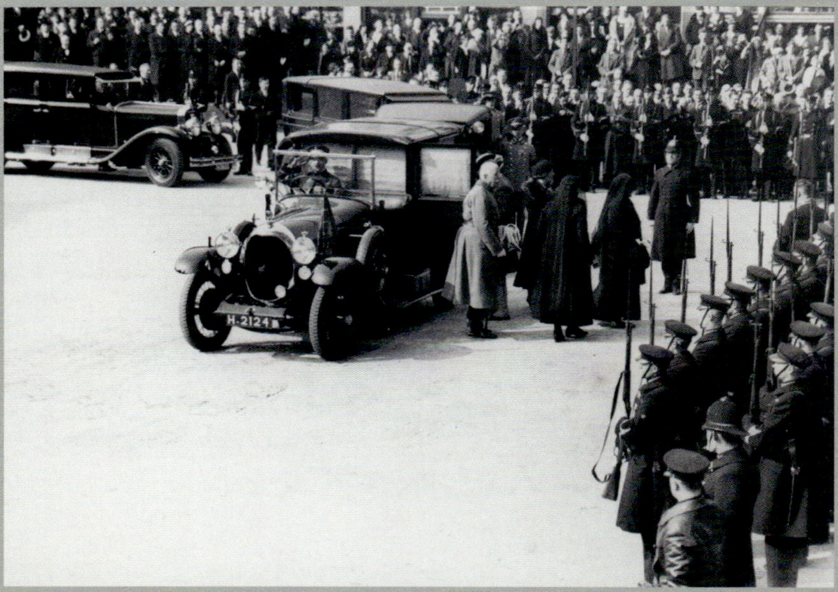


Queen Wilhelmina, Princess Juliana and their German relatives arrive at the Nieuwe Kerk church in Delft for the funeral of Queen Emma, 27 March 1934
Photographer unknown
National Archives, Elsevier photography collection

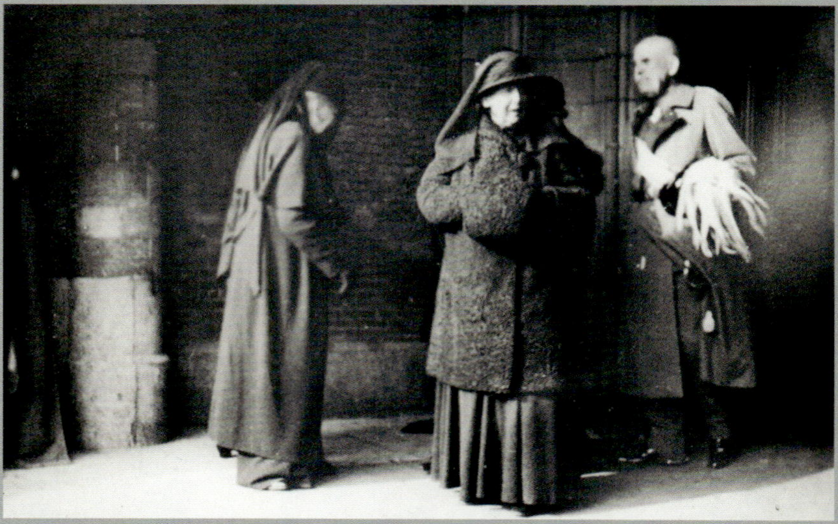

Queen Wilhelmina at Queen Emma's funeral, with relatives of her mother wearing full black mourning
Photographer unknown
Paleis Het Loo, Apeldoorn

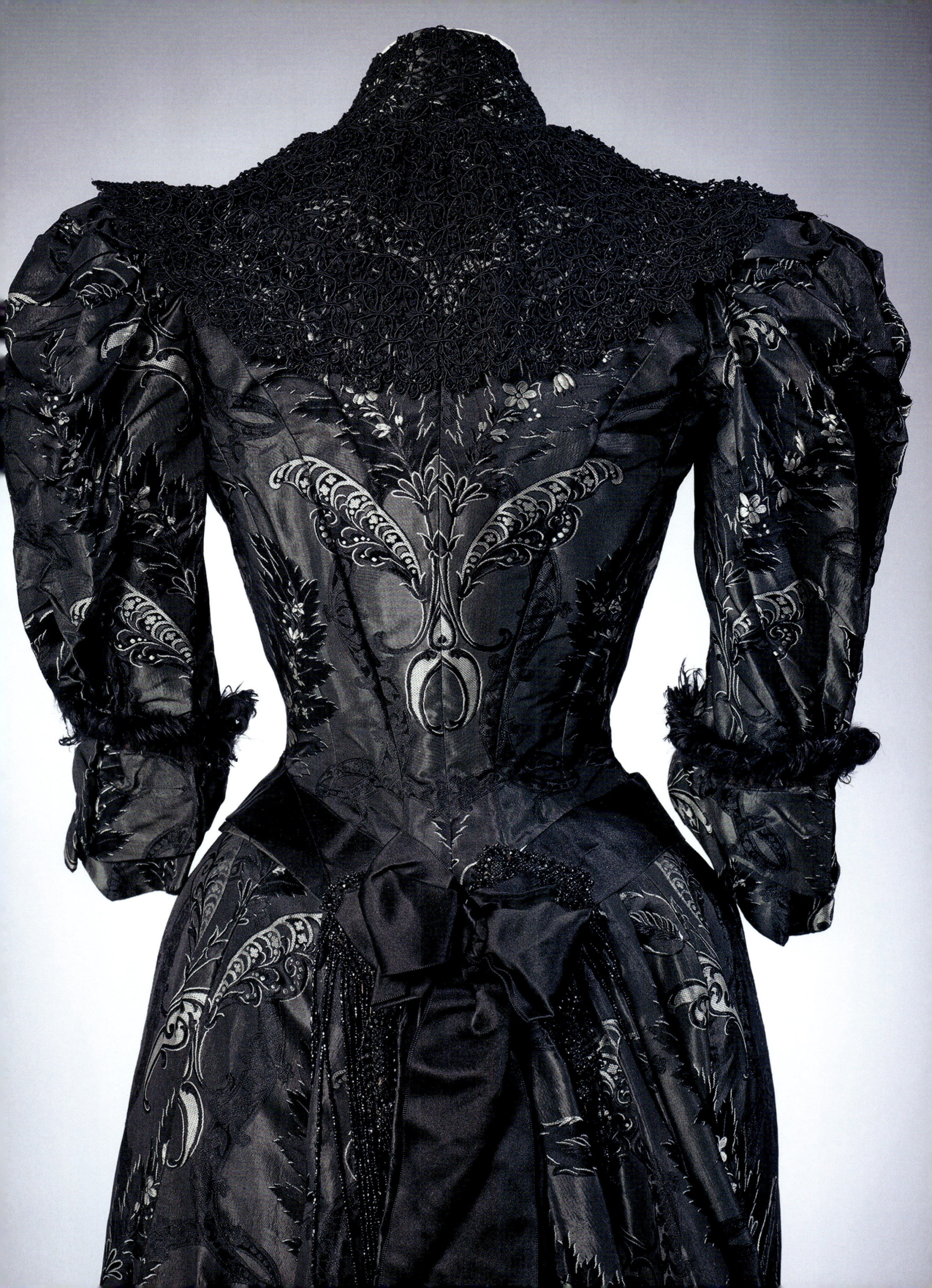

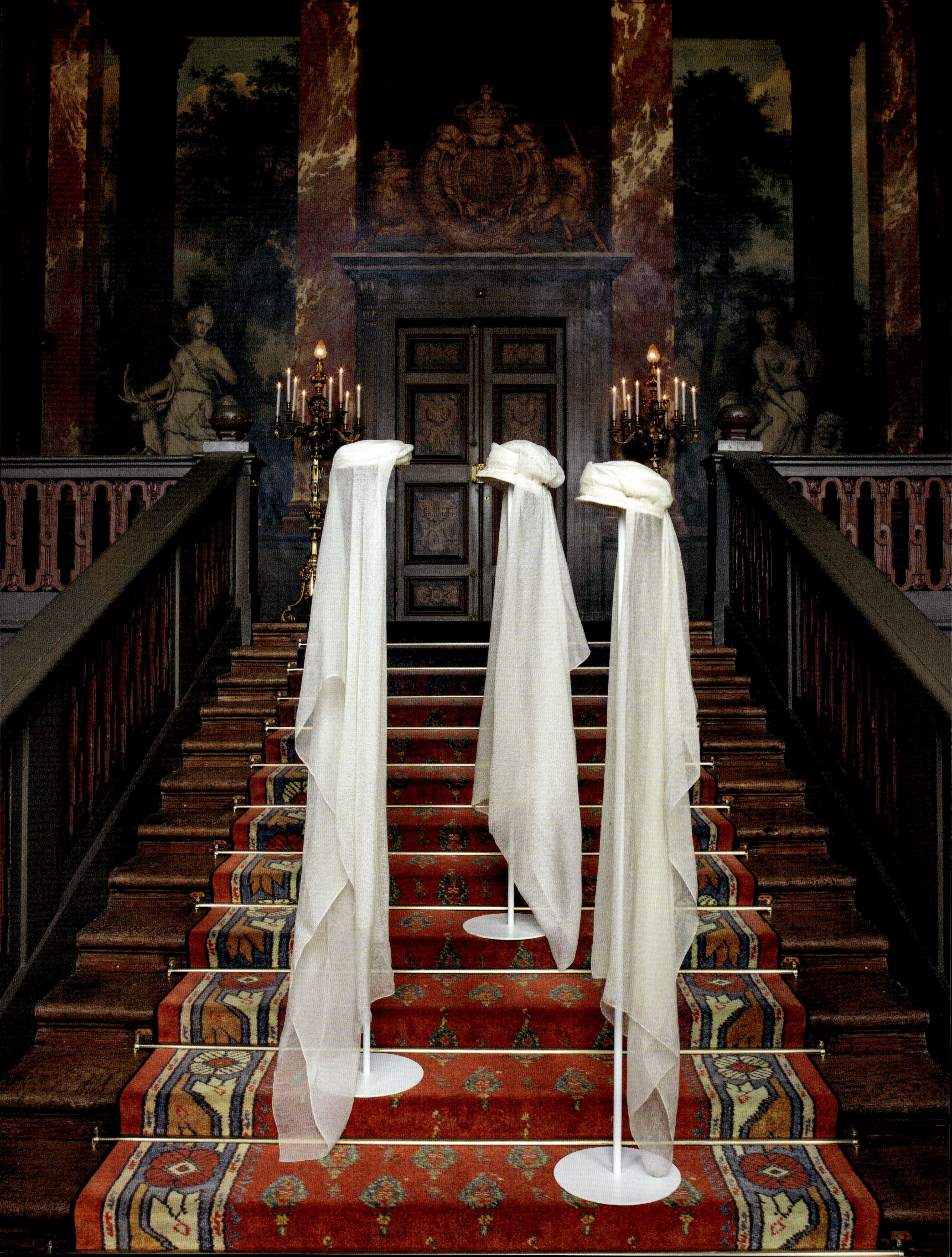

# WILHELMINA'S WHITE MOURNING BONNETS

Queen Emma, Wilhelmina's mother, died on 20 March 1934. The court was plunged into mourning. Full mourning, though grey and purple touches were by now permitted at a later stage, during the period of light mourning. Wilhelmina attended the funeral in black, even wearing a black veil over her face. A little over three months later, the royal family suffered another bereavement, when Wilhelmina's husband Prince Hendrik died. The sudden death of the prince-consort at the age of just 58 was entirely unexpected, as was the white mourning attire that Wilhelmina announced. The entire royal family – now in fact just Wilhelmina and Juliana – and the ladies-in-waiting all adapted their wardrobe to comply with the order that everything should now be spotlessly white, from hat to shoes. Accessories such as jewellery, handbags, fans, fur stoles and umbrellas were also white. Wilhelmina and Hendrik had chosen white mourning in the realisation that it would make a big impact on the public. 'Long before his passing, my husband and I had repeatedly discussed the meaning of death and the eternal life that follows', Wilhelmina said. 'We were both firm in our belief that death is the gateway to Life, and therefore promised each other that our funerals would take place entirely in white. We thus now acted accordingly.'[1]

Some of her widow's bonnets have survived, while others are known only from portrait photographs. The front of the hat seems to reference a royal tiara. The hats are covered in white crêpe. The veil – which shortened as the period of mourning progressed – was attached to the bonnet with mother-of-pearl headed pins or sewn on halfway back.

Like the British queen, Victoria, Queen Emma had always worn a white lace widow's bonnet with a white veil within the palace walls, although the white veil was also part of gala court attire during times when there was no mourning. Queen Wilhelmina wore her white veil at public events, including the official opening of parliament in the year of her husband's death, 1934. She observed two years of mourning, during which she wore shorter and shorter veils.

White mourning was also the dress code at Queen Wilhelmina's own funeral in 1962. Although the announcement of white mourning in 1934 and 1962 was unique for the Dutch court, it was in fact part of a long European tradition. Queen Mary Tudor of Scotland, widow of King François II of France from 1560, was known as *la reine blanche*, the white queen, because of the white mourning she adopted. Belgian queens Fabiola and Paola adopted white mourning after the death of King Baudouin. These days, court mourning involves cancelling public engagements in the period between death and internment.
Court mourning is also adopted when members of friendly royal families die. Exercising restraint in one's attire is now regarded as sufficient. However, at the funerals of their parents Juliana and Bernhard, Queen Wilhelmina and Prince Hendrik's four granddaughters were dressed entirely or largely in white, in accordance with the family tradition.
—PR

**Wilhelmina's veiled white mourning bonnets ◆**
The Hague, Mme G. de Cler-Smit, 1934-1935
Silk, cotton
Paleis Het Loo, on long-term loan
from the Royal Collections, The Hague

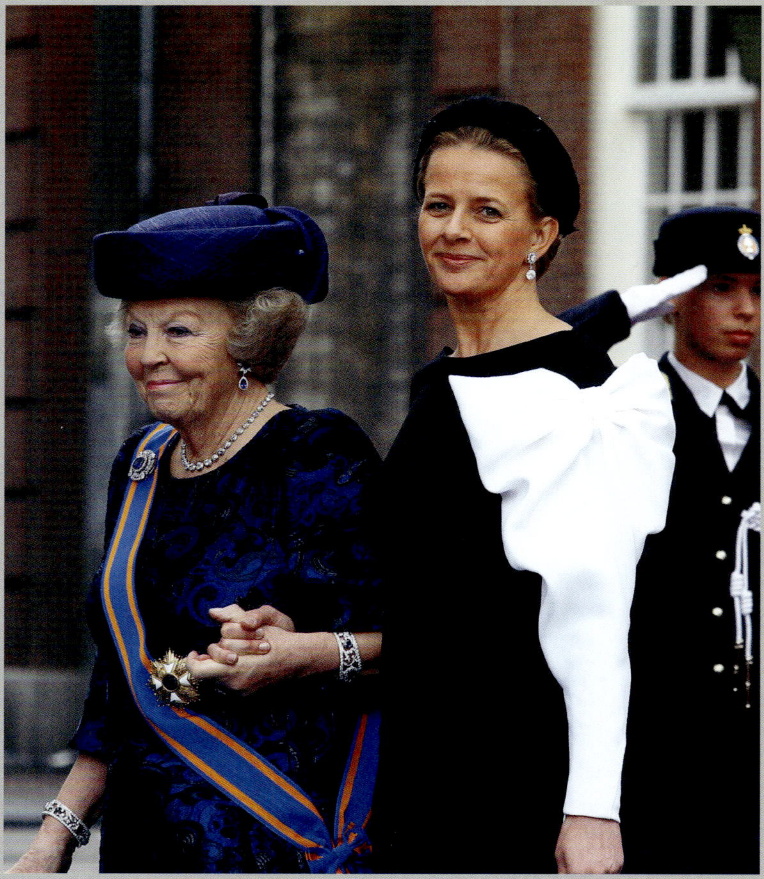

**Official portrait in white mourning dress**
Wilhelmina expressed her new role as a queen in mourning by having official photographs taken. She posed on the grand staircase at Paleis Het Loo in her white outfit, consisting of a high-necked dress with a train and long sleeves, white gloves and a mourning bonnet with a floor-length veil.

Photo Franz Ziegler, 1934
Paleis Het Loo, on long-term loan
from the Orange-Nassau Historical Society

**Personal mourning dress ◆**
At the investiture of King Willem-Alexander, Princess Mabel, who had lost her husband Prince Friso shortly before, wore a long black dress with a single white sleeve, created by designer duo Viktor & Rolf. They had also designed her white wedding dress, which was covered in bows. It was therefore a dress with personal symbolism, the white sleeve referring to the empty space beside her.

Photo Cees Buys, Abaca Press
Courtesy of HRH Princess Mabel /
Royal Collections, The Hague

**Prinsjesdag in white**
Queen Wilhelmina and Princess Juliana arrive at the entrance to the Knights' Hall for the official opening of the States-General in 1934. They are dressed entirely in white, apart from the orange and blue of the decorations of the Order of Orange-Nassau.

Photo Spaarnestad Photo
National Archives, Spaarnestad collection

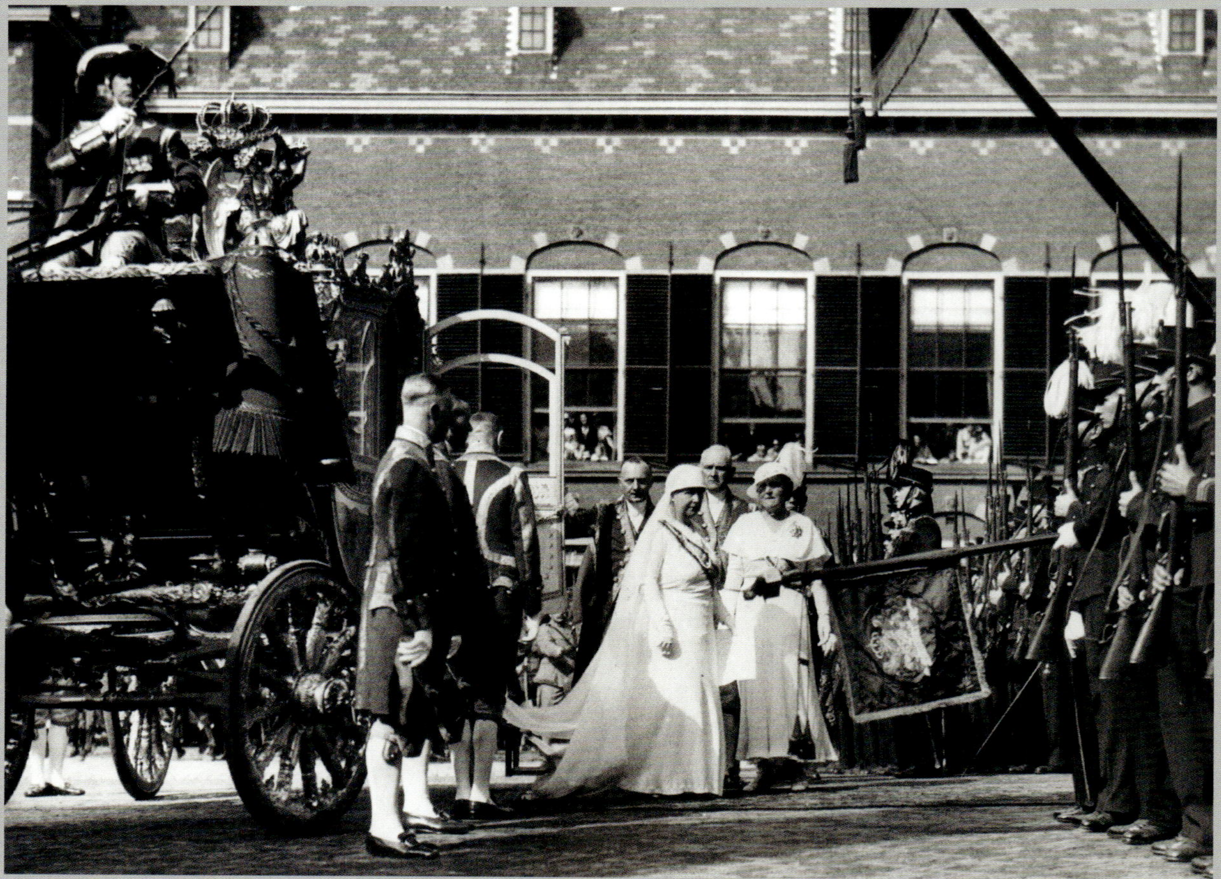

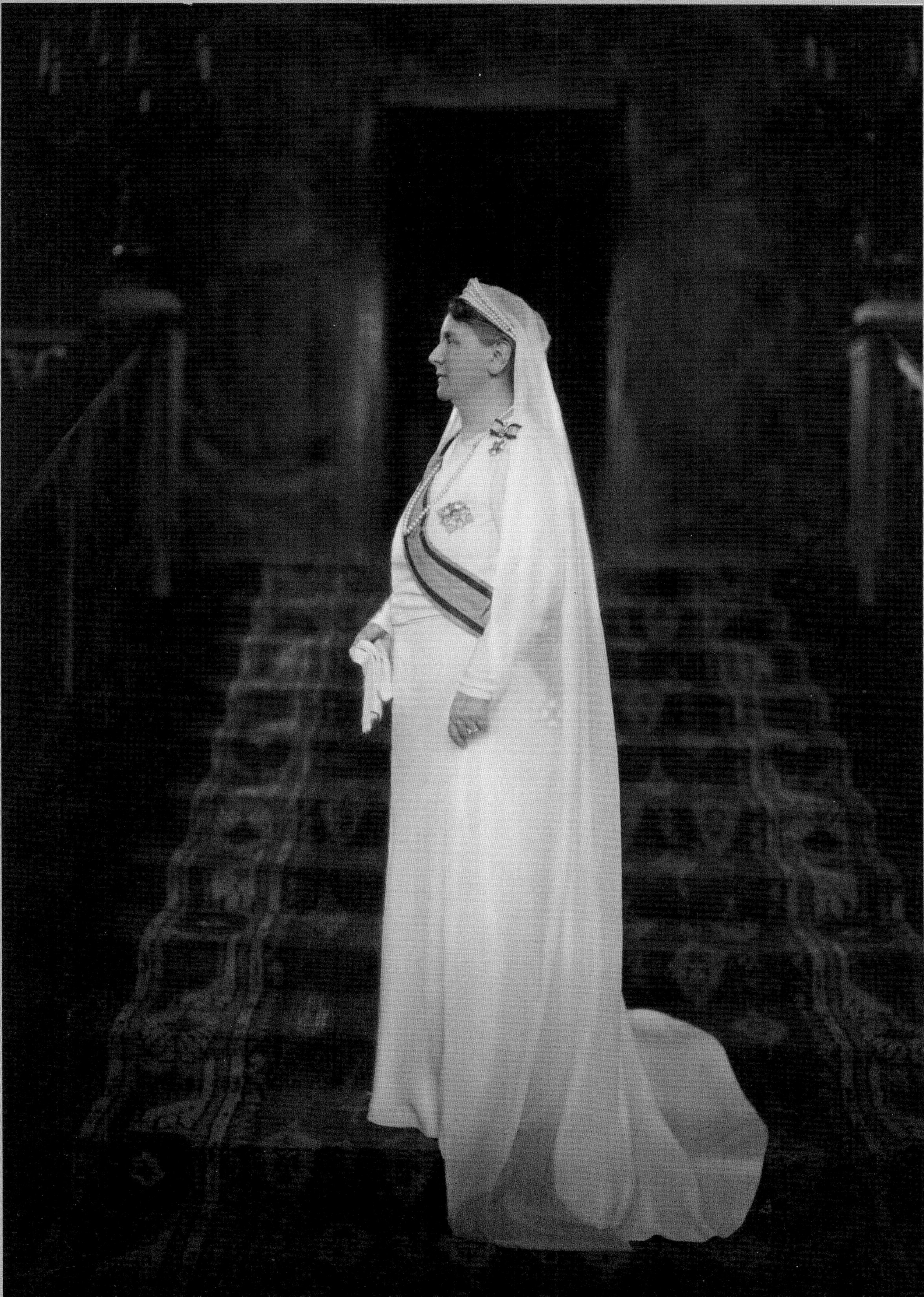

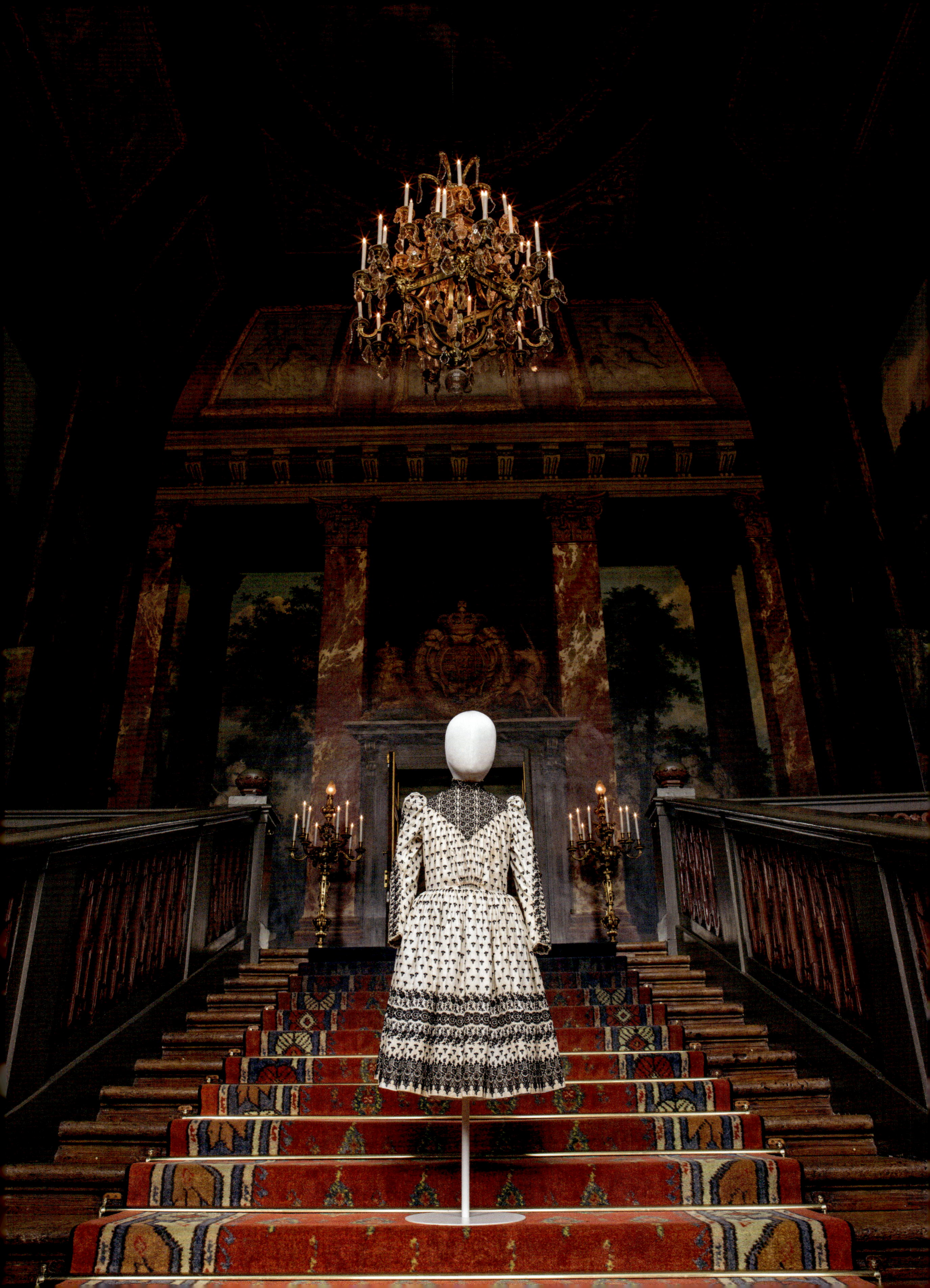

# A YOUNG QUEEN IN HALF MOURNING

The death of King Willem III at Paleis Het Loo on 23 November 1890 signified the end of the male line in the House of Orange. The king's three sons from his first marriage to Queen Sophie had all died. He had had a daughter, Princess Wilhelmina, with his second wife Emma. Wilhelmina was only ten years old when her father died. She had officially become queen, with her mother Emma as regent. Shortly after the king's death, Wilhelmina and her mother started wearing the required black mourning dress. The ladies-in-waiting and gentlemen of the court also followed the rules of mourning. Men simply had to cover the gleaming aiguillettes (shoulder cords) and epaulettes on their uniform with black crêpe. They also wore a black armband made of crêpe, the thin, black, slightly wrinkled, translucent wool or silk fabric that was used to make court mourning attire. Queen Emma had photographs taken of herself and her young daughter in full mourning. This was a poignant image to many Dutch people which, perhaps unintentionally, evoked feelings of sympathy and respect. The Dutch monarchy was in sore need of the latter, having been out of the public eye for some time during the final years of Willem III's reign.

The period immediately after the death of her father was traumatic for Wilhelmina. She even stopped growing for a while. 'And that deathly silence everywhere, and the shutters closed, all those black figures with long veils, even indoors, and above all my mother, so sad and dressed in terrifying amounts of crêpe. I could not stand it', to quote Wilhelmina herself.[1] Wilhelmina's dresses in full mourning style, ordered from Switzerland, England and France, were also made of crêpe, often with decorations in black tulle. Black jewellery was bought for her to wear with them, some of it made of jet, an organic mineraloid that could be polished to a shine.

It was not until 39 weeks later that the heavy mourning was replaced by half mourning. Ten weeks later, light mourning began, lasting three weeks. The young Queen Wilhelmina was in paternal mourning, which was lighter than widow's mourning. Wilhelmina appeared in a light mourning dress alongside the completely black figure of her mother, who had also taken to wearing a bonnet with a mourning veil. One of Wilhelmina's half mourning dresses was made of white cotton decorated with stylised machine-embroidered black floral motifs. The leg-of-mutton sleeves were in line with women's fashion at the time. Wilhelmina wore black stockings and black shoes with the dress, and a separate black belt around her waist. The large white hats she wore with the dress were decorated with black trimmings, such as ostrich feathers that had been dyed black. During her annual visit to the capital Amsterdam in 1891, her first without the king, Wilhelmina wore 'a white dress with black embroidery and a white hat with long feathers', according to *De Avondpost* newspaper's 28 May edition.

Even after the required period of mourning for Willem III, Queen Emma continued to wear a white widow's bonnet with a white lace veil within the palace walls. At gala events the veil would be attached to her tiara. The white widow's bonnet was a tradition among German female monarchs.
—PR

**Dress worn by the young Queen Wilhelmina in half mourning ◆**
Gonten (Switzerland),
atelier of Thérèse Hersche, 1891
Cotton, silk, mother-of-pearl
Paleis Het Loo, on long-term loan
from the Royal Collections, The Hague

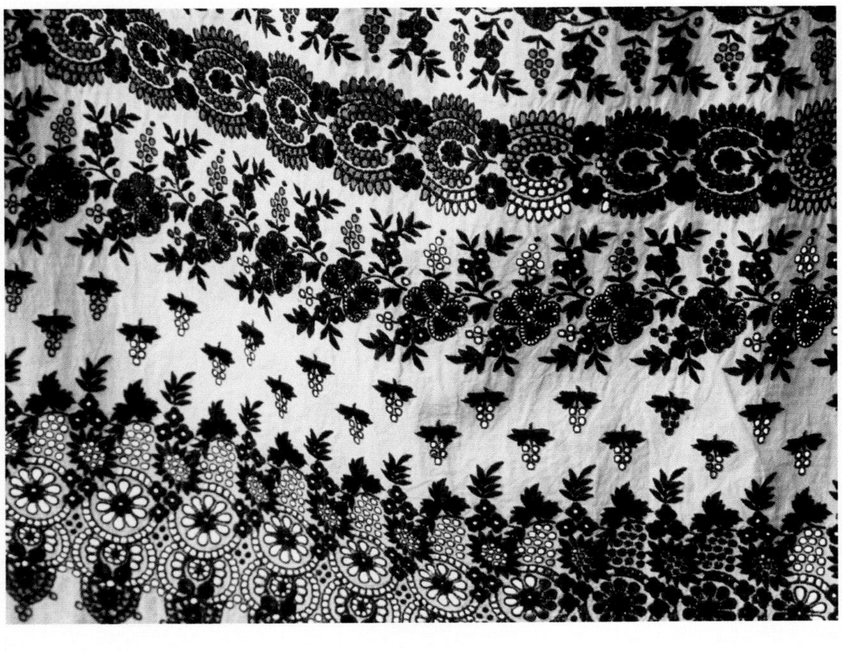

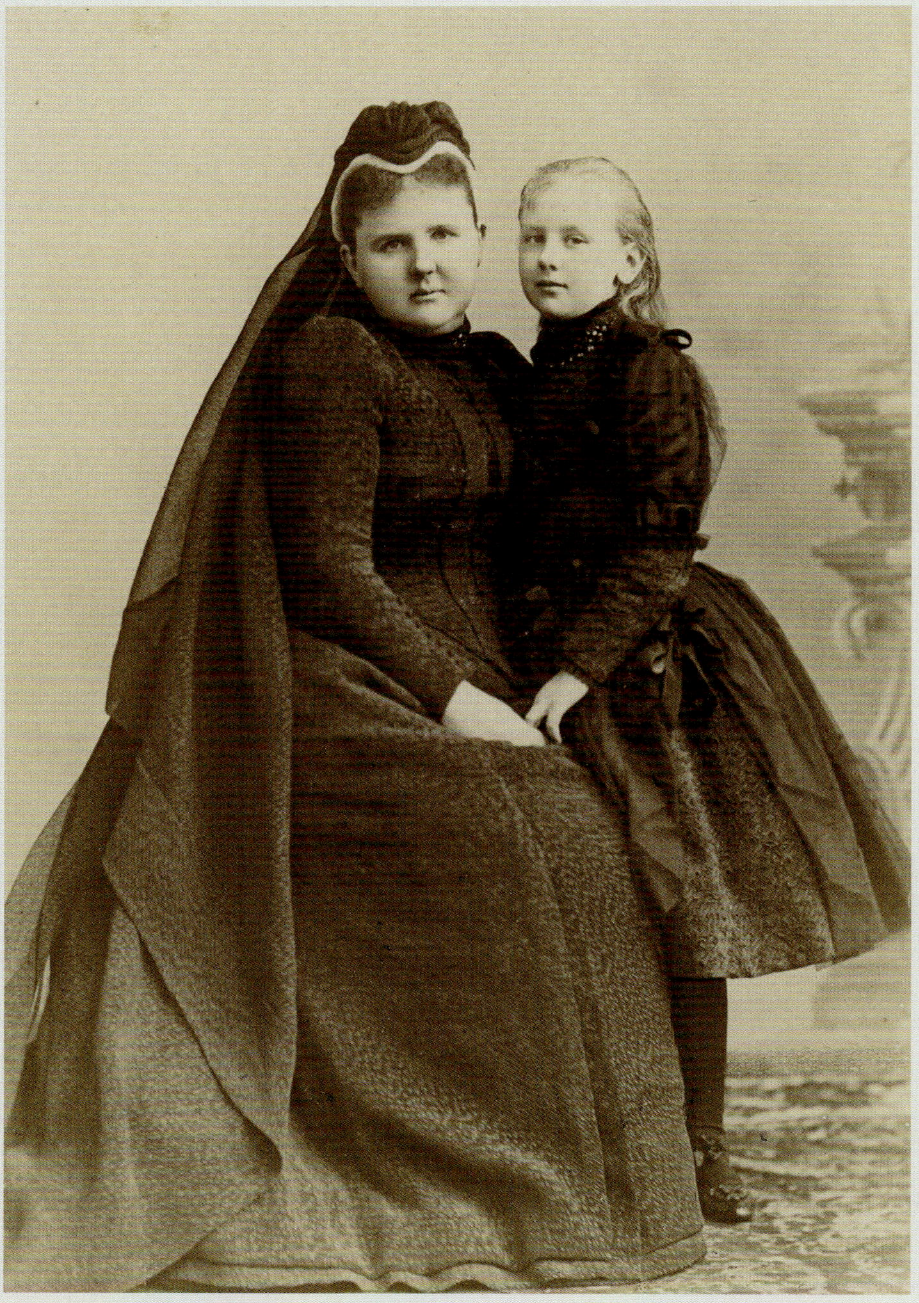

Queen Wilhelmina's Chief Equerry in court mourning dress, c. 1936 ◆
The chief equerry is in charge of the Royal Stables, the department at court that is responsible for the royal family's transport. On high days and holidays he would wear a full dress uniform, which was adapted when the court was in mourning.

Onbekende kleermaker
Wol, zijde, verguld metaal, leer
Collectie Paleis Het Loo

Two queens in full mourning
Almost four months after the death of King Willem III, dowager queen Emma and Queen Wilhelmina were photographed in full mourning. Queen Emma not only wore the black veil, but also a short veil in front of her face at public events outside the palace.

Photo Adolphe Zimmermans, 18 March 1891
Paleis Het Loo

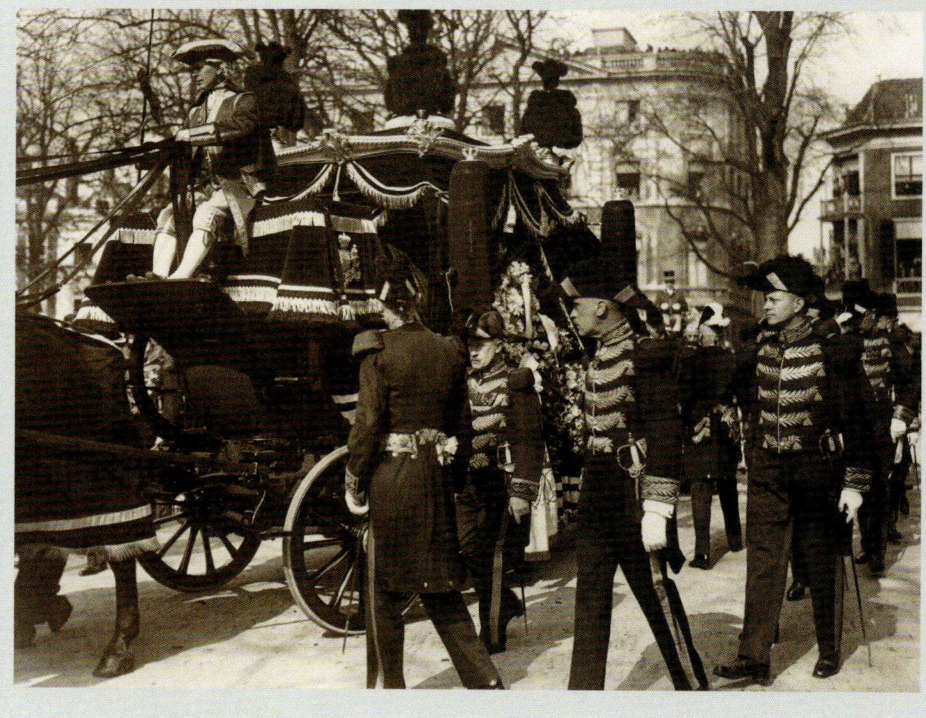

Funeral in black
On 27 March 1934 Queen Emma was interred in the royal crypt. The aides-de-camp walking alongside the hearse are all in full mourning, with a black armband over their left sleeve and the gleaming epaulettes and aiguillettes (shoulder cords) of their dress uniforms covered with black crêpe. The feathers on their hats are also black.

Photo N.V. Vereenigde Fotobureaux
Paleis Het Loo

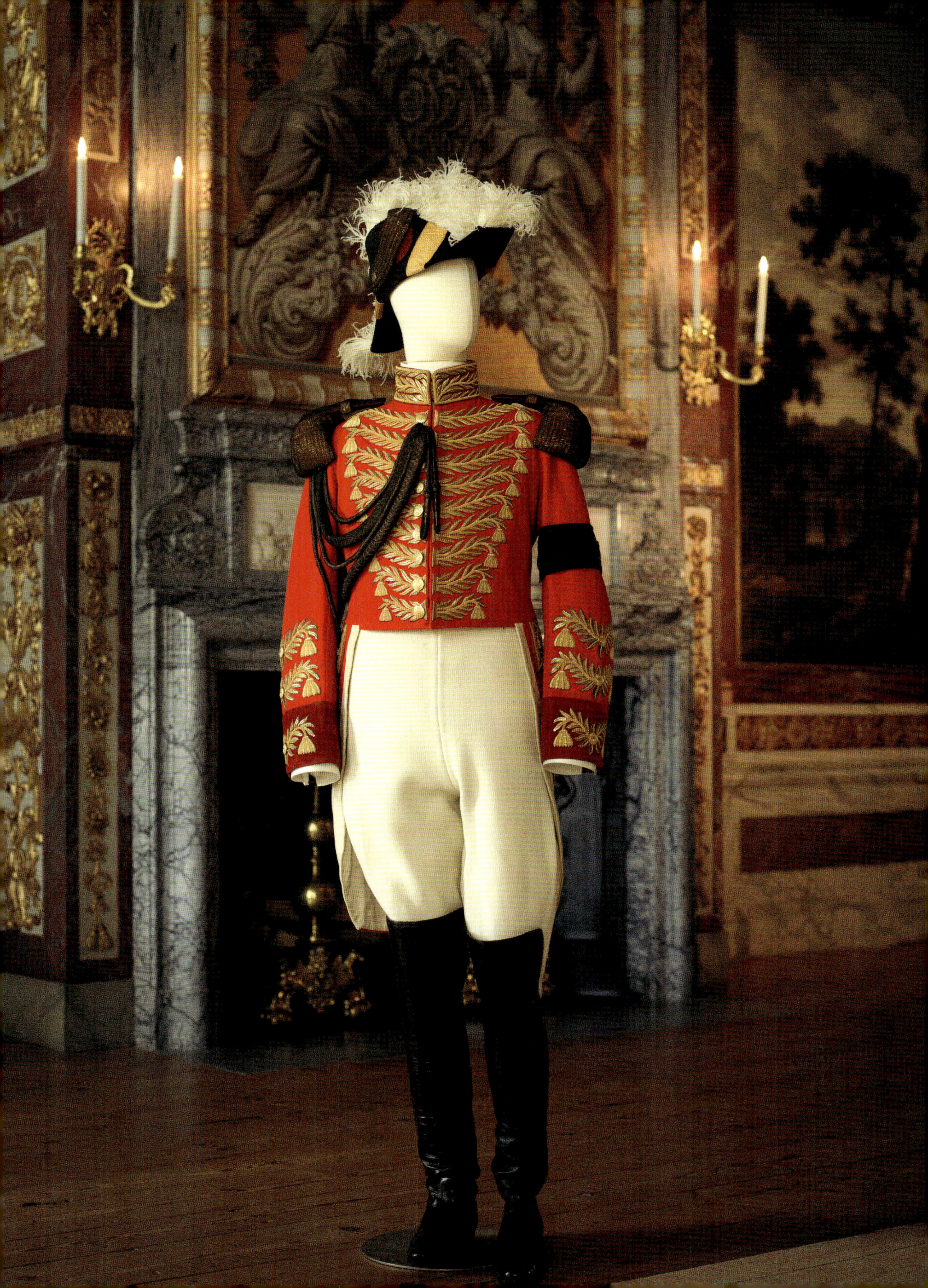

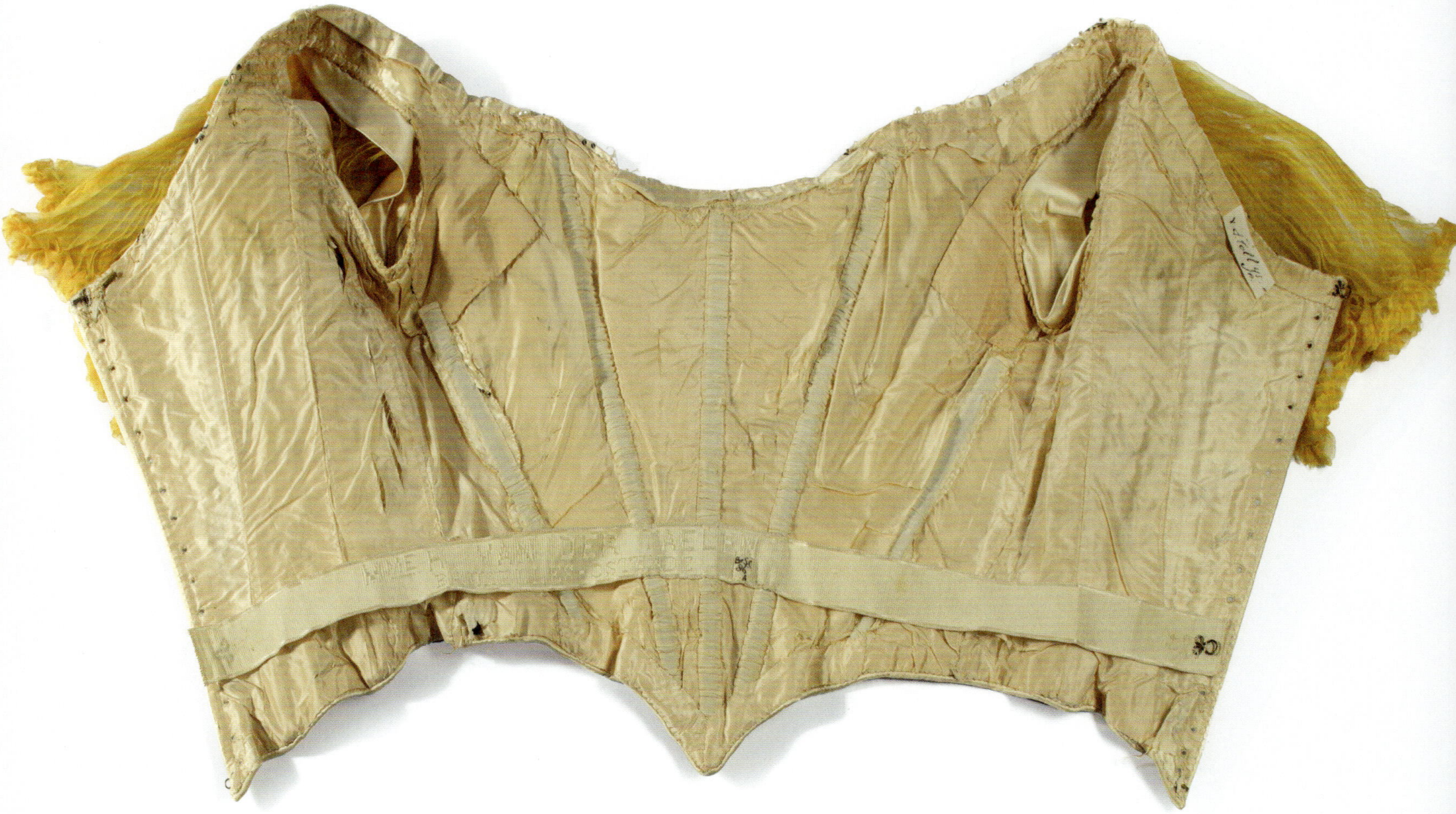

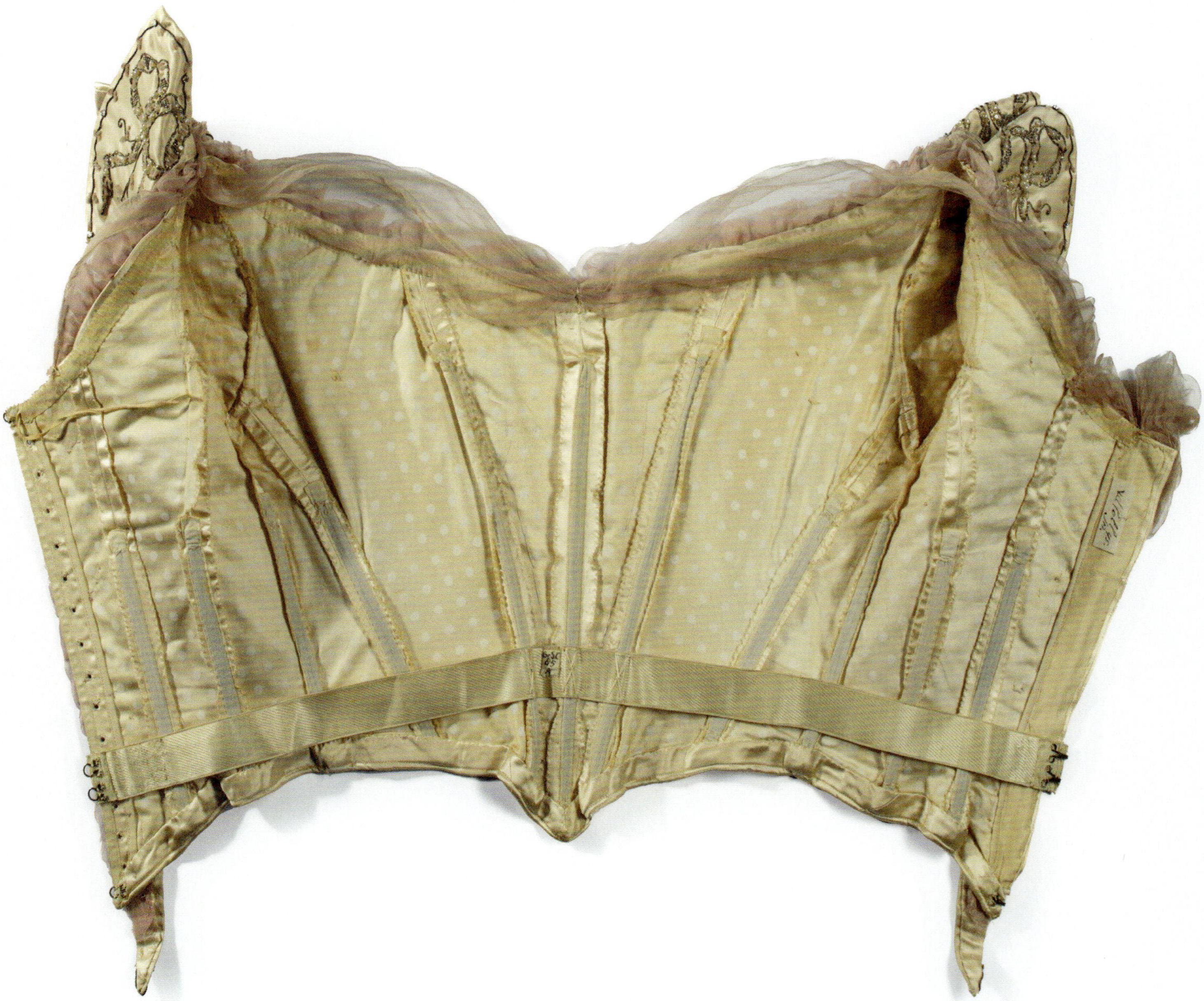

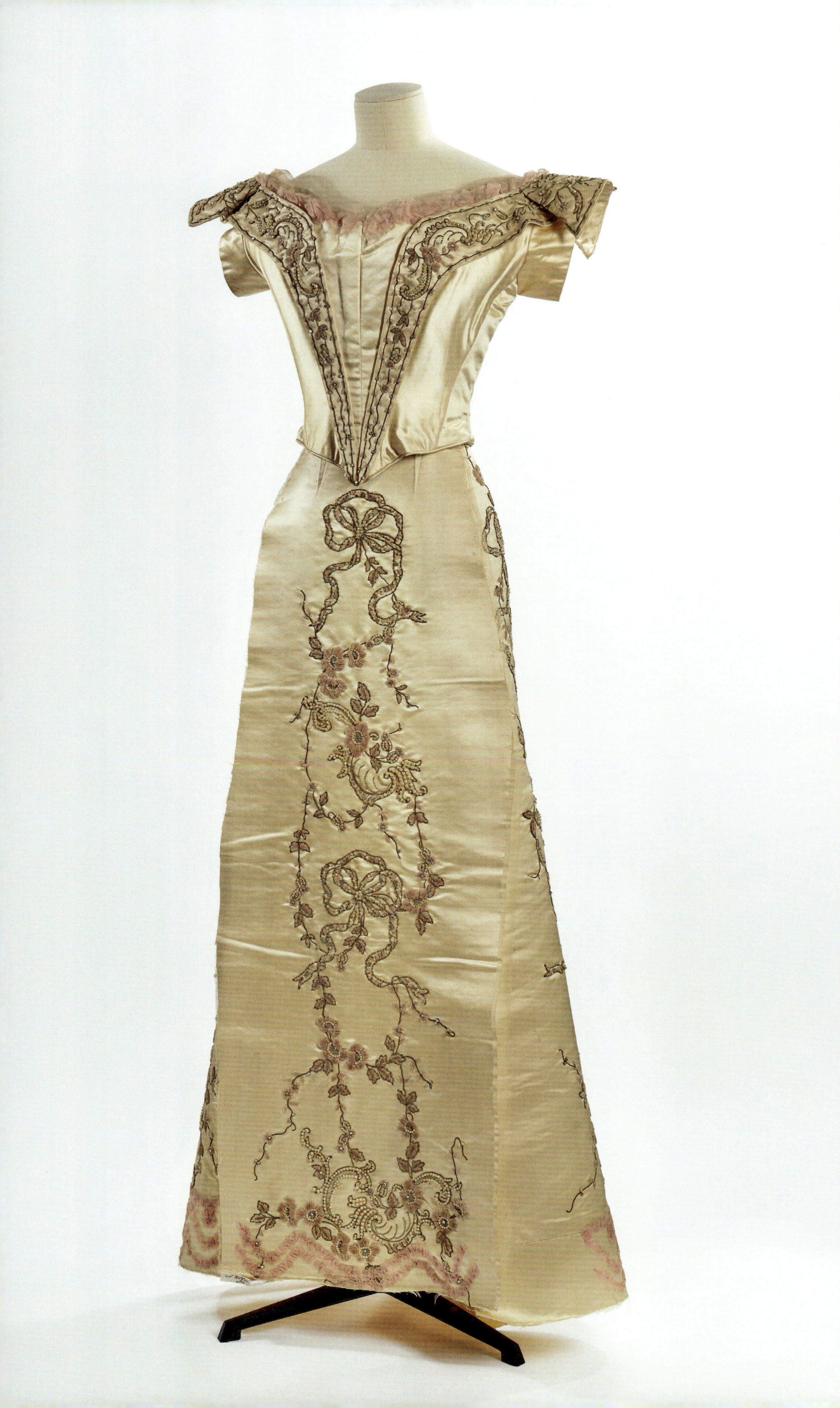

# MAKING AND ALTERING

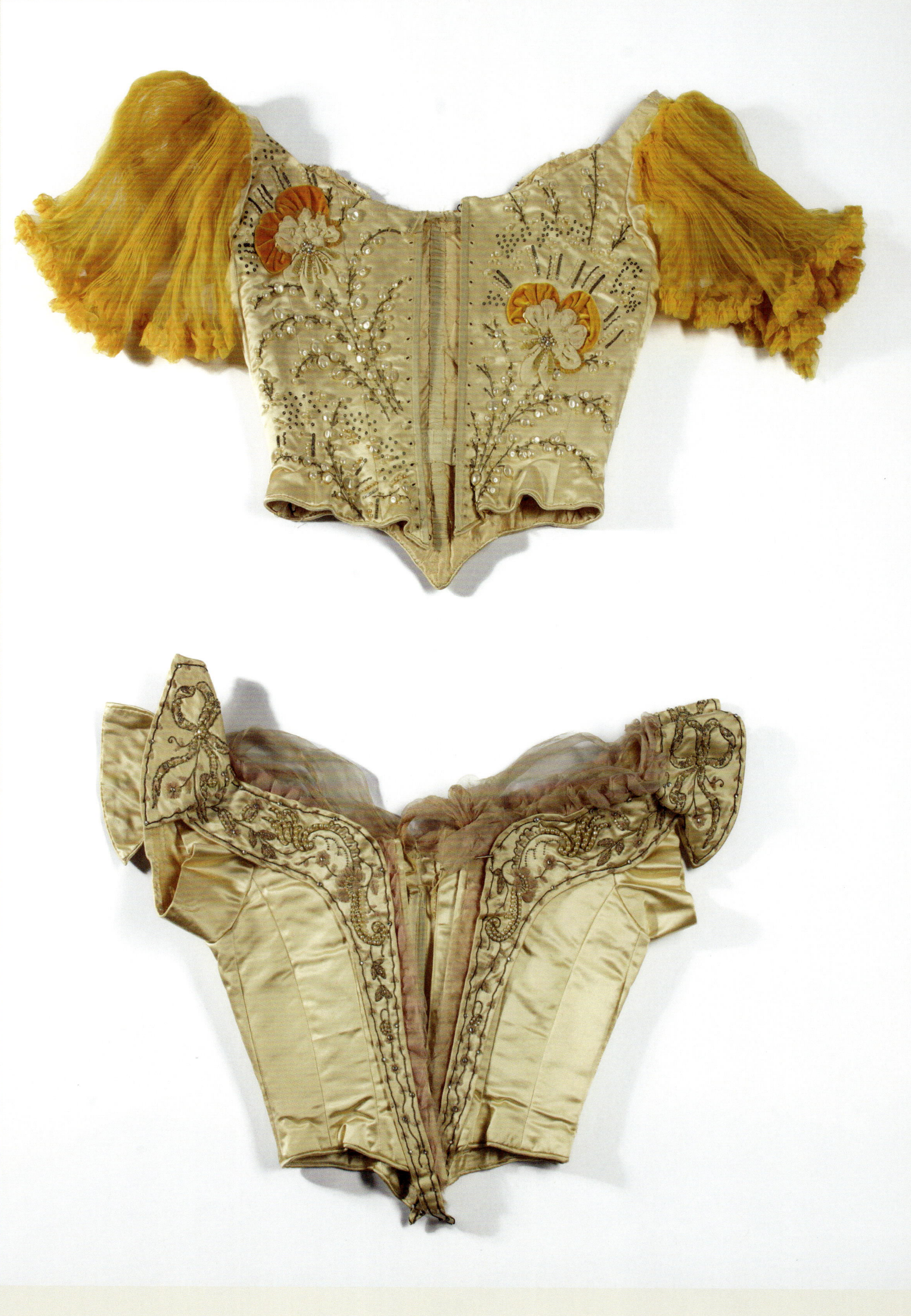

# REPAIRING AND 'REFRESHING'

At court, one was expected to wear appropriate clothing for every occasion. This was no simple matter, especially given the fact that many posts were honorary, and therefore unsalaried. Henriette van de Poll, lady-in-waiting to Queen Emma, wrote in May 1880 that 'concerns regarding outfits are most certainly the greatest difficulty in our position'. Henriette had just been appointed, and described in letters to her mother how she and fellow lady-in-waiting Elise van Ittersum often had to be very creative with money. In 1880, for example, they each decided to buy a gown for 80 guilders from Hague fashion store Trippelvitz, consisting of a satin bodice and a skirt in the cheaper tarlatan, saving themselves 60 guilders. Henriette reasoned that she could always order some silk later and have their dressers make skirts for them.[1]

Henriette's dressers – first Cécile and later Daatje – made many garments for her, but above all they altered many items, making small adjustments such as taking in a bodice, as well as major alterations, completely 'remodelling' an entire garment. An old 'sortie' (capelet) was transformed, with just a few adjustments and the addition of a fur trim, into an entirely new mantle. Hundreds of Henriette's letters have survived, and they indicate that she also altered dresses herself, particularly the decoration. This was a time-consuming activity, as she herself pointed out: 'there is always something to repair or refresh'.[2] Almost all of the dresses that once belonged to Henriette that are now in the collection at Kunstmuseum Den Haag have been altered, which was certainly not uncommon for the time, given that fabric was more expensive than labour.[3] With their limited clothes budget, gifts from the queen in the form of discarded clothes were always welcome.[4] For the investiture in 1898 Queen Emma actually gave her ladies-in-waiting extra funds, 500 guilders each, on one condition: that the gowns they chose be shown to her for approval. Henriette was secretly pleased about this, because 'then I shall be sure that the QR [Queen Regent] will like my gown'.[5] Following this generous gift, Henriette placed a large order with the Brussels fashion house run by Mme Van der Taelen. The bill, which has survived, shows that she not only ordered new gowns, but also had certain items repaired.[6] When the order arrived, Henriette was not entirely happy. She thought the bodice of the grey gown was too sparsely decorated, and other items were also somewhat disappointing. She wrote, 'I hope I shall not make too poor an impression among the others, and am remaining as calm as possible about the matter'.[7] Her concerns seem to have been unfounded, as her sister Joanna remarked after the investiture, 'you had great success with all your new gowns'.[8]

Besides Van der Taelen, Mme Coche's Brussels fashion house was another favourite of Henriette's. Correspondence with her sisters shows that Mme Coche travelled regularly to the Netherlands to meet her clients.[9] Besides making new gowns, Mme Coche also did alterations. Kunstmuseum Den Haag's collection includes several dresses made by Mme Coche that were made from older garments.[10] This is also reflected in the letters between Henriette and her sisters. In 1897, for example, Joanna told her sister that Mme Coche would be able to do a wonderful job of altering a gown from Henriette for her. On the same visit, her sister had sent Henriette some fabric samples, including a purple and white striped fabric which her sister and Mme Coche thought very suitable for her age and 'absolutement pas de deuil' ('absolutely not mourning').[11] Correspondence with her sisters also suggests that they regularly borrowed each other's accessories, including feathers, hats and mourning jewellery, and also bodices and coats.[12]

While in 1880 the younger Henriette regarded her 'concerns regarding outfits' as her greatest worry, she gradually became more relaxed about the matter. Just before Wilhelmina's wedding in 1901, she wrote, 'things are still proceeding slowly with my outfits, but they will fall into place'.[13]
—TW

**Two evening gown bodices ◆**
Worn by Lady Henriette van de Poll (1853-1946), lady-in-waiting to Queen Emma Brussels, Madame van der Taelen, circa 1900
Maker unknown, circa 1900
Silk, metal
Kunstmuseum Den Haag

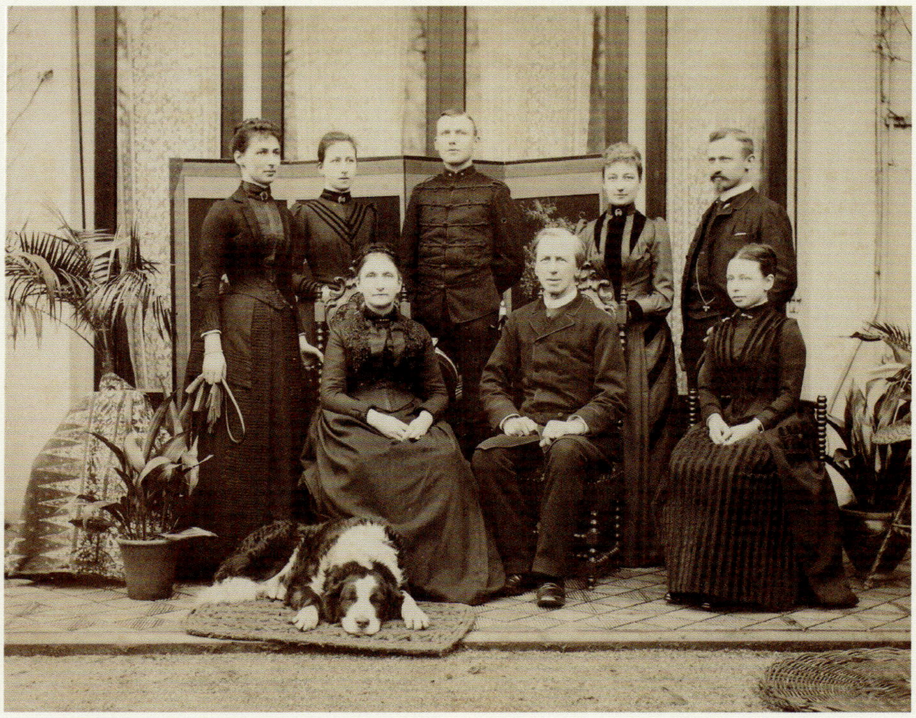

**Portrait of the Van der Poll family, Henriette is standing on the right.**
Unknown photographer, circa 1890.
RKD – National Institute for Art History, The Hague

**Two evening gown bodices (one inside out) and parts of skirt ◆**
Worn by Lady Henriette van de Poll (1853-1946), lady-in-waiting to Queen Emma
Maker unknown, circa 1895-1900
Silk, metal
Kunstmuseum Den Haag

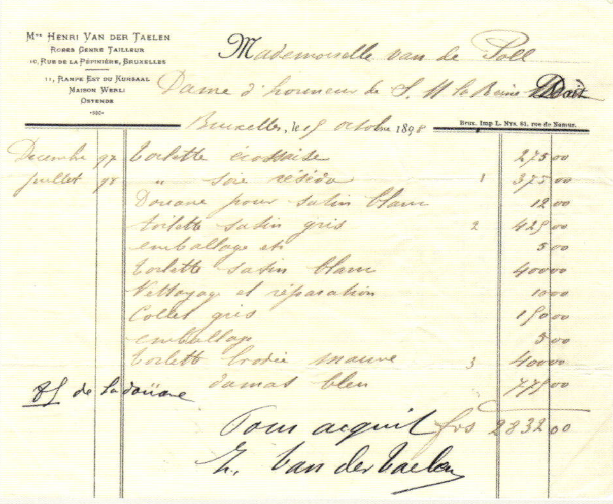

Mme Henri Van der Taelen
Robes Genre Tailleur
10, Rue de la Pépinière, Bruxelles
11, Rampe Est du Kursaal
Maison Werli
Ostende

Mademoiselle van de Poll
Dame d'honneur de S. M. la Reine Doit

Bruxelles, le 15 octobre 1898

Brux. Imp L. Nys, 61, rue de Namur.

| | | | |
|---|---|---|---|
| Décembre 97 | toilette écossaise | | 275 00 |
| juillet 98 | " soie résida | 1 | 375 00 |
| | Douane pour satin blanc | | 12 00 |
| | toilette satin gris | 2 | 425 00 |
| | emballage etc | | 5 00 |
| | toilette satin blanc | | 400 00 |
| | Nettoyage et réparation | | 10 00 |
| | Collet gris | | 150 00 |
| | emballage | | 3 00 |
| | toilette brodée mauve | 3 | 400 00 |
| 8 f de la douane | damas bleu | | 775 00 |

Pour acquit frs 2832 00
H. van der Taelen

**Bill**
Bill from Mme Henri Van der Taelen `
for an order placed by Van de Poll in 1898
Zeist municipal archives

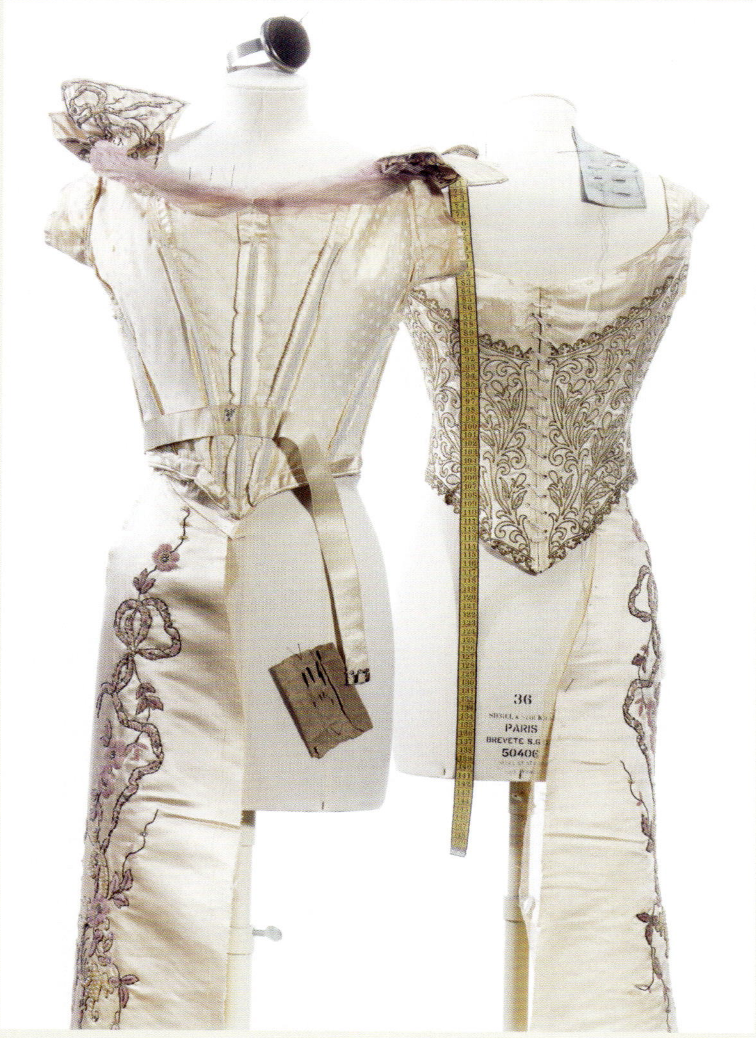



**Two evening gown bodices and parts of skirt ◆**
Worn by Lady Henriette van de Poll (1853-1946), lady-in-waiting to Queen Emma
Brussels, Madame van der Taelen, circa 1900 Maker unknown, circa 1900
Silk, metal
Kunstmuseum Den Haag

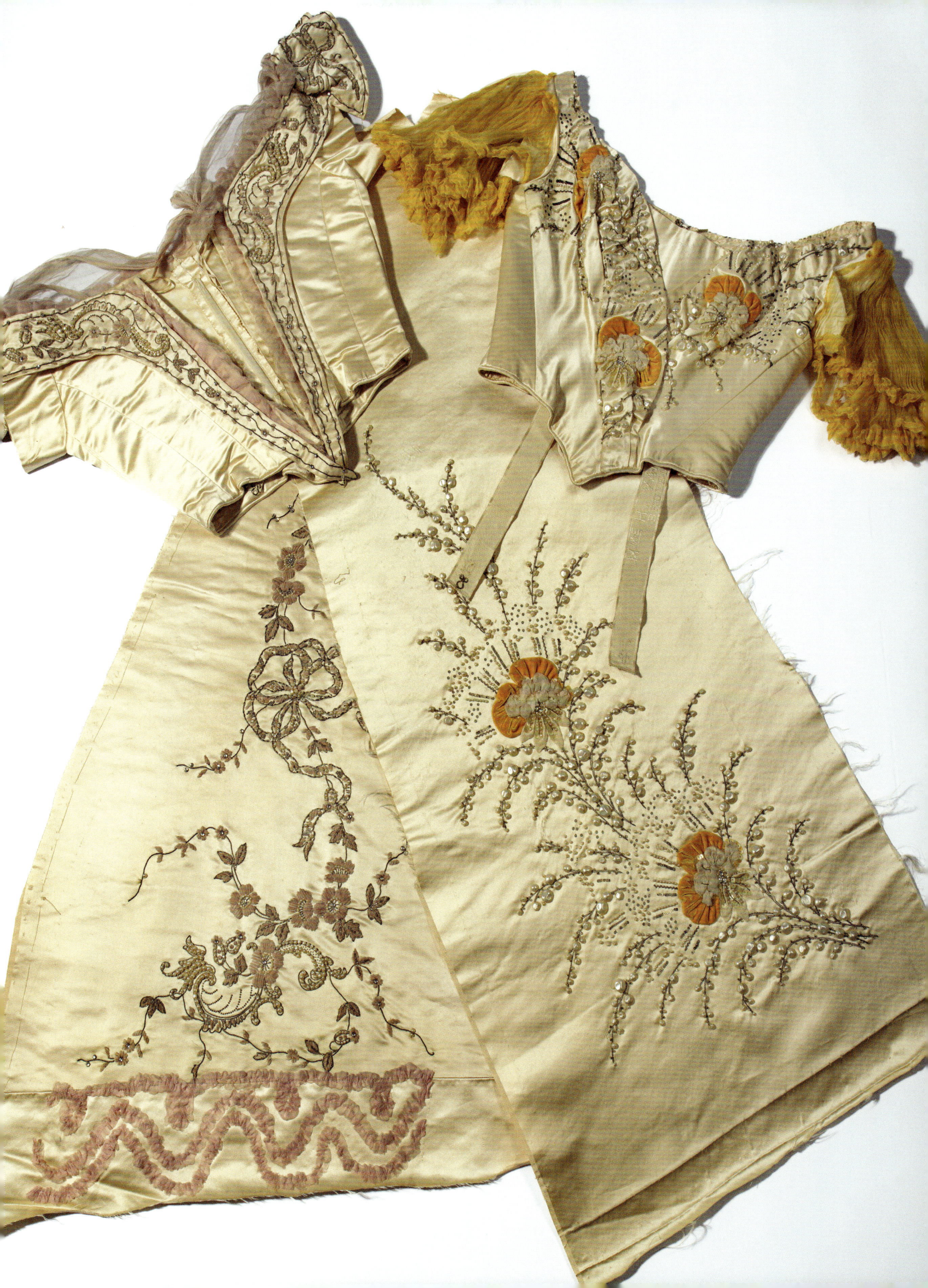

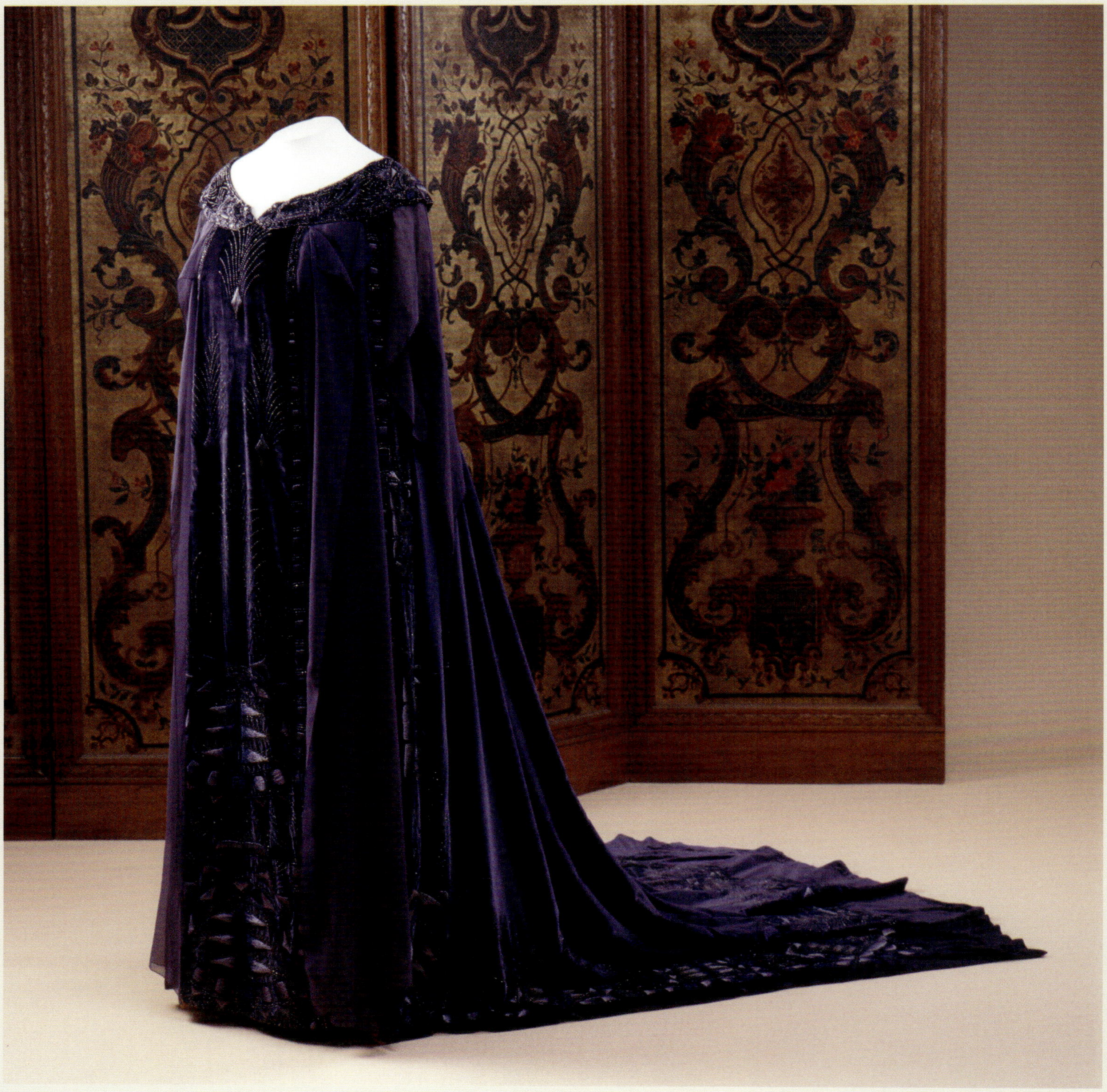

# EMMA'S ALTERED EVENING DRESS

Though Queen Emma, Queen Wilhelmina and Princess Juliana ordered fashionable dresses from Paris fashion houses, it cost less to select a dress from a French fashion magazine and have it copied by one's dresser or regular seamstress, in the atelier at the palace. The Dutch court was thrifty, so special expensive items would often be worn more than once, and dresses would be altered to suit a new occasion, or to conform to changing tastes and figures. One good example is an early 20th-century purple velvet evening dress – later altered – that Emma ordered from the Paris fashion house Nicaud. Emma was often photographed in it, always in black-and-white. The evening dress with train and other surviving garments that belonged to Emma show that she seemed to have a preference for purple, a colour that was popular among older ladies. Purple was also regarded as a colour of mourning.

The original slender bodice with a low neckline was retained, as was an embroidered band of velvet with beaded embroidery, a band of plain velvet and the lilac satin underskirt. A 'gala' dress code meant that the ladies at court had to wear a dress with a low-cut neckline and short sleeves. Older ladies who may have felt that their cleavage was no longer so lovely and youthful were also expected to conform. As she aged, therefore, Queen Emma continued to adhere to this traditional dress code. For a family party where 'evening dress' rather than 'gala' was required, she would turn to her by now rather old-fashion dress from Paris, showing as little flesh as possible. Queen Emma wore the purple evening dress at Queen Wilhelmina and Prince Hendrik's silver wedding party at Paleis Het Loo on 6 February 1926, for which it was altered to its current form: an overdress with a rectangular train and a flat velvet collar. The skirt falls open at the front and has embroidered edges in the Art Deco style of the 1920s. A visible underskirt was therefore needed.

The fact that parts of the original version of Queen Emma's purple evening dress have survived is evidence of the Queens' frugal tendencies. Emma, Wilhelmina and Juliana regularly had their dresses altered. Clothes worn at court were expensive, but a few major alterations could create an entirely new design. Queen Wilhelmina bought dresses from the Amsterdam fashion house Hirsch & Cie from time to time.[1] Some of them were later sent back for alterations. The grandson of one of the directors of Hirsch recalled the stories told within the family about the frugality of Queen Wilhelmina's court. 'Each strip of fabric that was removed had to be returned to Het Loo with the new design, along with the replaced buttons, piping, lace frills and even the remains of yarn used to sew the altered dress. If a reel of yarn was missing, a claim would immediately be submitted by a lady-in-waiting.'[2] Frugality with foresight: all the remnants were kept with the dress in case further alterations had to be made.
—PR

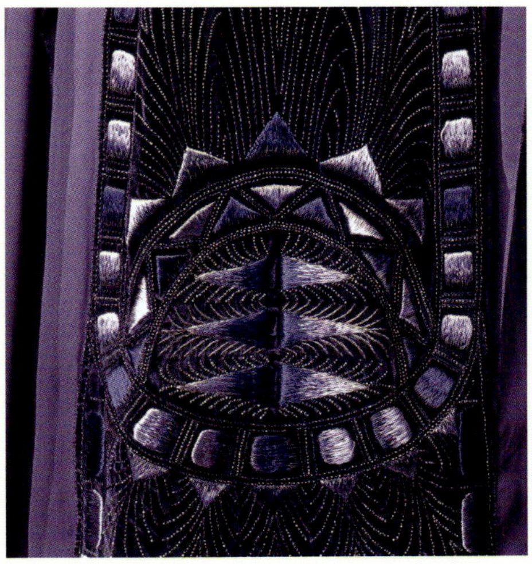

**Purple velvet evening dress belonging to Queen Emma ◆**
Paris, Nicaud Paris, circa 1900, altered circa 1925
Silk, beads
Paleis Het Loo, on long-term loan from the Royal Collections, The Hague

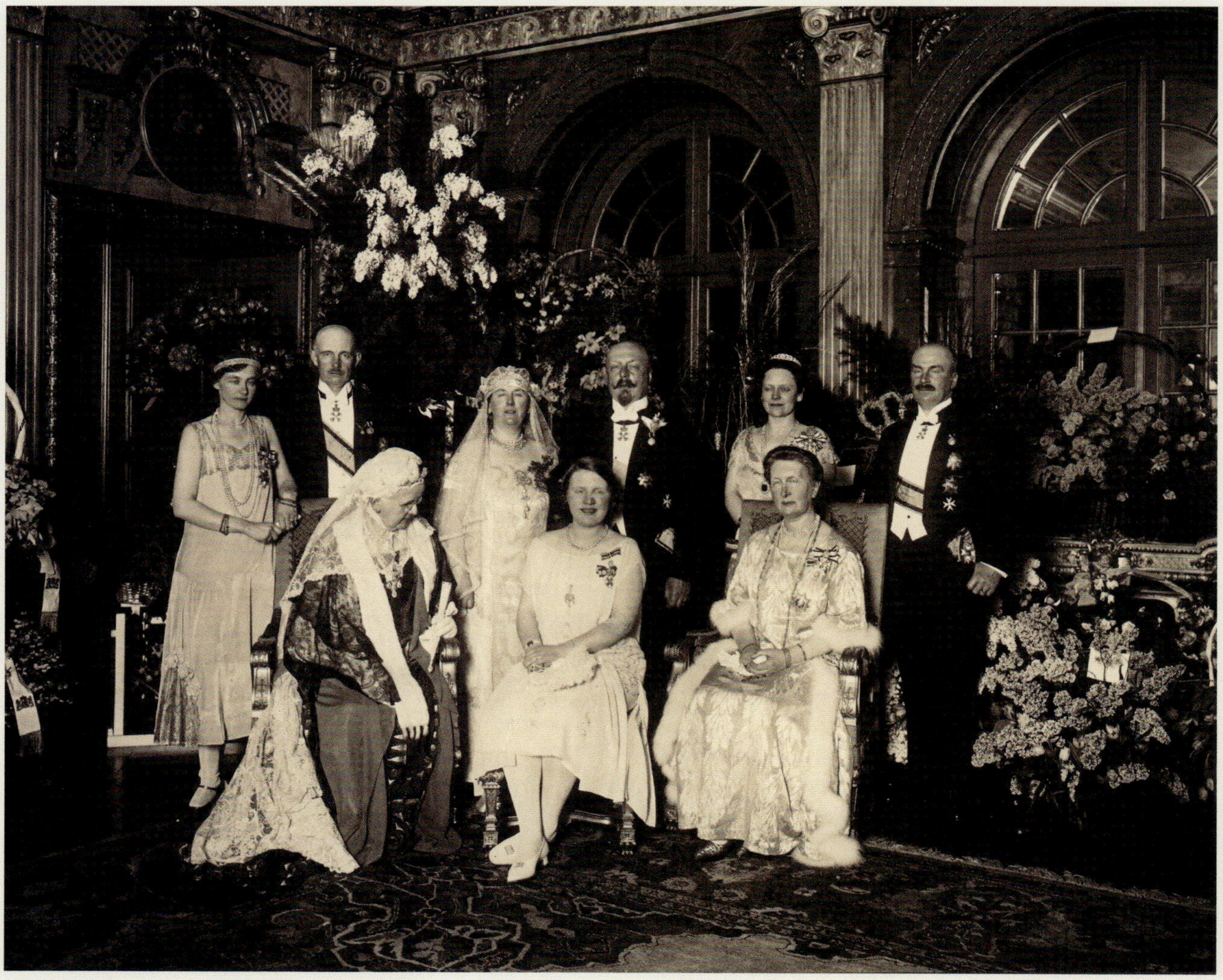

**Queen Emma at the silver wedding party in 1926 ◆**
Before the party in the main dining hall of Paleis Het Loo, the assembled company posed for a photograph in the vestibule. On the front row to the left, in front of the couple themselves, is Queen Emma wearing her purple evening dress. The Queen Mother, who was 67 at the time, also wore a black lace and ermine stole. Her long white lace veil was attached to the tiara from the jewellery set supplied by Parisian jeweller Mellerio.

Photo W.J.H. Coret, 1926
Royal Collections, The Hague

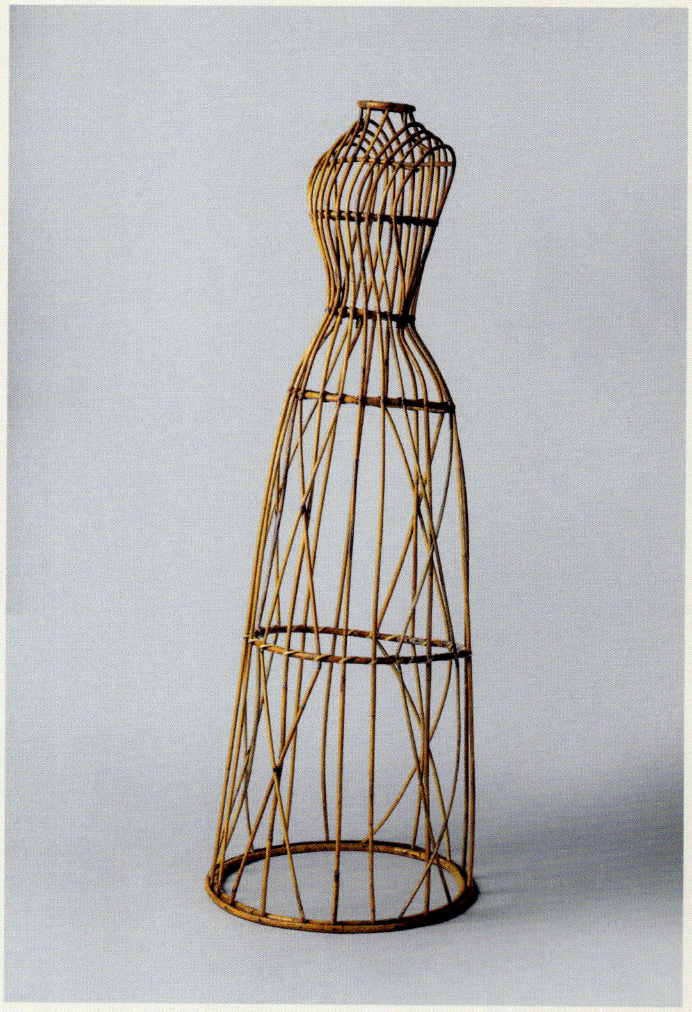

**Wilhelmina's mannequin ◆**
It was not only the sewing atelier at Hirsch & Cie that used 'mannequins' to fit their designs to Queen Wilhelmina's figure. The seamstresses at court who made dresses for the queen also used them. They would be covered in fabric so that pins could be stuck in them.

Probably Mandenmakersfabriek erven
N. van Vliet, The Hague, circa 1900
Rattan
Paleis Het Loo

**Parts of a ballgown ◆**
On her daughter's wedding day, Queen Emma wore a ballgown with an embroidered wisteria motif on a cream silk background. The dress was later dismantled and adapted to suit changing tastes.

Unknown fashion house, 1900-1901
Silk, glass, silver thread, glass pearls
Paleis Het Loo, on long-term loan
from the Royal Collections, The Hague

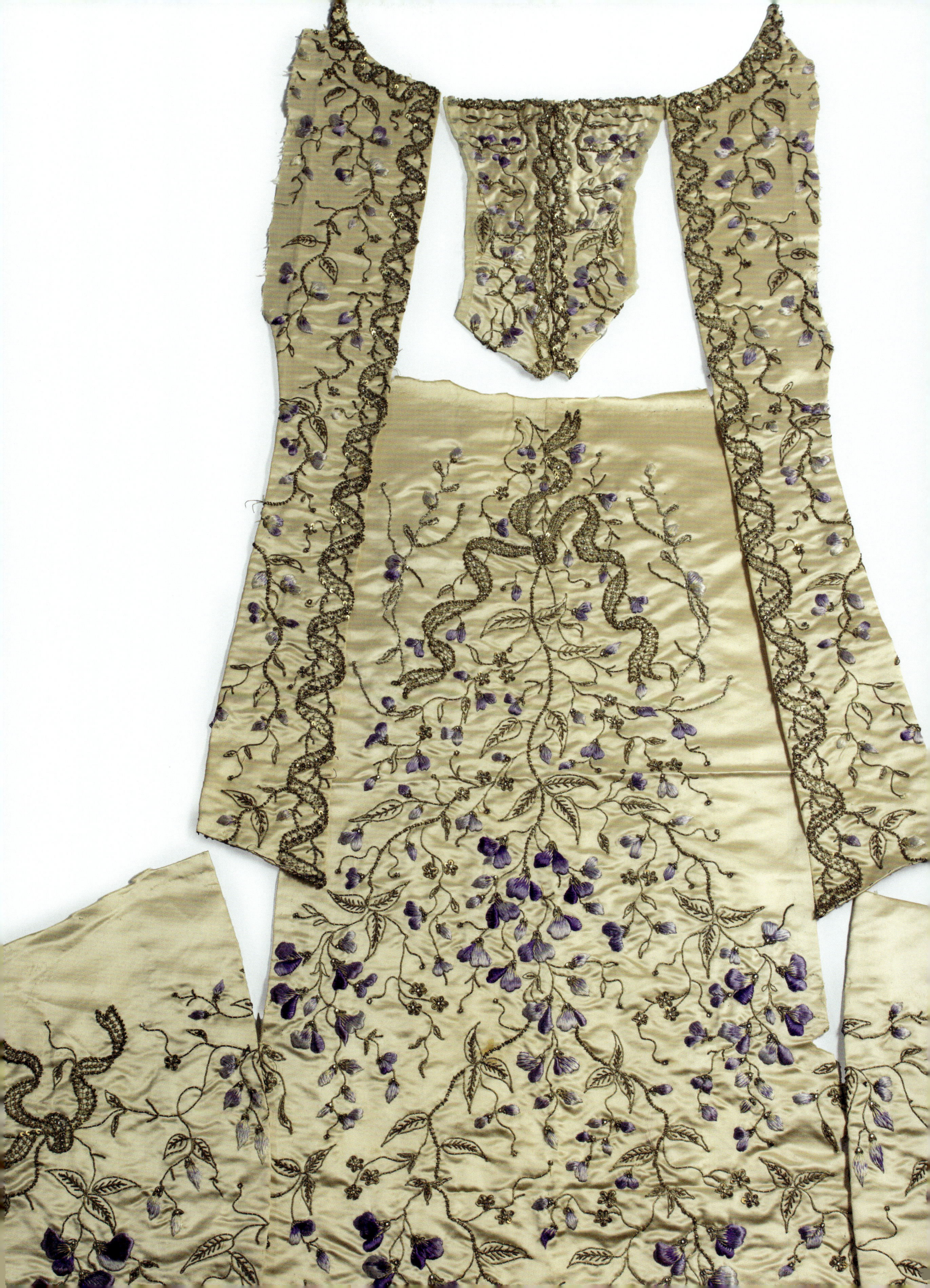

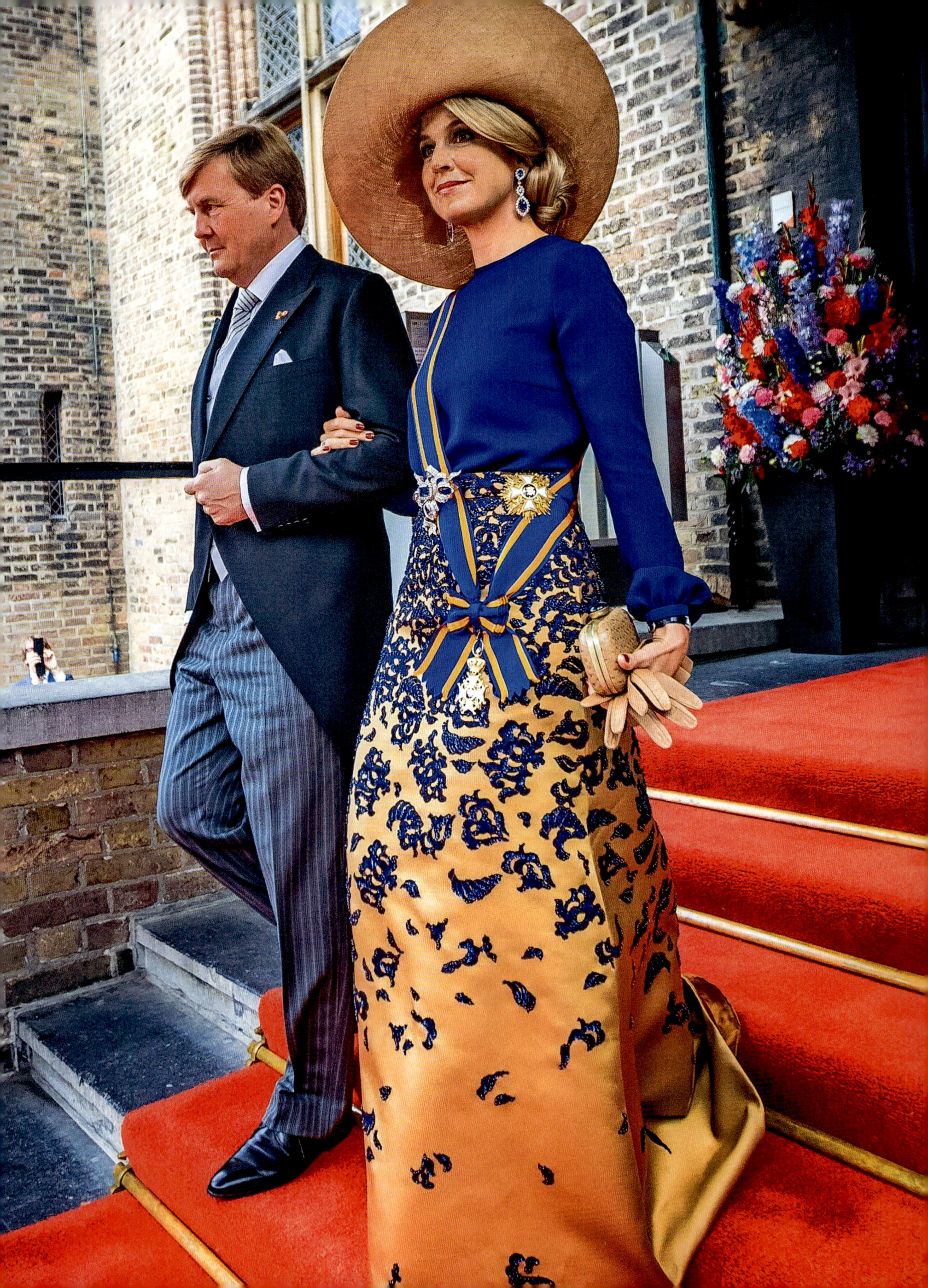

# FROM COURT CULTURE TO POP CULTURE

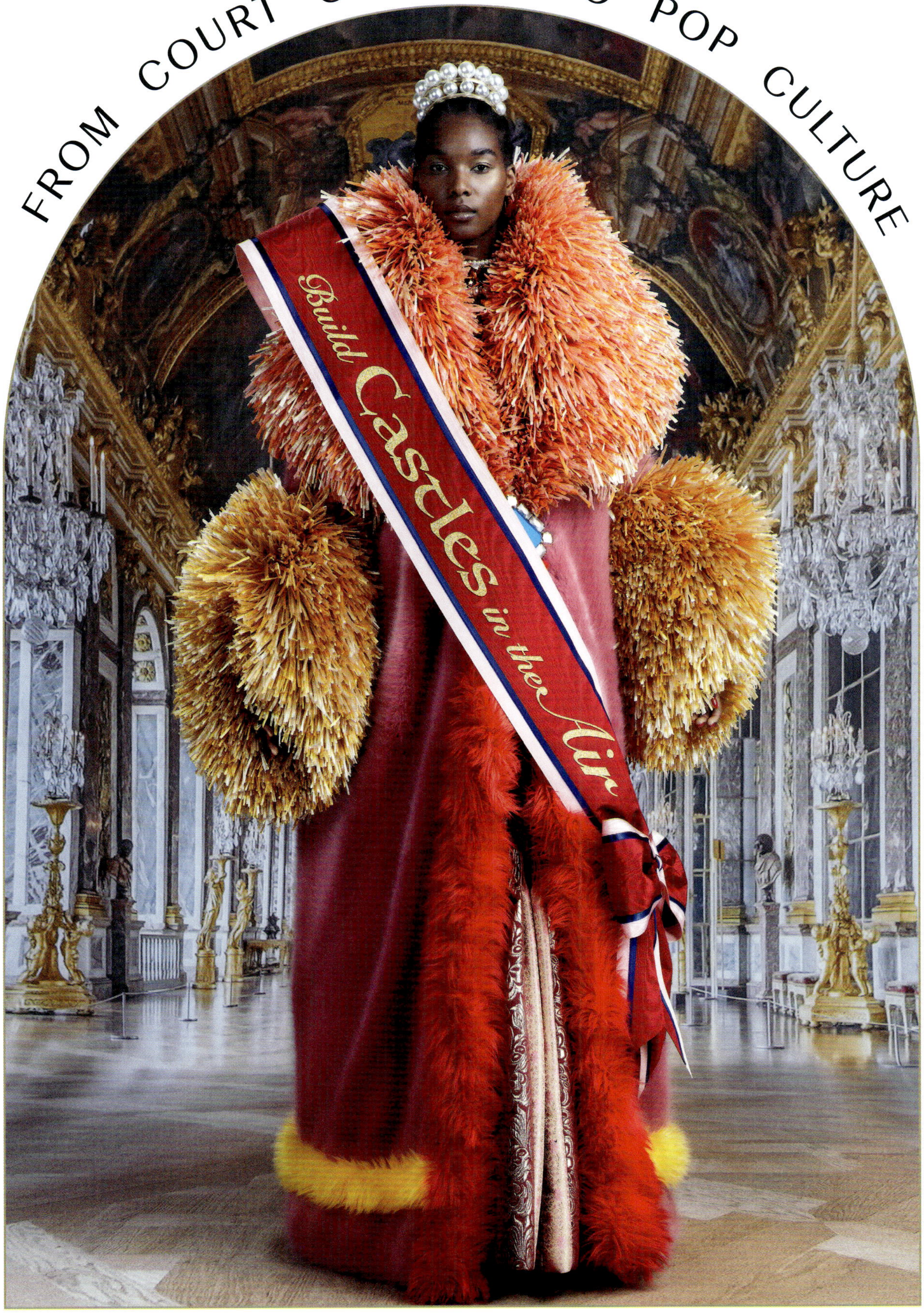


MADELIEF HOHÉ

← ← King Willem-Alexander and Queen Máxima on Prinsjesdag 2016. The king is wearing a morning suit, Queen Máxima is wearing an evening dress by Claes Iversen. Courtesy of Her Majesty Queen Máxima, Royal Collections, The Hague ◆

← 'Build Castles in the Air' ensemble by Viktor&Rolf, autumn/winter 2021, courtesy of Viktor&Rolf, Amsterdam ◆

## Tradition and innovation

*'The wedding was at noon. At 72nd Street and Madison, where the bride was dressing at her mother's house, the crowds started to gather before 9 a.m. and soon lined the entire route to St Thomas Church, twenty blocks away at 53rd Street and Fifth Avenue. At 72nd Street, no-one was allowed within a hundred and fifty feet of Alva Vanderbilt's new home, but all kind of tactics were deployed by certain individuals determined to subvert the rules. By 10.30 a.m. the crowd had grown to around two thousand people, and windows in every house in the neighbourhood were crammed with spectators enjoying small private parties of their own.' [...] the New York Times noted that halfway down the block towards Park Avenue, women could be seen standing in bay windows peering through opera glasses for glimpses of the bridal party.'*[1]

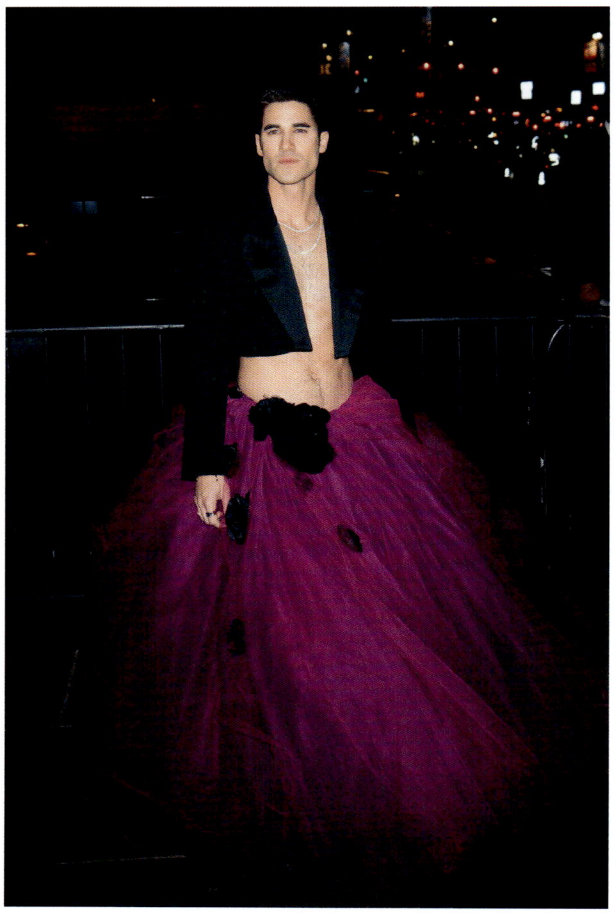

Darren Criss wearing an evening ensemble by Christian Siriano, 2024, at the CFDA Fashion Awards 2024 in New York, courtesy of Christian Siriano, New York ◆

This could be a description of a royal wedding, or a modern celebrity sighting, but it is in fact a report of a society wedding in New York in 1895 where, on 6 November, the spectacularly wealthy Consuelo Vanderbilt married the Brit Charles Spencer-Churchill, 9th Duke of Marlborough. The American bride was from a 'self-made' family, and was marrying a 'titled' British man for reasons of status. His wife's dowry would finally enable the aristocratic British bridegroom to renovate the family home, Blenheim Palace.[2] Such alliances between 'new money' from America and 'titles' from the old world occurred in what came to be known as the 'gilded age' (the late 19th century). The wealthy American brides were referred to in the press as 'the dollar princesses'.[3] It is fascinating to see how the press, and the public, treated these wealthy families like American royalty. The media devoted many column inches to American society life, and plenty of the newly wealthy were happy to cooperate.

Fashion reports such as these were actually part of a long tradition. The earliest fashion magazines of the 18th century emerged from detailed reports in the newspapers on the clothes worn at court, which people loved to read even back then.[4] The new media of the 19th century, including magazines, and the emerging art of photography, bolstered this tradition. The mother of bride Consuelo Vanderbilt even went so far as to send her daughter's underwear to American fashion magazine Vogue, where an illustration was made and published as part of her costly trousseau. Detailed descriptions subsequently appeared in the press, emphasising how expensive everything was. 'It is delightful to know that the clasps of Miss Vanderbilt's stocking supporters are of gold, and that her corset-covers and chemises are embroidered with rosebuds in relief.'[5] Talk about royalty!

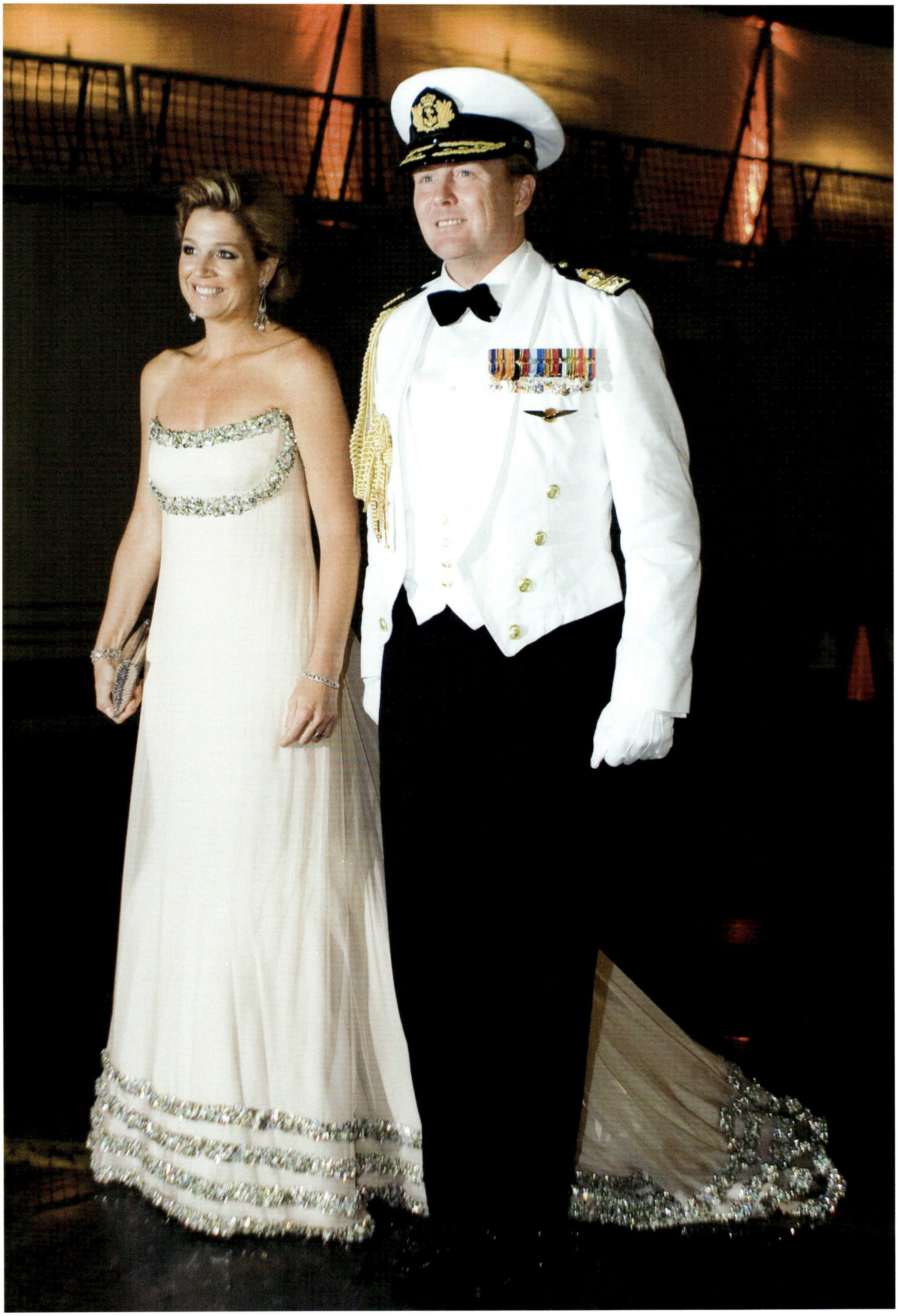

Queen Máxima wearing an evening dress by Jan Taminiau and King Willem-Alexander in the white dress uniform (tropical version) of the Royal Navy, attending the gala dinner on HNLMS Tromp in New York, 13 September 2009. Courtesy of Their Majesties King Willem-Alexander and Queen Máxima, Royal Collections, The Hague ◆

## Dressed like royalty

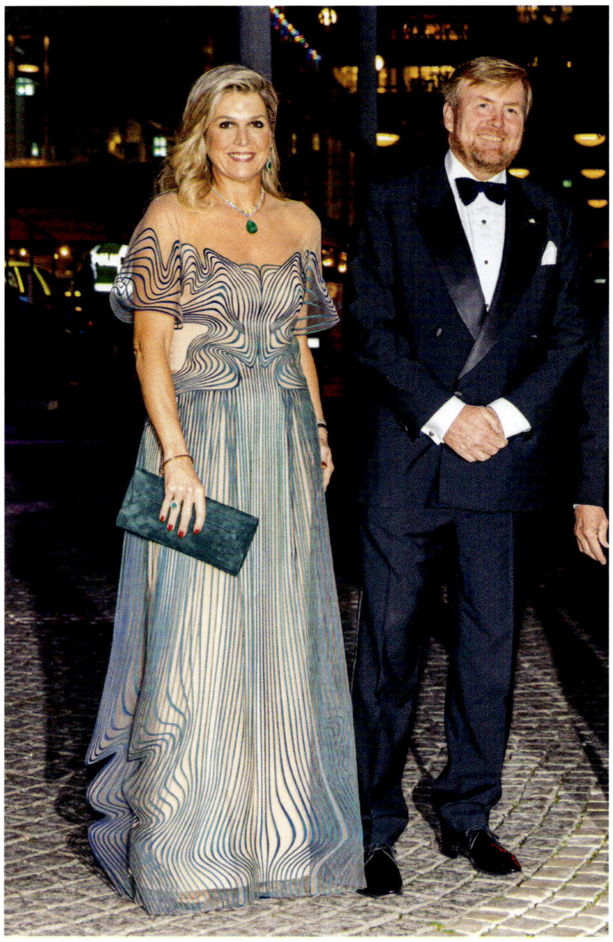

Queen Máxima wearing a design by Iris van Herpen during the state visit to Sweden, 12 October 2022. The queen had previously worn this dress at her 50th birthday celebrations in 2021. Courtesy of Her Majesty Queen Máxima, Royal Collections, The Hague ◆

Opulent, fashionable outfits equal to those worn by European royals were part of the image of high society. It is no coincidence that, in this gilded age, American women were among the leading clients of Paris couture houses, which dressed them like new royals. In the absence of a royal family in America, wealthy American women did not need to hold back or refrain from eclipsing the queen with their lavish outfits. Nothing therefore stopped them from flaunting their wealth, and even dressing as if they were royalty. The leading high-society families were the Vanderbilts, the Astors, the Whitneys, the Coulds, the Carnegies, the Morgans and the Rockefellers.[6] Their recently acquired wealth was reflected in the extravagant houses they had built, with equally extravagant interiors and over-the-top lifestyles, as well as, of course, in the clothes they wore. The newly wealthy aspired to the visual image projected by the kings and queens of Europe. Their clothing style imitated the court dress codes at royal courts. Low-cut gowns, long trains, gloves, opulent embroidery - you name it. As in previous centuries, clothes were used to signal membership of a particular group. Fashionable clothes were also used - deliberately or otherwise - to exclude others who could not afford such a sumptuous lifestyle.

The newly wealthy bought from famous couturiers in Paris like Charles Frederick Worth, Maison Paquin, Redfern and Doucet. Couturier Worth was delighted with his American clientele, who spent more than many royal families. 'Worth says that American women are the best customers he has - far better than queens. They ask the price: American women never do. They simply say, "Give me the best, the most beautiful, the most fashionable gown".'[7] American men also imitated the well-known traditions of royal courts, ordering bespoke clothes, like the traditional morning dress, frock coat and and morning suit. The dinner jacket gained in popularity in the 1920s, a tradition that would continue as 'black tie' after the Second World War. It was frequently worn, in combination with cocktail dresses for women, which were shorter than traditional evening dresses. Long evening gowns continued to be worn, alongside gentlemen in morning suits, a dress code known as white tie. And of course the best 'accessory' for a wealthy American woman was a genuine British 'titled' spouse beside her.

## The advent of celebrity culture

In the 19th century, the couturiers of Paris were proud to dress not only royals and other society figures - whether from old or new money - but also famous actresses, the 'it girls' of their day. Though many of them are now forgotten, a couturier like Charles Frederick Worth derived a lot of status from the fact that he dressed world-famous actresses and opera stars like Sarah Bernhardt.[8] Since actresses generally had to pay for their wardrobes themselves, they often chose clothes they could wear on stage and when out in public. Another fascinating aspect is the popularity of 'dressing-up costumes' in the 19th century. There were many costume balls, for which the costumes ordered were often more expensive than the outfits for a fashionable ball. To our way of thinking, a fancy dress party is not such a serious matter, but in the 19th century these events were an important part of society life. The Dutch elite and royal family also loved fancy dress parties and costume balls. They dressed as historical characters, often kings or queens, adding a little extra shine to their background and status. Society and fancy dress parties were much more intertwined, and were also associated in a natural way with the world of haute couture and the theatre. The influence of theatre and stage jewellery was in fact much greater than we realise today. The extravagant costumes worn by actresses and opera stars in the 19th century influenced fashion. The over-the-top fake jewellery they wore on stage led to the rise of 'costume jewellery', the fashionable fake jewels that Coco Chanel used to accessorise her little black dresses in the 1920s and 30s.[9] Fashion items would sometimes be worn on stage in historical plays, and Queen Wilhelmina also occasionally gave away a gown for this purpose. So it was that one of the queen's court dresses ended up as a semi-18th-century stage dress, that is now in the collection of Kunstmuseum Den Haag. Actress Theo Mann-Bouwmeester (1850-1939) wore it to great effect in her role as Madame de Pompadour in *Narcis*, performed in 1916 by the Dutch theatre company Nederlandsch Toneel.[10]

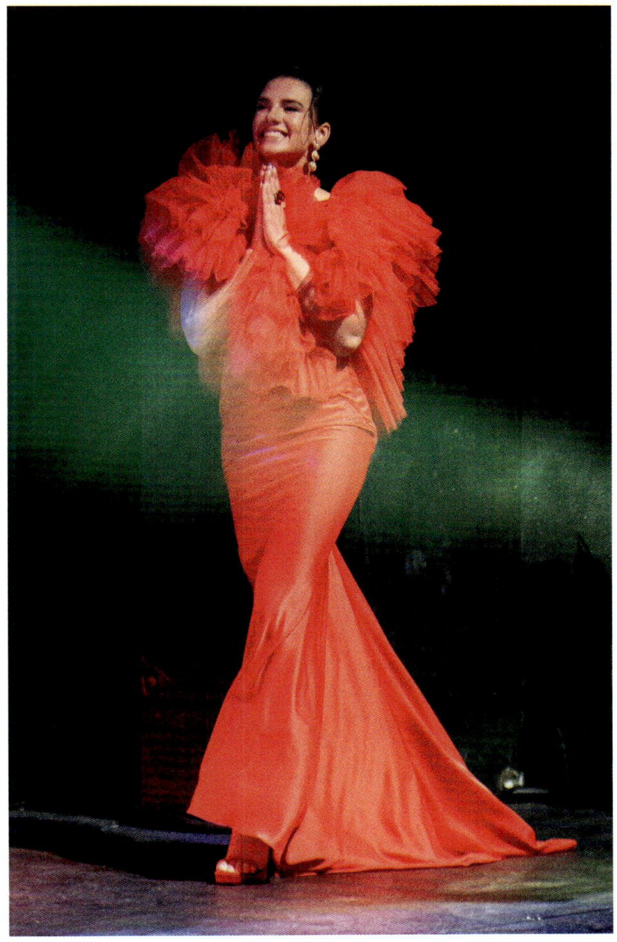

Maan wearing an evening dress by Edwin Oudshoorn, 'Thalassic' collection 2021, at the Edison Pop Awards 2022, courtesy of Edwin Oudshoorn, Leiden ◆

When cinema arrived, attention increasingly shifted from theatre and opera to film stars, who came to define tastes in fashion. We see this in the 1930s, when couturiers were in fact asked to help design film costumes. The 'red carpet dress' increasingly became a phenomenon. (Fun fact: the concept of 'red carpet treatment' originated in 1902, when the New York Central Railroad literally laid out a red carpet on the platform for passengers on the luxury train from New York to Chicago.[11]) This practice was eventually adopted by the film industry in 1922, and the 'red carpet moment' was born, and became a feature of galas, Oscar ceremonies and other glamorous events. In 1930s Hollywood some designers, like Americans Adrian and Edith Head, started specialising in film costumes.
In post-war America, French couture continued to influence the Hollywood film industry. Film star Audrey Hepburn became famous in outfits designed for her by couturier Hubert de Givenchy. She wore his couture designs both in her films and in her private life. Audrey Hepburn, whose mother was from a Dutch aristocratic family, did not dress any differently from her social peers – interesting to note if we consider the wardrobes of her contemporaries, the Dutch princesses at Paleis Soestdijk, and how they dressed in the 1960s. The wardrobes of this young film star and her royal contemporaries had in fact become completely interchangeable. The young Princess Beatrix was, for example, dressed by Maison Linette in Den Bosch. This fashion house, run by Lien Bergé-Farwick (1902-1980), made couture for Queen Juliana and her four daughters in the 1950s and 60s.[12] It appears on the buyers' lists of Maison Dior in Paris as early as autumn 1947.[13] This means that Maison Linette was able to make Paris couture for its Dutch clients under licence. Fabrics would be ordered from suppliers prescribed by the French couture house,

from which a Dutch copy of the French design would be made using a cotton toile. This had been a tradition in French couture since the 19th century. The 'American royal' Jackie Kennedy ordered her favourite Parisian couture designs in a similar way, through an American couture house.[14] The fact that she bought French couture was not mentioned, as critics had pointed out that, as first lady, Jackie Kennedy should really wear American fashion.

Jackie Kennedy became an important trendsetter, and her classic wardrobe of monochromatic outfits was emulated by many. For years afterwards, women like first lady Michelle Obama were inspired by the dress style of Jackie Kennedy, before developing their own distinctive style. Queen Máxima also appears to be a fan of the classic Jackie Kennedy style and her famous pillbox hats. This is reflected in a number of designs produced for her by fashion house Natan (Edouard Vermeulen) in Belgium, alongside influences from classic Dior and Balenciaga designs. Jackie Kennedy's status as an 'American royal' is also reflected in the references to her wedding dress in the design that John Galliano produced for Melania Knaus when she married businessman (and later president) Donald Trump in 2005. Jackie Kennedy wore her gown in 1953 when she married John F. Kennedy, who became president of the United States in 1961. It was designed by renowned African American designer Ann Lowe. Jackie Kennedy did not initially mention Lowe by name and, mortifyingly, she was described merely as 'a coloured dressmaker'.[15] The design that Galliano made for Melania Knaus, Trump's third wife, has very similar decoration to Jackie Kennedy's dress. Designer Galliano, for Christian Dior Haute Couture in Paris, incorporated similar large round rosettes into the skirt of the dress, which the media claimed cost over US$ 200,000 and weighed 25 kilos. Melania appeared on the cover of American *Vogue* wearing her extravagant bridal gown in 2005, in an apparent move to associate herself with the tradition of Jackie Kennedy, whom many Americans still regard as 'American royalty', just as the newly wealthy Americans of the gilded age imitated European royals.

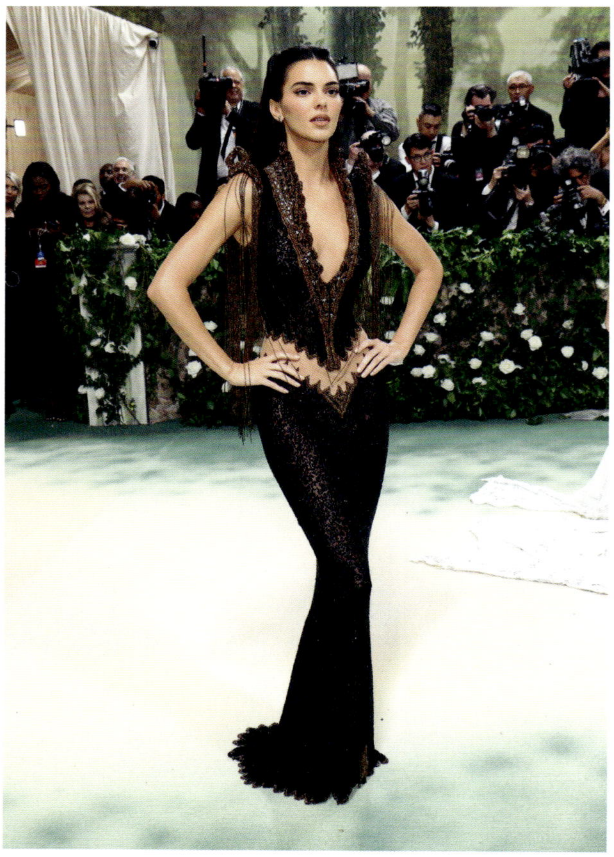

Kendall Jenner wearing an evening dress by Alexander McQueen for Givenchy, haute-couture collection autumn/winter 1999, at The Met Gala 2024 marking the exhibition *Sleeping Beauties: Reawakening Fashion*, courtesy of Givenchy, Paris ◆

## Princesses and film stars

One American film star who was not only seen as a classic, athletic beauty, but whose youthful and simple style appealed to many, was Grace Kelly. When she married Prince Rainier of Monaco in 1956, the movie princess suddenly became an actual princess, which only made her seem more glamorous. Her youthful, sporty style of dress was popular, and she too became a style icon. Princess Grace liked to wear clothes by French couturiers such as Christian Dior, Coco Chanel, Balenciaga, Givenchy and Yves Saint Laurent. Her hairstyles for special occasions were designed and created by the famous Parisian hair stylist Alexandre de Paris, who also designed a hairstyle for Princess Beatrix in the 1960s. Beatrix continued to wear her hair in this style for many years, and it eventually came to be known as the 'Beatrix coupe'. Princess Beatrix and her sisters – like Princess Grace of Monaco – lived through the era of more youthful fashions in the 1960s, the more relaxed 1970s with its flowing maxi dresses, and the more businesslike attire that became popular in the 1980s. Her death at a relatively young age means we recall Princess Grace of Monaco above all as a young woman in the prime of life. Princess Beatrix has been able to 'grow old gracefully', her wardrobe adapting to her age and her activities. Like Britain's Queen Elizabeth, Princess Beatrix drew a clear distinction between clothes for official duties, and the things she wore in private. Along with couturier Theresia Vreugdenhil, she developed the distinctive 'Beatrix look' in the 1980s and 90s, with respect for dress codes. Her wardrobe also includes outfits for private occasions, her outdoor outfits – like those of the late British head of state – very much in the tradition of the outdoor wear of yesteryear.

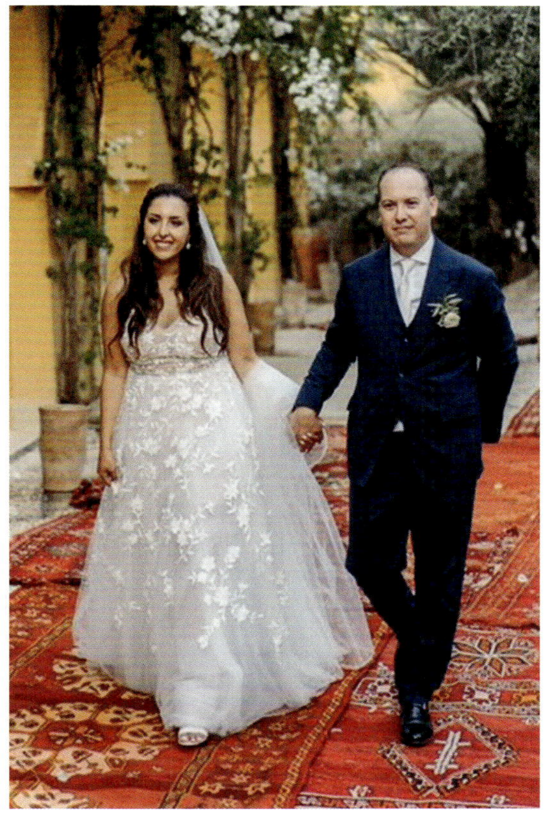

Wedding outfits worn by Hafida Abahai-Almarini and Mohamed Almarini, when they married in 2018. Hafida wore a custom-made gown by Oscar de la Renta ◆, and a white takchita, the traditional outfit for a Moroccan bride. Mohamed also wore both a western-style suit and a traditional Moroccan bridegroom's suit; courtesy of Hafida Abahai-Almarini and Mohamed Almarini

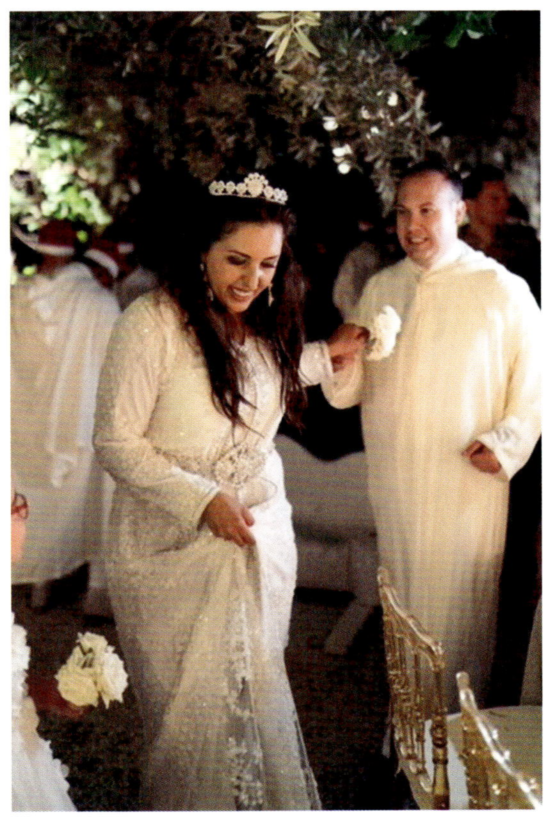

## Fashion for supermodels

While the 1960s and 70s were notable for the fashionable dress codes of film stars and royals, who brought glamour to fashion, the 1980s and 90s saw the growing influence of supermodels. They took over the roles of the stage actresses and film stars of the past, influencing fashion in their own way. They, too, emulated the old court culture, appearing at red carpet events in fabulous ballgowns with 'regal' trains, their hair up and bedecked with expensive jewellery (often borrowed). At important events, they became walking advertisements for the fashion houses with whom they worked to cultivate their 'look'. The Party of the Year, a fundraising event established by The Costume Institute of The Metropolitan Museum of Art in New York, which has raised funds for the costume department since 1948, evolved into a huge celebrity event in the 1990s. Since 1995, this annual fundraising dinner has been hosted by Anna Wintour, editor-in-chief of American *Vogue*, who helped to develop the celebrity cult of supermodels in the 1980s. With the advent of the internet and social media, reality TV stars and influencers are today's new celebrities. For many, what you wear is no longer a personal choice, but a question of collaboration with couture houses, with whom some celebrities sign a contract to become 'the face of'. The Met has been happily rolling out the red carpet since 2006, although since 2016 it has no longer actually been red, changing colour and design each year according to the theme of The Party of the Year.[16] These days, the dress codes that still apply at important events are more connected to the past than we might expect. Here, too, the royal dress codes of trains, low necklines and lavish embroidery are dominant. Anyone who wants to appear regal still puts their faith in the royal dress codes.

## From classic court culture to 'high & low'

While many, from 'new money' to film stars and influencers, presented themselves in accordance with royal dress codes in the 20th (and 21st) centuries, something else entirely was happening at the royal courts of Europe. The classic dress codes, including low-cut gowns for gala events, that applied at Queen Wilhelmina's wedding, would in fact go into decline at royal courts in the 20th century. This had everything to do with changes in general fashion and with the modernisation of old traditions that was gradually taking place. A simpler dress code was chosen for the ceremonial baptism of Wilhelmina's daughter Juliana in 1909, where ladies were required to wear the slightly more modern 'high neckline with hat'.[17] In 1937, too, at the wedding of Princess Juliana and Prince Bernhard, a more modern dress code applied for the ladies. The gentlemen wore the traditional black tie, while the ladies were asked to combine a long gown with a hat.[18] The bridegroom wore the uniform of a captain of the hussars,[19] while the bride was dressed in a fashionable gown of silk satin with a waterfall neckline, possibly designed by Maggy Rouff in Paris. We know that the gown was made by Kühne in The Hague, but the underdress has a label from fashion house Rouff.[20] This suggests that the dress may have been a Parisian design made under the couture licensing system at Maison Kühne. The princess's adult bridesmaids wore similar dresses in various pastel colours. This rainbow effect was Princess Juliana's idea.[21]

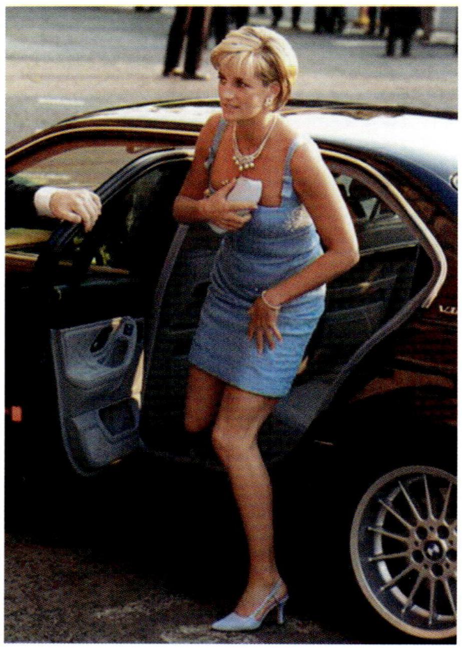

Princess Diana, London, 3 June 1997, wearing a dress by Jacques Azagury ◆

Prinses Juliana had a modern lifestyle, and like her peers she too went off to study. Her wardrobe, particularly the clothes she wore in private, changed with the times, and ranged from formal dress for official occasions to less formal for private moments or less official events. This was a result not only of her character – the princess on a bike – but also of the spirit of the times. A lot of court ceremony was abandoned in the 1930s, as befitted a time of economic crisis. After the Second World War, under the leadership of Queen Wilhelmina, the court was modernised and stripped of many of its trimmings. Queen Juliana continued this process after her investiture in 1948. Her daughters wore modern clothing, like their contemporaries. By now, fashion was so democratised that, for special occasions, the dress codes for film stars and princesses barely differed, as was also the case at times when it was appropriate to 'dress down'. Queen Beatrix wore businesslike outfits and retained the existing dress codes. By then, the monarch would be the only one wearing a long gown at grand ceremonies during the day, like Prinsjesdag, the official opening of Parliament, while guests would adhere to the 'tenue de ville' (formal daywear) dress code. Hats fell gradually out of fashion in the 1960s, but in the 1990s they became part of the tradition of Prinsjesdag once more. Indeed, this gave rise to a trend of wearing striking hat designs at this formal occasion, and in recent years hats and entire outfits have been used to make political or personal statements, as part of an entirely unique dress code tradition.

As fashion democratised in the 1960s, the influence of couture gradually declined, and boutiques and ready-to-wear increasingly set the tone. The way the crowned heads of Europe dressed also changed, partly as a reflection of the changing role of the royals in society. The public no longer appreciates too much distance between public and royalty, or excessive displays of wealth. In a modern monarchy, personal warmth and the human dimension, including in terms of lifestyle and clothes, have become gradually more important. Ceremonial display is now reserved for important occasions like an investiture or royal wedding. Otherwise, the royals dress much like you or I. Princess Diana was photographed in trendy sportswear in the 1990s, sparking a trend. The younger generations, like Princess Kate, Queen Máxima and Princess Amalia are known for wearing a lot of ready-to-wear clothes, as well as bespoke couture items. Meghan (Markle), Duchess of Sussex, often combines unique pieces with simple ready-to-wear items, which she herself describes as 'dressing high-low'.[22]
In reports on their outfits, royal dress watchers therefore always indicate where the clothes can be sourced, with the result that they often sell out immediately. Catherine, Duchess of Cambridge recently announced that she will no longer share information on who makes her outfits, as she believes it detracts attention from the purpose of the events she attends. Yet the reporting continues, and it is now simply a greater challenge for fashion journalists to be the first to report which label made a particular outfit. Countess Eloise of Orange-Nassau, who is of the same generation as Princess Amalia, has gone a step further in terms of royal innovation, by promoting 'vintage' clothing. She and her mother Princess Laurentien have opened vintage shops called My Lima Lima, where people can donate clothes that are sold as vintage, with the proceeds going to charity. Eloise's own style is difficult to copy because of her focus on vintage, making her all the more original and innovative among royalty.

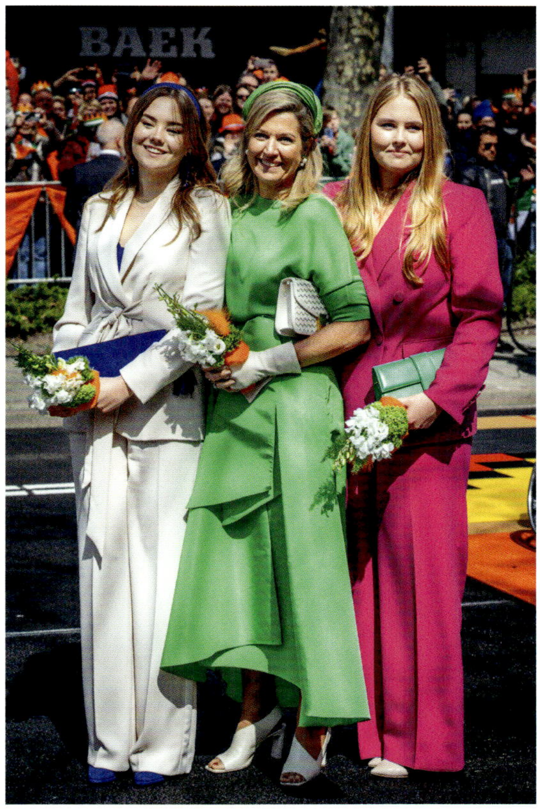

Princess Ariane, Queen Máxima and Princess Amalia in Rotterdam on King's Day 2023. Princess Amalia is wearing a trouser suit by Marina Rinaldi. Courtesy of HRH the Princess of Orange, Royal Collections, The Hague

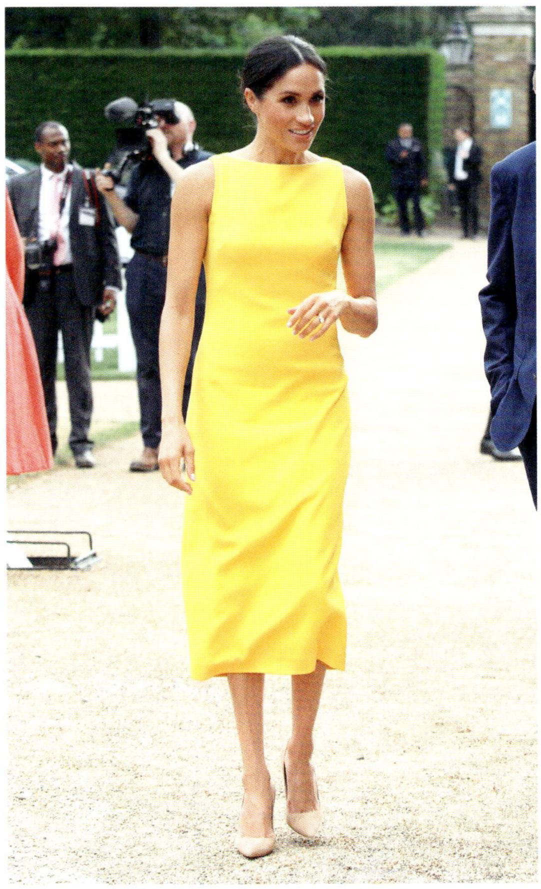

Meghan Markle, Duchess of Sussex, London, 5 July 2018, wearing a dress by Brandon Maxwell; same design courtesy of Sophie Huijts-Statema, London ◆

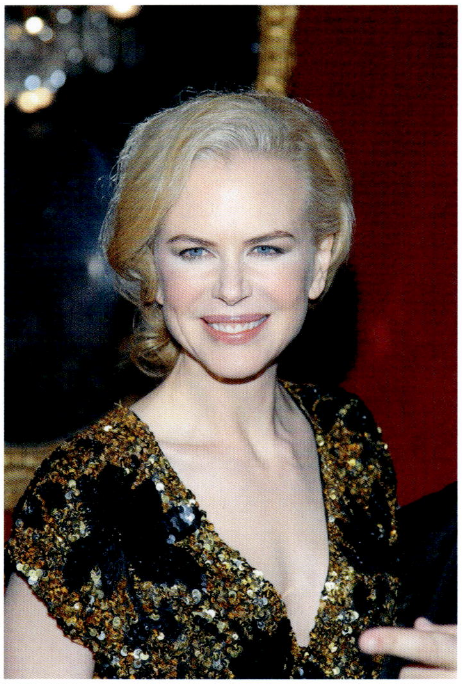

Nicole Kidman wearing an evening dress by Dries van Noten, Antwerp, spring/summer 2009, at the premiere of the film Australia, New York, 2008; same design on loan from Kunstmuseum Den Haag ◆

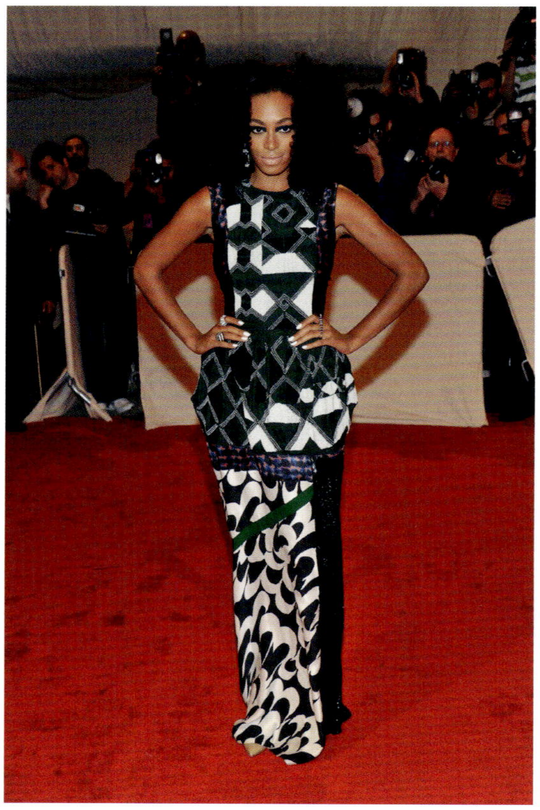

Solange Knowles wearing an evening dress by Dries van Noten, autumn/winter 2011, at The Met Gala 2011, marking the exhibition Alexander McQueen: Savage Beauty at The Metropolitan Museum of Art, autumn/winter 2011, courtesy of Dries van Noten, Antwerp ◆

## Fashion rebels

This brings us to those who break with dress codes, for rules are made to be broken. Many Dutch people will never forget the moment when Prince Claus took off his tie during a speech in 1998, entirely contrary to protocol. It has gone down in history as 'The Declaration of the Tie'.[23] When Queen Máxima caused a furore when she wore a denim jacket on Queen's Day 2004 - albeit a design by Natan - as denim is traditionally regarded as a fabric worn by manual workers, and wearing it at an official event was seen as a contravention of the dress codes. Queen Máxima's daughter Alexia wore the jacket in 2018, with a red beret. She herself achieved a 'first' by appearing in a modern combination that included a leather jacket on King's Day this year (2025). Leather jackets are traditionally regarded as rebellious, due to their association with film history and pop culture.[24] The 'postbag jacket' that Queen Máxima wore in 2009 also elicited a lot of comment, given that designer Jan Taminiau had literally made it from an old postbag. To her credit, Queen Máxima has chosen outfits by Dutch designers for many important events. Her favourite Dutch designers include Jan Taminiau, who designed her investiture gown, Frans Hoogendoorn, Spijkers & Spijkers, Claes Iversen, Mattijs van Bergen, Benchellal and Iris van Herpen. In 2021 Queen Máxima wore an Iris van Herpen gown that *Vogue* described as 'a mesmerising naked dress'.[25] She wore another striking creation by Iris van Herpen at the opening of an exhibition of her designs in Paris, which was also attended by Brigitte Macron. This highlights an interesting development. The designs of Iris van Herpen are worn by many celebrities on the red carpet, at The Met Gala in New York, for example. In choosing to wear her designs, Queen Máxima has also aligned herself with the dress code tradition of international celebrities, while at the same time promoting the work of a Dutch designer, and expressing her love of Dutch design.

Princess Diana was also no stranger to games of status and celebrity cults. After her divorce from Prince Charles in 1996, she developed a new look and a glamorous dress style, which put her on a par with the supermodels of the 1990s. Diana wore designs by star couturiers like Gianni Versace, Karl Lagerfeld for Chanel and British glamour designers Catherine Walker, Victor Edelstein and Jacques Azagury.[26] Five lavishly embroidered designs by Azagury have gone down in fashion history as 'the famous five'.[27] Some of these cocktail dresses were shorter than the princess would normally wear. She was worried that 'people might not like me wearing so short a skirt', but Azagury persuaded her to go three inches (approx. 7.5 cm) above the knee. The defiant princess was eventually happy with her choice, and told Azagury 'with a cheeky grin' that the short red cocktail dress he made for her was 'definitely one of my favourites now'.[28] The interesting thing here is that this was a princess emulating her glamorous, pop cult contemporaries. She caused a huge stir when, at The Met Gala in 1997, she wore a 'revealing' evening dress by John Galliano for Dior that resembled a négligé, and opted to go braless.[29] An employee of American *Vogue* introduced Diana to the work of Gianni Versace, from whom she ordered an ice-blue evening dress with extravagant

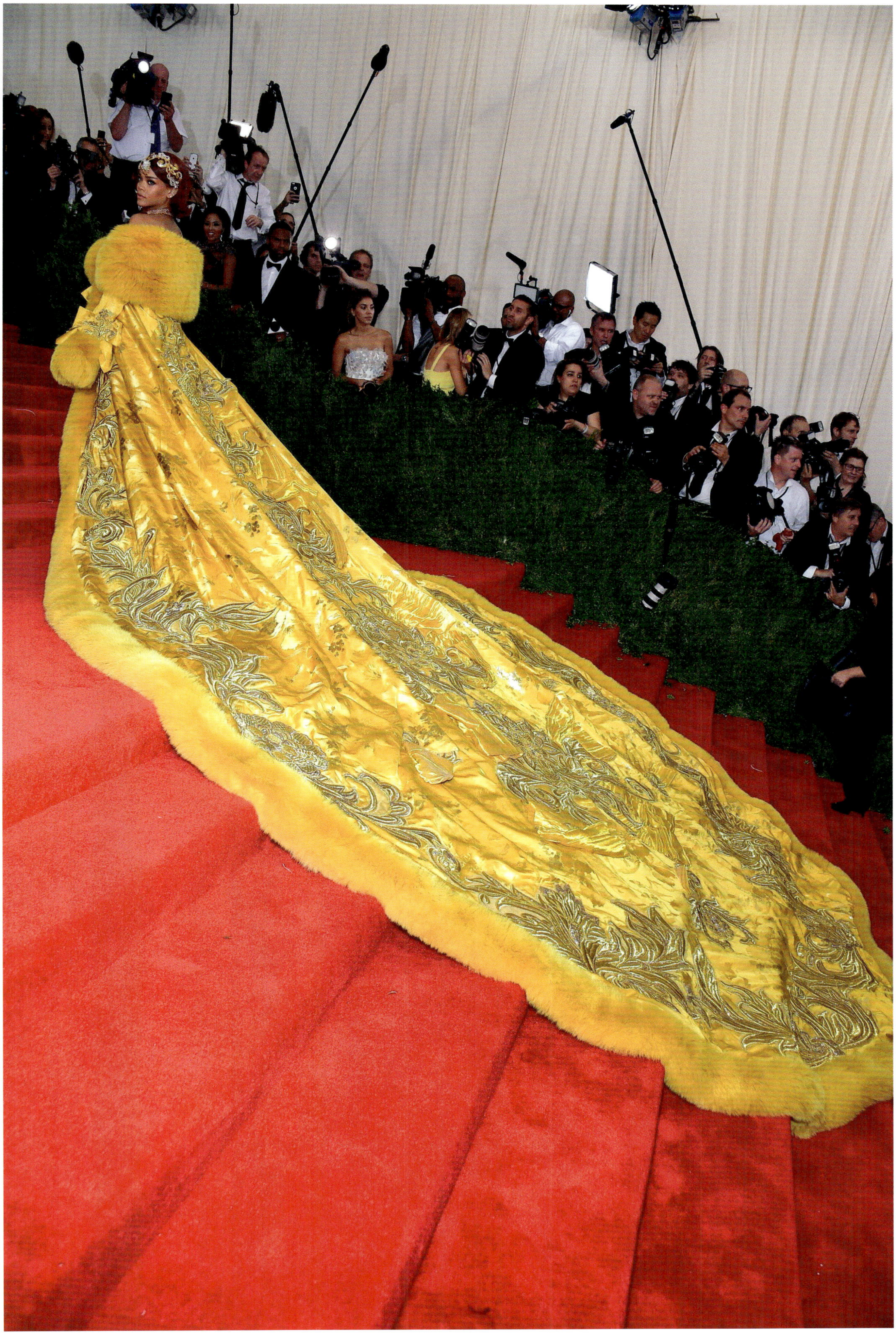

Rihanna wearing an ensemble by Guo Pei, China 2010, to The Met Gala 2015 marking the exhibition *China: Through the Looking Glass* at the Metropolitan Museum of Art in New York, courtesy of Guo Pei, Beijing

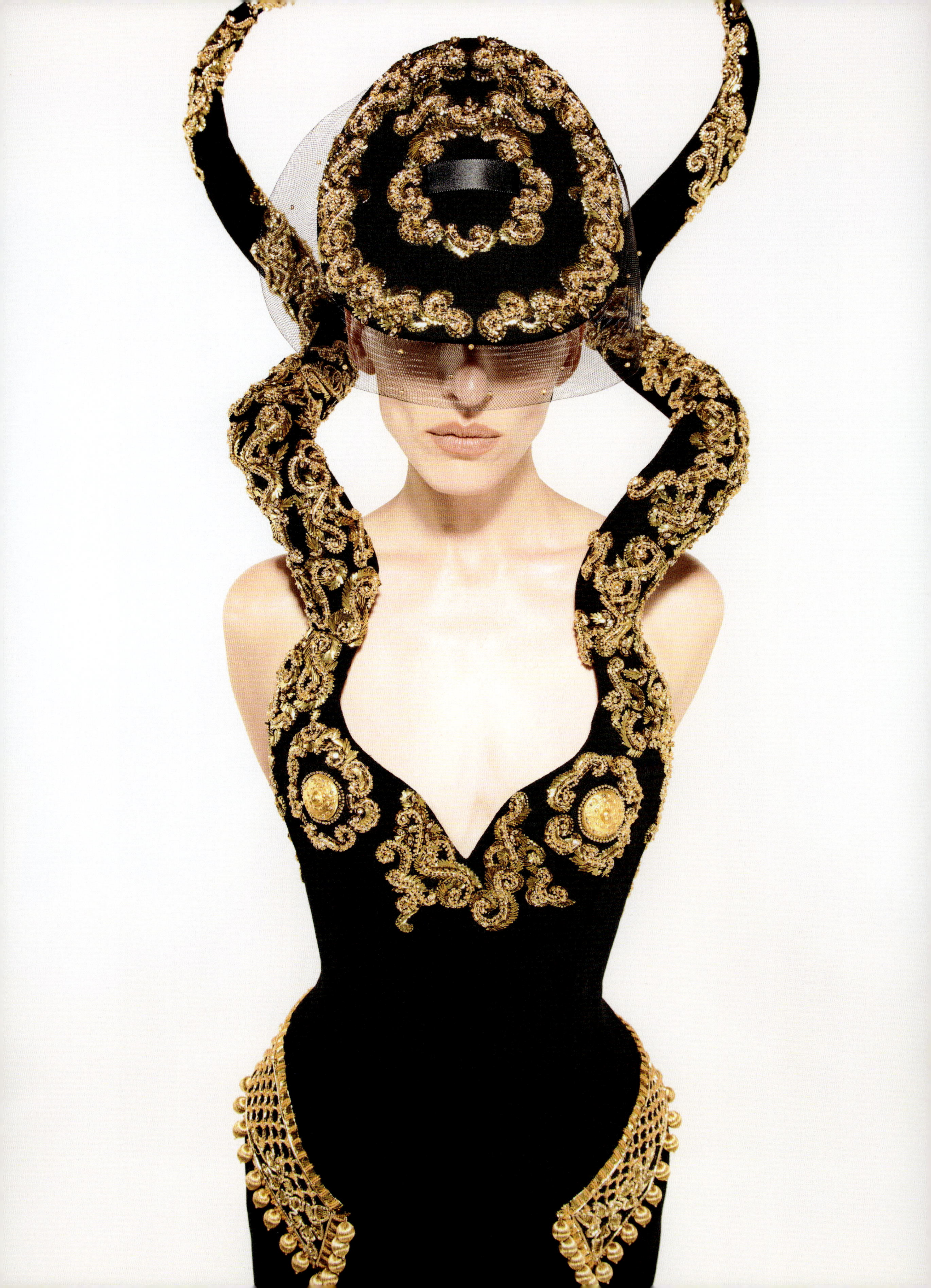

embroidery. The princess was photographed wearing this dress, supermodel-style, by star photographer Patrick de Marchellier, and the photograph was published in *Harpers & Queen* in 1991.[30] The roles were now reversed, and the princess received a lot of criticism from Britain's conservative royal family. History had moved from court culture to pop culture, the latter initially imitating the former, but now a royal had taken command of the dress codes of pop culture. A celebrity princess was born.

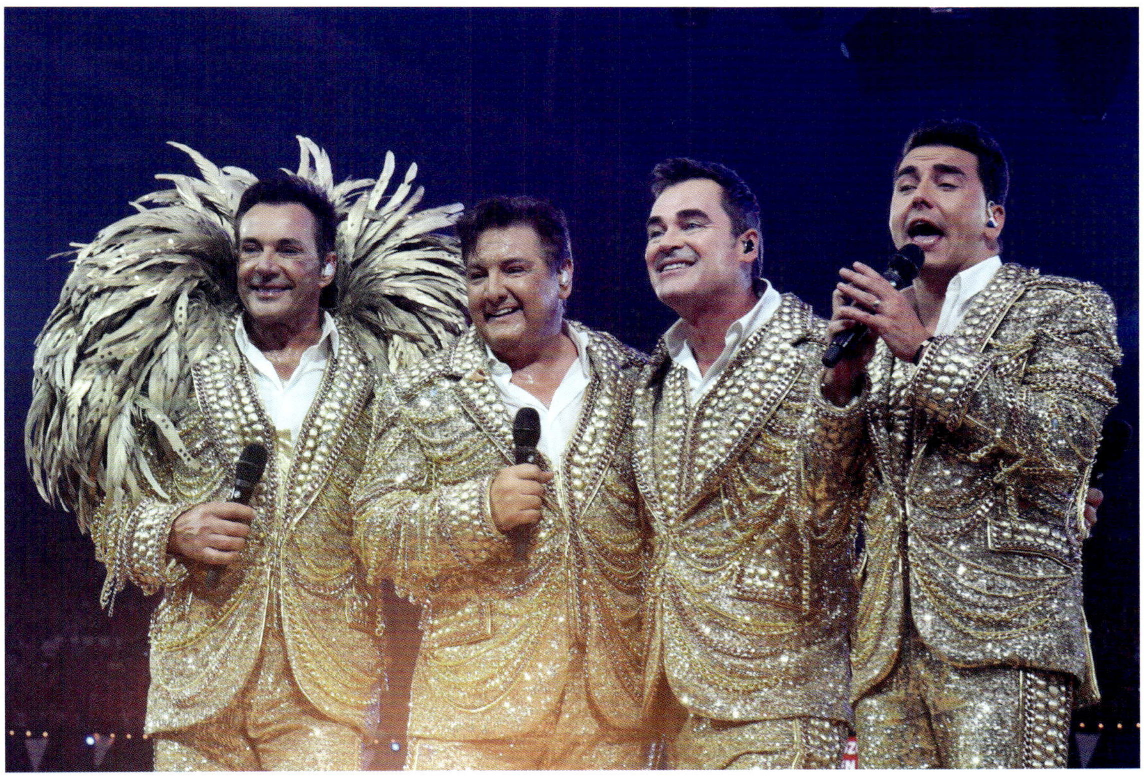

De Toppers in Concert, Amsterdam Arena, 1 June 2019

Daniel Roseberry for Schiaparelli
*Matador* collection, haute couture autumn/winter 2021.
Courtesy of Patriomoine Schiaparelli, Paris

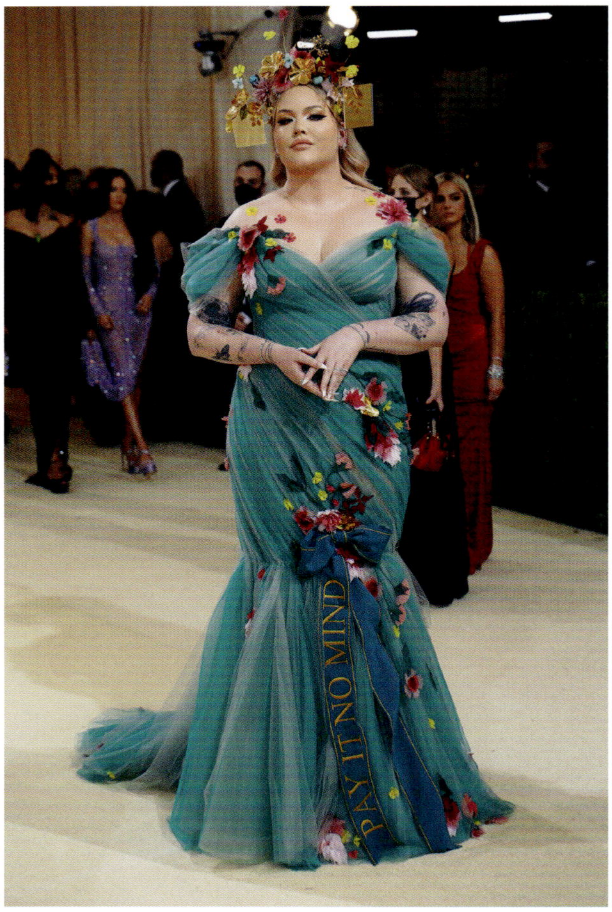


Nikkie de Jager wearing an evening dress by Edwin Oudshoorn, 2021, to The Met Gala 2021 marking the exhibition In America: A Lexicon of Fashion at The Metropolitan Museum of Art in New York, with the dress code 'American Independence', courtesy of Edwin Oudshoorn, Leiden. ◆

Hamish Bowles wearing a design by Valentino to The Met Gala 2018 marking the exhibition Heavenly Bodies: Fashion and the Catholic Imagination

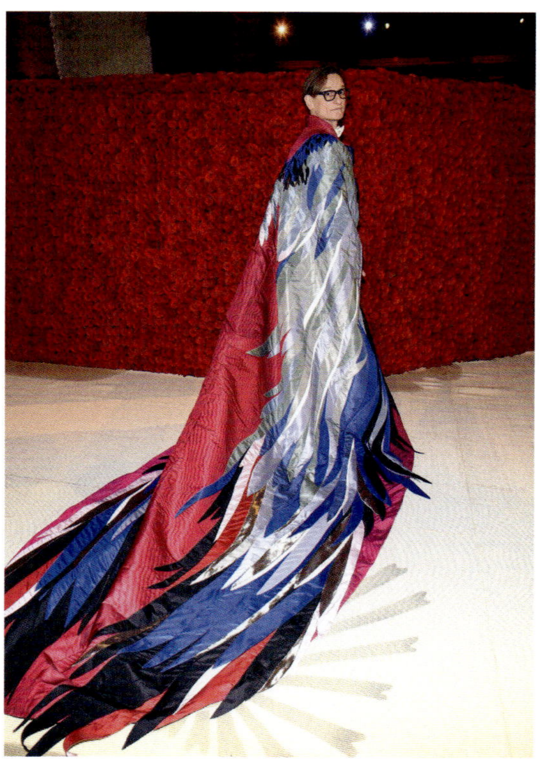

## New times, new dress codes

The royal dress codes of the past now not only influence celebrity culture, but are also used as familiar symbols by famous designers, sometimes with a large measure of irony. British designer Vivienne Westwood adored British tradition and loved to shock. She often played with the royals' dress codes in her catwalk collections. One of the most famous was her 'Harris Tweed' collection (autumn-winter 1987), which included a tweed crown and faux ermine capelets. Viktor & Rolf have also taken a few liberties with the traditional dress codes of the court and with modern celebrity culture in several of their collections. In spring 2019 all eyes were on their couture collection featuring gowns covered in layers of tulle, like exploded debutante dresses, with inscriptions like 'Sorry I am late, I did not want to come' and 'No photos please'. In autumn 2021 they took things a step further in their 'The New Queens of Fashion' collection, with models not only dressed in royal outfits, long or short, but also regal cloaks, sashes and crowns with humorous slogans like 'Size Queen', 'Don't be a Drag just be a Queen' and 'Princess? No Bitch, Queen!'. The message: 'Everybody can be a queen, and everybody is his or her own creation', according to Viktor & Rolf. Maximalist John Galliano had previously made an over-the-top collection for Dior based on royal traditions, where everything was larger than life, in line with his design aesthetic and sense of drama. The celebrity Rihanna wore a highly dramatic regal creation at The Met Gala in 2015, in the form of in a majestic yellow cloak by Chinese designer Guo Pei. The outfit was not only in the yellow colour associated in China with the empire, but also had a train several metres long and the kind of embroidery and fur seen in European court traditions. This statement had echoes of the large quantities of gold and fur worn on the hiphop scene in the 1980s and 90s, when the peak of extravagance was the white fur coat worn by P. Diddy at the height of his fame – before his public fall from grace – in which he presented himself as a 'royal'.

## From style icon to statement

Dress codes have been used for centuries to emphasise status and exclude people, but fortunately things have changed. For a long time (until the French Revolution) it was only possible to appear at court if you were able dress in opulent, fashionable attire – so if you had the means to do this. A dress code on an invitation was not even needed then: either you dressed fashionably, or you would not be admitted. Much has changed. Monarchs themselves now dress much like everyone else. And in order to make everyone feel welcome at the Dutch court, there is not always a dress code for a royal reception. At the annual 'shining stars' lunch hosted by King Willem-Alexander and Queen Máxima, people are specifically invited to wear clothes they feel comfortable in. Not a dress code in sight. In the world of celebrity, too, in recent years much-needed room has been created for diversity and recognition of other dress codes and cultural groups that had long been

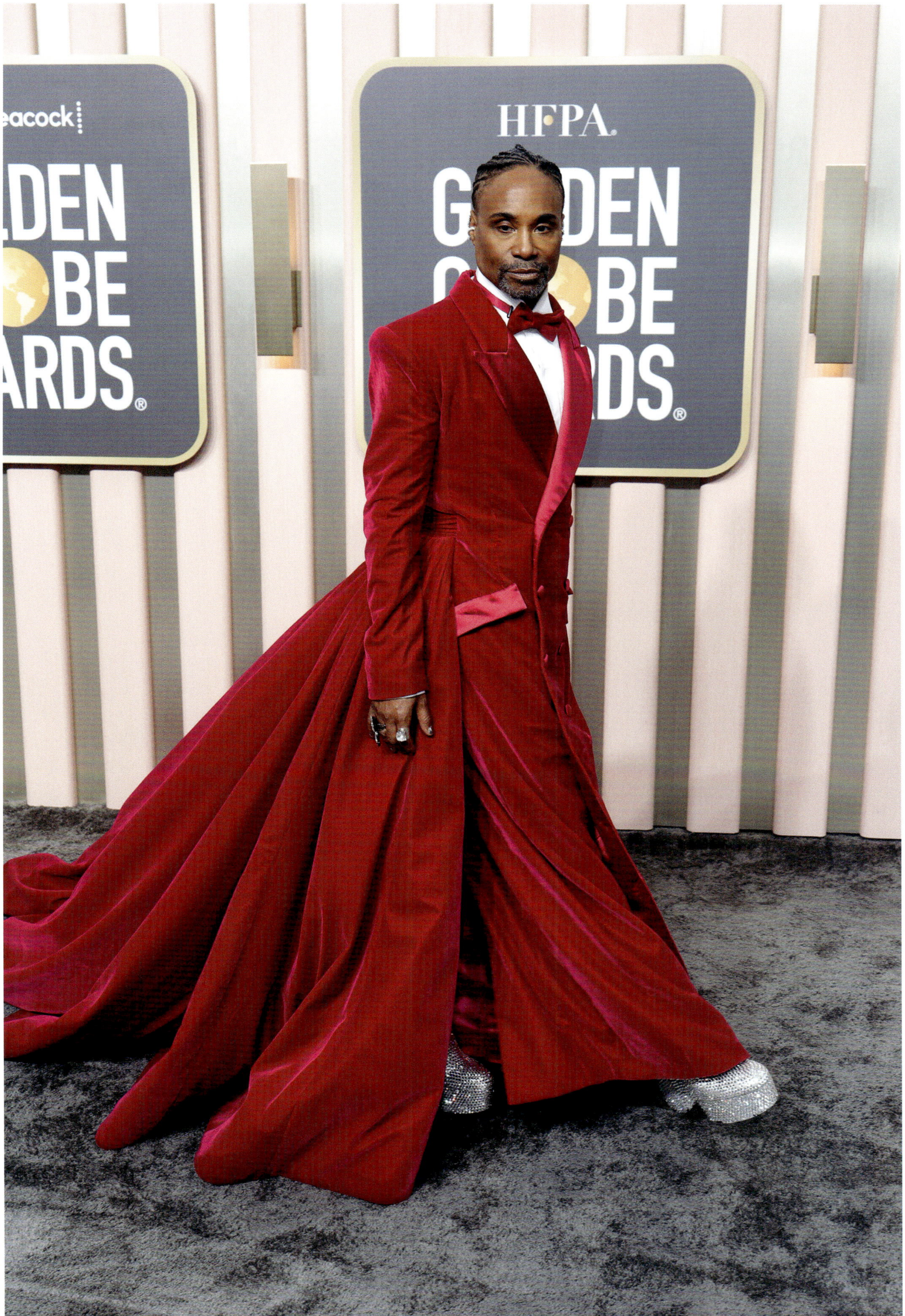


Billy Porter wearing an evening dress by Christian Siriano, 2023,
to the Golden Globe Awards 2023, courtesy of Christian Siriano, New York ◆

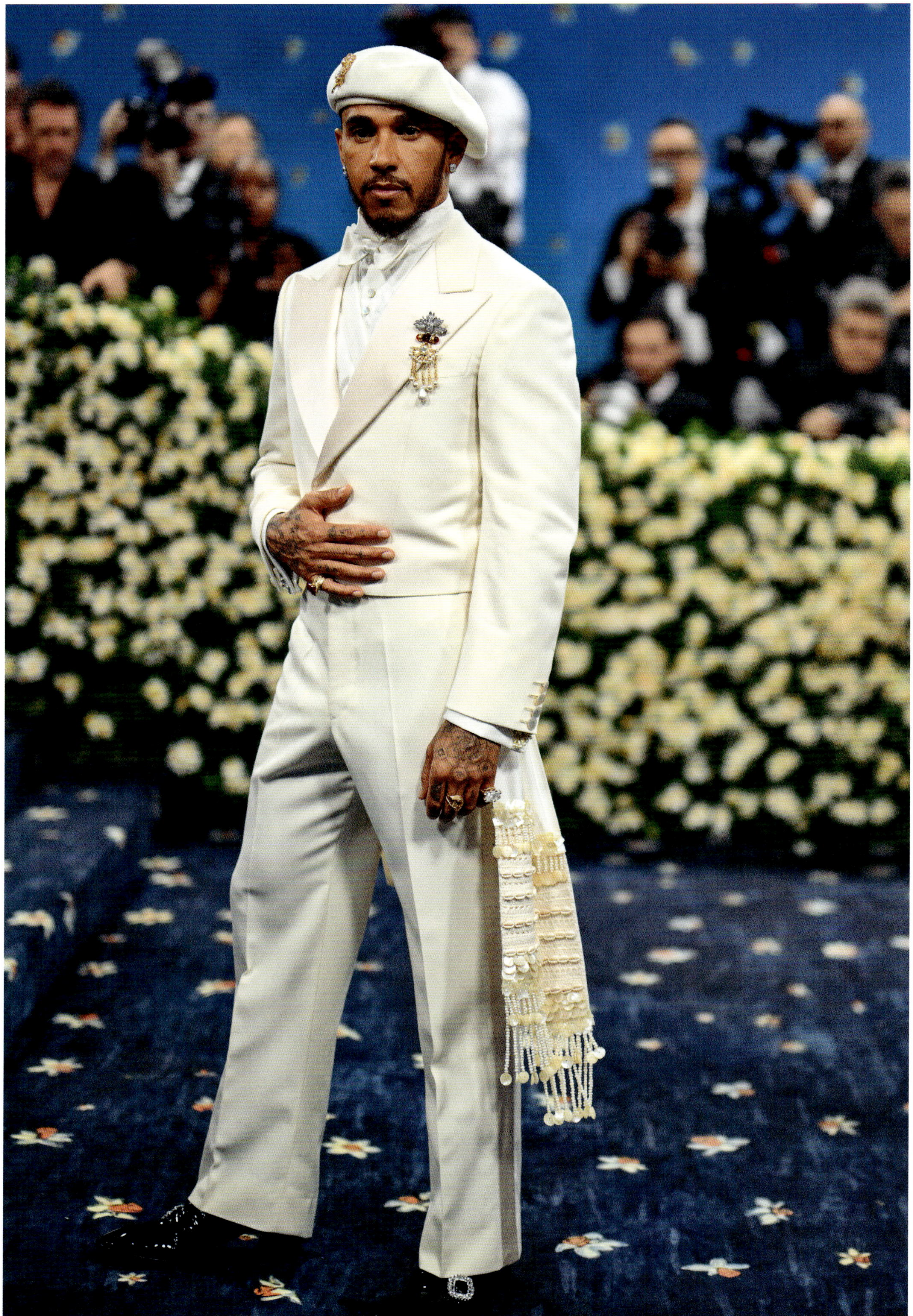

Lewis Hamilton wearing a design by Grace Wales Bonner to The Met Gala 2025 marking the exhibition *Superfine: Tailoring Black Style, at The Metropolitan Museum* of Art in New York, with the dress code 'Tailored for You'.

excluded or overlooked. One particularly good example of this is The Met Gala's theme in May 2025, which was all about The Black Dandy, related to the museum's new fashion exhibition *Superfine: Tailoring Black Style*, which celebrates Black fashion culture. The outfits that appeared on the red carpet were fantastic examples of the celebration and acknowledgement of dress codes other than the 'royal references' so often seen at such occasions. For once, the outfits referenced other examples of fashion, and a whole range of cultural heritages were highlighted and celebrated. The white outfit that racing driver Lewis Hamilton – a modern dandy himself – wore to The Met Gala included countless references. Grace Wales Bonner designed a white suit for him which he wore with a white beret. The outfit featured decorative baobab flower motifs (a metaphor for resilience), embroidered cowrie shells (used as a means of payment in the context of slavery) and mother-of pearl buttons: potent symbols honouring Black fashion culture and the Black dandy.[31]

In recent years, more and more designers and those who wear their designs have openly profiled their cultural heritage in their dress codes, in order to highlight and honour their own history. It is high time for this diversity of dress codes to be given the space and recognition it deserves. In today's modern society, the days when dress codes could only emulate the example and cultural heritage of the one-sided court culture of a century ago are long gone. This applies not only on the red carpet, but also in modern court culture. Dress codes at court have evolved, in an age when the court itself has also modernised. There is finally more room for innovation and change on the red carpet, too – the place where court culture lives on in pop culture – as well as in celebrity culture more generally. But apart from all this, the phenomenon of the dress code remains very much alive, in whatever form. As soon as people decide to form groups, dress codes emerge. Let us hope that, unlike in the past, these dress codes are no longer used to exclude, but to achieve a greater sense of belonging and connection.

Florence Welch wearing an evening ensemble by Gucci to The Met Gala 2019 at The Metropolitan Museum of Art marking the exhibition Camp: Notes on Fashion, courtesy of Gucci Archives, Florence ◆

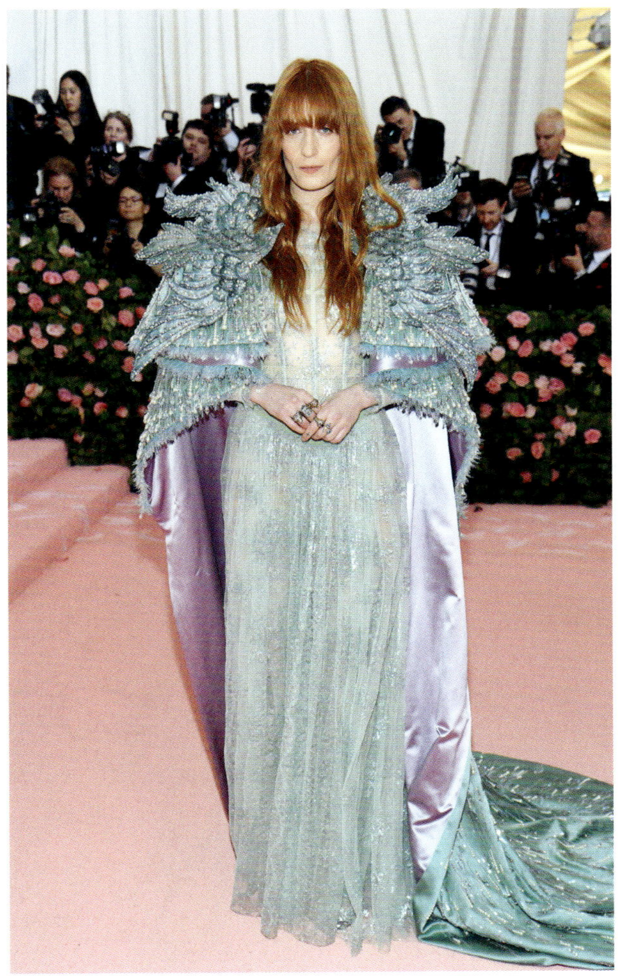

→ Heidi Klum wearing an evening dress with train by Elie Saab, 2025, at the Cannes Film Festival, courtesy of Elie Saab, Beirut/Paris ◆

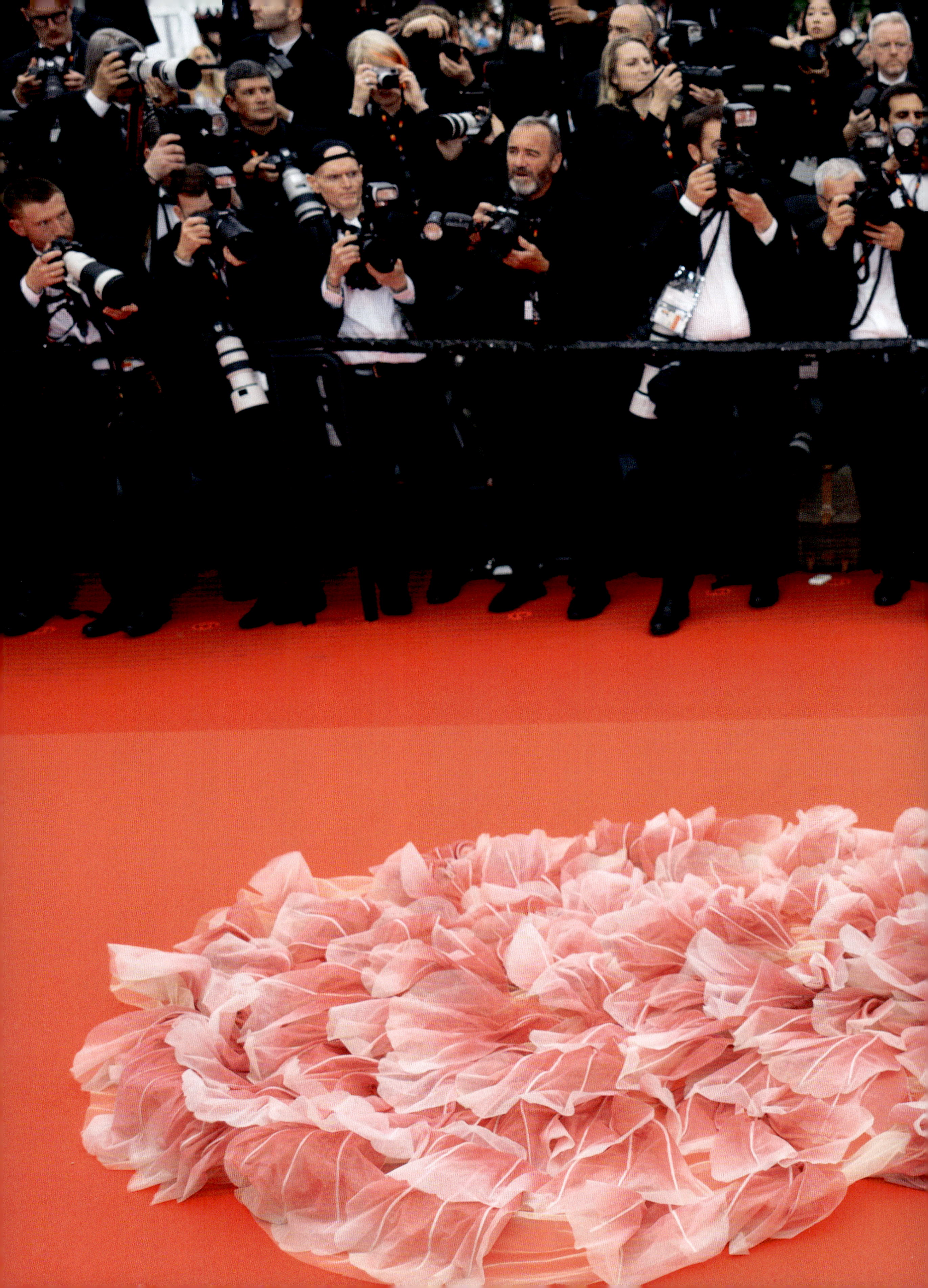

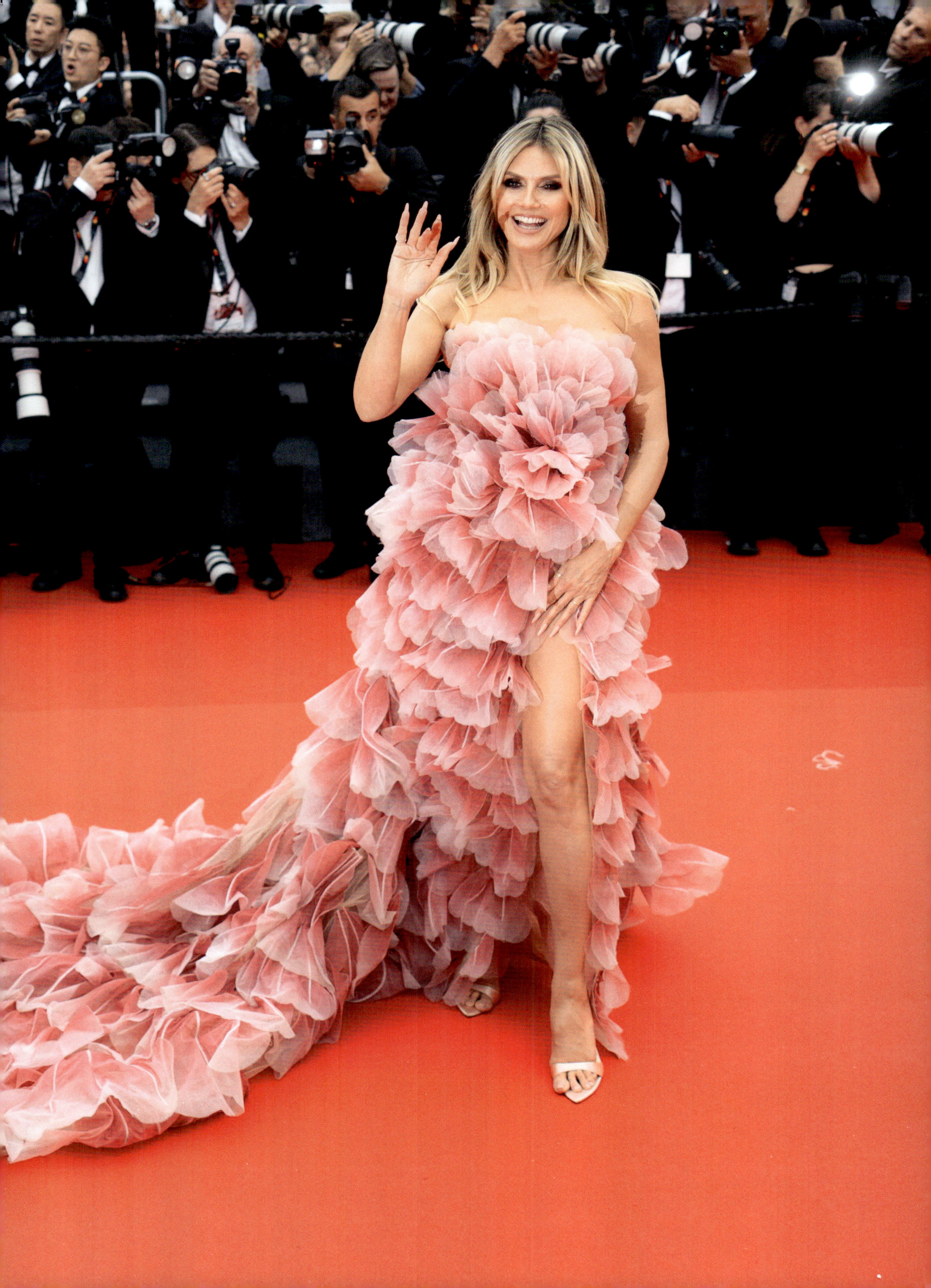

Captions to images on introductory pages

**P30-31 → Evening gown ◆**
Worn by Lady Henriette van de Poll (1853-1946), lady-in-waiting to Queen Emma.
Brussels, Madame Coche, circa 1901
Silk, cotton
Kunstmuseum Den Haag

**Evening gown ◆**
Worn by Baroness Sloet van Marxveld (1871-1941) when, as lady-in-waiting, she joined the bridal procession at the wedding of Queen Wilhelmina.
Maker unknown, 1901
Silk
Kunstmuseum Den Haag

**Evening gown ◆**
Brussels, Mesdames Coche, circa 1898-1900
Silk, cotton, metal
Kunstmuseum Den Haag

**Evening dress ◆**
Probably worn by Countess Marie Jacqueline van Lynden van Sandenburg (1903-1983)
Maker unknown, circa 1930
Silk
Kunstmuseum Den Haag

**Evening dress ◆**
Probably worn by Countess Marie Jacqueline van Lynden van Sandenburg (1903-1983)
Maker unknown, circa 1934
Artificial silk
Kunstmuseum Den Haag

**Evening dress ◆**
Worn by Agnes Margaretha van Beeck Calkoen, Baroness Schimmelpenninck van der Oije (1908-1991), lady-in-waiting to Queen Wilhelmina
Brussels, Mademoiselle Le Bel, circa 1937
Silk, artificial silk, metal
Kunstmuseum Den Haag

**P94-95 → Gown ◆**
Worn by Lady Anna Mathilda Meteler-kamp-den Tex (1861-1944)
Maker unknown, circa 1900-1905
Linen, cotton, metal
Kunstmuseum Den Haag

**P104-105 → Queen Wilhelmina's wedding dress ◆**
Nicaud Paris, 1900-1901
Silk, silver thread, cotton, glass pearls
Paleis Het Loo, on long-term loan from the Royal Collections, The Hague

**P126 → Bodice of an evening gown ◆**
Worn by Lady Henriette van de Poll (1853-1946), lady-in-waiting to Queen Emma
Brussels, Madame van der Taelen, circa 1900
Silk, metal
Kunstmuseum Den Haag

**Bodice of an evening gown ◆**
Worn by Lady Henriette van de Poll (1853-1946), lady-in-waiting to Queen Emma
Maker unknown, circa 1900
Silk, metal
Kunstmuseum Den Haag

**P127 → Parts of an evening gown ◆**
Worn by Lady Henriette van de Poll (1853-1946), lady-in-waiting to Queen Emma
Maker unknown, circa 1900
Silk, metal
Kunstmuseum Den Haag

Cover images

**'Build Castles in the Air' ensemble by Viktor&Rolf ◆**
Autumn/winter 2021, courtesy of Viktor&Rolf, Amsterdam; background, interior at Paleis Het Loo, Apeldoorn

**Portrait of Wilhelmina in Investiture Robe**
Thérèse Schwartze, 1897-1898
Paleis Het Loo

◆ This symbol denotes items that also feature in the exhibition.

# NOTES

P14
**DRESS CODES AT THE DUTCH COURT 1880-1940**

1
Pauw van Wieldrecht 1993, p. 72.
2
Cleverens 1994, p. 14.
3
Cleverens 1994, p. 55.
4
Withuis 2016, p. 110.
5
Withuis 2016, p. 207.

P32
**QUEEN WILHELMINA'S COURT TRAIN**

1
Van Wessem [1904], p. 309.
2
Pauw van Wieldrecht 1993, p. 73.

P36
**THE DAILY CYCLE OF COSTUME CHANGES**

1
Van Heuven 2012, p. 220.
2
Cleverens 1994, p. 22.

P44
**DRESS CODES AT COURT**

1
Catherine Join-Diéterle, 'Robes à transformation', in: *Sous l'empire des crinolines*, exh.cat. (Musée Galliera, musée de la mode de la ville de Paris) Paris 2008, pp. 101-103.
2
Cleverens 1994, p. 112, letter from The Hague, 4 Sept. 1898. The investiture took place on 6 September 1898.
3
In 1936 the three outfits were loaned to a costume exhibition at the Knights' Hall in The Hague by 'the honourable misses van de Poll of Zeist', i.e. Henriette van de Poll and her sisters. In the early 1950s these and other clothes belonging to the family were donated to the Dutch Costume Museum, now the fashion and costume department at Kunstmuseum Den Haag, inv.nos. BSC-89, 90 and 91. They were described on page 59 of the exhibition catalogue for 'Het Costuum onzer Voorouders' as: '142. Evening gown. Grand decolleté, bodice and skirt with long train. Decorated with sequined lace and pleated silk organza bands. Salmon-coloured satin, 1898; 143. Evening gown. Grand decolleté, bodice and skirt with long train. Decorated with encrusted sequined lace and pleated silk organza bands. Pale yellow and cream bound satin, bow motif [1898, dated by photograph p. 75]; 144. Afternoon dress. Long-sleeved bodice and skirt. Decorated with soutache of cream cord and lace encrusted. Bodice with white satin revers and three velvet bows; pale lilac rib-woven-silk, 1898.'
4
Information from *Programma van de feestelijkheden en plechtigheden ter gelegenheid van het huwelijk van Hare Majesteit Koningin Wilhelmina der Nederlanden met Zijne Hoogheid Hertog Hendrik van Mecklenburg*, Royal Family Archives, no. E10-IVba-12 (491).

P48
**DRESSED AS A COURTIER**

1
*Bepalingen omtrent de Hof-Costumes, Behoort tot het besluit van den 17de Maart 1815, no. 20*, articles 3 and 11.
2
Hohé 2007, p. 48.
3
Cleverens 1994, p. 31, letter from Het Loo, 28 May 1880.
4
Cleverens 1994, p. 33, letter from Het Loo, 9 July 1880.
5
Cleverens 1994, p. 112, letter from The Hague, 27 March 1898.

P52
**FASHION FROM PARIS**

1
Elzenga, Loonstra, Meij (eds.), 1998, p. 36-38, 115-117. Hohé 2010, pp. 69-70. See also Wedding of Queen Wilhelmina of the Netherlands and Duke Heinrich of Mecklenburg-Schwerin, 1901 – Herstoric Royal Dress, accessed on 5 May 2025. A. Corbay, later Corbay-Wenzel, is believed to have been a well-known fashion house. Its designs are now in the collections of the Philadelphia Museum of Art, Royal Ontario Museum in Toronto, The Metropolitan Museum of Art in New York. Empress Maria Feodorovna of Russia ordered a gown there in 1886 that is now at the State Historical Museum in Moscow.
2
Hohé 2010, Royal Archives, Queen Emma Archives, A 47, III, multiple accounts
3
De Marly 1980, Hohé 2010, pp. 23-24.
4
De Marly 1980, p. 103, Hohé 2010, p. 25.
5
De Marly 1980, p. 103.
See: Charles Dickens, *All the Year Round*, June-December 1867, vol. IX, p. 9.
6
Magdinson, 2013, p.107-130
7
See Elzenga, Loonstra, Meij (eds.) 1998, pp. 60-62, 70. For closed houses in Amsterdam, see also Du Mortier, 2007.
8
Cleverens 1994, p. 26, letter from the Palace, 21 March 1880.
9
Cleverens 1985, p. 30.
10
Cleverens 1994, p. 230. Rijksmuseum Amsterdam inv.no. BK-NM-13089-AB.

P78
**WILHELMINA'S INVESTITURE GOWN**

1
Van Heuven 2012, p. 215.
2
Lady-in-waiting Henriette van de Poll wrote to her mother in a letter of 5 January 1899: 'The gala ball went well, the queen looked lovely in the gown from the investiture'. Zeist municipal archives, Van de Poll archive, 2092, inv.no. 487.

P82
**LADY-IN-WAITING AT A ROYAL WEDDING**

1
Zeist municipal archives, Van de Poll Family, Zeist branch, 1765-1970, finding aid 2092, inv.no. 488.
2
Zeist municipal archives, NL-ZtGAZ_2092-487.
3
Zeist municipal archives, NL-ZtGAZ_2092-488.
4
Overijssel provincial collection, Zwolle site, Civil Wedding Ceremony, Overijssel Register of Births, Deaths and Marriages, Vollenhove, archive 0123, inv. no. 12314, 21 07 1904, Registers of Marriages and Divorces, Vollenhove, file no. 5.
5
Object information on gown with inv.no. K 266-1982, Kunstmuseum Den Haag.

P90
**QUEEN EMMA'S GALA DRESS AND COAT**

1
Wardle 1998, p. 24-59.

P96
**SIMPLE OUTDOOR DRESSES**

1
The Hague, 12 April 1898, in: *Soerabaijasch Handelsblad*, Surabaya, 12-04-1898, p. 1. Accessed via Delpher.nl on 07-05-2025.
2
'NEDERLAND. Den Haag, 23 Juni 1898', in: *Sumatra-courant : nieuws- en advertentieblad*'. Padang, 25-07-1898, p. 1. Accessed via Delpher.nl on 07-05-2025.
3
*Stadsnieuws..', in: Het nieuws van den dag : kleine courant*'. Amsterdam, 03-09-1898, p. 9. Accessed via Delpher.nl on 07-05-2025. According to this article, the painting shows Queen Wilhelmina in the garden of Paleis Het Loo.
4
Jones 2012, pp. 29-61.
5
Braams et al. 1998, pp. 126-129.
6
Idem, pp. 236-237.
7
Hohé 2023, pp. 61-62.
8
Zeist municipal archives, Van de Poll Family, Zeist branch, 1765-1970, finding aid 2092, cat. no. 569.
9
Zeist municipal archives, NL-ZtGAZ_2092-1232.
10
Jones 2012, pp. 255-285.

P106
**QUEEN WILHELMINA'S WEDDING DRESS**

1
Cleverens 1994, p. 230.

P110
**PRINCESS JULIANA'S WEDDING DRESS**

1
Berville 2022, p. 83.
2
Meij 1998, p. 55.
3
De Bas 1937, p. 358.

P114
**IN MOURNING**

1
Cleverens 1994, pp. 60-61, letter from Het Loo, 10 September 1881. This refers to the death of Prince Willem Frederik Karel ('Prince Frederik'), second son of King Willem I, at Huize de Paauw in Wassenaar, 8 September 1881.
2
Hohé and Rosa de Carvalho 2007, pp. 12, 13.
3
Cleverens 1994, p. 60, letter from Het Loo, 10 September 1881.
4
Cleverens 1994, p. 80, letter from Kissingen, 27 June 1884.
5
Hohé 2010, p. 34; Cleverens 1984.
6
Cleverens 1994, p. 61, letter from The Hague, 23 Sept. 1881.
7
Cleverens 1994, p. 96, letter from Het Loo, 27 Nov. 90.
8
Cleverens 1994, p. 62.

P118
**WILHELMINA'S WHITE MOURNING BONNETS**

1
Wilhelmina 1959, p. 251.

P122
**A YOUNG QUEEN IN HALF MOURNING**

1
Wilhelmina 1959, p. 29-30.

P128
**REPAIRING AND 'REFRESHING'**

1
Zeist municipal archives, Van de Poll family, Zeist branch, 1765-1970, finding aid 2092, inv.no. 477.
2
Zeist municipal archives, NL-ZtGAZ_2092-486.
3
Collection of Henriette van de Poll's gowns at in Kunstmuseum Den Haag, De Jonge 2012, pp. 34-51.
4
Zeist municipal archives, NL-ZtGAZ_2092-477.
5
Zeist municipal archives, NL-ZtGAZ_2092-486.
6
Zeist municipal archives, NL-ZtGAZ_2092-846.
7
Zeist municipal archives, NL-ZtGAZ_2092-486.
8
Zeist municipal archives, NL-ZtGAZ_2092-698.
9
NL-ZtGAZ_2092-713.
10
Not only dresses from Mme Coche worn by Henriette van de Poll were altered or made from older garments. Dress K 80-1963 from circa 1913 was also made from an older dress.
11
Zeist municipal archives, NL-ZtGAZ_2092-698.
12
Zeist municipal archives, NL-ZtGAZ_2092-713.
13
Zeist municipal archives, NL-ZtGAZ_2092-488.

P132
**EMMA'S ALTERED EVENING DRESS**

1
Knoop 2018.
2
Weyel 2018, p. 138.

P136
**FROM COURT CULTURE TO POP CULTURE**

1
Mackenzie Stuart 2006, pp. 2-3.
2
Mackenzie Stuart 2006.
3
King 2009, p. 212.

4
Ross 2023, p. 12.
5
Mackenzie Stuart 2006, p. 2.
6
King 2009, p. 2.
7
King 2009, p. 213.
8
De Marly 1980, pp. 174-175.
9
Stibbe, Fronty 2024.
10
Inv.no. CMC-0504, Kunstmuseum Den Haag. Thanks to Tirza Westland, who found a photograph of the actress in this role. When it came into the collection, it was noted that the dress was 'worn in Brachvogel's [Albert Emil Brachvogel, the author] *Narcis*. Originally made for Her Majesty Queen Wilhelmina'.
11
Ross 2023, p. 13.
12
Grijpma 1999, pp. 49-50. All of the dresses worn by Queen Juliana on Prinsjesdag between 1957 and 1973 were made by Maison Linette, as was Princess Beatrix's wedding dress in 1966.
13
The list of buyers at Dior in Paris for autumn 1947 (Maison Dior's second couture collection) includes fashion house Linette of 1 Torenstraat in 'Bois-le-Duc' ('s Hertogenbosch). The list of buyers for the spring 1947 collection has not been preserved in the archive; it is not known whether Linette attended this first show. Research performed in 2014-2024 by Madelief Hohé, with the help of Soizic Pfaff, Perrine Scherrer, Joana Tosta, Solène Aureal-Lamy, Séverine Breton, to whom many thanks for their kind assistance. Hohé 2024, p. 47.
14
Bowles 2001, p. 31.
15
Fawnia Soo Hoo, 'The Powerful Story Behind Jackie Kennedy's Wedding Dress, in: *Vanity Fair*, 18 January 2023, accessed online in May 2025.
16
Instagram post @atlasofshows, 4 May 2025.
17
Invitation to the christening at Willemskerk in The Hague on Saturday 5 June 1909, addressed to Henriette van de Poll, in Zeist Archives.
18
Wedding invitation for 7 January 1937, addressed to Henriette van de Poll, in Zeist Archives.
19
Eelco Elzenga, *Ja, ik wil. Koninklijke Huwelijken 1791-2022*, exh. cat. (De Nieuwe Kerk, Amsterdam / Paleis Het Loo, Apeldoorn) Zwolle 2001, p. 18.
20
This was important for the Dutch court, indicating that the bridal gown had been made in the Netherlands. At the time, it was never communicated that anyone other than Kühne had designed it. Photographs of Kühne's sewing atelier appeared in the press, showing Dutch seamstresses working on the dress. The label in the wedding dress reads: 'Maggy Rouff, Av. Des Champs-Elysées 136, Paris, no. 43119, modéle déposé, Made in France, Paris.' Thanks to Hans Schuite, Paleis Het Loo, Apeldoorn.
21
'Juliana bruid van Nederland', in: *Eva*, vol. 19, 6 January 1962, accessed via Delpher.nl in May 2025. These floral dresses are very similar to the bridal gown, and were also supplied by Kühne, as were the outfits for the four young bridesmaids and pages. Might they also have been designed by Maison Rouff?
22
Rebekah Absalom, Eliza Scarborough, 'Meghan's high-low Netflix wardrobe', *Mail Online*, 6 March 2025, accessed in May 2025.
23
'Prins Claus werpt stropdas af (1998)', *NOS Nieuws online*, 6 April 2011, accessed in May 2025.
24
Boyer 2006.
25
'Koningin Máxima draagt haar 'viral' Iris van Herpen jurk opnieuw in Zweden', *Vogue* online article (Dutch edition), 13 October 2022, accessed in May 2025.
26
Joseph 2022.
27
Joseph 2022, pp. 172-174.
28
Joseph 2022, p. 174.
29
Desmoulins 2024, pp. 87-89.
30
Joseph 2022, pp. 212-213.
31
Hannah Jackson, 'Lewis Hamiltons look voor het Met Gala 2025 zit vol symboliek', *Vogue Netherlands online,* 6 May 2025, accessed in May 2025.

De Bas 1937
Bas, W.G. de, *Gedenkboek Oranje-Nassau – Mecklenburg / Lippe-Biesterfeld. Uitgegeven ter gelegenheid van het huwelijk van H.K.H. Prinses Juliana met Z.D.H. Prins Bernhard*, Amsterdam 1937.

Berville 2022
Berville, Eva, *La maison de haute couture Maggy Rouff de 1929 à 1948*, Master's dissertation, Université de Picardie-Jules Vernes, Amiens, Sciènces de l'Homme et Société department, 2022.

Bowles 2001
Hamish Bowles et al., *Jacqueline Kennedy: The White House Years*, exh. cat. New York (The Metropolitan Museum of Art), New York 2001.

Boyer 2006
G. Bruce Boyer, *Rebel Style. Cinematic Heroes of the 1950s*, New York 2006.

Cleverens 1984
R.W.A.M. Cleverens, *Rose Villa. Herinnering aan Mevrouw H.A. Insinger-van Loon, dame du Paleis van H.M. Koningin Emma voor Amsterdam, 1825-1902*, Middelburg 1984.

Cleverens 1994
René Cleverens, *Niet verder dan ons Huis...de Koninklijke Hofhouding. Het dagelijks leven in de paleizen Noordeinde en Het Loo*, 1870-1918, Middelburg 1994.

Desmoulins 2024
Lucile Desmoulins, 'Lady Diana', in: Madelief Hohé et al., *Dior: A New Look*, exh. cat. (Kunstmuseum Den Haag), Zwolle 2024, pp. 87-89.

Elzenga, Loonstra and Meij (eds.) 1998
E. Elzenga, M. Loonstra, I. Meij (eds.), *Koninklijk Gekleed. Wilhelmina, 1880-1962*, exh. cat. Apeldoorn (Museum Paleis het Loo), Zwolle 1998.

Elzenga 2001
Eelco Elzenga, *Ja, ik wil. Koninklijke Huweiijken 1791-2022*, exh. cat. (De Nieuwe Kerk, Amsterdam / Paleis Het Loo, Apeldoorn) Zwolle 2001.

Grijpma 1999
Dieuwke Grijpma, *Kleren voor de elite. Nederlandse couturiers en hun klanten 1882-2000*, Amersfoort 1999.

Van Heuven 2012
Heuven-van Nes (ed.), van, Emerentia, *Dear Old Bones, Brieven van Koningin Wilhelmina aan haar Engelse gouvernante Miss Elizabeth Saxton Winter, 1886-1935*, Bussum 2012.

Hohé and Rosa de Carvalho 2007
Madelief Hohé, Trudie Rosa de Carvalho, *Haagse Hofmode*, exh. cat. (Gemeentemuseum Den Haag), Zwolle 2007.

Hohé 2010
Madelief Hohé, Georgette Koning, *Voici Paris! Haute Couture*, exh. cat. (Gemeentemuseum Den Haag) Zwolle 2010.

Hohé 2023
Madelief Hohé et al., *Royals & Rebels: British Fashion*, exh. cat. (Kunstmuseum Den Haag) Zwolle 2023.

Hohé 2024
Madelief Hohé et al., *Dior: A New Look*, exh. cat. (Kunstmuseum Den Haag), Zwolle 2024.

Hyland 2022
Véronique Hyland, *Dress Code: Unlocking Fashion from the New Look to Millennial Pink*. New York 2022.

Joseph 2022
Claudia Joseph, *Diana: A Life in Dresses: From Debutante to Style Icon*, Woodbridge 2022.

Join-Diéterle 2008
Catherine Join-Diéterle, 'Robes à transformation', in: *Sous l'empire des crinolines*, exh. cat. (Musée Galliera, musée de la mode de la ville de Paris) Paris 2008, pp. 101-103.

De Jonge 2012
Jacoba de Jonge, 'Tot de laatste draad', in: *Een leven in de mode. Vrouwenkleding 1750-1950. Uit de collectie Jacoba de Jong*, exh. cat., (MoMu Antwerp), Tielt 2012, pp. 34-51.

Jones 2012
Kevin L. Jones, *Sporting Fashion, Outdoor Girls 1800 to 1960*, exh. cat., (ASU FIDM Museum Los Angeles), New York 2012, pp. 29-61.

King 2009
Greg King, *A Season of Splendor: The Court of Mrs. Aster in Gilded Age New York*, Hoboken 2009.

Knoop 2018
Knoop, Femke, *Hirsch & Cie Amsterdam (1882-1976). Haute Couture aan het Leidseplein*, Hilversum 2018.

Mackenzie Stuart 2006
Amanda Mackenzie Stuart, *Consuelo and Alva Vanderbilt: The Story of a Daughter and a Mother in the Gilded Age*, New York 2006 (1st ed. 2005).

Magidson 2013
Phyllis Magidson, 'A Fashionable Equation: Maison Worth and the Clothes of the Gilded Age, in: Donald Albrecht and Jeannine Falino (eds.) *Gilded New York. Design, Fashion and Society*, exh.cat., (The City Museum of New York), New York, pp. 107-130.

Mansel 2005
Philip Mansel, *Dressed to Rule: Royal and Court Costume from Louis XIV to Elizabeth II*, Yale 2005.

De Marly 1980
Diana de Marly, *Worth: Father of Haute Couture*, London 1980 (I).

Du Mortier 2007
Bianca M. du Mortier, 'Mode op maat: over naaisters, coupeuses en gesloten huizen in Amsterdam, in: Annemarie den Dekker, Bianca M. du Mortier et al., *Modepaleizen in Amsterdam, 1880-1960*, exh. cat. Amsterdam (Amsterdams Historisch Museum), Bussum 2007, pp. 104-115.

Pauw van Wieldrecht 1993
Agnies Pauw van Wieldrecht, *Vin-je dat we een hoed op moeten?*, Amsterdam 1993.

Ross 2023
Colleen Ross, 'Did you know?', in: *Crown to Couture: The Magazine*, exh.cat. (Hampton Court Palace) London 2023.

Stibbe, Fronty 2024
Isabelle Stibbe, Jérôme Fronty, *Bijoux de scène de l'Opéra de Paris*, exh. cat. (Opéra National de Paris), Paris 2024.

Thompson Ford 2021
Richard Thompson Ford, *Dress Codes: How the Laws of Fashion Made History*, New York 2021.

Vanderbilt Balsan 2012
Consuelo Vanderbilt Balsan, *The Glitter and the Gold: The American Duchess – In Her Own Words*, London 2012 (1st ed. 1953).

Wells 2025
Chester S. Wells, *Wearing Freedom: The Evolution of Black Dandyism and its Cultural Validation at the Met Gala*, 2025.

Van Wessem [1904]
Henriette J. van Wessem, *Ik kan kostuumnaaien, Geïllustreerd handboek voor degenen, die tot haar kostumes en alles wat tot de garderobe behoort, thuis willen gereedmaken*. (Voor de Nederlandsche dames bewerkt door Henriette J. van Wessem, Leerares aan de Industrieschool te 's-Gravenhage), Leiden 1908.

Weyel 2018
Weyel, Ivo, *Het verleden ruist voorbij*, Amsterdam/Antwerp 2018.

Wilhelmina 1959
Wilhelmina, *Eenzaam maar niet alleen*, Amsterdam 1959.

Withuis 2016
Withuis, Jolande, *Juliana. Vorstin in een mannenwereld*, Amsterdam 2016.

# CREDITS

This publication accompanies the exhibition: *Dress Codes - From statement to Style Icon* at Paleis Het Loo, Apeldoorn from 9 October 2025 to 8 March 2026.

*Dress Codes – From Statement to Style Icon* is an exhibition by Paleis Het Loo in collaboration with Kunstmuseum Den Haag.

paleis het loo

KUNSTMUSEUM DEN HAAG

Authors
Madelief Hohé
Cécile Narinx
Paul Rem
Tirza Westland

Image editing
Angelique van den Eerenbeemd

Translation
Sue McDonnell

Photography
Adriaan van Dam
Alice de Groot

Design
Studio Marline Bakker

Publishers
Waanders Publishers, Zwolle

Lithography
Benno Slijkhuis, Wilco Art Books

Printing
Wilco Art Books, Amersfoort

Lenders
ABN AMRO History Department / long-term loans from the Dutch Silver Museum, MoMu | ModeMuseum Antwerpen, Dries van Noten Antwerp, Princess Diana Museum | The Princess & The Platypus Foundation Los Angeles, Givenchy Patrimoine Paris, Viktor&Rolf Amsterdam, Dutch Cavalry Museum Amersfoort, Gucci Archive Florence, Elie Saab France (SARL), Guo Pei Peking/ Paris, Frans Hoogendoorn The Hague, Patriomoine Schiaparelli, Paris, Christian Siriano New York, The Royal Collections of The Netherlands, Kunstmuseum The Hague, H.M. the King, H.M. the Queen, and Their Royal Highnesses Princesses Amalia, Irene, and Mabel / The Royal Collections of the Netherlands, The Hague, Geschiedkundige Vereniging Oranje-Nassau, Stichting tot Instandhouding van het Museum van de Kanselarij der Nederlandse Orden, Edwin Oudshoorn Leiden, Toppers in Concert, Studio Exactitudes Rotterdam and various private collections.

Photography locations
Paleis Het Loo, Apeldoorn
Escher in Het Paleis, The Hague
Noordeinde Palace, The Hague

Image credits
Marijke Aerden, 2, 137
AFP, Angela Weiss, 151
ANP, Fred Boer, 66;
Hollandse Hoogte/ Berlinda van Dam 69, 71/ Ruud Morijn, 64/ Robin Utrecht, 140, 145; KIPPA/ Paul Bergen, 141; Lex van Lieshout, 139
AP Photo, Jacqueline Arzt, 144
Atlas van Stolk, Rotterdam, 80
Gregorio T. Binuya, Everett Collection, 147
Cees Buys, Abaca Press, 120
Camera Press Ltd, Rota, 145
Centraal Museum Utrecht, 50;
Ernst Moritz, 34; Adriaan van Dam, 50
Gamma Press Images, Harvey, Stills, 71
Municipal archives Zeist, 130
Getty Images, Tim Graham, 71; Stephen Lovekin, 146; Jamie McCarthy, 142; MG18/ Dimitrios Kambouris, 150, 153; Sean Zanni/ Patrick McMullan, 150
Alice de Groot/ Adriaan van Dam, photographed at Paleis Het Loo, 8-9, 14, 21, 27, 32, 33, 38, 39, 40, 43, 47, 48, 50, 51, 55, 56, 76-77, 86, 90, 93, 96, 100, 104-105, 107, 108, 109, 118, 122, 125, 135
Alice de Groot/ Adriaan van Dam, photographed at Paleis Noordeinde, The Hague, 34, 35
Alice de Groot/ Adriaan van Dam, photographed at Museum Escher, The Hague, 30-31, 44, 52, 82, 94-95, 99, 114, 116
Frazer Harrison, WireImage, 148
Andreas Holm, 143
IMAGO, Christian Ender, 156-157
Royal Collections, The Hague, 15, 19, 20, 23, 24, 25, 60, 79, 84, 85, 88, 89, 98, 106, 110, 134
Kunstmuseum The Hague, 54, 83, 84;
Alice de Groot, 117, 126, 127, 128, 130, 131
Jan Lankveld, 70
Michael Loccisano, FilmMagic, 146
Maison Schiaparelli, Paris, 152
J. Mayer, Shutterstock, 138
Museum Van Loon, Amsterdam, 54
National Archives, The Hague, 97, 112, 116, 120
Dutch Open Air Museum, Arnhem, 63
Paleis Het Loo, 22, 26, 28, 36, 38, 39, 46, 50, 58, 59, 79, 88, 92, 98, 102, 103, 113, 116, 121, 124, 134; Robert Mulder, 16, 17, 18, 78, 80, 81, 123, 132, 133
RKD, The Hague, 46, 84, 130
Royal Collection Trust, His Majesty King Charles III, London, 54
Rijksmuseum Amsterdam, 33, 42, 92
SIPA USA, Anthony Behar, 61
Robin Utrecht, 12-13, 68, 136
Ari Versluis, Ellie Uyttenbroek, Rotterdam, 62, 72, 73, 74, 75
Roger-Violett Agence Photographique, Maurice-Louis Branger, 67
World History Archive, 64
Frans van Zijst, 149

Partner of Modemuze

MODE MUZE

ISBN 9789462626447
NUR: 644

This publication has also been published in a Dutch edition.
ISBN 9789462626430



waanders.nl
paleishetloo.nl
kunstmuseum.nl

The publication and exhibition have been made possible thanks to

VRIENDENLOTERIJ
Mogelijk gemaakt door Apeldoorn
mondriaan fund
FONDS 21
het cultuurfonds
ZABAWAS
GRAVIN VAN BYLANDT STICHTING
Hendrik Muller fonds
nederlandse kostuum vereniging

MIX Paper | Supporting responsible forestry FSC® C004472